Bangkok

written and researched by

Paul Gray and Lucy Ridout

ROUGH
GUIDES

NEW YORK · LONDON · DELHI

www.roughguides.com

Contents

Bangkok by boat colour
section following p.64

Thai cuisine colour
section following p.192

Colour maps following
p.288

◄◄ Longtail boat ◄ Buddha image for sale, Thanon Damrung Muang

Introduction to

Bangkok

The headlong pace and flawed modernity of Bangkok match few people's visions of the capital of exotic Siam. Spiked with scores of high-rise buildings of concrete and glass, it's a vast flatness which holds a population of at least nine million, and feels even bigger. But under the shadow of the skyscrapers you'll find a heady mix of chaos and refinement, of frenetic markets and hushed golden temples, of early-morning alms-giving ceremonies and ultra-hip designer boutiques.

Bangkok is a relatively young capital, established in 1782 after the Burmese sacked Ayutthaya, the former capital. A temporary base was set up on the western bank of the Chao Phraya River, in what is now Thonburi, before work started on the more defensible east bank, where the first king of the new dynasty, Rama I, built his fabulously ornate palace within a protective ring of canals. Around the temples and palaces of this "royal island", there spread an amphibious city of shops and houses built on bamboo rafts moored on the river and canals.

Ever since its foundation, but with breakneck acceleration in recent years, Bangkok has attracted internal migration from all over Thailand, pushing the city's boundaries ever outwards in an explosion of modernization that has seen the canals on the east side of the river concreted over and left the city without an obvious centre. The capital now sprawls over 330 square kilometres and, with a population forty times that of the second city, Chiang Mai, is far and away the country's dominant city. Bangkokians own four-fifths of the nation's automobiles, and there's precious little chance to escape from the pollution in green space: the city has only 0.4 square metres of public parkland per inhabitant, the lowest figure in the world, compared, for example, to London's 30.4 square metres per person. In the make-up of its population, however, Bangkok bucks world trends, with over half of its inhabitants under thirty, so helping to consolidate its position as one of Asia's liveliest and most fashionable cities.

▲ A spirit house

What to see

Rama I named his royal island **Ratanakosin**, and it remains the city's spiritual heart, not to mention its culturally most rewarding quarter. No visit to the capital would be complete without seeing the star attractions here – if necessary, the dazzling ostentation of **Wat Phra Kaeo** and the **Grand Palace**, the grandiose decay of **Wat Pho** and the **National Museum**'s hoard of exquisite works of art can all be crammed into a single action-packed day.

One of the other great pleasures of the city is a ride on its remaining waterways; the majestic **Chao Phraya River** is served by frequent ferries and longtail boats, and is the backbone of a network of canals, floating markets

▼ Early morning in Thonburi

▲ Monks collecting alms, Wat Benjamabophit

and waterside temples – including the striking five-towered **Wat Arun** – that remains fundamentally intact in the west-bank **Thonburi** district. Inevitably the waterways have earned Bangkok the title of "Venice of the East", a tag that seems all too apt when you're wading through flooded streets in the rainy season.

Bangkok began to assume its modern guise at the end of the nineteenth century, when the forward-looking Rama V relocated the royal family to a neighbourhood north of Ratanakosin called **Dusit**. Here he commissioned grand European-style boulevards, built the new Chitrlada Palace (still used by the royal family today), had his charming, teakwood **Vimanmek Palace** reconstructed nearby, and capped it all with the erection of a sumptuous new temple, **Wat Benjamabophit**, built from Italian marble. When political modernization followed in 1932, Dusit was the obvious choice of home for Thailand's new parliament, which now sits in Parliament House.

Modern Bangkok's commercial heart lies to the southeast of Dusit, where sleek glass towers and cool marble malls lend an air of energy and big-city drama to the districts of **Silom**, **Siam Square** and **Sukhumvit**. These areas shelter a few noteworthy tourist sights, too, best of which is **Jim Thompson's House**, a small, personal museum of Thai design. **Shopping**

▲ Soi Issaranuphap, Chinatown

downtown varies from touristic outlets selling silks and handicrafts to international fashion emporia and boutiques showcasing Thailand's increasingly desirable home-grown contemporary designs. For livelier scenes, explore the dark alleys of the bazaars in **Chinatown** or the Indian district, **Pahurat**, or head out to the enormous, open-air **Chatuchak Weekend Market**. Similarly, the city offers wildly varied entertainment, ranging from traditional dancing and the orchestrated bedlam of Thai boxing, through hip bars and clubs in the backpackers' enclave of **Banglamphu**, to the farang-only sex bars of the notorious Patpong district.

▲ Garland seller, Nonthaburi

City of Angels

When Rama I was crowned in 1782, he gave his new capital a grand 43-syllable name to match his ambitious plans for the building of the city. Since then 21 more syllables have been added.

Krungthepmahanakhornbowornratanakosinmahintarayutthaya-mahadilokpopnopparatratchathaniburiromudomratchaniwet-mahasathanamornpimanavatarnsathitsakkathattiyavisnukarprasit is Guinness-certified as the longest place name in the world and roughly translates as "Great city of angels, the supreme repository of divine jewels, the great land unconquerable, the grand and prominent realm, the royal and delightful capital city full of nine noble gems, the highest royal dwelling and grand palace, the divine shelter and living place of the reincarnated spirits". Fortunately, all Thais refer to the city simply as Krung Thep ("City of Angels"), though plenty can recite the full name at the drop of a hat. Bangkok – "Village of the Plum Olive" – was the name of the original village on the Thonburi side; with remarkable persistence, it has remained in use by foreigners since the 1660s, when the French built a short-lived garrison fort in the area.

▲ Pak Khlong Talat flower market

North and west of the city, the unwieldy urban mass of Greater Bangkok peters out into the vast, well-watered central plains, a region that for centuries has grown the bulk of the nation's food. The atmospheric ruins of Thailand's fourteenth-century capital **Ayutthaya** lie here, ninety minutes' train ride from Bangkok and, together with the ornate palace at nearby **Bang Pa-In**, make a rewarding excursion from the modern metropolis. Further west, the massive stupa at **Nakhon Pathom** and the floating markets of **Damnoen Saduak** are also easily manageable as a day-trip, and combine well with a visit to the historic town of **Phetchaburi**, famous for its charming old temples. Riverside **Amphawa** is similarly evocative and makes a perfect escape from the city, with its untouristed floating markets and traditional canalside neighbourhoods. An overnight stay at **Kanchanaburi** is also well worth the effort: impressively sited on the River Kwai, it holds several moving World War II sights, including the notorious Death Railway.

▼ Sugar cane and bananas for sale

Rat or raja?

There's no standard system of transliterating Thai script into Roman, so you're sure to find that the Thai words in this book don't always match the versions you'll see elsewhere. Maps and street signs are the biggest sources of confusion, so we've generally gone for the transliteration that's most common on the spot. However, sometimes you'll need to do a bit of lateral thinking, bearing in mind that a classic variant for the town of Ayutthaya is Ayudhia, while among street names, Thanon Rajavithi could come out as Thanon Ratwithi – and it's not unheard of to find one spelling posted at one end of a road, with another at the opposite end. See p.259 for an introduction to the Thai language.

When to go

▲ Fruit stall, Banglamphu

Bangkok's climate is governed by three seasons, though in reality the city sits firmly within the tropics and so enjoys warm days and nights year-round. The so-called **cool season**, which runs from November to February, is the most pleasant time to visit; days are invariably bright and clear, and temperatures average a manageable 27°C (though they can still reach a broiling 31°C at midday). Not surprisingly this is high season for the tourist industry, so it's well worth booking accommodation and flights in advance over this period; prices for hotel rooms are at their highest during this time, rising to a peak at Christmas and New Year. March sees the beginning of the **hot season**, when temperatures can rise to 36°C, and continue to do so beyond the end of April. During these sweltering months you may find yourself spending more money than at other times, simply in order to secure the benefits of air-conditioning, whether in hotel rooms, restaurants, taxis or buses. The daily downpours that characterize the **rainy season** can come as a welcome relief, though being hot and wet is a sensation that doesn't appeal to everyone. The rainy season varies in length and intensity from year to year, but usually starts with a bang in May, gathers force between June and August, and comes to a peak in September and October, when whole districts of the capital are flooded. Rain rarely lasts all day however, so as long as you're armed with an umbrella there's no reason to reschedule your trip – and you'll get more for your money, too, as many hotels and airlines drop their prices right down at this time of year.

	Jan	Feb	Mar	Apr	May	Jun	Jul	Aug	Sep	Oct	Nov	Dec
Average daily temperatures (°C)												
Maximum	28	28	29	30	31	31	30	31	31	30	29	28
Minimum	21	21	21	22	23	23	23	23	23	23	23	22
Average monthly rainfall (mm)												
Rainfall	11	28	31	72	190	152	158	187	320	231	57	9

22

things not to miss

It's not possible to see everything Bangkok has to offer on a short trip – and we don't suggest you try. What follows is a subjective selection of the highlights, from extravagant palaces and frenetic markets to tranquil neighbourhoods and cutting-edge nightlife and shopping, plus great day-trip destinations around the city. They're arranged in colour-coded categories to help you find the very best things to see, do and experience. All entries have a page reference to take you straight into the guide, where you can find out more.

01 The Grand Palace Page **61** • Sheltering Thailand's holiest temple, Wat Phra Kaeo, and its most sacred image, the Emerald Buddha, this huge complex is a beautiful kaleidoscope of strange colours and shapes.

03 Nightlife Page **193** • Pack your party gear for high-style nights on the town.

04 Amulet market Page **04** • Nearly all Thais wear a sacred talisman – often a miniature Buddha image – to ward off misfortune, and the huge amulet market at Wat Rajnadda is a great place for browsing.

02 Wat Pho Page **68** • This lavish and lively temple is home to the awesome Reclining Buddha and a great massage school.

05 63rd-floor sundowner Page **197** • Fine cocktails and jaw-dropping views, especially at sunset, at *The Sky Bar* and *Distil*.

06 **Muang Boran Ancient City** Page **138** • Escape from the city to this attractively landscaped open-air museum, which features beautifully crafted replicas of Thailand's finest monuments.

08 **Jim Thompson's House** Page **114** • An elegant and very personal museum of Thai crafts and architecture.

07 **Traditional Thai Puppet Theatre** Page **205** • The last troupe of its kind, this is the only authentic form of Thai dance-drama performed to a high standard every night of the week.

09 Thai boxing Page **205** • Nightly bouts at the national stadia are accompanied by live music and frenetic betting.

10 Exploring traditional neighbourhoods Page **34** • Venture beyond the downtown gloss on a bicycle tour through the city's rural fringes.

11 Vimanmek Palace Page **107** • This elegant late-nineteenth-century summer palace was built from golden teakwood, without a single nail.

12 Wat Arun Page **104** • The Temple of Dawn looks great from the river – and even better close up.

14 **Chatuchak Weekend Market** Page **129** • Bangkok's top shopping experience features over eight thousand stalls selling everything from hill-tribe jewellery to jeans and designer lamps to kitchen china.

13 **Ayutthaya** Page **140** • Razed by the Burmese, the old capital is a grassy, brooding graveyard of temples, an hour to the north by train.

15 **Kanchanaburi and the River Kwai** Page **158** • Poignant World War II sights, a scenic train ride, and a glorious riverine setting make this a memorable excursion from the capital.

16 **National Museum** Page **72** • The cornucopia of Thailand's artistic heritage, ranging from sculptural treasures to fantastic royal funeral chariots.

17 **Contemporary design**
Page **213** • Traditional East meets minimalist West.

18 **Songkhran** Page **45** • Thai New Year is the excuse for a national waterfight - don't plan on getting much done if you come in mid-April, just join in the fun.

19 **Chinatown** Page **89** • This atmospheric neighbourhood of kilometre-long alleyway markets, centuries-old traditions and evocative temples is also home to the world's largest solid-gold Buddha.

20 **Erawan Shrine** Page **116** • The full spiritual monty: Buddhism, Hinduism and animism, dancing, lottery tickets and enough jasmine and gold to knock you out.

21 **The Thonburi canals** Page **100** • The best way to explore the city's waterside communities is to travel as its residents do – by boat.

22 **Thanon Khao San** Page **77** • Legendary mecca for Southeast Asian backpackers: the place for cheap sleeps, baggy trousers and tall tales.

Basics

Basics

Getting there

Up to late 2006, all international flights into Bangkok used Don Muang Airport. However, as this book was going to press, the capital's new Suvarnabhumi Airport had just opened. It will now handle all scheduled flights, with charters remaining at Don Muang. See p.30 for more information about both airports.

Airfares to Bangkok always depend on the **season**, with the highest being around mid-November to mid-February, when the weather is best (with premium rates charged for flights between mid-Dec and New Year), and in July and August to coincide with school holidays. You will need to book several months in advance to get reasonably priced tickets during these peak periods.

Flights from the UK and Ireland

The fastest and most comfortable way of reaching Bangkok **from the UK** is to fly nonstop from London with Qantas/British Airways, Thai Airways or Eva Airways – a journey time of about eleven and a half hours. These airlines usually keep their prices competitive, at around £510/730 plus tax in low season/high season. Fares on indirect scheduled flights to Bangkok – with a change of plane en route – are always cheaper than nonstop flights and start at £330/590, though these journeys can take anything from two to twelve hours longer.

There are no nonstop flights from any regional airports in Britain or from any **Irish airports**, and rather than routing via London, you may find it convenient to fly to another hub such as Amsterdam (with KLM), Frankfurt (with Lufthansa), Paris (with Air France), Zurich (with Swiss) or even Dubai (with Emirates), and take a connecting flight from there. Note, however, that changing planes at Charles de Gaulle airport in Paris is a perennial nightmare, partly due to the huge queues at security checks in the transit area, and that KLM can be less than reliable. Flights from Glasgow via Dubai with Emirates, for example, start at around £490, from Dublin via Zurich with Swiss, at around €690.

Flights from the US and Canada

Thai Airways operate **nonstop flights** to Bangkok from New York (4 weekly; around US$1100/1250 low season/high season) and Los Angeles (4–6 weekly; US$1150/1350). Otherwise, plenty of airlines run daily flights to Bangkok from major East and West Coast cities with only **one stop** en route; it's generally easier to find a reasonable fare on flights via Asia than via Europe, even if you're departing from the East Coast. From New York expect to pay around US$1100/1250 in low season/high season, from LA US$825/950. Air Canada has the most convenient service to Bangkok from the largest number of Canadian cities; from Vancouver, expect to pay around US$1400/1600 in low season/high season; from Toronto, C$1600/1850. Cheaper rates are often available if you're prepared to make two or three stops and take more time.

Although layover times can vary, the actual **flying time** is approximately 17 hours from either New York or LA. From Canada, you can expect to spend something like 16 hours in the air flying from Vancouver (via Tokyo) or at least twenty hours from Montréal (via Europe).

Flights from Australia and New Zealand

There's no shortage of **scheduled flights** to Bangkok **from Australia**, with direct services from major cities operated by Thai Airways, Qantas/British Airways and Emirates (around nine hours from Sydney and seven from Perth), and plenty of indirect flights via Asian hubs, which take at least eleven and a half hours. There's often not much difference between the fares on

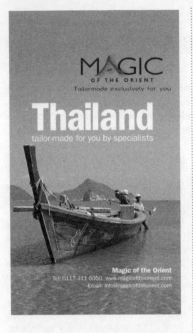

MAGIC
OF THE ORIENT
Tailormade exclusively for you

Thailand
tailor-made for you by specialists

Magic of the Orient
Tel: 0117 311 6050 www.magicoftheorient.com
Email: info@magicoftheorient.com

nonstop and indirect flights, with fares start-ing from around A$800/1200 (excluding taxes) in low/high season from Sydney and most major eastern Australian cities; special promotions are quite common, however, so you could be looking at low-season flights for as little as A$730. Fares from Perth and Darwin are up to A$100/200 cheaper.

From **New Zealand**, Thai Airways runs nonstop twelve-hour flights between Auckland and Bangkok, charging from NZ$1250/1700 (excluding taxes) in low/high season. BA/Qantas and Emirates flights from Auckland make brief stops in Sydney, adding at least a couple of hours to the trip, and other major Asian airlines offer indirect flights via their hubs (from 17 hours): fares for indi-rect flights also start at about NZ$1250/1700. From Christchurch and Wellington you'll pay NZ$150–300 more than from Auckland.

Flights from South Africa

There are no nonstop flights **from South Africa** to Bangkok, but Singapore Airlines can get you there from Johannesburg, via a brief stop in Singapore, in 14 hours. From Cape Town it's a minimum of 18 hours, going

via Kuala Lumpur. Other airlines, including South African Airways, make a stop either in the Middle East or in Hong Kong or South-oast Asia. Fares start at about R10,000/7600 for high/low season, including taxes.

Online booking

Ⓦ www.expedia.co.uk (in UK), Ⓦ www.expedia .com (in US), Ⓦ www.expedia.ca (in Canada)
Ⓦ www.lastminute.com (in UK)
Ⓦ www.opodo.co.uk (in UK)
Ⓦ www.orbitz.com (in US)
Ⓦ www.travelocity.co.uk (in UK), Ⓦ www .travelocity.com (in US), Ⓦ www.travelocity .ca (in Canada), Ⓦ www.zuji.com.au (in Australia), Ⓦ www.zuji.co.nz (in New Zealand)

Airlines

Air France US ☎ 1-800/237-2747, Canada ☎ 1-800/667-2747, UK ☎ 0870/142 4343, Australia ☎ 1300/390 190, Ⓦ www.airfrance.com.
Air New Zealand US ☎ 1-800/262-1234, Canada ☎ 1-800/663-5494, UK ☎ 0800/028 4149, Republic of Ireland ☎ 1800/551 447, New Zealand ☎ 0800/737 000, Ⓦ www.airnewzealand.com.
British Airways US and Canada ☎ 1-800/ AIRWAYS, UK ☎ 0870/850 9850, Republic of Ireland ☎ 1890/626 747, Australia ☎ 1300/767 177, New Zealand ☎ 09/966 9777, Ⓦ www.ba.com.
Cathay Pacific US ☎ 1-800/233-2742, UK ☎ 020/8834 8888, Australia ☎ 13 1747, New Zealand ☎ 09/379 0861; Ⓦ www.cathaypacific.com.
China Airlines US ☎ 917/368-2003, UK ☎ 020/7436 9001, Australia ☎ 02/9232 3336, New Zealand ☎ 09/308 3364, Ⓦ www.china-airlines.com.
Delta US and Canada ☎ 1-800/221-1212, Ⓦ www .delta.com.
Emirates US ☎ 1-800/777-3999, UK ☎ 0870/243 2222, Australia ☎ 02/9290 9700, New Zealand ☎ 09/968 2200, South Africa ☎ 0861-364728, Ⓦ www.emirates.com.
Etihad Airways Canada ☎ 905/858 8998, UK ☎ 020/8735 6700, South Africa ☎ 0861-ETIHAD, Ⓦ www.etihadairways.com.
EVA Air US and Canada ☎ 1-800/695-1188, UK ☎ 020/7380 8300, Australia ☎ 02/8338 0419, New Zealand ☎ 09/358 8300, Ⓦ www.evaair.com.
Finnair US ☎ 1-800/950-5000, UK ☎ 0870/241 4411, Republic of Ireland ☎ 01/844 6565, Australia ☎ 02/9244 2299, Ⓦ www.finnair.com.
Garuda Indonesia US ☎ 212/279-0756, UK ☎ 020/7467 8600, Australia ☎ 1300/365 330 or 02/9334 9944, New Zealand ☎ 09/366 1862, Ⓦ www.garuda-indonesia.com.

Fly less – stay longer! Travel and climate change

Climate change is the single biggest issue facing our planet. It is caused by a build-up in the atmosphere of carbon dioxide and other greenhouse gases, which are emitted by many sources – including planes. Already, flights account for around 3–4% of human-induced global warming: that figure may sound small, but it is rising year on year and threatens to counteract the progress made by reducing greenhouse emissions in other areas.

Rough Guides regard travel, overall, as a global benefit, and feel strongly that the advantages to developing economies are important, as are the opportunities for greater contact and awareness among peoples. But we all have a responsibility to limit our personal "carbon footprint". That means giving thought to how often we fly and what we can do to redress the harm that our trips create.

Flying and climate change

Pretty much every form of motorized travel generates CO_2, but planes are particularly bad offenders, releasing large volumes of greenhouse gases at altitudes where their impact is far more harmful. Flying also allows us to travel much further than we would contemplate doing by road or rail, so the emissions attributable to each passenger become truly shocking. For example, one person taking a return flight between Europe and California produces the equivalent impact of 2.5 tonnes of CO_2 – similar to the yearly output of the average UK car.

Less harmful planes may evolve but it will be decades before they replace the current fleet – which could be too late for avoiding climate chaos. In the meantime, there are limited options for concerned travellers: to reduce the amount we travel by air (take fewer trips, stay longer!), to avoid night flights (when plane contrails trap heat from Earth but can't reflect sunlight back to space), and to make the trips we do take "climate neutral" via a carbon offset scheme.

Carbon offset schemes

Offset schemes run by **climatecare.org**, **carbonneutral.com** and others allow you to "neutralize" the greenhouse gases that you are responsible for releasing. Their websites have simple calculators that let you work out the impact of any flight. Once that's done, you can pay to fund projects that will reduce future carbon emissions by an equivalent amount (such the distribution of low-energy lightbulbs and cooking stoves in developing countries). Please take the time to visit our website and make your trip climate neutral.

www.roughguides.com/climatechange

KLM US ☎1-800/225-2525, UK ☎0870/507 4074, Australia ☎1300/303 747, New Zealand ☎09/309 1782, ⓦwww.klm.com.
Korean Air US and Canada ☎1-800/438-5000, UK ☎0800/0656 2001, Republic of Ireland ☎01/799 7990, Australia ☎02/9262 6000, New Zealand ☎09/914 2000, ⓦwww.koreanair.com.
Lufthansa US ☎1-800/645-3880, Canada ☎1-800/563-5954, UK ☎0870/837 7747, Republic of Ireland ☎01/844 5544, Australia ☎1300/655 727, New Zealand ☎09/303 1529, ⓦwww .lufthansa.com.
Malaysia Airlines US ☎1-800/552-9264, UK ☎0870/607 9090, Republic of Ireland ☎01/676 2131, Australia ☎293/13 26 27, New Zealand ☎0800/777 747, South Africa ☎011/880-9614 ⓦwww.malaysia-airlines.com.

Northwest/KLM US ☎1-800/225-2525, ⓦwww .nwa.com.
Qantas Airways US and Canada ☎1-800/227-4500, UK ☎0845/774 7767, Republic of Ireland ☎01/407 3278, Australia ☎13 13 13, New Zealand ☎0800/808 767 or 09/357 8900, ⓦwww .qantas.com.
Qatar Airways US ☎1-877/777-2827, Canada ☎1-888/366-5666, UK ☎020/7896 3636, ⓦwww .qatarairways.com.
Royal Brunei UK ☎020/7584 6660, Australia ☎1300/721 271, New Zealand ☎09/977 2209, ⓦwww.bruneiair.com.
Royal Jordanian US ☎1-800/223-0470, Canada ☎1-800/363-0711 or 514/288-1647, UK ☎020/7878 6300, Australia ☎02/9244 2701, New Zealand ☎03/365 3910, ⓦwww.rj.com.

Singapore Airlines US ☎1-800/742-3333, Canada ☎1-800/ 663-3046, UK ☎0844/800 2380, Republic of Ireland ☎01/671 0722, Australia ☎13 1011, New Zealand ☎0800/808 909, South Africa ☎021/674-0601, ⓦwww .singaporeair.com.
South African Airways US and Canada ☎1-800/722-9675, UK ☎0870/747 1111, Australia ☎1800/221 699, New Zealand ☎09/977 2237, South Africa ☎011/978-1111, ⓦwww.flysaa.com.
Swiss US and Canada ☎1-877/359-7947, UK ☎0845/601 0956, Republic of Ireland ☎1890/200 515, Australia ☎1300/724 666, New Zealand ☎09/977 2238, South Africa ☎0860/040506, ⓦwww.swiss.com.
Thai Airways US ☎212/949-8424, Canada ☎416/971-5181, UK ☎0870/606 0911, Australia ☎1300/651 960, New Zealand ☎09/377 3886; ⓦwww.thaiair.com.
Turkish Airlines US and Canada ☎1-800/874-8875, UK ☎020/7766 9300, Australia ☎02/9299 8400, ⓦwww.thy.com.

Travel agents and tour operators worldwide

For Bangkok travel agents selling onward international flights, see p.64.

An exotic land blending jungles, temples and beaches with an infectious sense of fun and irrepressible charm. The natural exuberance and endless variety of Thailand mean no matter how many times you visit, you'll forever want to return.

Thailand

SILVERBIRD
THE FAR EAST TRAVEL SPECIALISTS

For information or a brochure call:
Tel: 020 8875 9090 Fax: 020 8875 1874
Email: sales@silverbird.co.uk
Website: www.silverbird.co.uk

Creative Events Asia Thailand ⓦwww .creativeeventsasia.com. Wedding specialists for everything from paperwork to the ceremony and guest accommodation.
ebookers UK ☎0800/082 3000, ⓦwww .ebookers.com, Republic of Ireland ☎01/488 3507 ⓦwww.ebookers.ie. Low fares on an extensive selection of scheduled flights and package deals.
Educational Travel Center US ☎1-800/747-5551 or 608/256-5551, ⓦwww.edtrav.com. Low-cost fares, student/youth discount offers and tours.
Flight Centre US ☎1-866/967 5351, Canada ☎1-877/967 5302, UK ☎0870/499 0040, Australia ☎13 31 33, New Zealand ☎0800/243 544, South Africa ☎0860/400 727, ⓦwww.flightcentre.com. Guarantee to offer the lowest air fares; also sell a wide range of package holidays.
gohop Republic of Ireland ☎01/241 2389, ⓦwww.gohop.ie. Irish-owned agent, offering flights, packages and hotels.
North South Travel UK ☎01245/608 291, ⓦwww.northsouthtravel.co.uk. Competitive travel agency, offering discounted fares worldwide. Profits are used to support projects in the developing world, especially the promotion of sustainable tourism.
Origin Asia Thailand ☎02 259 4896, ⓦwww .alex-kerr.com. Cultural programmes that teach and explain living Thai arts such as dance, music, martial arts, textiles, flower offerings and cooking. Courses last from one day to a week and are held in Bangkok.
STA Travel US ☎1-800/781-4040, Canada ☎1-888/427-5639, UK ☎0870/1630 026, Australia ☎1300/733 035, New Zealand ☎0508/782 872, South Africa ☎0861/781 781, ⓦwww.statravel .com. Worldwide specialists in independent travel; also student IDs, travel insurance, car rental, and more. Good discounts for students and under-26s.
Thompsons Tours South Africa ☎011/770-7700, ⓦwww.thompsons.co.za. Flights and package holidays.
Trailfinders UK ☎0845/058 5858, Republic of Ireland ☎01/677 7888, Australia ☎1300/780 212, ⓦwww.trailfinders.com. One of the best-informed and most efficient agents for independent travellers.
Travel Cuts US ☎1-800/592-CUTS, Canada ☎1-866/246-9762, ⓦwww.travelcuts.com. Popular, long-established specialists in budget travel, including student and youth discount offers.
USIT Republic of Ireland ☎01/602 1904, Northern Ireland ☎028/9032 7111, with branches in Athlone, Belfast, Cork, Dublin, Galway, Limerick and Waterford, ⓦwww.usit.ie. Ireland's main outlet for discounted, youth and student fares.

From neighbouring countries

Sharing **land borders** with Burma, Laos, Cambodia and Malaysia, Thailand works well as part of many overland itineraries, both across Asia and between Europe and Australia. Bangkok is also one of the major regional flight hubs for Southeast Asia – indeed, on many flights between Europe and Vietnam, Laos and Cambodia you have no choice but to be routed via Bangkok.

The main restrictions on overland routes in and out of Thailand are determined by **visas**, and by where the permitted land crossings lie. At any of the land borders described below, most passport holders should be able to get an on-the-spot thirty-day entry stamp into Thailand, which can be extended for ten days at Thai provincial immigration offices for a swingeing B1900. It's easy enough, however, to hop across one of the land borders and return on the same day with another, free thirty-day stamp, or you might want to apply for a sixty-day tourist visa instead, obtainable in advance from Thai embassies.

Full details of visa requirements are given on p.25.

You may need to buy visas for your next port of call when in Thailand; details of visa requirements for travel to Thailand's immediate neighbours are outlined below, but these can change so it's worth checking in advance before you travel. Contact details for **Asian embassies** in Bangkok are given on p.53. Many Khao San tour agents offer to get your visa for you, but beware: some are reportedly **faking the stamps**, which could get you in pretty serious trouble, so it's safer to go to the embassy yourself.

From Burma

At the time of writing, there is no overland access from **Burma** into Thailand and access in the opposite direction is mostly restricted to day-trips. There are, however, numerous flights between Bangkok and Burma, and tourists who intend to enter Burma by air can buy four-week tourist visas at the Burmese embassy in Bangkok for about B800; apply to the embassy and you may be able to collect the same day, or definitely the following day.

From Cambodia

At the time of writing, six overland crossings on the **Thai-Cambodian border** are open to non-Thais, but regulations are changeable so check with the Cambodian Embassy in Bangkok and consult Ⓦwww.talesofasia .com/cambodia-overland.htm for travellers' recent experiences. All Cambodian borders open daily from 7am to 8pm. Numerous **flights** operate between Bangkok and Cambodia.

Visas for Cambodia are issued to travellers on arrival at Phnom Penh and Siem Reap airports, and at the Aranyaprathet–Poipet and Hat Lek–Koh Kong land borders; you need US$20 and two photos for this. If you do need to buy an advance thirty-day visa, you can do so from the Cambodian Embassy in Bangkok (about B1000; apply before noon and you can collect your visa the following day after 5pm).

The most commonly used land crossing is at **Poipet**, which lies just across the border from the Thai town of **Aranyaprathet** and has public-transport connections with Sisophon, Siem Reap and Phnom Penh. There are two trains a day from Aranyaprathet to Bangkok (about 6hr), departing at 6.35am and 1.05pm, and two in the opposite direction, departing Bangkok at 5.55am and 1.05pm. Tuk-tuks will take you the 4km between the train station and the border post. Buses also run from Aranyaprathet to Bangkok's Northern (Mo Chit) Bus Terminal (at least hourly; 4hr 30min); in the reverse direction the last bus leaves Bangkok at 6pm. In Aranyaprathet you'll need to take a tuk-tuk from the bus station to the border. It's also possible to buy a **through-ticket to Siem Reap** from Bangkok from almost any travel agent in Banglamphu for B400–600 but this option is dogged by **scams** (including a visa "service charge" scam, described in detail at Ⓦwww.talesofasia .com/cambodia-overland-bkksr-package .htm), can take up to ten hours longer than doing it independently, and nearly always uses clapped-out buses or even pick-ups, despite the promised "luxury" bus.

The other main border crossing is from **Koh Kong** (with transport to and from Sihanoukville and Phnom Penh) to **Hat**

Lek near Trat on Thailand's east coast. Hat Lek–Koh Kong is the fastest option if you're travelling nonstop from Bangkok to Cambodia. The usual route into Thailand is to get the speedboat from Sihanoukville to Koh Kong, then a motorcycle taxi to the Hat Lek border post. Minibuses and songthaews run from Hat Lek to Trat, 91km northwest, where you can pick up a bus straight to Bangkok's Eastern or Northern Bus Terminal (4–6hr). In the reverse direction, buses run frequently from Bangkok to Trat, where minibuses depart for Hat Lek every 45 minutes between 6am and 5pm.

From Laos and Vietnam

Tourists can cross into Thailand at five points along the Lao border, all of which have frequent bus connections with Bangkok's Northern (Mo Chit) Bus Terminal: Houayxai (for Chiang Khong; 10 daily buses to and from Bangkok; 13–14hr); Vientiane (for Nong Khai; frequent buses to and from Bangkok; 10hr; and 4 trains daily; 10hr 30min–12hr 30min); Khammouan (aka Tha Khaek, for Nakhon Phanom; frequent buses to and from Bangkok; 12hr); Savannakhet (for Mukdahan; frequent buses to and from Bangkok; 11hr); and Pakxe (for Chong Mek; daily buses to and from Bangkok; 11hr). In addition there are numerous flights between Bangkok and Laos.

Visas are required for all non-Thai visitors to Laos. A fifteen-day visa on arrival can be bought for US$30 (plus two photos) at Vientiane Airport, Louang Phabang Airport, and all the above-listed land borders. However, these visas cost roughly the same but are valid for half the period of visas bought in advance from the Lao Embassy in Bangkok, which issues thirty-day visas for around B1400, depending on nationality. For this, you need two passport photos; processing takes up to three days – or less than an hour if you pay an extra B200.

If you have the right Lao visa and Vietnamese exit stamp, you can travel from Vietnam to Thailand via Savannakhet in a matter of hours; you'll need to use Vietnam's Lao Bao border crossing, west of Dong Ha, where you can catch a bus to Savannakhet and then a ferry across the Mekong to Mukdahan

(a bridge across the river near Mukdahan is due to be completed by the end of 2007, which should make the journey even quicker). All travellers into Vietnam need to buy a visa in advance. Thirty-day visas can take up to four working days to process at the embassy in Bangkok and cost about B1800, depending on your nationality.

From Malaysia and Singapore

Travelling between Thailand and Malaysia and Singapore has in the past been a straightforward and very commonly used overland route, with plentiful connections by bus, minibus, share-taxi and train, most of them routed through the southern Thai city and transport hub of Hat Yai. However, because of the ongoing sectarian violence in Thailand's deep south, all major Western governments are currently advising people not to travel to or through Songkhla, Pattani, Yala and Narathiwat provinces, unless essential. This encompasses Hat Yai and the following border crossings to and from Malaysia: at Padang Besar, on the main rail line connecting Butterworth in Malaysia (and, ultimately, Kuala Lumpur and Singapore) with Hat Yai and Bangkok; at Sungai Kolok, terminus of a railway line from Hat Yai and Bangkok, and at adjacent Ban Taba, both of which are connected by road to nearby Kota Bharu in Malaysia; and at the road crossings at Sadao, south of Hat Yai, and at Betong, south of Yala. (The routes towards Kota Bharu and Betong pass through particularly volatile territory, with martial law declared in Pattani, Yala and Narathiwat provinces; however, martial law is not in effect in Hat Yai itself nor the districts of Songkhla province through which the Bangkok–Butterworth rail line and the Hat Yai–Sadao road pass.) For up-to-the-minute advice, consult your government travel advisory (see p.46).

Nevertheless, the provinces of Trang and Satun on the west coast are not affected, and it's still perfectly possible to travel overland via Satun: by share-taxi between Alor Setar and Satun town, or by boat between Kuala Perlis (45min) or the island of Langkawi (1hr) and Satun's Thammalang pier. There are two daily buses from Satun to Bangkok's Southern Bus Terminal and the journey takes sixteen hours.

In addition, there are numerous daily **flights** from Malaysia and Singapore to Bangkok.

Most Western tourists can spend thirty days in Malaysia and fourteen days in Singapore without having bought a **visa** beforehand, and there are useful Thai embassies or consulates in Kuala Lumpur, Kota Bahru, Penang and Singapore (see p.26).

Visas

There are three main entry categories for visitors to Thailand; for all of them your passport must be valid for at least six months from the date of entry.

As **visa** requirements are often subject to change, you should always check before departure with a Thai embassy or consulate, a reliable travel agent, or on the Thai Ministry of Foreign Affairs' website at ⓦwww .mfa.go.th/web/12.php. For further, unofficial details on related matters, such as the perils of overstaying your visa, go to ⓦwww .thaivisa.com.

Most Western passport holders (that includes citizens of the UK, Ireland, the US, Canada, Australia, New Zealand and South Africa) are allowed to enter the country for **stays of up to thirty days** without having to apply for a visa (officially termed the "tourist visa exemption"); the period of stay will be stamped into your passport by immigration officials upon entry. You're supposed to be able to somehow show proof of means of living while in the country (B10,000/person, B20,000/family), and in theory you may be put back on the next plane without it or sent back to get a sixty-day tourist visa from the nearest Thai embassy, but this is unheard of.

If you're fairly certain you may want to stay longer than thirty days, then from the outset you should apply for a **sixty-day tourist visa** from a Thai embassy or consulate, accompanying your application – which generally takes several days to process – with your passport and two photos. The sixty-day visa currently costs B1000 or equivalent (though it's a rip-off £25 in the UK); multiple-entry versions are available, costing B1000 per entry, which may be handy if you're going to be leaving and re-entering Thailand. Tourist visas are valid for three months, ie you must enter Thailand within three months of the visa being issued by the Thai embassy or consulate. Visa application forms can be downloaded from, for example, ⓦwww .thaiembassyuk.org.uk/visaapplicationform_ internet.pdf.

Thai embassies also consider applications for **ninety-day non-immigrant visas** (B2000 or equivalent single-entry, B5000 multiple-entry) as long as you can offer a good reason for your visit, such as study or business (there are different categories of non-immigrant visa for which different levels of proof are needed). As it's quite a hassle to organize a ninety-day visa from outside the country (and generally not feasible for most tourists), it's generally easier, though more expensive, to apply for a thirty-day extension to your sixty-day visa once inside Thai borders.

It's not a good idea to **overstay** your visa limits. Once you're at the airport or the border, you'll have to pay a fine of B500/ day before you can leave Thailand. More importantly, however, if you're in the country with an expired visa and you get involved with police or immigration officials for any reason, however trivial, they are obliged to take you to court, possibly imprison you, and deport you.

Extensions and re-entry permits

Thirty-day stays can be **extended** in Thailand for a further seven days, sixty-day tourist visas for a further thirty days, at the discretion of officials; extensions cost B1900 and are issued over the counter at immigration offices (*kaan khao muang*; ⓦwww .immigration.go.th) across Thailand. You'll need two extra photos, plus two photocopies of the main pages of your passport including your Thai arrival card, arrival stamp and visa. Immigration offices also issue **re-entry permits** (B1000 single re-entry, B3800 multiple) if you want to leave the country and come back again while maintaining the validity of your existing visa.

The **immigration office in Bangkok** is about 600m down Soi Suan Phlu, off Thanon Sathorn Tai (Mon–Fri 8.30am–4.30pm; ☏02 287 3101–10; ⓦwww.immigration.go.th); visa extensions take about an hour. They also send a weekly mobile office to Bumrungrad Hospital, 3rd Floor, Sukhumvit Soi 3 (Wed 9am–3pm). It's difficult to get through to the Suan Phlu office by phone, so you may be better off calling the Department of Employment's One-Stop Service Centre for advice on ☏02 693 9333–9. Be very wary of any Khao San tour agents who offer to organize a visa extension for you: some are reportedly faking the relevant stamps and this has caused problems at immigration. However, many places organize "visa-run" trips, which take you and your passport, usually in a minivan, to the Cambodian border at Poipet and back within a day, charging around B2000 all in (the 30-day stamp itself is free); East Meets West Travel, Sukhumvit Soi 12 (☏02 251 5230, ⓦwww .eastmeetswesttravel.com), specializes in this service.

Thai embassies and consulates abroad

For a full listing of Thai diplomatic missions abroad, consult the Thai Ministry of Foreign Affairs' website at ⓦwww.mfa.go.th/web/10.php

Australia 111 Empire Circuit, Yarralumla, Canberra ACT 2600 ☏02/6273 1149, ⓦwww.thaiembassy .org.au; plus consulate at 131 Macquarrie St, Sydney, NSW 2000 ☏02/9241 2542–3, ⓦthaisydney.idx.com.au.
Burma 73 Manawhari Street, Dagon Township, Rangoon ☏01/224647.
Cambodia 196 Preah Norodom Blvd, Sangkat Tonle Bassac, Khan Chamcar Mon, Phnom Penh ☏023/726306–10, ⓦwww.thaiembassy .org/phnompenh.
Canada 180 Island Park Drive, Ottawa, ON, K1Y 0A2 ☏613/722-4444, ⓦwww.magma .ca/~thaiott; plus consulate at 1040 Burrard St, Vancouver, BC, V6Z 2R9 ☏604/687-1143, ⓦwww .thaicongenvancouver.org.
Laos Route Phonekheng, Vientiane, PO Box 128 ☏021/214581–3; plus consulate at Khanthabouly District, Savannakhet Province, PO Box 513 ☏041/212373.
Malaysia 206 Jalan Ampang, 50450 Kuala Lumpur ☏03/2148 8222; plus consulates at 4426 Jalan Pengkalan Chepa, 15400 Kota Bharu ☏09/748 2545; and 1 Jalan Tunku Abdul Rahman, 10350 Penang ☏04/226 9484.
New Zealand 2 Cook St, PO Box 17226, Karori, Wellington 6005 ☏04/476 8618–9, ⓦwww .thaiembassynz.org.nz.
Singapore 370 Orchard Road, Singapore 238870 ☏6737 2158 or 6835 4991, ⓦwww .thaiembsingapore.org.
South Africa 428 Pretorius/Hill St, Arcadia, Pretoria 0083 ☏012/342 1600.
UK and Ireland 29–30 Queens Gate, London SW7 5JB ☏020/7589 2944, ⓦwww.thaiembassyuk.org .uk. Visa applications by post are not accepted here, but can be sent to various honorary consulates around the UK and Ireland – see ⓦwww .thaiembassyuk.org.uk/instruction/htm.
US 1024 Wisconsin Ave NW, Suite 401, Washington, DC 20007 ☏202/944-3600, ⓦwww.thaiembdc .org; plus consulates at 700 North Rush St, Chicago, IL 60611 ☏312/664-3129, ⓦwww.thaichicago.net; 351 E 52nd St, New York, NY 10022 ☏212/754-1770, ⓦwww.thaiconsulnewyork.com; and 611 North Larchmont Blvd, 2nd Floor, Los Angeles, CA 90004 ☏323/962-9574–7, ⓦwww.thai-la.net.
Vietnam 63–65 Hoang Dieu St, Hanoi ☏04/823-5092–3; plus consulate at 77 Tran Quoc Thao St, District 3, Ho Chi Minh City ☏08/932-7637–8, ⓦwww.thaiembassy.org/hochiminhcity.

Information and maps

The efficient Tourism Authority of Thailand, or TAT (ⓦwww.tourismthailand.org), maintains offices in several cities abroad, where you can pick up a few glossy brochures and get fairly detailed answers to specific pre-trip questions. More comprehensive local information is given at the TAT offices in Bangkok and at the branches of the city's Bangkok Tourist Bureau.

The **Bangkok Tourist Bureau** (BTB) provides a decent information service from its headquarters, the **Bangkok Information Centre**, located next to Phra Pinklao Bridge at 17/1 Thanon Phra Athit in Banglamphu (daily 9am–7pm; ☏02 225 7612–4, ⓦwww .bangkoktourist.com; see map on p.80), and this is supported by 27 strategically placed satellite booths around the capital (daily 9am–5pm), including in front of the Grand Palace, at the Erawan Shrine, at River City and Mah Boon Krong shopping centres, in front of Robinson Department Store on Thanon Silom, and in front of Banglamphu's Wat Chana Songkhram.

The city's branches of the nationwide **Tourism Authority of Thailand** can also be useful. TAT maintains a booth in the airport arrivals concourse and runs a Tourist Service Centre at 4 Rajdamnoen Nok, Banglamphu (daily 8.30am–4.30pm; ☏02 283 1500, freephone tourist assistance 8am–8pm ☏1672, ⓦwww .tourismthailand.org; see colour map), a twenty-minute stroll from Thanon Khao San, or a short ride in air-conditioned bus #503. TAT's headquarters (daily 8.30am–4.30pm; ☏02 250 5500) are rather inconveniently located out at 1600 Thanon Phetchaburi Mai, 350m west of the junction with Sukhumvit Soi 21 and the Phetchaburi subway stop, or 150m east of the junction with Sukhumvit Soi 3 and Tha Nana Nua on the Khlong Saen Saeb canal boat service (see the Thanon Sukhumvit map on p.126). In addition, you can contact the TAT Call Centre from anywhere in the country on ☏1672 daily from 8am to 8pm.

Note, however, that the many other shops and offices across the capital displaying signs announcing "TAT Tourist Information" or similar are **not official Tourism Authority of Thailand centres** and will not be dispensing impartial advice: the Tourism Authority of Thailand never uses the acronym "TAT" on its office-fronts or in its logo.

TAT offices abroad

Australia and New Zealand Level 2, 75 Pitt St, Sydney, NSW 2000 ☏02/9247 7549, ⓦwww .thailand.net.au.
South Africa Contact the UK office.
UK and Ireland 3rd Floor, Brook House, 98–99 Jermyn St, London SW1Y 6EE ☏020/7925 2511, recorded information on ☏0870/900 2007, ⓦwww.thaismile.co.uk.
US and Canada 61 Broadway, Suite 2010, New York, NY 10006 ☏212/432-0433, ⓔinfo@tatny.com; 611 North Larchmont Blvd, 1st Floor, Los Angeles, CA 90004 ☏323/461-9814, ⓔtatla@ix.netcom.com.

Maps

To get around Bangkok on the cheap, you'll need to buy a **bus map**. Of the several available at bookshops, hotels and some guest houses, the most useful is Bangkok Guide's *Bus Routes & Map*, which not only maps all major air-conditioned and non-air-conditioned bus routes but also carries detailed written itineraries of some two hundred bus routes. The long-running bright blue and yellow bus map published by Tour 'n' Guide also maps bus routes and dozens of smaller sois, but its street locations are not always reliable, and it can be hard to decipher exact bus routings. The bus routes on *Litehart's Groovy Map and Guide* are clearly colour-coded but only selected ones are given. Serious shoppers will want to buy a copy of the idiosyncratic *Nancy Chandler's Map of Bangkok*, which has lots of annotated recommendations on shops, markets and interesting neighbourhoods across the city and is reliably accurate; it's available in most tourist areas and from ⓦwww.nancychandler.net.

Health

Thailand's climate, wildlife and cuisine present Western travellers with fewer health worries than in many Asian destinations.

For a start, there's no need to bring huge supplies of non-prescription medicines with you, as Thai **pharmacies** (*raan khai yaa*; typically open daily 8.30am–8pm) are well stocked with local and international branded medicaments, and of course they are generally much less expensive than at home. Nearly all pharmacies – including the city-wide branches of Boots the Chemist (most usefully on Thanon Khao San, in the Siam Centre on Thanon Rama I, on Patpong and inside the Emporium on Thanon Sukhumvit) – are run by trained English-speaking pharmacists, who are usually the best people to talk to if your symptoms aren't acute enough to warrant seeing a doctor.

Medical resources for travellers

UK and Ireland

British Airways Travel Clinics London ☎0845/600 2236, ⓦwww.ba.com/travel/healthclinintro.
Hospital for Tropical Diseases Travel Clinic London ☎020/7387 5000 or ☎0845/155 5000, ⓦwww.thehtd.org.
MASTA (Medical Advisory Service for Travellers Abroad) UK ⓦwww.masta.org or ☎0113/238 7575 for the nearest clinic.
NHS Travel Health Website ⓦwww.fitfortravel.scot.nhs.uk.
Royal College of Surgeons Travel Health Centre Dublin ☎01/402 2337.
Travel Medicine Services Belfast ☎028/9031 5220.
Tropical Medical Bureau Dublin ☎1850/487 674, ⓦwww.tmb.ie.

US and Canada

Canadian Society for International Health ⓦwww.csih.org. Extensive list of travel health centres.
CDC ⓦwww.cdc.gov/travel. Official US government travel health site.

International Society for Travel Medicine ⓦwww.istm.org. Lists travel health clinics.

Australia, New Zealand and South Africa

Travellers' Medical and Vaccination Centre ⓦwww.tmvc.com.au, in Australia ☎1300/658 844. Lists travel clinics in Australia, New Zealand and South Africa.

Inoculations

There are no compulsory **inoculation** requirements for people travelling to Thailand from the West, but you should consult a doctor or other health professional, preferably at least four weeks in advance of your trip, for the latest information on recommended immunizations. Most doctors strongly advise vaccinations or boosters against polio, tetanus, typhoid, diphtheria and hepatitis A, and in some cases they might also recommend protecting yourself against rabies, hepatitis B and other diseases. If you forget to have all your inoculations before leaving home, or don't leave yourself sufficient time, you can get them in Bangkok at, for example, the Thai Red Cross Society's Queen Saovabha Memorial Institute (QSMI) and Snake Farm on the corner of Thanon Rama IV and Thanon Henri Dunant (Mon–Fri 8.30am–noon & 1–4.30pm; ☎02 252 0161–4, ⓦwww.redcross.or.th; see also p.121), or the Travmin Medical Centre (see p.30).

Mosquito-borne diseases

Only certain regions of Thailand are now considered malarial, and **Bangkok is malaria-free**, so if you are restricting yourself to the capital you do not have to take malaria prophylactics. Bangkok does however have its fair share of **mosquitoes**; though nearly all the city's hotels and guest houses have screened windows, you will probably want to take mosquito repellent with you (or buy it there from any supermarket or pharmacy).

A further reason to protect yourself is the (remote) possibility of contracting **dengue fever**, a viral disease spread by mosquitoes that's on the increase throughout tropical Asia. There's no inoculation against it, though it's rarely fatal; symptoms usually develop between five and eight days after being bitten and include fever, headaches, severe joint and muscle pain ("breakbone fever" is another name for dengue), and possibly a rash. There are occasional outbreaks of dengue fever in Bangkok, particularly during and just after the rainy season; the only treatment is bed rest, liquids and non-aspirin-based painkillers, though more serious cases may require hospitalization.

Digestive problems

By far the most common travellers' complaint in Thailand, **digestive troubles** are often caused by contaminated food and water, or sometimes just by an overdose of unfamiliar foodstuffs. Break your system in gently by avoiding excessively spicy curries and too much raw fruit in the first few days, and then use your common sense about choosing where and what to eat: if you stick to the most crowded restaurants and noodle-stalls you should be perfectly safe. You need to be more rigorous about **drinking water**, though: stick to bottled water (even when brushing your teeth), which is sold everywhere, or else opt for boiled water or tea.

Stomach trouble usually manifests itself as simple **diarrhoea**, which should clear up without medical treatment within three to seven days and is best combated by drinking lots of fluids. If this doesn't work, you're in danger of getting **dehydrated** and should take some kind of rehydration solution, either a commercial sachet of ORS (oral rehydration solution), sold in all Thai pharmacies, or a do-it-yourself version, which can be made by adding a handful of sugar and a pinch of salt to every litre of boiled or bottled water (soft drinks are *not* a viable alternative). If you can eat, avoid fatty foods. Anti-diarrhoeal agents such as Imodium are useful for blocking you up, but only attack the symptoms and may

prolong infections; an antibiotic such as ciprofloxacin, however, can often reduce a typical attack of self-limiting traveller's diarrhoea to one day. If diarrhoea persists for a week or more, or if you have blood or mucus in your stools, or an accompanying fever, go to a doctor or hospital.

Other diseases

Between four and seven percent of dogs in Bangkok are reported to be rabid, so steer well clear of them, as **rabies** is transmitted by bites, scratches or even licks; cats and monkeys also carry rabies. Rabies is invariably fatal if the patient waits until symptoms begin, though modern vaccines and treatments are very effective and deaths are rare. The important thing is, if you are bitten, licked or scratched by an animal, to vigorously clean with soap and disinfect the wound, preferably with something containing iodine, and to seek medical advice regarding treatment right away.

AIDS is widespread in Thailand, primarily because of the sex trade (see p.124). Condoms (*meechai*) are sold in pharmacies, department stores, hairdressers, even on street markets. Due to rigorous screening methods, the country's medical blood supply is now considered safe.

There have been outbreaks of **avian influenza (bird flu)** in domestic poultry and wild birds in Thailand which have led to a small number of human fatalities, believed to have arisen through close contact with infected poultry. There has been no evidence of human-to-human transmission in Thailand, however, and the risk to humans is believed to be very low. Nevertheless, as a precaution, you should avoid visiting live animal markets and other places where you may come into close contact with birds, and ensure that poultry and egg dishes are thoroughly cooked.

Hospitals, clinics and dentists

Hospital (*rong phayaabahn*) cleanliness and efficiency vary, but generally hygiene and healthcare standards are good, the ratio of medical staff to patients is considerably higher than in most parts of the West, and the doctors speak English. In the event of a major health crisis, get someone to contact your embassy (see p.53) and insurance company. Most expats rate the private Bumrungrad International Hospital, 33 Sukhumvit Soi 3 (☎02 667 1000, emergency ☎02 667 2999, ⓦwww.bumrungrad.com), with its famously five-star accommodation, as the best and most comfortable in the city, followed by the BNH (Bangkok Nursing Home) Hospital, 9 Thanon Convent (☎02 686 2700, ⓦwww.bnhhospital.com); Bangkok International Hospital, 2 Soi Soonvijai 7, Thanon Phetchaburi Mai (☎02 310 3000, emergency ☎02 310 3102, ⓦwww.bangkokhospital.com); and the Samitivej Sukhumvit Hospital, 133 Sukhumvit Soi 49 (☎02 711 8000, ⓦwww.samitivej.co.th). Other recommended private hospitals include Bangkok Mission Hospital, 430 Thanon Phitsanulok, cnr Thanon Lan Luang, just east of Banglamphu (☎02 282 1100,

ⓦwww.tagnet.org/mission-net), and Bangkok Christian Hospital, 124 Thanon Silom (☎02 233 6981–9).

Among **general clinics**, the Australlan-run Iravmin Bangkok Medical Centre, 8th Floor, Alma Link Building, next to the Central Department Store at 25 Soi Chitlom, Thanon Ploenchit (☎02 655 1024–5; B650/consultation), is recommended.

For **dental problems**, try the Bumrungrad Hospital's dental department on ☎02 667 2300, or the following dental clinics (not 24hr): Care Dental Clinic 120/26 Soi Prasamnit 3, Sukhumvit Soi 23 ☎02 259 1604; Dental Hospital 88/88 Sukhumvit Soi 49 ☎02 260 5000–15, ⓦwww.dentalhospitalbangkok.com; Glas Haus Dental Centre, mouth of Sukhumvit Soi 25, ☎02 260 6120–2; Siam Family Dental Clinic 292/6 Siam Square Soi 4 ☎02/255 6664–5, ⓦwww.siamfamilydental.com.

Arrival

Unless you arrive in Bangkok by train, be prepared for a long journey into the centre. Both the old airport at Don Muang and its brand-new replacement, Suvarnabhumi Airport, are a slow 25km from the city centre. The three main coach stations are also a good way out, though at least the Northern Terminal is handily placed for the Skytrain and subway, the Eastern Terminal for the Skytrain.

By air: Suvarnabhumi Airport

At the time of going to press, the new **Suvarnabhumi Airport** (pronounced "soo-wanna-poom"; ⓦwww.suvarnabhumiairport.com, or go to ⓦwww.2bangkok.com or ⓦwww.bangkokairportonline.com for the latest news) had just opened, 25km east of central Bangkok off the main Bang Na–Trat highway towards Chonburi, at inauspiciously named Nong Ngu Hao (meaning "cobra swamp"). It now handles all scheduled international and domestic flights, while the old Don Muang Airport may continue handling charter airlines.

Facilities at Suvarnabhumi include tourist information and accommodation-booking desks in the Arrivals hall, plenty of cafés and restaurants (on Level 6), two 24-hour clinics, a spa and an airport hotel. Left-luggage storage is located between the international and domestic arrivals areas and costs B100 per 24hr; it's open 24 hours. However, Suvarnabhumi's facilities and transport connections are still a work in progress so some of the following transport information may change; check with the information desks at the airport for latest details.

Getting into town from Suvarnabhumi

There are several ways of getting into the city from Suvarnabhumi. Air-conditioned **Airport Express buses** (frequent departures; B150) depart from outside the Arrivals hall on Level 2 and serve four main areas of the city: route AE1 goes to Thanon Silom (via expressway); route AE2 serves Banglamphu (via expressway); route AE3 runs the length of Thanon Sukhumvit; and route AE4 heads for Hualamphong train station (via expressway).

To catch a **metered taxi**, however, you may need to head for levels 4 or 1; in addition to the standard meter rate for all Bangkok taxis (about B300 to Silom for example), you'll need to pay a B50 airport surcharge plus around B70 in tolls. Be sure to get a licensed metered taxi and to avoid any freelance unmetered taxi touts: see below for a warning about this.

For all other (cheaper) airport transport, particularly public buses, plus **rental car** pick-up, you need to first make your way from the passenger terminal to the main transportation centre, elsewhere in Suvarnabhumi's vast airport complex. This involves taking a free ten-minute ride on the "express route" shuttle bus from outside Arrivals (Level 2) or Departures (Level 4) to the transportation centre (be sure not to confuse this with the "ordinary route" shuttle bus, which ferries airport staff around the various buildings). At the transportation centre, you can catch **public buses** to the following destinations in the capital (all for no more than B40), though it is likely that more routes will be added in the future. Currently, the most useful are: #552 to On Nut Skytrain station at the far eastern end of Thanon Sukhumvit; #551 to Victory Monument (via expressway); #554 to Don Muang Airport (via expressway); and #553 to Samut Prakan. A route to the Southern Bus Terminal is also on the cards.

If you're aiming to get into town by **public taxi** from the transportation centre, avoid any tout who may offer a cheap ride in an unlicensed and unmetered vehicle, as newly arrived travellers are seen as easy prey for robbery, and the cabs are untraceable; instead take a metered, air-conditioned cab (with a distinctive "TAXI METER" sign on top).

Airport transport should become a lot less complicated when the planned high-speed **rail** link is completed (possibly in 2008). This will run to Phaya Thai Skytrain station in downtown Bangkok (connected to Phetchaburi subway station).

Accommodation at and around Suvarnabhumi

There is one **airport hotel** on site at Suvarnabhumi, a three-minute walk from the main passenger terminal, via a walkway. This is the *Novotel Suvarnabhumi* (☎02 131 1111, ⓦwww.accorhotels.com; ➒), which offers Thai, Japanese and international restaurants, a swimming pool, health spa and fitness centre, plus kids' play area and babysitting services.

Otherwise, the closest accommodation options are some 15km from the airport, on the far eastern edge of Bangkok: in **Bang Na** and around **Sukhumvit sois 71 and 77**. These include *Hotel Ibis Huamark Bangkok* at 7 Soi Ramkamhaeng 15, off Thanon Ramkamhaeng (☎02 308 7888, ⓦwww.ibishotel.com; 6x); *Avana Hotel* at 23/1 Soi 14/1, Thanon Bangna–Trad (☎02 744 4280, ⓦwww.avanahotel.com; 8x); and *Royal Princess Srinakarin* at 905 Thanon Srinakarin (☎02 721 8400, ⓦbangkok-srinakarin.royalprincess.com; 8x).

Transport to Suvarnabhumi

The Airport Express buses will likely be less reliable for **transport from the city to Suvarnabhumi**, as the Bangkok traffic will make it difficult for them to stick to their schedules. Instead, you'll probably be better off using the private minibuses to Suvarnabhumi arranged by travel agents, guest houses and hotels, especially in Banglamphu, with pick-ups from your accommodation. Alternatively, from downtown areas, ride the Skytrain to On Nut in the east of the city and then either take bus #552 for the last few kilometres to Suvarnabhumi, or flag down a taxi.

By train

Travelling to Bangkok by **train** from Malaysia and most parts of Thailand, you arrive at **Hualamphong Station**, which is centrally located, at the southern end of the subway line. The most useful of the numerous city buses serving Hualamphong are #53 (non-air-con), which stops on the east side (left-hand exit) of the station and runs to the budget accommodation in Banglamphu; and the #25 (ordinary and air-con), which runs east to Siam Square and along Thanon Sukhumvit to the Eastern Bus Terminal, or west through Chinatown to Tha Chang (for the Grand Palace). See box on p.36 for bus-route details.

Station **facilities** include a post office, an exchange booth, several ATMs, an Internet centre and a **left-luggage** office (daily 4am–11pm), which charges B20–30 per day, depending on the size of the bag (almost any rucksack counts as large). A more economical place to store baggage is at the *TT2 Guest House* (see p.173), about fifteen minutes' walk from the station, which provides the same service for only B10 per item per day, whatever the size.

One service the station does not provide is itinerant tourist assistance staff – anyone who comes up to you in or around the station concourse and offers help/information/ transport or ticket-booking services is almost certainly a **con-artist**, however many official-looking ID tags are hanging round their neck. This is a well-established scam to fleece new arrivals and should be avoided at all costs (see p.47 for more details). For train-related questions, contact the 24-hour "Information" counter close by the departures board. The station area is also fertile ground for **dishonest tuk-tuk drivers**, so you'll need to be extra suspicious to avoid them – take a metered taxi or public transport instead.

By bus

Long-distance buses come to a halt at a number of far-flung spots. All services from the north and northeast terminate at the **Northern Bus Terminal** (**Mo Chit**) on Thanon Kamphaeng Phet 2; some east-coast buses also use Mo Chit (rather than the Eastern Terminal), including several daily services from Chanthaburi and Trat (for the Cambodian border). The quickest way to get into the city centre from Mo Chit is to hop onto the Skytrain (see p.38) at the Mo

Chit Station, or the subway at the adjacent Chatuchak Park Station (see p.39), fifteen minutes' walk from the bus terminal on Thanon Phaholyothin, and then change onto a city bus if necessary. Otherwise, it's a long bus or taxi ride into town: city buses from the Northern Bus Terminal include ordinary #159 to Siam Square, Hualamphong Station, Banglamphu and the Southern Bus Terminal; and ordinary and air-conditioned #3, and air-conditioned #509 and #512 to Banglamphu; for details of these routes see the box on p.36.

Most buses from the east coast use the **Eastern Bus Terminal** (**Ekamai**) between sois 40 and 42 on Thanon Sukhumvit. This bus station is right beside the Ekamai Skytrain stop and is also served by lots of city buses, including air-conditioned #511 to Banglamphu and the Southern Bus Terminal (see box on p.36 for details), or you can take a taxi down Soi 63 to Tha Ekamai, a pier on Khlong Saen Saeb, to pick up the canal boat service to the Golden Mount near Banglamphu (see p.38). There's a left-luggage booth at the bus terminal (daily 8am–6pm; B30/day).

Bus services from Malaysia and the south, as well as from Kanchanaburi, use the **Southern Bus Terminal** (**Sai Tai Mai**) at the junction of Thanon Borom Ratchonni and the Nakhon Chaisri Highway, west of the Chao Phraya River in Thonburi. Drivers on these services always make a stop to drop passengers on the east side of Thanon Borom Ratchonni, in front of a Toyota dealer, before doing a time-consuming U-turn for the terminus on the west side of the road; if you're heading across the river to Banglamphu or downtown Bangkok you should get off here, along with the majority of the other passengers. Numerous **city buses** cross the river from this bus stop, including air-con #507 to Banglamphu, Hualamphong Station and Thanon Rama IV, air-con #511 to Banglamphu and Thanon Sukhumvit, and non-air-con #159 to the Northern Bus Terminal (see box on p.36 for routes). This is also a better place to grab a **taxi** into town, as rides are faster and cheaper when started from here.

Orientation

Bangkok can be a tricky place to get your bearings as it's huge and ridiculously congested, with largely featureless modern buildings and no obvious centre. The boldest line on the map is the Chao Phraya River, which divides the city into Bangkok proper on the east bank, and Thonburi, part of Greater Bangkok, on the west.

The historical core of Bangkok proper, site of the original royal palace, is **Ratanakosin**, which nestles into a bend in the river. Three concentric canals radiate eastwards around Ratanakosin: the southern part of the area between the canals is the old-style trading enclave of **Chinatown** and Indian **Pahurat**, linked to the old palace by Thanon Charoen Krung (aka New Road); the northern part is characterized by old temples and the **Democracy Monument**, west of which is the backpackers' ghetto of **Banglamphu**. Beyond the canals to the north, **Dusit** is the site of many government buildings and the nineteenth-century palace, which is linked to Ratanakosin by the three stately avenues, Thanon Rajdamnoen Nok, Thanon Rajdamnoen Klang and Thanon Rajdamnoen Nai.

"New" Bangkok begins to the east of the canals and beyond the main rail line and Hualamphong Station, and stretches as far as the eye can see to the east and north. The main business district and most of the embassies are south of **Thanon Rama IV**, with the port of Khlong Toey at the southern edge. The diverse area north of Thanon Rama IV includes the sprawling campus of Chulalongkorn University, huge shopping centres around **Siam Square** and a variety of other businesses. A couple of blocks northeast of Siam Square stands the tallest building in Bangkok, the 84-storeyed **Baiyoke II Tower** whose golden spire makes a good point of reference. To the east lies the swish residential quarter off **Thanon Sukhumvit**.

Bangkok addresses

Thai **addresses** can be confusing, as property is often numbered twice, firstly to show which real-estate lot it stands in, and then to distinguish where it is on that lot. Thus 154/7–10 Thanon Rajdamnoen means the building is on lot 154 and occupies numbers 7–10.

A minor road running off a major road is often numbered as a **soi** ("lane" or "alley", though it may be a sizeable thoroughfare), rather than given its own street name. Thanon Sukhumvit, for example, has minor roads numbered Soi 1 to Soi 103, with odd numbers on one side of the road and even on the other; so a Thanon Sukhumvit address could read something like 27/9–11 Soi 15, Thanon Sukhumvit, which would mean the property occupies numbers 9–11 on lot 27 on minor road number 15 running off Thanon Sukhumvit.

City transport

The main form of transport in the city is **buses**, and once you've mastered the labyrinthine complexity of the route maps you'll be able to get to any part of the city, albeit slowly. Catching the various kinds of **taxi** is more expensive, and you'll still get held up by the daytime traffic jams.

Boats are obviously more limited in their range, but they're regular and as cheap as buses, and you'll save a lot of time by using them whenever possible – a journey between Banglamphu and the GPO, for instance, will take around thirty minutes by water, half what it would take on land. The **Skytrain** and **subway** each have a similarly limited range but are also worth using whenever suitable for all or part of your journey; their networks roughly coincide with each other at the east end of Thanon Silom, at the corner of Thanon Sukhumvit and Thanon Asok Montri (Soi 21), and on Thanon Phaholyothin by

Tours of the city

If you can't face negotiating the public transport network, any taxi or tuk-tuk driver can be hired for the day to take you around the major or minor sights (B700–800), and every travel agent in the city can arrange this for you as well; read the advice on avoiding tuk-tuk tout scams on p.47 first. Alternatively, the Bangkok Tourist Bureau (BTB; see p.27) runs occasional **tours of the capital**, including a night-time bicycle tour of Ratanakosin (Sat 6.30–9.30pm; minimum five people; B390 including bicycle), weekend walking tours according to demand (B100), and a tourist "tram" (more like an open-topped single-decker bus) which covers a forty-minute circuit from the Grand Palace down to Wat Pho, up to Banglamphu, and back to the palace, roughly every half an hour (daily 9.30am–5pm; B30). Real Asia (T02 665 6364, W www.realasia.net) does canal and walking tours through Thonburi and leads outings to the historic fishing port of Samut Sakhon (from B1800), and Tamarind Tours runs imaginative and well-regarded tours of the city and nearby provinces, including specialized options such as Bangkok X-Files and Bangkok After Dark (T02 238 3227, W www.tamarindtours.com; from US$59).

Unlikely as it sounds, there are several companies offering **cycle tours** of the city's outer neighbourhoods and beyond; these are an excellent way to gain a different perspective on Thai life and offer a unique chance to see traditional communities close up. The most popular, longest-running bicycle tour is the ABC Amazing Bangkok Cyclist Tour, which starts in the Thanon Sukhumvit area and takes you across the river to surprisingly rural khlong- and riverside communities; tours operate every day year-round, cover up to 30km depending on the itinerary, and need to be reserved in advance through Real Asia (T02 665 6364, W www.realasia .net; B1000–2000 including bicycle). Bangkok Bike Rides (T02 712 5305 W www .bangkokbikerides.com; $25–50 per person, minimum two people) also operates from the Sukhumvit area and runs a programme of different daily tours within Greater Bangkok as well as to the floating markets and canalside neighbourhoods of Damnoen Saduak and Samut Songkhram in the central plains. Grasshopper Adventures runs half-day cycle tours from Banglamphu around the sights of Ratanakosin (departs every Sun at 8am from the Viengtai Hotel on Thanon Ram Bhuttri; T087 929 5208, W www.grasshopperadventures.com; B800).

For details of Thonburi canal tours, see p.100; for Chao Phraya express tourist boats, see p.36; and for dinner cruises along the Chao Phraya River, see p.183.

Chatuchak Park (Mo Chit), while the Skytrain joins up with the Chao Phraya express boats at the vital hub of Sathorn/Saphan Taksin (Taksin Bridge) and the subway intersects the mainline railway at Hualamphong and Bang Sue stations. **Walking** might often be quicker than travelling by road, but the heat can be unbearable, distances are always further than they look on the map, and the engine fumes are stifling.

At the back of this guide you'll find full-colour route maps of the Skytrain, subway and Khlong Saen Saeb longtail boats and of the Chao Phraya express boats.

Buses

Bangkok is served by over four hundred bus routes, reputedly the world's largest bus network, on which operate three main types of bus service. On **ordinary** (non-air-con) buses, which are either red and white, blue and white, or small and green, fares range from B6 to B9; most routes operate from about 4am to 10pm, but some maintain a 24-hour service, as noted in the box on p.36. **Air-conditioned** buses are either blue, orange or white (some are articulated) and charge between B12 and B24 according to distance travelled; most stop in the late evening, but a few of the more popular routes run 24-hour services. As buses can only go as fast as the car in front, which at the moment is averaging four kilometres per hour, you'll probably be spending a long time on each journey, so you'd be well advised to pay the extra for cool air – and the air-conditioned buses are usually less crowded, too. It's also possible to travel certain routes (until 9pm) on pink, air-conditioned private **microbuses**, which were designed with the commuter in mind and offer the certainty of a seat (no standing allowed). The fare is generally a flat B25 (exact money only), which is dropped into a box beside the driver's seat.

Some of the most useful city-bus routes are described in the box p.36; for a comprehensive roundup of bus routes in the capital, buy a copy of Bangkok Guide's *Bus Routes & Map* (see p.27), or log onto the Bangkok Mass Transit Authority website (Ⓦwww.bmta.co.th), which gives details of all city-bus routes, bar microbuses and airport buses.

Boats

Bangkok was built as an amphibious city around a network of canals – or **khlongs** – and the first streets were constructed only in the second half of the nineteenth century. Many canals remain on the Thonburi side of the river, but most of those on the Bangkok side have been turned into roads. The Chao Phraya River itself is still a major transport route for residents and non-residents alike, forming more of a link than a barrier between the two halves of the city. See the colour section, *Bangkok by boat*, for more on riverine travel in the capital.

Express boats

The Chao Phraya Express Boat Company operates the vital **express-boat** (*reua duan*; Ⓦwww.chaophrayaboat.co.th) service, using large water buses to plough up and down the river, between clearly signed piers (*tha*), which appear on all Bangkok maps. Tha Sathorn, which gives access to the Skytrain network at Saphan Taksin Station, has been designated "Central Pier", with piers to the south of here numbered S1, S2, etc, those to the north N1, N2 and so on – the important stops in the centre of the city are outlined in the box on p.00 and marked on our colour maps at the back of the book. Its basic route, one hour thirty minutes in total, runs between Wat Rajsingkorn, just upriver of Krung Thep Bridge, in the south, and Nonthaburi in the north. These **"standard"** boats set off every fifteen/twenty minutes between around 6am and 7.30pm (6.40pm on Sat & Sun). Boats do not necessarily stop at every landing – they only pull in if people want to get on or off, and when they do stop, it's not for long – so when you want to get off, be ready at the back of the boat in good time for your pier. During busy periods, certain **"special express"** boats operate limited-stop services on set routes, flying either a **blue flag** (Nonthaburi to Tha Sathorn in 35min, stopping only at Wang Lang; Mon–Fri roughly 6–9am & 5–7pm), a **yellow flag** (Nonthaburi to Rajburana, far downriver beyond Krung Thep Bridge, in about 50min; Mon–Fri roughly 6–9am & 4–7.30pm) or an **orange flag** (Nonthaburi to Wat Rajsingkorn in 1hr; Mon–Fri roughly 6–9am & 2.30–7pm).

Useful bus routes

For more details on Banglamphu bus stops and routes, see p.78.

#3 (ordinary and air-con, 24hr): Northern Bus Terminal–Chatuchak Weekend Market–Thanon Phaholyothin–Thanon Samsen–Thanon Phra Athit (for Banglamphu guest houses)–Thanon Sanam Chai–Thanon Triphet–Memorial Bridge (for Pak Khlong Talat)–Taksin Monument–Wat Suwan.

#15 (ordinary): Krung Thep Bridge–Thanon Charoen Krung–Thanon Silom–Thanon Rajdamri–Siam Square–Thanon Lan Luang–Sanam Luang–Thanon Phra Athit.

#16 (ordinary and air-con): Thanon Srinarong–Thanon Samsen–Thewes (for guest houses)–Thanon Phitsanulok–Thanon Phrayathai–Siam Square–Thanon Suriwong.

#25 (ordinary and air-con, 24hr): Eastern Bus Terminal–Thanon Sukhumvit–Siam Square–Hualamphong station–Thanon Yaowarat (for Chinatown)–Pahurat–Wat Pho–Tha Chang (for the Grand Palace). Note, however, that some #25 buses (ordinary only) only go as far as Hualamphong Station, while during rush hours some #25 buses take the expressway, missing out Siam Square.

#29 (ordinary and air-con): Don Muang Airport–Chatuchak Weekend Market–Siam Square–Thanon Phrayathai–Thanon Rama IV–Hualamphong Station.

#38 (ordinary): Chatuchak Weekend Market–Victory Monument–Thanon Phrayathai–Thanon Phetchaburi–Thanon Asok Montri–Thanon Sukhumvit–Eastern Bus Terminal.

#39 (ordinary, 24hr): Chatuchak Weekend Market–Victory Monument–Thanon Phetchaburi–Thanon Lan Luang–Democracy Monument–Rajdamnoen Klang (for Thanon Khao San guest houses)–Sanam Luang. Note, however, that some #39 buses only run as far south as Victory Monument.

#53 circular (also anti-clockwise; ordinary): Thewes–Thanon Krung Kasem–Hualamphong Station–Thanon Yaowarat–Pahurat–Pak Khlong Talat–Thanon Maharat (for Wat Pho, the Grand Palace and Wat Mahathat)–Sanam Luang (for National Museum)–Thanon Phra Athit and Thanon Samsen (for Banglamphu guest houses)–Thewes.

#56 circular (also clockwise; ordinary): Thanon Phra Sumen–Wat Bowoniwes–Thanon Pracha Thipatai–Thanon Ratchasima (for Vimanmek Palace)–Thanon Rajwithi–Krung Thon Bridge–Thonburi–Phrapokklao Bridge–Thanon Chakraphet (for Chinatown)–Thanon Mahachai–Democracy Monument–Thanon Tanao (for Khao San guest houses)–Thanon Phra Sumen.

#59 (ordinary and air-con, 24hr): Don Muang Airport–Chatuchak Weekend Market–Victory Monument–Thanon Phrayathai–Thanon Phetchaburi–Phan Fah (for Khlong Saen Saeb and Golden Mount)–Democracy Monument (for Banglamphu guest houses)–Sanam Luang.

Tickets can be bought on board, and cost B9–13 on standard boats according to distance travelled, B13 flat rate on orange-flag boats, B18–27 on yellow-flag boats and B22–32 on blue-flag boats. Don't discard your ticket until you're off the boat, as the staff at some piers impose a B1 fine on anyone disembarking without one.

The Chao Phraya Express Boat Company also runs **tourist boats**, distinguished by their light-blue flags, between Sathorn (departs every 30min 9.30am–3pm on the hour and half-hour) and Banglamphu piers (departs every 30min 10am–3.30pm on the hour and half-hour). In between (in both directions), these boats call in at Oriental, Si Phraya, Rachawongse, Saphan Phut, the Princess Mother Memorial Park in Thonburi, Thien, Maharaj (near Wat Mahathat and the Grand Palace) and Wang Lang; there are also free connecting boats from Tha Banglamphu across to the Royal Barge Museum. On-board guides provide running commentaries, and a one-day ticket for unlimited trips, which also allows you to use other express boats within the same route between 9am

#124 (ordinary): Southern Bus Terminal–Phra Pinklao Bridge–Sanam Luang (for Banglamphu guest houses).

#159 (ordinary): Southern Bus Terminal–Phra Pinklao Bridge–Democracy Monument–Hualamphong Station–MBK Shopping Centre–Thanon Rajaprarop–Victory Monument–Chatuchak Weekend Market–Northern Bus Terminal.

#503 (air-con): Sanam Luang (for Banglamphu guest houses)–Democracy Monument–Rajdamnoen Nok (for TAT and boxing stadium)–Wat Benjamabophit–Thanon Sri Ayutthaya (for Thewes guest houses)–Victory Monument–Chatuchak Weekend Market–Rangsit. Note, however, that during rush hours, some #503 buses take the expressway, missing out Chatuchak Weekend Market.

#504 (air-con): Don Muang Airport–Thanon Rajaprarop–Thanon Rajdamri–Thanon Silom–Thanon Charoen Krung–Krungthep Bridge.

#507 (air-con): Southern Bus Terminal–Phra Pinklao Bridge (for Banglamphu guest houses)–Sanam Luang–Thanon Charoen Krung (New Road)–Thanon Chakraphet–Thanon Yaowarat (for Chinatown and Wat Traimit)–Hualamphong Station–Thanon Rama IV (for Soi Ngam Duphli guest houses)–Bang Na Intersection–Pak Nam (for Ancient City buses).

#508 (air-con): Thanon Maharat–Grand Palace–Thanon Charoen Krung–Siam Square–Thanon Sukhumvit–Eastern Bus Terminal–Pak Nam (for Ancient City buses). Note, however, that during rush hours, some #508 buses take the expressway, missing out the Eastern Bus Terminal.

#509 (air-con): Northern Bus Terminal–Chatuchak Weekend Market–Victory Monument–Thanon Rajwithi–Thanon Sawankhalok–Thanon Phitsanulok–Thanon Rajdamnoen Nok–Democracy Monument–Rajdamnoen Klang (for Banglamphu guest houses)–Phra Pinklao Bridge–Thonburi.

#511 (air-con, 24hr): Southern Bus Terminal–Phra Pinklao Bridge–Wat Bowoniwes (for Banglamphu guest houses)–Democracy Monument–Thanon Lan Luang–Thanon Phetchaburi–Thanon Sukhumvit–Eastern Bus Terminal–Pak Nam (for Ancient City buses). Note, however, that during the day, some #511 buses take the expressway, missing out the Eastern Bus Terminal.

#512 (air-con): Northern Bus Terminal–Chatuchak Weekend Market–Thanon Phetchaburi–Thanon Lan Luang–Democracy Monument (for Banglamphu guest houses)–Sanam Luang–Tha Chang (for Grand Palace)–Pak Khlong Talat.

#513 (air-con): Don Muang Airport–Victory Monument–Thanon Phrayathai–Thanon Sri Ayutthaya–Thanon Rajaprarop–Eastern Bus Terminal–Thanon Sukhumvit. Note, however, that some #513 buses take the expressway, missing out the section from Victory Monument to the Eastern Bus Terminal.

and 7.30pm, costs B100; one-way tickets are also available, costing, for example, B20 from Tha Sathorn to Maharaj.

Cross-river ferries

Smaller than express boats are the slow **cross-river ferries** (*reua kham fak*), which shuttle back and forth between the same two points. Found at or beside every express stop and plenty of other piers in between, they are especially useful for exploring Thonburi and for connections to

Chao Phraya special-express-boat stops during rush hours. Fares are B2–3, which you usually pay at the entrance to the pier.

Longtail boats

Longtail boats (*reua hang yao*) ply the khlongs of Thonburi like commuter buses, stopping at designated shelters (fares are in line with those of express boats), and are available for individual rental here and on the river (see box on p.98). On the Bangkok side, **Khlong Saen Saeb** is well served by

Central stops for the Chao Phraya express boats

Piers are marked on the colour maps at the back of the book.

N15 Thewes (all boats except blue flag) – for Thewes guest houses.

N14 Rama VIII Bridge (standard) – for Samsen Soi 5.

N13 Phra Athit (standard and orange flag) – for Thanon Phra Athit, Thanon Khao San and Banglamphu guest houses.

N12 Phra Pinklao Bridge (all boats except blue flag) – for Royal Barge Museum and Thonburi shops.

N11 Thonburi Railway Station (or Bangkok Noi; standard) – for trains to Kanchanaburi.

N10 Wang Lang (or Siriraj; all standard and special express boats) – for Siriraj Hospital and hospital museums.

N9 Chang (standard and orange flag) – for the Grand Palace.

N8 Thien (standard) – for Wat Pho, and the cross-river ferry to Wat Arun.

N7 Ratchini (aka Rajinee; standard).

N6 Saphan Phut (Memorial Bridge; standard and orange flag) – for Pahurat, Pak Khlong Talat and Wat Prayoon.

N5 Rachawongse (aka Rajawong; all boats except blue flag) – for Chinatown.

N4 Harbour Department (standard and orange flag).

N3 Si Phraya (all boats except blue flag) – walk north past the *Sheraton Royal Orchid Hotel* for River City shopping complex.

N2 Wat Muang Kae (standard) – for GPO.

N1 Oriental (standard and orange flag) – for Thanon Silom.

Central Sathorn (all standard and special express boats) – for the Skytrain (Saphan Taksin Station) and Thanon Sathorn.

longtails, which run at least every fifteen minutes during daylight hours from the Phan Fah pier at the Golden Mount (handy for Banglamphu, Ratanakosin and Chinatown), and head way out east to Wat Sribunruang, with useful stops at Thanon Phrayathai, aka Saphan Hua Chang (for Jim Thompson's House and Ratchathevi Skytrain stop); Pratunam (for the Erawan Shrine); Soi Chitlom; Thanon Witthayu (Wireless Road); and Soi Nana Nua (Soi 3), Thanon Asok Montri (Soi 21, for TAT headquarters and Phetchaburi subway stop), Soi Thonglo (Soi 55) and Soi Ekamai (Soi 63), all off Thanon Sukhumvit. This is your quickest and most interesting way of getting between the west and east parts of town, if you can stand the stench of the canal. You may have trouble actually locating the piers as few are signed in English and they all look very unassuming and rickety; keep your eyes peeled for a plain wooden jetty – most jetties serve boats running in both directions. Once on the boat,

state your destination to the conductor when he collects your fare, which will be between B8 and B18. Due to the construction of some low bridges, all passengers change onto a different boat at Tha Pratunam and then again at the stop way out east on Sukhumvit Soi 71 – just follow the crowd.

The Skytrain

Although its network is limited, the **BTS Skytrain**, or *rot fai faa* (ⓦ www.bts.co.th), provides a much faster alternative to the bus, and is clean, efficient and vigorously air-conditioned. There are only two Skytrain lines, both running every few minutes from around 6am to midnight, with **fares** of B10–40 per trip depending on distance travelled. You'd really have to be motoring to justify buying a day **pass** at B100, while the ten-trip, fifteen-trip and thirty-trip cards, for B250, B300 and B540 respectively (valid for thirty days), are designed for long-distance commuters.

The **Sukhumvit Line** runs from Mo Chit (stop N8) in the northern part of the city (near Chatuchak Market and the Northern Bus Terminal) south via Victory Monument (N3) to the interchange, **Central Station**, at Siam Square, and then east along Thanon Ploenchit and Thanon Sukhumvit, via the Eastern Bus Terminal (Ekamai; E7), to On Nut (Soi 77, Thanon Sukhumvit; E9); the whole journey to the eastern end of town from Mo Chit takes around thirty minutes.

The **Silom Line** runs from the National Stadium (W1), just west of Siam Square, through Central Station, and then south along Thanon Rajdamri, Thanon Silom and Thanon Sathorn, via Sala Daeng near Patpong (S2), to Saphan Taksin (Sathorn Bridge; S6), to link up with the full gamut of express boats on the Chao Phraya River. Free feeder buses for Skytrain passholders, currently covering six circular routes, mostly along Thanon Sukhumvit, are geared more for commuters than visitors, but pick up a copy of the ubiquitous free BTS **map** if you want more information.

The subway

Bangkok's underground rail system, the **subway** or metro (in Thai, *rot fai tai din*; ⓦ www.bangkokmetro.co.th), has similar advantages to the Skytrain, though its current single line connects few places of interest for visitors. With fares of between B14 and B36, the subway runs a frequent service (every 2–7min) between around 6.30am and 11.30pm from Hualamphong train station, first heading east along Thanon Rama IV, with useful stops at Sam Yan (for Si Phraya and Phrayathai roads), Silom (near the Sala Daeng Skytrain station) and Lumphini (Thanon Sathorn/southeast corner of Lumphini Park). The line then turns north up Thanon Asok Montri/Thanon Ratchadapisek via the Queen Sirikit National Convention Centre, Sukhumvit Station (near Asoke Skytrain station), Phetchaburi (handy for Khlong Saen Saeb boats) and the Thailand Cultural Centre, before looping around via Chatuchak Park (near Mo Chit Skytrain station) and Kampaeng Phet (best stop for the weekend market) to terminate at Bang Sue railway station in the north of the city.

Taxis

Bangkok **taxis** come in three forms, and are so plentiful that you rarely have to wait more than a couple of minutes before spotting an empty one of any description. Neither tuk-tuks nor motorbike taxis have meters, so you should agree on a price before setting off, and expect to do a fair amount of haggling.

For nearly all journeys, the best and most comfortable option is to flag down one of Bangkok's metered, air-conditioned **taxi cabs**; look out for the "TAXI METER" sign on the roof, and a red light in the windscreen in front of the passenger seat, which means the cab is available for hire. Fares start at B35, and are displayed on a clearly visible meter that the driver should reset at the start of each trip, and increase in stages on a combined distance/time formula; as an example, a medium-range journey from Thanon Ploenchit to Thanon Sathorn will cost around B50 at a quiet time of day. Try to have change with you as cabs tend not to carry a lot of money; tipping of up to ten percent is common, though occasionally a cabbie will round down the fare on the meter. If a driver tries to quote a flat fare rather than using the meter, let him go, and avoid the now-rare unmetered cabs (denoted by a "TAXI" sign on the roof). If you want to book a metered taxi (B20 surcharge), call Siam Taxi Co-operative on ⓣ1661 or Taxi Radio on ⓣ1681.

Somewhat less stable though typically Thai, **tuk-tuks** have little to recommend them. These noisy, three-wheeled, open-sided buggies, which can carry three medium-sized passengers comfortably, fully expose you to the worst of Bangkok's pollution and weather. Locals might use tuk-tuks for short journeys – though you'll have to bargain hard to get a fare lower than the taxi-cab flagfall of B35 – while a longer trip from Thanon Ploenchit to Thanon Sathorn, for example, will set you back up to B100. Be aware, also, that tuk-tuk drivers tend to speak less English than taxi drivers – and there have been cases of robberies and attacks on women passengers late at night. During the day it's quite common for tuk-tuk drivers to try and **con** their passengers into visiting a jewellery or expensive souvenir shop with them, for which they get a hefty commission; the usual tactic involves falsely informing tourists that the Grand Palace, or whatever their destination might be, is closed (see p.47), and offering instead a ridiculously cheap, even free, city tour.

Motorbike taxis generally congregate at the entrances to long sois – pick the riders out by their numbered, coloured vests – and charge around B10 for short trips down into the side streets. If you're short on time and have nerves of steel, it's also possible to

charter them for hairy journeys out on the main roads (a trip from Thanon Ploenchit to Thanon Sathorn should cost around B50). Crash helmets are compulsory on all main roads in the capital (traffic police fine non-wearers on the spot), though they're rarely worn on trips down the sois and the local press has reported complaints from people who've caught head-lice this way (they suggest wearing a headscarf under the helmet).

Mail, phones and Internet access

Mail

Overseas mail should take around seven days to reach its destination from Bangkok. Post offices are the best places to buy **stamps**, though hotels and guest houses often sell them too, charging an extra B1 per stamp. An airmail letter of under 10g costs B17 to send to Europe or Australia and B19 to North America; standard-sized postcards cost B12, larger ones and aerogrammes B15, regardless of where they're going.

All **parcels** must be officially boxed and sealed (for a small fee) at special counters within main post offices, or in a private outlet just outside. Be prepared to queue, first for the packaging, then for the weighing and then again for the buying of stamps. The **surface** rate for parcels to the UK is B950 for the first kg, then B175/kg; to the US B550 for the first kg, then B140/kg; and to Australia B650 for the first kg, then B110/kg; the package should reach its destination in three months. The **airmail** rate for parcels to the UK is B900 for the first kg, then B380/kg; to the US B950 for the first kg, then B500/kg; and to Australia B750 for the first kg, then B350/kg; the package should reach its destination in one or two weeks.

The **GPO** is at 1160 Thanon Charoen Krung, a few hundred metres left of the exit for Wat Muang Kae express-boat stop. The

parcel-packing service operates Mon–Fri 8.30am–4.30pm, Sat 9am–noon, but most other services at the GPO are open Mon–Fri 8am–8pm, Sat & Sun 8am–1pm. If you're staying on or near Thanon Khao San in Banglamphu, it's more convenient to use one of the two post offices in Banglamphu itself. The one closest to Khao San is Ratchadamnoen Post Office on the eastern stretch of Soi Damnoen Klang Neua (Mon–Fri 8am–5pm, Sat 9am–1pm), with an efficient parcel-packing and sending service in the same building. Banglamphu's other post office is on Soi Sibsam Hang, just west of Wat Bowoniwes (Mon–Fri 8am–5pm, Sat 9am–1pm). The Thanon Sukhumvit post office is between sois 4 and 6 (Mon–Fri 8.30am–5.30pm, Sat 9am–noon).

Phones

Inter-provincial **calls within Thailand** can cost as much as B12/minute, but **local calls within Bangkok** are very cheap (as little as B1 for 3min from a coin payphone). To save fiddling around with coins, you may want to get hold of a domestic TOT **phonecard** for B100; this comes with a PIN number, is available from hotels and a wide variety of shops, and can be used in designated orange or green cardphones or in stainless steel payphones. For **directory enquiries** within Thailand, call ☎1133.

When **dialling** any number in Thailand, you must now always preface it with what used to be the area code, even when dialling from the same area; in this book we've separated off this code, for easy recognition (you'll still come across plenty of business cards and brochures which give only the old local number, to which you'll need to add the area code). Where we've given several line numbers – eg ☎02 431 1802–9 – you can substitute the last digit, 2, with any digit between 3 and 9.

All mobile phone numbers in Thailand have recently been changed from nine to ten digits, by adding the number "8" after the initial zero (again you're likely to come across cards and brochures giving the old number). Note also, however, that Thais tend to change mobile-phone providers – and therefore numbers – comparatively frequently, in search of a better deal. One final local idiosyncrasy: Thai phone books list people by their first name, not their family name.

The largest and most convenient **public telephone office** is in the compound of the GPO on Thanon Charoen Krung (daily 7am–8pm), which also offers a fax and Internet service, a free collect-call service and even video-conferencing. The post offices at Hualamphong Station, on Thanon Sukhumvit and in Banglamphu also have international telephone offices attached, but these close at 5pm (see p.40 for location details of these offices).

Mobile phones

An increasing number of tourists are taking their **mobile phones** to Thailand. Visitors from the US may well need to have a dual- or tri-band phone, but GSM 900Hz and 1800Hz, the systems most commonly found in other parts of the world, are both available in Thailand. Most foreign networks have links with Thai networks, but it's worth checking with your phone provider before you travel. For a full list of network types and providers in Thailand, along with coverage maps and roaming partners, go to ⓦwww.gsmworld .com/roaming.

If you want to use your mobile a lot in Thailand, it may well be worth getting hold of a rechargeable **Thai SIM card** with a local phone number, such as an AIS 1-2-Call card (ⓦwww.ais.co.th). Their call rates are B5 for the first minute, then B2 per minute within Thailand; international calls can cost as much as around B30 per minute, but you can get far cheaper rates (B7/min to the UK, for example) by using voice-over-internet protocol (VOIP; see below), prefixing the relevant country code with ☎009. Texts cost B2 domestic, around B9 international, and top-up cards are available at 7-11 stores around Bangkok.

Your own network operator may be able to give you useful advice about **exchanging SIM cards** before you leave home, but the best place in Bangkok to buy a card and have any necessary technical adjustments made is the Mah Boon Krong Centre (see p.212); an AIS 1-2-Call SIM card, for example, will cost you around B220, including your first B50 worth of calls. Because of heightened security fears, you'll need to take your passport along and fill in a simple registration form when you buy a rechargeable Thai SIM card.

International calls

There are two basic ways of making **international calls** from Thailand: by international direct-dialling (IDD), prefixing the relevant country code with ☎001; and far more cheaply, by voice-over-internet protocol (VOIP), prefixing the relevant country code with ☎009.

001 calls to North America cost B9/ minute, to Australia or the UK B18/minute and to New Zealand B22/minute. For most other countries, there are three time periods with different **rates**: the most expensive, or **standard**, time to call is from 7am to 9pm (economy rate applies on Sundays); the **economy** period runs from 9pm to midnight and 5am to 7am; the **reduced** rate applies between midnight and 5am. The per-minute rate for a direct-dial call to Ireland is B30 standard, B24 economy and B24 reduced, to South Africa B45/B36/B32.

You can use these government rates by buying a **Thaicard**, the international phonecard issued by CAT (Communications Authority of Thailand). Available in

International dialling codes

Calling from abroad, the international **country code** for Thailand is ☏**66**, after which you leave off the initial zero of the Thai number.

Calling from Thailand, for Burma, Cambodia, Laos or Malaysia dial ☏007 then the subscriber number, or for cheap-rate calls to Malaysia ☏002 then the subscriber number. For anywhere else, dial ☏001 or ☏009 and then the relevant country code:

Australia ☏61

Canada ☏1

Ireland ☏353

New Zealand ☏64

South Africa ☏27

UK ☏44

US ☏1

For **international directory enquiries** and operator services, call ☏100.

B100–3000 denominations at post offices and many shops, Thaicards can be used in designated purple cardphones, which are dotted all over the city, and at government telephone centres.

There's also a private international cardphone system called **Lenso**, whose yellow phones are also dotted all over the city. To use them, you either need a special Lenso phonecard (available from shops near the phones in B200, B300 and B500 denominations), or you can use a credit card. Rates, however, are ten percent higher than government IDD rates.

You can take advantage of the cheaper rates of **009 calls** by buying one of CAT's **Phone Net** cards, which come in denominations of B300 and B500. They're available from the same outlets as Thaicards (see above) and can be used in the same cardphones. Whatever time of day it is, tariffs are B5/minute to North America, B6/minute to Australia, South Africa and the UK, B14/minute to New Zealand and B24/minute to Ireland. Many private international call offices (where your call is timed and you pay at the end) in tourist areas such as Thanon Khao San now use VOIP to access these rates – plus a service charge to the customer, of course.

Internet access

Banglamphu is packed with places offering **Internet access**, in particular along Thanon Khao San, where competition keeps prices very low. To surf in style, head for True, housed in a beautiful early-twentieth-century villa at the back of *Tom Yam Kung* restaurant at the western end of Thanon Khao San, where you also can sip coffee, recline on retro sofas and browse lifestyle mags. Outside Banglamphu, mid-range and upmarket hotels also offer Internet access, but at vastly inflated prices. Thanon Sukhumvit has a number of makeshift phone/Internet offices, as well as several more formal and more clued-up Internet cafés, including one opposite the 7/11 on Soi 11 (daily 9am–midnight), and the Time Internet Centre on the second floor of Times Square, between sois 12 and 14 (daily 9am–midnight). On the north side of Thanon Silom, between Soi 4 and Soi 2/1, *Mr Bean* offers civilized surfing (daily 9am–10pm) and very good coffee. Elsewhere in the downtown area, during the day, there are several, rather noisy, places on Floor 7 of the MBK Shopping Centre, while *Chart Café* on the ground floor of River City shopping centre offers a bit more style and tranquillity, as well as food and drink while you're online.

There are **Catnet** centres at the Ratchadamnoen Post Office on Banglamphu's Soi Damnoen Klang Neua (Mon–Fri 8.30am–4.30pm) and in the public telephone office adjacent to the GPO on Thanon Charoen Krung (daily 7am–8pm). To use the service, you need to buy a B100 card with a Catnet PIN (available at all phone offices), which gives you around three hours of Internet time at any of these public terminals.

If you plan to email from your **laptop** in Bangkok, be advised that very few budget guest houses and cheap hotels have telephone sockets in the room. At the other end of the scale, luxury hotels charge astronomical rates for international calls, though many now offer broadband, or even wireless access. One potentially useful way round the cost issue is to become a temporary subscriber to the Thai ISP CS Loxinfo (☎02 263 8222, ⓦwww.csloxinfo .com). Their Webnet deal, for example, is aimed at international businesspeople and tourists and can be bought online; it allows you 12 hours of Internet access for B160, 30 hours for B380 or 63 hours for B750. The usual phone plug in Thailand is the American standard RJ11 phone-jack. See ⓦwww.kropla.com for detailed advice on how to set up your modem before you go, and how to hardwire phone plugs where necessary.

The media

To keep you abreast of world affairs, there are several English-language newspapers in Thailand, though a mild form of censorship affects the predominantly state-controlled media, even muting the English-language branches on occasion.

Newspapers and magazines

Of the hundreds of **Thai-language newspapers and magazines** published every week, the sensationalist tabloid *Thai Rath* attracts the widest readership, and the independent *Siam Rath*, founded by M.R. Kukrit Pramoj (see p.123), and the broadly similar *Matichon*, are the most intellectual.

Alongside these, two daily **English-language papers** – the *Bangkok Post* (ⓦwww.bangkokpost.com) and the *Nation* (ⓦwww.nationmultimedia.com) – are capable of adopting a fairly critical attitude to governmental goings-on and cover major domestic and international stories as well as tourist-related issues. Of the two, the *Bangkok Post* tends to focus more on international stories, while the *Nation* has the most in-depth coverage of Thai and Southeast Asian issues. Both are sold at most newsstands in Bangkok.

Bangkok Metro, the capital's monthly English-language listings **magazine**, as well as reviews and previews of events in the city, carries lively articles on cultural and contemporary life in Thailand. The more traveller-oriented monthly magazine *Untamed Travel* (formerly *Farang*) reviews bars, clubs, restaurants and guest houses in Thailand's most popular dozen tourist destinations and also prints some interesting features on contemporary Southeast Asian culture.

You can also pick up **foreign publications** such as *Newsweek*, *Time* and the *International Herald Tribune* in Bangkok; from Monday to Friday, the *IHT* now carries an English-language supplement devoted to Thailand, *Thai Day*. English-language bookstores such as Bookazine and some expensive hotels carry air-freighted copies of foreign national newspapers for at least B50 a copy. The weekly current affairs magazine *Far Eastern Economic Review* is also worth looking out for; available in major bookshops and at newsstands in tourist areas, it generally offers a very readable selection of articles on Thailand and the rest of Asia.

Television

There are five government-controlled **TV channels** in Thailand: channels 3, 5, 7 and 9 transmit a blend of news, documentaries, soaps, talk and quiz shows, while the more serious-minded 11 is a public-service channel, owned and operated by the government's public relations department. ITV is the only supposedly independent channel, owned and operated by Shin Corp, a communications conglomerate that was founded by Thaksin Shinawatra, but was recently sold, under controversial circumstances, to Temasek Holdings of Singapore; what effect, if any, this will have on editorial policy is unclear. **Cable** networks – available in many mid-range and most upmarket hotel rooms – carry channels from all around the world, including CNN from the US, BBC World from the UK, ABC from Australia, English-language movie channels, MTV and various sports and documentary channels. Both the *Bangkok Post* and the *Nation* print the daily TV and cable **schedule**.

Radio

Thailand boasts over five hundred **radio stations**, mostly music-oriented, ranging from Virgin Radio's Eazy (105.5 FM), which serves up Western pop, to Fat Radio, which plays Thai indie sounds (104.5 FM). At the opposite end of the taste spectrum, Chulalongkorn University Radio (101.5 FM) plays classical music from 9.30pm to midnight every night. Meanwhile, the government-controlled Radio Thailand broadcasts news in English on 95.5 FM and 105 FM every day at 7am, noon and 7pm.

With a shortwave **radio** – or by going **online** – you can pick up the BBC World Service (ⓦwww.bbcworldservice .com), Radio Australia (ⓦwww.abc.net. au/ra), Voice of America (ⓦwww.voa.gov), Radio Canada (ⓦwww.rcinet.ca) and other international stations right across Thailand. Times and wavelengths change regularly, so get hold of a recent schedule just before you travel or consult the websites for frequency and programme guides.

Festivals

Nearly all Thai festivals have some kind of religious aspect. The most theatrical are generally Brahmanic (Hindu) in origin, honouring elemental spirits with ancient rites and ceremonial costumed parades. In Buddhist celebrations, merit-making plays an important role and events are usually staged at the local temple, but a light-hearted atmosphere prevails, as the wat grounds are swamped with food- and trinket-vendors and makeshift stages are set up to show *likay* folk theatre, singing stars and beauty contests; there may even be funfair rides as well.

Few of the dates for religious festivals are fixed, so check with TAT for specifics or consult ⓦwww.thailandgrandfestival.com.

January/February Chinese New Year (new moon of the first lunar month: some time between mid-Jan and late Feb; Thanon Yaowarat and Charoen Krung). Even more foodstalls than usual in Chinatown and plenty to feast your eyes on too, including Chinese opera shows and jaunty parades led by traditional Chinese dragons and lions.

February Bangkok International Film Festival (usually takes place over ten days in Feb; at many downtown cinemas). Annual chance to preview new and unusual Thai films alongside features and documentaries from around the world. Check ⓦwww.bangkokfilm.org for programmes and dates.

February Maha Puja (on the day of full moon). A day of merit-making marks the occasion when 1250 disciples gathered spontaneously to hear the Buddha preach. Best experienced at Wat

Benjamabophit, where the festival culminates with a candlelit procession round the temple.

Late February to mid-April Kite fights and flying contests (Sanam Luang, Ratanakosin). Sanam Luang next to the Grand Palace is the venue for demonstrations and competitions of kite-flying and fighting (see p.71).

April 13–15 Songkhran: Thai New Year. The Thai New Year is welcomed in with massive waterfights and no one, least of all foreign tourists, escapes a good-natured soaking. Trucks roam the streets spraying passers-by with hosepipes and half the city carries a huge water pistol for the duration. Don't wear your favourite outfit as water is sometimes laced with dye. Celebrated throughout the city but famously raucous on Thanon Silom and, especially, on Thanon Khao San, which also stages special organized entertainments.

May Raek Na, Royal Ploughing Ceremony (early in the month; Sanam Luang). To mark the beginning of the rice-planting season, ceremonially clad Brahmin leaders parade sacred oxen and the royal plough across Sanam Luang, interpreting omens to forecast the year's rice yield (see also p.72).

May/June Visakha Puja (on the day of full moon of the sixth lunar month). Temples across the city are the focus of this holiest day of the Buddhist calendar, which commemorates the birth, enlightenment and death of the Buddha. The most photogenic event is the candlelit evening procession around the wat, particularly at Wat Benjamabophit in Dusit.

October 23 Chulalongkorn Day. Bangkokians mark the anniversary of the death of the widely loved Rama V, King Chulalongkorn (1868–1910), by laying offerings around the famous equestrian statue of the king, at the Thanon U-Thong-Thanon Sri Ayutthaya crossroads in Dusit (see p.106).

October Awk Pansa (on the day of full moon). Devotees at temples across the city make offerings to monks and there's general merrymaking to celebrate the end of the Buddhist retreat period.

October/November Loy Krathong (on the full moon day of the twelfth lunar month, between late Oct and early Nov). Wishes and prayers wrapped up in banana-leaf baskets full of flowers and lighted candles are released on to the Chao Phraya River and Thonburi canals in this charming festival that both honours the water spirits and celebrates the end of the rainy season.

October/November Vegetarian Festival (Ngan Kin Jeh) (held over nine days during the ninth lunar month in the Chinese calendar; Chinatown). Many Chinese people become vegetarian for this annual nine-day Taoist detox, so most food vendors and restaurants in Chinatown, and many outlets in other parts of the city, turn veggie too, displaying a yellow pennant to alert their customers (see p.186 for more).

November Ngan Wat Saket (first week; Wat Saket, near Democracy Monument). Probably Thailand's biggest temple fair, held around Wat Saket and the Golden Mount, with funfairs, folk theatre, music and tons of food.

November Bangkok Pride (for one week, usually mid-month; Thanon Silom and Lumphini Park). The capital's gay community struts its stuff in a week of parades, cabarets, fancy-dress shows and sports contests that culminates with a jamboree in Lumphini Park on the Saturday. See ⓦwww .bangkokpride.org.

December 2 Trooping the Colour (Suan Amporn, Dusit). An extraordinary array of sumptuous uniforms makes this annual marshalling of the Royal Guards a sight worth stopping for.

December 5 King's Birthday (Sanam Luang, Ratanakosin). In the evening thousands of people gather in Sanam Luang to light candles and sing the king's anthem, after which there's free entertainment into the night from pop stars and folk theatre troupes, capped by a huge fireworks display. Nearby Rajadamnoen Klang is prettily decorated with special lights and portraits of the king.

December 31 Western New Year's Eve The new year is greeted with fireworks along the river and at Sanam Luang, and huge crowds gather for a mass countdown around the Central World Plaza and Siam Square area, which is all pedestrianized for the night.

Crime and personal safety

As long as you keep your wits about you, you shouldn't encounter much trouble in Bangkok. Theft and pickpocketing are two of the main problems, but the most common cause for concern is the number of con-artists who dupe gullible tourists into parting with their cash.

To **prevent theft**, most travellers prefer to carry their valuables with them at all times, but it's sometimes possible to leave your valuables in a hotel or guest-house locker – the safest lockers are those that require your own padlock, as there are occasional reports of valuables being stolen by hotel staff. **Padlock your luggage** when leaving it in hotel or guest-house rooms, as well as when consigning it to storage or taking it on public transport. Padlocks also come in handy as extra security on your room.

Personal safety

Be wary of accepting food and drink from strangers as it may be drugged. This might sound paranoid, but there have been enough **drug-muggings** for TAT to publish a specific warning about the problem. Drinks are sometimes spiked in bars and clubs, especially by sex-workers who later steal from their victim's room.

Violent crime against tourists is not common, but it does occur, and there have been several serious attacks on women travellers in the last few years. However, bearing in mind that over five million foreign tourists visit Thailand every year, the statistical likelihood of becoming a victim is extremely small. **Obvious precautions** for travellers of either sex include locking accessible windows and doors at night – preferably with your own padlock (doors in many of the simpler guest houses and beach bungalows are designed for this) – and not travelling alone at night in a taxi or tuk-tuk. Nor should you risk jumping into an unlicensed taxi at the airport in Bangkok at any time of day: there have been some very violent robberies in these, so take the well-marked licensed, metered taxis instead, or the airport bus.

Unfortunately, it is also necessary for female tourists to think twice about spending time alone with a **monk**, as not all men of the cloth uphold the Buddhist precepts and there have been rapes and murders committed by men wearing the saffron robes of the monkhood. See p.241 for more about the changing Thai attitudes towards the monkhood.

Though unpalatable and distressing, Thailand's high-profile **sex industry** is relatively unthreatening for Western women, with its energy focused exclusively on farang men; it's also quite easily avoided, being contained within certain pockets of the capital. As for **harassment** from men, it's hard to generalize, but most Western women find it less of a problem in Thailand than they do back home.

Governmental travel advisories

Australian Department of Foreign Affairs Ⓦ www.dfat.gov.au, Ⓦ www.smartraveller .gov.au.

British Foreign & Commonwealth Office Ⓦ www.fco.gov.uk.

Canadian Department of Foreign Affairs Ⓦ www.dfait-maeci.gc.ca.

Irish Department of Foreign Affairs Ⓦ www.foreignaffairs.gov.ie.

New Zealand Ministry of Foreign Affairs Ⓦ www.mft.govt.nz.

South African Department of Foreign Affairs Ⓦ www.dfa.gov.za.

US State Department Ⓦ travel.state.gov.

For advice on safe travelling in Thailand, consult your government's travel advisory.

Scams

Despite the best efforts of guidebook writers, TAT and the Thai tourist police, countless travellers to Thailand get scammed every year. Nearly all **scams** are easily avoided if you're on your guard against anyone who makes an unnatural effort to befriend you. We have outlined the main scams in the relevant sections of this guide, but con-artists are nothing if not creative, so if in doubt walk away at the earliest opportunity.

Many Bangkok **tuk-tuk drivers** earn most of their living through securing **commissions** from tourist-oriented shops and will do their damnedest to get you to go to a gem shop (see below). The most common tactic is for drivers to pretend that the Grand Palace or other major sight you intended to visit is closed for the day (they usually invent a plausible reason, such as a festival or royal occasion), and to then offer to take you on a round-city tour instead, perhaps even for free. The tour will invariably include a visit to a gem shop. The easiest way to avoid all this is to take a **metered taxi**; if you're fixed on taking a tuk-tuk, ignore any tuk-tuk that is parked up or loitering and be firm about where you want to go.

Self-styled **tourist guides**, **touts** and anyone else who might introduce themselves as **students** or **businesspeople** and offer to take you somewhere of interest, or invite you to meet their family, are often the first piece of bait in a well-honed chain of con-artists. If you bite, chances are you'll end up either at a gem shop or in a gambling den, or, at best, at a tour operator or hotel that you had not planned to patronize. This is not to say that you should never accept an invitation from a local person, but be extremely wary of doing so following a street encounter in Bangkok or the resorts. Tourist guides' ID cards are easily faked.

For many of these characters the goal is to get you inside a dodgy **gem shop**,

nearly all of which are located in Bangkok. There is a full run-down of advice on how to avoid falling for the notorious low-grade gems scam on p.218, but the bottom line is that if you are not experienced at buying and trading in valuable gems you will definitely be ripped off, possibly even to the tune of several thousand pounds or dollars. Check the 2Bangkok website's account of a typical gem scam (@www.2bangkok.com/2bangkok/Scams/Sapphire.shtml) before you shell out any cash at all.

A less common but potentially more frightening scam involves a similar cast of warm-up artists leading tourists into a **gambling** game. The scammers invite their victim home on an innocent-sounding pretext, get out a pack of cards, and then set about fleecing the incomer in any number of subtle ways. Often this can be especially scary as the venue is likely to be far from hotels or recognizable landmarks. You're unlikely to get any sympathy from police, as gambling is **illegal** in Thailand.

Reporting a crime or emergency

For all emergencies, either contact the English-speaking **tourist police** who maintain a 24-hour toll-free nationwide line (☎1155) and also have a booth in the Suan Lum Night Bazaar on Thanon Rama IV; visit the Banglamphu Police Station at the west end of Thanon Khao San; or contact the Tourist Police Headquarters, CMIC Tower, 209/1 Soi 21 (Thanon Asok Montri), Thanon Sukhumvit ☎02 664 4000.

The role of the tourist police is to offer advice and tell you what to do next, but they do not file crime reports, which must be done at the nearest police station. TAT has a special department for mediating between tourists, police and accused persons (particularly shopkeepers and tour agents) – the Tourist Assistance Center, or **TAC**; it's based in the TAT office on Thanon Rajdamnoen Nok in Banglamphu (daily 8.30am– 4.30pm; ☎02 281 5051).

Culture, etiquette and the law

Tourist literature has marketed Thailand as the "Land of Smiles" so successfully that a lot of farangs arrive in Bangkok expecting to be forgiven any outrageous behaviour. This is just not the case: there are some things so universally sacred in Thailand that even a hint of disrespect will cause deep offence. TAT publishes a special leaflet on the subject, entitled *Dos and Don'ts in Thailand*, reproduced at Ⓦ www.tourismthailand.org.

The monarchy

It is both socially unacceptable and a criminal offence to make critical or defamatory remarks about the **royal family**. Thailand's monarchy might be a constitutional one, but almost every household displays a picture of King Bhumibol and Queen Sirikit in a prominent position, and respectful crowds mass whenever either of them makes a public appearance. The second of their four children, Crown Prince Vajiralongkorn, is the heir to the throne; his younger sister, Princess Royal Maha Chakri Sirindhorn, is often on TV and in the English newspapers as she is involved in many charitable projects. When addressing or speaking about royalty, Thais use a special language full of deference, called *rajasap* (literally "royal language").

Aside from keeping any anti-monarchy sentiments to yourself, you should be prepared to stand when the **king's anthem** is played at the beginning of every cinema programme, and to stop in your tracks if the neighbourhood you're in plays the **national anthem** over its public address system – many small towns do this twice a day at 8am and again at 6pm, as do some train stations and airports. A less obvious point: as the king's head features on all Thai currency, you should never step on a coin or banknote, which is tantamount to kicking the king in the face.

Religion

Almost equally insensitive would be to disregard certain **religious** precepts. **Buddhism** plays an essential part in the lives of most Thais, and Buddhist monuments should be treated with respect – which basically means wearing long trousers or knee-length skirts, covering your arms and removing your shoes whenever you visit one.

All **Buddha images** are sacred, however small, tacky or ruined, and should never be used as a backdrop for a portrait photo, clambered over, placed in a position of inferiority or treated in any manner that could be construed as disrespectful. In an attempt to prevent foreigners from committing any kind of transgression the government requires a special licence for all Buddha statues exported from the country.

Monks come only just beneath the monarchy in the social hierarchy, and they too are addressed and discussed in a special language. If there's a monk around, he'll always get a seat on the bus, usually right at the back. Theoretically, monks are forbidden to have any close contact with women, which means, as a female, you mustn't sit or stand next to a monk, or even brush against his robes; if it's essential to pass him something, put the object down so that he can then pick it up – never hand it over directly. Nuns, however, get treated like ordinary women.

See Contexts p.238 for more on religious practices in Thailand.

The body

The Western liberalism embraced by the Thai sex industry is very unrepresentative of the majority Thai attitude to the body. **Clothing** – or the lack of it – is what bothers Thais most about tourist behaviour. As mentioned above, you need to dress modestly when entering temples, but the same also applies to other important buildings and all public places. Stuffy and sweaty as it sounds, you should keep short shorts and vests for the beach.

According to ancient Hindu belief, the **head** is the most sacred part of the body and the **feet** are the most unclean. This belief, imported into Thailand, means that it's very rude to touch another person's head or to point your feet either at a human being or at a sacred image – when sitting on a temple floor, for example, you should **tuck your legs beneath you** rather than stretch them out towards the Buddha. These hierarchies also forbid people from wearing **shoes** (which are even more unclean than feet) inside temples and most private homes, and – by extension – Thais take offence when they see someone sitting on the "head", or prow, of a boat. **Putting your feet up** on a table, a chair or a pillow is also considered very uncouth, and Thais will always take their shoes off if they need to stand on a train or bus seat to get to the luggage rack, for example. On a more practical note, the **left hand** is used for washing after defecating, so Thais never use it to put food in their mouth, pass things or shake hands – as a farang though, you'll be assumed to have different customs, so left-handers shouldn't worry unduly.

Social conventions

Thais very rarely shake hands, instead using the *wai* to greet and say goodbye and to acknowledge respect, gratitude or apology. A prayer-like gesture made with raised hands, the *wai* changes according to the relative status of the two people involved: Thais can instantaneously assess which *wai* to use, but as a farang your safest bet is to go for the "stranger's" *wai*, which requires that your hands be raised close to your chest and your fingertips placed just below your chin. If someone makes a *wai* at you, you should generally *wai* back, but it's safer not to initiate.

Public displays of **physical affection** in Thailand are more common between friends of the same sex than between lovers, whether hetero- or homosexual. Holding hands and hugging is as common among male friends as with females, so if you're caressed by a Thai acquaintance of the same sex, don't assume you're being propositioned.

Finally, there are three specifically Thai **concepts** you're bound to come across, which may help you comprehend a sometimes laissez-faire attitude to delayed buses and other inconveniences. The first, **jai yen**, translates literally as "cool heart" and is something everyone tries to maintain – most Thais hate raised voices, visible irritation and confrontations of any kind, so losing one's cool can have a much more inflammatory effect than in more combative cultures. Related to this is the oft-quoted response to a difficulty, **mai pen rai** – "never mind", "no problem" or "it can't be helped" – the verbal equivalent of an open-handed shoulder shrug, which has its basis in the Buddhist notion of karma. And then there's **sanuk**, the wide-reaching philosophy of "fun", which, crass as it sounds, Thais do their best to inject into any situation, even work. Hence the crowds of inebriated Thais who congregate at parks and other beauty spots on public holidays (travelling solo is definitely not *sanuk*), the inability to do almost anything without high-volume musical accompaniment, and the national waterfight which takes place every April on streets right across Thailand.

Thai names

Although all Thais have a first **name** and a family name, everyone is addressed by their first name – even when meeting strangers – prefixed by the title "**Khun**" (Mr/Ms); no one is ever addressed as Khun Surname, and even the phone book lists people by their given name. In Thailand you will often be addressed in an Anglicized version of this convention, as "Mr Paul" or "Miss Lucy" for example. Bear in mind, though, that when a man is introduced to you as Khun Pirom, his wife will definitely not be Khun Pirom as well (that would be like calling them, for instance, "Mr and Mrs Paul"). Among friends and relatives, **Phii** ("older brother/sister") is often used instead of Khun when addressing older familiars (though as a tourist you're on surer ground with Khun), and **Nong** ("younger brother/sister") is used for younger ones.

Many Thai **first names** come from ancient Sanskrit and have an auspicious meaning; for example, Boon means good deeds, Porn means blessings, Siri means glory and Thawee means to increase. However, Thais of all ages are commonly known by the nickname given them soon after birth rather than by their official first name. This tradition arises out of a deep-rooted superstition that once a child has been officially named the spirits will begin to take an unhealthy interest in them, so a nickname is used instead to confuse the spirits. Common nicknames – which often bear no resemblance to the adult's personality or physique – include Yai (Big), Oun (Fat) and Muu (Pig); Lek or Noi (Little), Nok (Bird), Noo (Mouse) and Kung (Shrimp); Neung (Number One/Eldest), Sawng (Number Two), Saam (Number Three); and English nicknames like Apple, Joy or even Pepsi.

Family names were only introduced in 1913 (by Rama VI, who invented many of the aristocracy's surnames himself), and are used only in very formal situations, always in conjunction with the first name. It's quite usual for good friends never to know each other's surname. Ethnic Thais generally have short surnames like Somboon or Srisai, while the long, convoluted family names – such as Sonthanasumpun – usually indicate Chinese origin, not because they are phonetically Chinese but because many Chinese immigrants have chosen to adopt new Thai surnames and Thai law states that every newly created surname must be unique. Thus anyone who wants to change their surname must submit a shortlist of five unique Thai names – each to a maximum length of ten Thai characters – to be checked against a database of existing names. As more and more names are taken, Chinese family names get increasingly unwieldy, and more easily distinguishable from the pithy old Thai names.

Age restrictions and other laws

Thai law requires that tourists **carry their original passports** at all times, though sometimes it's more practical to carry a photocopy and keep the original locked in a safety deposit. It is illegal for **under-18s** to buy cigarettes or alcohol, or to drive. The **age of consent** is 15, but it is against the law to have sex with a prostitute who is under 18. You must be 21 to be allowed into a **bar or club** (ID checks are often enforced in Bangkok). It is illegal for anyone to **gamble**

in Thailand (though many do). **Smoking** is prohibited in all air-conditioned public buildings (including restaurants but usually excluding bars and clubs) and on air-conditioned trains, buses and planes; violators are subject to a B2000 fine. Dropping cigarette butts, **littering** and spitting in public places can also earn you a B2000 fine. There are fines for **overstaying your visa** (see p.25), **working without a permit**, and **not wearing a motorcycle helmet** and violating other **traffic laws**.

Drugs

Drug-smuggling carries a maximum penalty in Thailand of death. **Dealing drugs** will get you anything from four years to life in a Thai prison; penalties depend on the drug and the amount involved. Travellers caught with even the smallest amount of drugs at airports and international borders are prosecuted for trafficking, and no one charged with trafficking offences gets bail. Heroin, amphetamines, LSD and ecstasy are classed as Category 1 drugs and carry the most severe penalties: even **possession** of Category 1 drugs for personal use can result in a **life sentence**. Away from international borders, most foreigners arrested in possession of small amounts of cannabis are released on bail, then fined and deported, but the law is complex and prison sentences are possible.

Despite occasional royal pardons, don't expect special treatment as a farang: you only need to read one of the first-hand accounts by foreign former prisoners (reviewed in "Books" on p.252) to get the picture, but if that doesn't put you off you could always visit an inmate in a Bangkok jail – details on how to do this are given on p.25. The **police** actively look for tourists doing drugs, reportedly searching people regularly and randomly on Thanon Khao San, for example. They have the power to order a urine test if they have reasonable grounds for suspicion, and even a positive result for marijuana consumption could lead to a year's imprisonment. Be wary also of **being shopped** by a farang or local dealer keen to earn a financial reward for a successful bust, or having substances slipped into your luggage (simple enough to perpetrate unless all fastenings are secured with padlocks).

If you are arrested, ask for your embassy to be contacted immediately, which is your right under Thai law (see p.53 for phone numbers), and embassy staff will talk you through procedures. The British charity Prisoners Abroad (ⓦ www.prisonersabroad .org.uk) carries a detailed Survival Guide on its website, which outlines what to expect if arrested in Thailand, from the point of apprehension through trial and conviction to life in a Thai jail; if contacted, the charity may also be able to offer direct support to a British citizen facing imprisonment in a Thai jail.

Travel essentials

Airlines, international

Aeroflot ☎ 02 254 1180–2; **Air Asia** ☎ 02 515 9999; **Air Canada** ☎ 02 670 0400; **Air France** ☎ 02 635 1186–7; **Air India** ☎ 02 235 0557–8; **Air New Zealand** ☎ 02 254 8440; **Bangkok Airways** ☎ 02 265 5555; **Biman Bangladesh Airlines** ☎ 02 233 3896–7; **British Airways** ☎ 02 627 1701; **Cathay Pacific** ☎ 02 263 0606; **China Airlines** ☎ 02 250 9888; **Druk Air** ☎ 02 535 1960; **Emirates** ☎ 02 664 1040; **Eva Air** ☎ 02 240 0890; **Finnair** ☎ 02 635 1234; **Garuda** ☎ 02 679 7371–2; **Gulf Air** ☎ 02 254 7931–4; **Japan Airlines** ☎ 02 649 9500; **KLM** ☎ 02 679 1100; **Korean Air** ☎ 02 635 0465–9; **Lao Airlines** ☎ 02 236 9822; **Lauda Air** ☎ 02 267 0873; **Lufthansa** ☎ 02 264 2400; **Malaysia Airlines** ☎ 02 263 0565–71; **Pakistan International (PIA)** ☎ 02 234 2961–5; **Philippine Airlines** ☎ 02 633 5713; **Qantas Airways** ☎ 02 627 1701; **Royal Brunei** ☎ 02 637 5151; **Royal Jordanian** ☎ 02 638 2960; **Singapore Airlines** ☎ 02 353 6000; **Sri Lankan Airlines** ☎ 02 236 8450; **Swiss** ☎ 02 636 2150; **Thai Airways** ☎ 02 356 1111; **United Airlines** ☎ 02 253 0558; **Vietnam Airlines** ☎ 02 655 4137–40.

Airport enquiries

Suvarnabhumi Airport General enquiries ☎ 02 132 1888; departures ☎ 02 132 9324-5; arrivals ☎ 02 132 9328-9.

Car rental

Theoretically, foreigners need an international driver's licence to rent a car, but most companies accept national licences. Prices for a small car start at about B1200 per day; petrol currently costs B26 a litre. Thais drive on the left, and the speed limit is 60km/h within built-up areas and 90km/h outside them.

Avis 2/12 Thanon Witthayu (Wireless Road) ☎ 02 255 5300–4, ⓦ www.avis.com.

Budget 19/23 Building A, Royal City Avenue, Thanon Phetchaburi Mai ☎ 02 203 0250; Suvarnabhumi Airport ☎ 089 896 4539, ⓦ www .budget.co.th.

SMT Rent-A-Car (part of National) 727 Thanon Srinakharin ☎ 02 722 8487, ⓦ www.smtrentacar .com.

Charities and volunteer projects

Reassured by the plethora of well-stocked shopping plazas, efficient services and abundance of bars and restaurants, it is easy to forget that life is extremely hard for many people in Bangkok. Countless **charities** work with Thailand's many poor and disadvantaged communities: listed below are a few that would welcome help in some way from visitors. The website of the *Bangkok Post* also carries an extensive list of charitable foundations and projects in Thailand at ⓦ www.bangkokpost.com/ outlookwecare.

Human Development Foundation 100/11 Kae Ha Klong Toey 4, Thanon Damrongrathhaphipat, Klong Toey, Bangkok ☎ 02 671 5313, ⓦ www .mercycentre.org. Since 1972, this organization – founded by locally famous Catholic priest Father Joe

Maier – has been providing education and support for Bangkok's street kids and slum-dwellers as well as caring for those with HIV-AIDS. It now runs more than thirty kindergartens in Bangkok's slums and is staffed almost entirely by people who grew up in the slums themselves. Contact the centre for information about donations, sponsorship and volunteering, or visit it to purchase cards and gifts. Father Joe's book, *Welcome to the Bangkok Slaughterhouse*, is an eye-opening insight into this side of Thai life that tourists rarely encounter; it's available from most Bangkok bookshops and profits go to the Foundation (see p.252 for a review).

Students' Education Trust (SET) ⓦwww .thaistudentcharity.org. High-school and further education in Thailand is a luxury that the poorest kids cannot afford – not only is there a lack of funds for fees, books, uniforms and even bus fares, but they often need to work to help support the family. Many are sent to live in temples to ease the burden on their relatives. The SET was founded by British-born Phra Peter Pannapadipo to help these kids pursue their education and escape from the poverty trap. He lived as a Thai monk for ten years and tells the heartbreaking stories of some of the boys at his temple in his book, *Little Angels: The real-life stories of twelve Thai novice monks* (see p.252 for a review). SET welcomes donations and sponsorship; see their website for details.

We-Train International House Bangkok ☎02 967 8550–4, ⓦwww.we-train.co.th. Run by the Association for the Promotion of the Status of Women (APSW), this is a comfortable, air-con hotel (❸; dorms from B100) set beside a lake close to Don Muang Airport, whose profits go towards helping APSW support, house and train disadvantaged women and children. Contact the hotel for help with transport.

Contact lens solutions

Opticians throughout the city sell international brand-name contact lens solutions.

Cookery classes

Nearly all the five-star hotels will arrange Thai cookery classes for guests if requested.

Basil At the *Sheraton Grande*, between sois 12 and 14 on Thanon Sukhumvit ☎02 649 8366, ⓦwww.sheratongrandesukhumvit.com. Afternoon classes at this contemporary, five-star hotel restaurant (Mon–Sat; B1950).

Blue Elephant 233 Thanon Sathorn Tai ☎02 673 9353–8, ⓦwww.blueelephant.com. Held in a grand, century-old building, the courses here range from B2800 for a half-day to a five-day private course for professional chefs for B68,000.

May Kaidee 117/1 Thanon Tanao, Banglamphu ☎089 137 3173, ⓦwww.maykaidee.com. Banglamphu's famous veggie cook shares her culinary expertise at her restaurant for B1000 per day.

Nipa Restaurant Third floor of the Landmark Plaza, between sois 4 and 6 on Thanon Sukhumvit ☎02 254 0404, ⓦwww.landmarkbangkok.com. Runs one- to five-day cookery courses on demand (B1950/person/day, but cheaper in groups and for longer courses), and add-on fruit-carving lessons (daily 2–4pm; B450).

Oriental Hotel 48 Oriental Avenue, off Thanon Charoen Krung ☎02 659 9000, ⓦwww .mandarinoriental.com. This is the most famous of the city's five-star-hotel courses. The focus is on demonstrating culinary techniques (Mon–Thurs each week), with a chance for hands-on practice on Fri and Sat. US$120/day.

Thai House ☎02 903 9611 or 02 997 5161, ⓦwww.thaihouse.co.th. Set in an orchard in a rural part of Nonthaburi, this place runs one- (B3500) to three-day (B16,650) cooking courses, the latter including vegetable- and fruit-carving and home-stay accommodation in traditional wooden houses.

Costs

Bangkok can be a very cheap place to visit. At the bottom of the scale, you can manage on a **daily budget** of about B600 (£9/US$15) if you're willing to opt for basic accommodation and eat, drink and travel as the locals do. With extras like air conditioning, taxis and a meal and a couple of beers in a more touristy restaurant, a day's outlay would look more like B1000 (£15/US$25). Staying in comfortable, upmarket hotels and eating in the more exclusive restaurants, you should be able to live in great comfort for around B2000 a day (£30/US$50).

Bargaining is expected practice for a lot of commercial transactions, particularly at markets and when hiring tuk-tuks and motorbike taxis (though not in supermarkets or department stores). It's a delicate art that requires humour, tact and patience. If your price is way out of line, the vendor's vehement refusal should be enough to make you increase your offer; never forget that the few pennies or cents you're making such a fuss over will go a lot further in a Thai person's hands than in your own.

Couriers

DHL Worldwide has several central Bangkok depots, including on Thanon Silom and Thanon Sukhumvit; call ☎02 345 5000 or visit ⓦwww.dhl.co.th for details.

Customs regulations

The **duty-free** allowance on entry to Thailand is 200 cigarettes (or 250g of tobacco) and a litre of spirits or wine.

To **export antiques or religious artefacts** – especially Buddha images – from Thailand, you need to have a licence granted by the Fine Arts Department, which can be obtained through the Office of Archeology and National Museums, 81/1 Thanon Sri Ayutthaya (near the National Library), Bangkok (☎02 628 5032). Applications take at least two working days and need to be accompanied by the object itself, two postcard-sized colour photos of it, taken face-on and against a white background, and photocopies of the applicant's passport; furthermore, if the object is a Buddha image, the passport photocopies need to be certified by your embassy in Bangkok. Some antiques shops can organize all this for you.

Departure taxes

The international **departure tax** on all foreigners leaving Thailand by air is B500, due to rise to B700 on February 1, 2007. Domestic departure taxes are generally included in the price of the ticket.

Electricity

Mains **electricity** is supplied at 220 volts AC. If you're packing phone and camera chargers, a hair-dryer, laptop or other appliance, you'll need to take a set of travel-plug adapters with you as several plug types are commonly in use, most usually with two round pins, but also with two flat-blade pins, and sometimes with both options. Check out ⓦwww.kropla.com for a very helpful list, complete with pictures, of the different sockets, voltage and phone plugs used in Thailand.

Embassies and consulates

See ⓦwww.mfa.go.th for a full list, with links.

Australia 37 Thanon Sathorn Tai ☎02 344 6300; **Burma** (Myanmar) 132 Thanon Sathorn Nua ☎02 233 2237; **Cambodia** 185 Thanon Rajdamri (enter via Thanon Sarasin) ☎02 254 6630; **Canada** 15th floor, Abdulrahim Place, 990 Thanon Rama IV ☎02 636 0540; **China** 57 Thanon Rajadapisek ☎02 245 7030–45; **Germany** 9 Thanon Sathorn Tai ☎02 287 9000; **India** 46 Sukhumvit Soi 23 ☎02 258 0300–5; **Indonesia** 600–602 Thanon Phetchaburi ☎02 252 3135–40; **Ireland** 12th Floor, Tisco Tower, 48/20 Thanon Sathorn Nua ☎02 638 0303; **Laos** 502/1–3 Soi Sahakarnpramoon, Thanon Pracha Uthit ☎02 539 6667–8, ext 1053; **Malaysia** 35 Thanon Sathorn Tai ☎02 679 2190–9; **Nepal** 189 Sukhumvit Soi 71 ☎02 391 7240; **Netherlands** 15 Soi Tonson, between Thanon Witthayu (Wireless Road) and Soi Langsuan ☎02 309 5200; **New Zealand** 14th Floor, M Thai Tower, All Seasons Place, 87 Thanon Witthayu ☎02 254 2530; **Pakistan** 31 Sukhumvit Soi 3 ☎02 253 0288; **Philippines** Mouth of Sukhumvit Soi 30/1, ☎02 259 0139–40; **Singapore** 129 Thanon Sathorn Tai ☎02 286 2111; **South Africa** 6th Floor, The Park Place, 231 Thanon Sarasin ☎02 253 8473–6; **Sri Lanka** 13th Floor, Ocean Tower II, Sukhumvit Soi 19 ☎02 261 1934; **UK** 14 Thanon Witthayu ☎02 305 8333; **US** 120 Thanon Witthayu ☎02 205 4000; **Vietnam** 83/1 Thanon Witthayu ☎02 251 5836–8, ext 112.

Insurance

Most visitors to Thailand will need to take out **specialist travel insurance**, though you should check exactly what's covered. Rough Guides has teamed up with Columbus Direct to offer you travel insurance that can be tailored to suit your needs. Products include a low-cost **backpacker** option for long stays; a **short break** option for city getaways; a typical **holiday package** option; and others. There are also annual **multi-trip** policies for those who travel regularly. Different sports and activities, such as trekking, can usually be covered if required. See our website (ⓦwww.roughguidesinsurance.com) for eligibility and purchasing options. Alternatively, call in the UK ☎0870/033 9988, in the US ☎1-800/749-4922, in Australia ☎1300/669 999 or elsewhere ☎+44 870/890 2843.

Language classes

The most popular place to **study Thai** is at the AUA (American University Alumni; ⓦ www.auathai.com). Other language schools include Jentana and Associates (ⓦ www.thai-lessons.com), and Nisa Thai Language School (ⓔ nisathai@cscoms.com). For more information and directories of language schools, see ⓦ www.learningthai .com.

Laundry

Guest houses and hotels all over the city run low-cost, same-day **laundry** services. In some places you pay per item, in others you're charged by the kilo (generally from B30–50/kg); ironing is often included in the price. There are several self-service laundries on Banglamphu's Thanon Khao San.

Living in Bangkok

The most common source of **employment** in Bangkok is **teaching English** and a good place to search for openings is ⓦ www .ajarn.com; the website also features extensive advice on all sorts of issues to do with teaching and living in Thailand. In addition, keep an eye on guest-house noticeboards as teachers often advertise for replacements here. The *Bangkok Post* and *Bangkok Metro* listings magazine also sometimes carry teachers-wanted ads.

A tourist visa does not entitle you to work in Thailand, so, legally, you'll need to apply for a **work permit**.

Money and exchange

Thailand's unit of currency is the **baht** (abbreviated to "B"), divided into 100 satang – which are rarely seen these days. Notes come in B20, B50, B100, B500 and B1000 denominations, inscribed with Western as well as Thai numerals, and increasing in size according to value. The coinage is more confusing, because new shapes and sizes circulate alongside older ones, which sometimes have only Thai numerals. There are three different silver one-baht coins, all legal tender; the smallest of these is the newest

version, and the one accepted by public call-boxes. Silver two-baht pieces are slightly bigger; silver five-baht pieces are bigger again and have a copper rim; ten-baht coins have a small brass centre encircled by a silver ring.

At the time of writing, **exchange rates** were averaging B40 to US$1, B50 to €1 and B70 to £1. A good site for current exchange rates is ⓦ www.xe.com. Note that Thailand has no black market in foreign currency. Because of severe currency fluctuations in the late 1990s, some tourist-oriented businesses now quote their prices in **US dollars**, particularly luxury hotels.

Banking hours are Monday to Friday from 8.30am to 3.30 or 4.30pm, but exchange kiosks in the main tourist areas are always open till at least 5pm, sometimes 10pm, and upmarket hotels change money 24 hours a day. Sterling and US dollar traveller's cheques are accepted by banks, exchange booths and upmarket hotels, and most places also deal in a variety of other currencies; everyone offers better rates for cheques than for straight cash. Generally, a total of B33 in commission and duty is charged per cheque, so you'll save money if you deal in larger cheque denominations.

American Express, Visa and MasterCard **credit and debit cards** are accepted at top hotels as well as in posh restaurants, department stores, tourist shops and travel agents, but surcharging of up to seven percent is rife, and theft and forgery are major industries – always demand the carbon copies, and never leave cards in baggage storage. If you have a personal identification number (PIN) for your debit or credit card, you can also withdraw cash from hundreds of 24-hour **ATMs** around the city and at the airport.

For an up-to-the-minute list of ATM locations in Bangkok that accept Visa/Plus cards or MasterCard/Cirrus cards, check ⓦ www .visa.com or ⓦ www.mastercard.com.

Opening hours and public holidays

Most **shops** open at least Monday to Saturday from about 8am to 8pm, while department stores operate daily from around 10am to 9pm. Private office hours are generally

Monday to Friday 8am to 5pm and Saturday 8am to noon, though in tourist areas these hours are longer, with weekends worked like any other day. Government offices work Monday to Friday 8.30am to noon and 1 to 4.30pm, and national museums tend to stick to these hours too, but some close on Mondays and Tuesdays rather than at weekends.

Many tourists only register **national holidays** because trains and buses suddenly get extraordinarily crowded: although banks and government offices shut on these days, most shops and tourist-oriented businesses carry on regardless, and TAT branches continue to dispense information. The only time an inconvenient number of shops, restaurants and hotels do close is during **Chinese New Year**, which, though not marked as an official national holiday, brings many businesses to a standstill for several days in late January or February.

Thais use both the Western Gregorian **calendar** and a Buddhist calendar – the Buddha is said to have died (or entered Nirvana) in the year 543 BC, so Thai dates start from that point: thus 2007 AD becomes 2550 BE (Buddhist Era).

National holidays

Jan 1 Western New Year's Day
Feb (day of full moon) Maha Puja: commemorates the Buddha preaching to a spontaneously assembled crowd of 1250.
April 6 Chakri Day: the founding of the Chakri dynasty.
April (usually 13–15) Songkhran: Thai New Year.
May 1 National Labour Day
May 5 Coronation Day
May (early in the month) Royal Ploughing Ceremony: marks start of rice-planting season.
May (day of full moon) Visakha Puja: the holiest of all Buddhist holidays, which celebrates the birth, enlightenment and death of the Buddha.
July (day of full moon) Khao Pansa: the start of the annual three-month Buddhist rains retreat, when new monks are ordained.
Aug 12 Queen's birthday
Oct 23 Chulalongkorn Day: the anniversary of Rama V's death.
Dec 5 King's birthday: also celebrated as national Fathers' Day.
Dec 10 Constitution Day
Dec 31 Western New Year's Eve

Photographic services

Most camera shops in Bangkok will download your **digital photos** onto a CD for about B150; there's no need to bring your own cables as they have card readers. In Banglamphu, try Center Digital Lab at 169 Thanon Khao San, next to *Grand Guest House*; on Sukhumvit, 11 Digital Photo has branches in Nana Square at the mouth of Soi 3 and near the *Federal Hotel* on Soi 11. Many Internet cafés also offer CD-burning services, though if you want to email your pictures, bringing your own cable will make life easier.

Prison visits

A number of foreigners are serving long sentences in Bangkok's prisons, most of them in Nonthaburi's Bang Kwang jail, and they appreciate visits from other foreigners. When visiting, you need to know the name of the prisoner, which block number they're in, and the relevant visiting hours. Embassy staff keep this information, and guest-house noticeboards often have more details as well as accounts from recent prison visitors; similar info is available at Ⓦ www.bangkwang.net and Ⓦ www.khaosanroad.com/bangedup .htm. Prisoners are only allowed one visitor at a time, and visitors must look respectable (no shorts or singlets); all visitors must show their passports at the jail. You can only bring certain gifts with you (such as books, newspapers, fruit, sweets and clothes), as other stuff has to be bought at the prison shop. For directions to Nonthaburi, see p.132; at Nonthaburi pier, take the road ahead, and then turn first left for the prison visitor centre.

Tampons

Few Thai women use **tampons**, which are not widely available, except from branches of Boots.

Time

Bangkok is seven hours ahead of GMT, twelve hours ahead of US Eastern Standard Time and three hours behind Australian Eastern Standard Time.

Tipping

It is usual to **tip** hotel bellboys and porters B20, and to round up taxi fares to the nearest B10. Most guides, drivers, masseurs, waiters and maids also depend on tips, and although some upmarket hotels and restaurants will add an automatic ten percent service charge to your bill, this is not always shared out.

Travel agents

Asian Trails 9th Floor, SG Tower, 161/1 Soi Mahadlek Luang 3, Thanon Rajdamri ℡ 02 626 2000, ⓦ www.asiantrails.net. Sells flights and tours and runs scheduled and private transfers from Bangkok hotels and the airport.
Diethelm Travel 12th Floor, Kian Gwan Building II, 140/1 Thanon Witthayu ℡ 02 255 9205–18, ⓦ www.diethelm-travel.com. Especially good for travel to Burma, Cambodia, Laos and Vietnam.
ETC (Educational Travel Centre) Ground floor, **Royal Hotel**, 2 Thanon Rajdamnoen Klang, Banglamphu ℡ 02 224 0043, ⓦ www.etc.co.th; 180 Thanon Khao San, Banglamphu ℡ 02 282 7021; and 5/3 Soi Ngam Duphli ℡ 02 286 9424. Sells air tickets and Thailand tours.
Olavi Travel Opposite Gullivers' Tavern at 53 Thanon Chakrabongse, Banglamphu ℡ 02 629 4711–4, ⓦ www.olavi.com. Sells air tickets and budget transfers.
Royal Exclusive 21 Thanon Silom ℡ 02 267 1536, ⓦ www.royalexclusive.com. Good for travel to Burma, Cambodia, Laos and Vietnam, and also sells air and train tickets.
STA Travel 14th Floor, Wall Street Tower, 33 Thanon Suriwong ℡ 02 236 0262, ⓦ www .statravel.co.th. The Bangkok branch of the worldwide chain is a reliable outlet for cheap international flights.
Thai Overlander 407 Thanon Sukhumvit, between sois 21 and 23, ℡ 02 258 4778–80,

ⓦ www.thaioverlander.com. Helpful place selling flights, train tickets and day-trips.

Travellers with disabilities

Thailand makes few provisions for its disabled citizens and this obviously affects **travellers with disabilities**, but taxis, comfortable hotels and personal tour guides are all more affordable than in the West and most travellers with disabilities find Thais only too happy to offer assistance where they can. Hiring a local tour guide to accompany you on a day's sightseeing is particularly recommended: government tour guides can be arranged through any TAT office.

Most **wheelchair users** end up driving on Bangkok's roads because it's too hard to negotiate the uneven pavements, which are high to allow for flooding and invariably lack dropped kerbs. Crossing the road can be a trial, as it's usually a question of climbing steps up to a bridge rather than taking a ramped underpass. Few buses and trains have ramps but some Skytrain stations and all subway stations have lifts.

Several **tour companies** in Thailand specialize in organizing trips featuring adapted facilities, accessible transport and escorts. Adventure Holidays Thailand (℡ 038 233502, ⓦ www.adventure-holidays-thailand.com) has a reputation for its can-do attitude to travel for disabled and physically challenged people and its tailor-made tours reflect this. The Help and Care Travel Company (℡ 02 720 5395, ⓦ www.wheelchairtours.com), which designs accessible holidays in Thailand for slow walkers and wheelchair users, can provide transport and escort services; its website carries a (short) list of wheelchair-accessible hotels in the main tourist centres.

The City

The City

Ratanakosin

When Rama I developed **Ratanakosin** as his new capital in 1782, after the sacking of Ayutthaya and a temporary stay across the river in Thonburi, he paid tribute to its precursor by imitating Ayutthaya's layout and architecture – he even shipped the building materials downstream from the ruins of the old city. Like Ayutthaya, the new capital was sited for protection beside a river and turned into an artificial island by the construction of defensive canals, with a central **Grand Palace** and adjoining royal temple, **Wat Phra Kaeo**, fronted by an open cremation field, **Sanam Luang**; the Wang Na (Palace of the Second King), now doing service as the **National Museum**, was also built at this time. **Wat Pho**, which predates the capital's founding, was further embellished by Rama I's successors, who have consolidated Ratanakosin's pre-eminence by building several grand European-style palaces (now housing government institutions); Wat Mahathat, the most important centre of Buddhist learning in southeast Asia; the National Theatre; the National Gallery; and Thammasat and Silpakorn universities.

Bangkok has expanded eastwards away from the river, leaving the Grand Palace a good 5km from the city's commercial heart, and the royal family have long since moved their residence to Dusit, but Ratanakosin remains the ceremonial centre of the whole kingdom – so much so that it feels as if it might sink into the boggy ground under the weight of its own mighty edifices. The stately feel is lightened by traditional shophouses and noisy markets along the riverside strip and by **Sanam Luang**, still used for cremations and royal ceremonies, but also functioning as a popular open park and the hub of the modern city's bus system. Despite containing several of the country's main sights, the area is

Getting to and from Ratanakosin

Ratanakosin is within easy walking distance of Banglamphu, but is best approached from the river, via the **express-boat** piers of Tha Chang (for the Grand Palace and Sanam Luang) or Tha Thien (for Wat Pho). Coming from the downtown area or Thanon Sukhumvit, the most comfortable and scenic approach is to catch a Skytrain to Saphan Taksin station, then an express boat from Central Pier (Sathorn). From Soi Kasemsan 1 (Tha Saphan Hua Chang) and from several piers near Thanon Sukhumvit, you might also consider the regular **longtails** along Khlong Saen Saeb and a walk from their Golden Mount terminus, which make up in speed for their lack of comfort and scenery. Otherwise take your pick from the scores of **buses** that stop or terminate on Sanam Luang and the surrounding streets – many of them after a slow crawl through congested Chinatown streets.

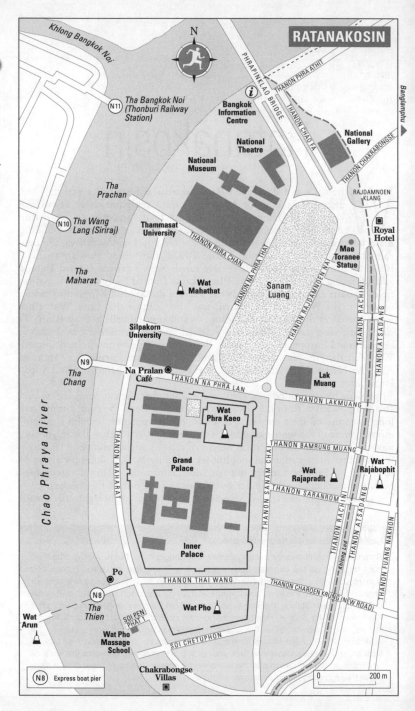

Khlong Bangkok Noi

N

RATANAKOSIN

Banglamphu ▶

PHRAPINKLAO BRIDGE

THANON PHRA ATHIT

THANON CHAD FA

N11 Tha Bangkok Noi
(Thonburi Railway
Station)

Bangkok
Information
Centre

National
Theatre

National
Gallery

THANON CHAKRABONGSE

RAJDAMNOEN
KLANG

National
Museum

Tha
Prachan

Thammasat
University

THANON PHRA CHAN

Royal
Hotel

N10 Tha Wang
Lang (Siriraj)

Mae
Toranee
Statue

THANON RACHINI

Tha
Maharat

Wat
Mahathat

THANON NA PHRA THAT

Sanam
Luang

THANON RAJDAMNOEN NAI

THANON ATSADANG

Silpakorn
University

N9

Tha
Chang

Na Pralan ◉
Café

THANON NA PHRA LAN

Lak
Muang

THANON LAKMUANG

Wat
Phra
Kaeo

THANON BAMRUNG MUANG

Wat
Rajabophit

Grand
Palace

THANON MAHARAT

Chao Phraya River

Wat
Rajapradit

THANON SARANROM

THANON SANAM CHAI

THANON RACHINI

Khlong Lod

THANON ATSADANG

THANON FUANG NAKHON

Inner
Palace

Po ◉

THANON THAI WANG

THANON CHAROEN KRUNG (NEW ROAD)

N8

Tha
Thien

SOI PEN
PHAT 1

Wat Pho

Wat
Arun

Wat Pho
Massage
School

SOI CHETUPHON

Chakrabongse
Villas ◻

N8 Express boat pier

0   200 m

busy enough in its own right not to have become a swarming tourist zone, and strikes a neat balance between liveliness and grandeur.

A **word of warning**: when you're heading for the Grand Palace or Wat Pho, you may well be approached by someone pretending to be a student or an official, who will tell you that the sight is closed when it's not, because they want to lead you on a shopping trip (see p.47 for details). Although the opening hours of the Grand Palace are sometimes erratic because of state occasions, it's far better to put in a bit of extra legwork and check it out for yourself.

Wat Phra Kaeo and the Grand Palace

Hanging together in a precarious harmony of strangely beautiful colours and shapes, **Wat Phra Kaeo** (ⓦ www.palaces.thai.net) is the apogee of Thai religious art and the holiest Buddhist site in the country, housing the most important image, the **Emerald Buddha**. Built as the private royal temple, Wat Phra Kaeo occupies the northeast corner of the huge **Grand Palace**, whose official opening in 1785 marked the founding of the new capital and the rebirth of the Thai nation after the Burmese invasion. Successive kings have all left their mark here, and the palace complex now covers 61 acres, though very little apart from the wat is open to tourists.

The only **entrance** to the complex in 2km of crenellated walls is the Gate of Glorious Victory in the middle of the north side, on Thanon Na Phra Lan. This brings you onto a driveway with a tantalizing view of the temple's glittering spires on the left and the dowdy buildings of the Offices of the Royal Household on the right; this is the powerhouse of the kingdom's ceremonial life, providing everything down to chairs and catering, even lending an urn when someone of rank dies (a textile museum under the auspices of the queen is scheduled to open among these buildings, perhaps in 2007). Turn left at the end of the driveway for the ticket office and entrance turnstiles.

Wat Phra Kaeo

Entering the temple is like stepping onto a lavishly detailed stage set, from the immaculate flagstones right up to the gaudy roofs. Although it receives hundreds of foreign sightseers and at least as many Thai pilgrims every day, the temple, which has no monks in residence, maintains an unnervingly sanitized look, as if it were built only yesterday. Its jigsaw of structures can seem complicated at first, but the basic layout is straightforward: the turnstiles in the west

---

Admission to Wat Phra Kaeo and the palace is B250 (daily 8.30am–3.30pm, palace halls and weapons museum closed Sat & Sun; 2hr personal audioguide B200, with passport or credit card as surety), which includes a free brochure and map, as well as admission (within seven days) to the Vimanmek Palace in the Dusit area (see p.107). As it's Thailand's most sacred site, you have to show respect by **dressing in smart clothes** – no vests, shorts, see-through clothes, sarongs, mini-skirts or fisherman's trousers – but if your rucksack won't stretch that far, head for the office to the right just inside the Gate of Glorious Victory, where suitable garments can be provided (free) as long as you leave some identification (passport or driver's licence) as surety or pay a deposit of B100 per item.

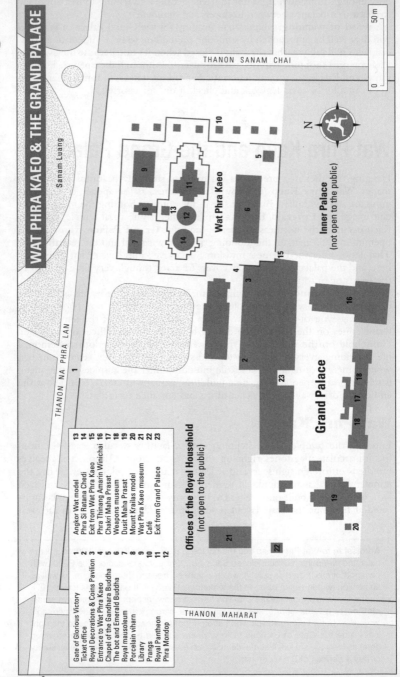

WAT PHRA KAEO & THE GRAND PALACE

Thanon Sanam Chai

Sanam Luang

Wat Phra Kaeo

Inner Palace
(not open to the public)

Grand Palace

Offices of the Royal Household
(not open to the public)

Thanon Na Phra Lan

Thanon Maharat

Tha Chang

N

0   50 m

Gate of Glorious Victory	**1**
Ticket office	**2**
Royal Decorations & Coins Pavilion	**3**
Entrance to Wat Phra Kaeo	**4**
Chapel of the Gandhara Buddha	**5**
The bot and Emerald Buddha	**6**
Royal mausoleum	**7**
Porcelain viharn	**8**
Library	**9**
Prangs	**10**
Royal Pantheon	**11**
Phra Mondop	**12**
Angkor Wat model	**13**
Phra Si Ratana Chedi	**14**
Exit from Wat Phra Kaeo	**15**
Phra Thinang Amarin Winichai	**16**
Chakri Maha Prasat	**17**
Weapons museum	**18**
Dusit Maha Prasat	**19**
Mount Krailas model	**20**
Wat Phra Kaeo museum	**21**
Café	**22**
Exit from Grand Palace	**23**

wall open onto the back of the bot, which contains the Emerald Buddha; to the left, the upper terrace runs parallel to the north side of the bot, while the whole temple compound is surrounded by arcaded walls, decorated with extraordinary murals of scenes from the *Ramayana* (see box on p.65).

The approach to the bot

Immediately inside the turnstiles, you're confronted by six-metre tall *yaksha*, gaudy demons from the *Ramayana*, who watch over the Emerald Buddha from every gate of the temple and ward off evil spirits. Less threatening is the tooth-less old codger, cast in bronze and sitting on a plinth by the back wall of the bot, who represents a Hindu hermit credited with inventing yoga and herbal medicine. In front of him is a large grinding stone where, previously, herbal practitioners could come to grind their ingredients – with enhanced powers, of course. Skirting around the bot, you'll reach its **main entrance** on the eastern side, in front of which stands a cluster of grey **statues**, which have a strong Chinese feel: next to Kuan Im, the Chinese goddess of mercy, are a sturdy pillar topped by a lotus flower, which Bangkok's Chinese community presented to Rama IV during his 27 years as a monk, and two handsome cows which commemorate Rama I's birth in the Year of the Cow. Worshippers make their offerings to the Emerald Buddha in among the statues, where they can look at the image through the open doors of the bot without messing up its pristine interior with candle wax and joss-stick ash.

Nearby, in the southeastern corner of the temple precinct, look out for the beautiful country scenes painted in gold and blue on the doors of the **Chapel of the Gandhara Buddha**, a building that was crucial to the old royal rain-making ritual and which is still used during the Royal Ploughing Ceremony (see p.72). Adorning the roof are thousands of nagas (serpents), symbolizing water; inside the locked chapel, among the paraphernalia used in the ritual, is kept the Gandhara Buddha, a bronze image in the gesture of calling down the rain with its right hand, while cupping the left to catch it. In times of drought the king would order a week-long rainmaking ceremony to be conducted, during which he was bathed regularly and kept away from the opposite sex while Buddhist monks and Hindu Brahmins chanted continuously.

The bot and the Emerald Buddha

The **bot**, the largest building of the temple, is one of the few original structures left at Wat Phra Kaeo, though it has been augmented so often it looks like the work of a wildly inspired child. Eight *sema* stones mark the boundary of the consecrated area around the bot, each sheltering in a psychedelic fairy castle, joined by a low wall decorated with Chinese porcelain tiles, which depict deli-cate landscapes. The walls of the bot itself, sparkling with gilt and coloured glass, are supported by 112 golden garudas (birdmen) holding nagas, representing the god Indra saving the world by slaying the serpent-cloud that had swallowed up all the water. The symbolism reflects the king's traditional role as a rainmaker.

Inside the bot, a nine-metre-high pedestal supports the tiny **Emerald Buddha**, a figure whose mystique draws pilgrims from all over Thailand – as well as politicians accused of corruption, who traditionally come here to publicly swear their innocence. Here, especially, you must act with respect, sitting with your feet pointing away from the Buddha. The spiritual power of the sixty-centimetre jadeite image derives from its legendary past. Reputed to have been created in Sri Lanka, it was discovered when lightning cracked open an ancient chedi in Chiang Rai in northern Thailand in the early fifteenth century. The image was then moved around the north, dispensing miracles wherever it went, before being taken to Laos for two hundred years. As it was believed to bring great fortune to its possessor, the future Rama I snatched it back when he captured Vientiane in 1779, installing it at the heart of his new capital as a talisman for king and country.

The Emerald Buddha has three costumes, one for each season: the crown and ornaments of an Ayutthayan king for the hot season; a gilt monastic robe dotted with blue enamel for the rainy season, when the monks retreat into the temples; and a full-length gold shawl to wrap up in for the cool season. To this day it's the job of the king himself to ceremonially change the Buddha's costumes – though in recent years, due to the present king's age, the Crown Prince has conducted proceedings. (The Buddha was granted a new set of these three costumes in 1997: the old set is now in the Wat Phra Kaeo Museum – see p.68 – while the two costumes of the new set that are not in use are put on display among the blinding glitter of crowns and jewels in the Royal Decorations and Coins Pavilion, which lies between the ticket office and the entrance to Wat Phra Kaeo.) Among the paraphernalia in front of the pedestal is the tiny, black Victory Buddha, which Rama I always carried with him into war for luck.

The upper terrace

The eastern end of the **upper terrace** is taken up with the **Prasat Phra Thep Bidorn**, known as the **Royal Pantheon**, a splendid hash of styles. The pantheon has its roots in the Khmer concept of *devaraja*, or the divinity of kings: inside are bronze and gold statues, precisely life-size, of all the kings since Bangkok became the Thai capital. The building is open only on special occasions, such as Chakri Day (April 6), when the dynasty is commemorated.

From here you get the best view of the **royal mausoleum**, the **porcelain viharn** and the **library** to the north (all of which are closed to the public), and, running along the east side of the temple, a row of eight bullet-like **prangs**, each of which has a different nasty ceramic colour. Described as "monstrous vegetables" by Somerset Maugham, they represent, from north to south, the Buddha, Buddhist scripture, the monkhood, the nunhood, the Buddhas who attained enlightenment but did not preach, previous emperors, the Bodhisattva and the future Buddha.

In the middle of the terrace, dressed in deep-green glass mosaics, the **Phra Mondop** was built by Rama I to house the *Tripitaka*, or Buddhist scripture. It's famous for the mother-of-pearl cabinet and solid-silver mats inside, but is never open. Four tiny **memorials** at each corner of the mondop show the symbols of each of the nine Chakri kings, from the ancient crown representing Rama I to the present king's sun symbol, while the bronze statues surrounding the memorials portray each king's lucky white elephants, labelled by name and pedigree. A contribution of Rama IV, on the north side of the mondop, is a **scale model of Angkor Wat**, the prodigious Cambodian temple, which during his reign (1851–68) was under Thai rule. At the western end of the terrace, you can't miss the golden dazzle of the **Phra Si Ratana Chedi**, which Rama IV erected to enshrine a piece of the Buddha's breastbone.

The murals

Extending for over a kilometre in the arcades that run inside the wat walls, the **murals of the Ramayana** depict every blow of this ancient story of the triumph of good over evil, using the vibrant buildings of the temple itself as backdrops, and setting them off against the subdued colours of richly detailed

Bangkok by boat

With traffic on the roads frequently gridlocked, Bangkok's waterways are often the fastest way of getting around – and they boast all the best views too . The city was founded on the east bank of the Chao Phraya River and designed to be negotiated by water, so many of its finest monuments and temples, not least the Grand Palace and Wat Arun, are to this day best approached by river.

▲ Monk paddling down a Thonburi khlong

The Chao Phraya – "River of Kings" – has been the lifeblood of Bangkok ever since Rama I chose to establish his capital here in 1782. A network of khlongs (canals) provided extra defence and though many of these have since been concreted over, those that survive remain crucial to the free flow of people and goods around the capital. They are particularly important in the city's Thonburi district, on the west bank of the Chao Phraya, where traditional stilted homes still line the labyrinth of canals and a boat is more useful than a car.

The Chao Phraya River

The easiest and most economical way to enjoy sights along the Chao Phraya is to leap aboard the **express-boat service** that transports commuters and visitors some 21km from near Krung Thep Bridge in the south to **Nonthaburi** in the north. The full ride takes an hour and a half and costs B13. There's always plenty to look at both on and alongside the river: longtail taxis and sightseeing boats roar up and down, cross-river ferries beetle between the two banks, and tug-boats lug their convoys of barges weighed down with rice, sugar and tapioca

▲ Canalside home, Thonburi

grown in Thailand's fertile central plains and destined for the capital's cargo port at Khlong Toey. Pastel-painted colonial-era facades, obtruding skyscrapers and glittering temple rooftops dominate downriver vistas, while upstream frontages include the Bangyikan distillery, home of Thailand's fiery Mekhong whisky.

Of the dozen bridges across the Chao Phraya, the beautiful, modern, cable-stayed **Rama VIII Bridge** stands out, hanging asymmetrically from a single pylon erected on the Thonburi bank to comply with a law prohibiting tall structures within sight of the Grand Palace.

Exploring the canals

Public boats also ply some of the **canals**, most usefully Khlong Saen Saeb, which zips eastwards

◄ Longtail boatmen wait for a fare, Nonthaburi

The longtail boat

Like its road-bound counterpart the tuk-tuk, the **longtail boat** (*reua hang yao*) is a Bangkok icon: fast, colourful, ubiquitous – and excessively noisy and polluting. The nerve-wearying roar is produced by the boat's diesel-powered Isuzu engine, appropriated from pick-up trucks and operated by an elongated propeller shaft, the eponymous longtail. But much else about the design is graceful, not least the streamlined wooden hulls whose improbably steep prows enable the longtails to shoot across the water at an amazing speed, and their rainbow-hued livery, often with matching multi-coloured canopies. The look barely varies, whether it's a taxi-style longtail seating eight, or one that plies scheduled routes and crams in fifty passengers or more. Most longtail drivers festoon the prow – which is considered sacred, like the human head – with garlands of plastic flowers to both honour and ask protection from the spirits; this special status also means that it's offensive to sit on or astride the prow. Plastic sheets rigged along the sides of the boats provide more pragmatic protection – from health-endangering contact with the foetid canal water, at its vilest inky-black along the east–west artery, Khlong Saen Saeb.

from Banglamphu to Sukhumvit and beyond. But for a glimpse of the more scenic khlong-side neighbourhoods you're best off chartering your own longtail taxi for a tour around the much-visited but undeniably atmospheric backwaters of Thonburi. Homes here range from rickety wooden shacks to plush concrete villas with waterside lawns, and though the once-photogenic floating markets are now undisguised tourist traps, individual vendors do still paddle up and down flogging everything from plastic buckets to hot noodle soup; banking services and mail delivery are still waterborne in some corners, monks do their early-morning alms rounds by canoe and some residents brave the murky waters for an evening bathe.

For details of tours and charters around the Thonburi canals, see p.100.

▼ Doing the dishes

▼ The Chao Phraya River at dusk

River views

Many of Bangkok's finest **hotels** are built along the banks of the Chao Phraya. The *grande dame* of the river has long been the *Oriental Hotel* (see p.177), built here in 1876 and renowned for its impressive roster of famous guests. Among these was the author Somerset Maugham, who first stayed in the 1920s; convalescing from malaria, he appreciated having "nothing to do except look at the river". Across on the opposite, Thonburi, bank, the swanky 21st-century *Peninsula Bangkok* (see p.177) is an even more luxurious alternative, not least for the sweeping river vistas enjoyed from every room. Further upriver, across the Chao Phraya from the Grand Palace, the tiny, three-room *Ibrik Resort on the River* (see p.173) fosters a far more intimate experience: buried in a lively Thonburi neighbourhood you are literally at the water's edge, close enough to dip your toe in.

Dining beside the river – and even on it – is another good way of absorbing riverine life: once the sun sets and the river traffic quietens, locals flock to *Tonpoh* in Banglamphu for the seafood and river breezes (see p.183), and to nearby *Kinlom Chom Saphan* (see p.185) for its fine outlook on the elegant Rama VIII Bridge. Dinner cruises along the Chao Phraya, some of them on converted teakwood barges, also offer a memorable perspective on the floodlit riverside sights: see p.183 for details.

The Ramayana

The **Ramayana** is generally thought to have originated as an oral epic in India, where it appears in numerous dialects. The most famous version is that of the poet Valmiki, who as a tribute to his king drew together the collection of stories over two thousand years ago. From India, the *Ramayana* spread to all the Hindu-influenced countries of South Asia and was passed down through the Khmers to Thailand, where as the **Ramakien** it has become the national epic, acting as an affirmation of the Thai monarchy and its divine Hindu links. As a source of inspiration for literature, painting, sculpture and dance-drama, it has acquired the authority of holy writ, providing Thais with moral and practical lessons, while its appearance in the form of films and comic strips shows its huge popular appeal. The version current in Thailand was composed by a committee of poets sponsored by Rama I, and runs to three thousand pages (available in an abridged English translation by M.L. Manich Jumsai – see p.154).

The central story of the *Ramayana* concerns **Rama** (in Thai, Phra Ram), son of the king of Ayodhya, and his beautiful wife **Sita**, whose hand he wins by lifting and stringing a magic bow. The couple's adventures begin when they are exiled to the forest, along with Rama's good brother, **Lakshaman** (Phra Lak), by the hero's father under the influence of his evil stepmother. Meanwhile, in the city of Lanka (Longka), the demon king **Ravana** (Totsagan) has conceived a passionate desire for Sita and, disguised as a hermit, sets out to kidnap her. By transforming one of his subjects into a beautiful deer, which Rama and Lakshaman go off to hunt, Ravana catches Sita alone and takes her back to Lanka. Rama then wages a long war against the demons of Lanka, into which are woven many battles, spy scenes and diversionary episodes, and eventually kills Ravana and rescues Sita.

The Thai version shows some characteristic differences from the Indian. Hanuman, the loyal monkey king, is given a much more playful role in the *Ramakien*, with the addition of many episodes which display his cunning and talent for mischief, but the major alteration comes at the end of the story, when Phra Ram doubts Sita's faithfulness after rescuing her from Totsagan. In the Indian story, this ends with Sita being swallowed up by the earth so that she doesn't have to suffer Rama's doubts any more; in the *Ramakien* the ending is a happy one, with Phra Ram and Sita living together happily ever after.

---

landscapes. Because of the damaging humidity, none of the original work of Rama I's time survives: maintenance is a never-ending process, so you'll always find an artist working on one of the scenes. The story is told in 178 panels, labelled and numbered in Thai only, starting in the middle of the northern side: in the first episode, a hermit, while out ploughing, finds the baby Sita, the heroine, floating in a gold urn on a lotus leaf and brings her to the city. Panel 109 shows the climax of the story, when Rama, the hero, kills the ten-headed demon Totsagan (Ravana), and the ladies of the enemy city weep at the demon's death. Panel 110 depicts his elaborate funeral procession, and in 113 you can see the funeral fair, with acrobats, sword-jugglers and tightrope-walkers. In between, Sita – Rama's wife – has to walk on fire to prove that she has been faithful during her fourteen years of imprisonment by Totsagan. If you haven't the stamina for the long walk round, you could sneak a look at the end of the story, to the left of the first panel, where Rama holds a victory parade and distributes thankyou gifts.

The palace buildings

The exit in the southwest corner of Wat Phra Kaeo brings you to the palace proper, a vast area of buildings and gardens, of which only the northern edge

△ Chinese statue, the Grand Palace

is on show to the public. Though the king now lives in the Chitrlada Palace in Dusit, the Grand Palace is still used for state receptions and official ceremonies, during which there is no public access to any part of the palace; in addition the weapons museum and the interiors of the Phra Thinang Amarin Winichai and the Dusit Maha Prasat are closed at weekends.

Phra Maha Monthien

Coming out of the temple compound, you'll first of all see to your right a beautiful Chinese gate covered in innumerable tiny porcelain tiles. Extending in a straight line behind the gate is the **Phra Maha Monthien**, which was the grand residential complex of earlier kings.

Only the **Phra Thinang Amarin Winichai**, the main audience hall at the front of the complex, is open to the public. The supreme court in the era of the absolute monarchy, it nowadays serves as the venue for the king's birthday speech; dominating the hall is the *busbok*, an open-sided throne with a spired roof, floating on a boat-shaped base. The rear buildings are still used for the most important part of the elaborate coronation ceremony, and each new king is supposed to spend a night there to show solidarity with his forefathers.

Chakri Maha Prasat and the Inner Palace

Next door you can admire the facade of the "farang with a Thai hat", as the **Chakri Maha Prasat** is nicknamed. Rama V, whose portrait you can see over its entrance, employed an English architect to design a purely Neoclassical residence, but other members of the royal family prevailed on the king to add the three Thai spires. This used to be the site of the elephant stables. The large red tethering posts are still there and the bronze elephants were installed as a reminder. The building displays the emblem of the Chakri dynasty on its gable, which has a trident (*ri*) coming out of a *chak*, a discus with a sharpened rim. The only part of the Chakri Maha Prasat open to the public is the **weapons museum**, which occupies two rooms on the ground floor on either side of the grand main entrance, and houses a forgettable display of hooks, pikes, tridents, guns and cannon.

The **Inner Palace**, which used to be the king's harem (closed to the public), lies behind the gate on the left-hand side of the Chakri Maha Prasat. The harem was a town in itself, with shops, law courts and a police force for the huge all-female population: as well as the current queens, the minor wives and their servants, this was home to the daughters and consorts of former kings, and the daughters of the aristocracy who attended the harem's finishing school. Today, the Inner Palace houses a school of cooking, fruit-carving and other domestic sciences for well-bred young Thais.

Dusit Maha Prasat

On the western side of the courtyard, the delicately proportioned **Dusit Maha Prasat**, an audience hall built by Rama I, epitomizes traditional Thai architecture. Outside, the soaring tiers of its red, gold and green roof culminate in a gilded *mongkut*, a spire shaped like the king's crown, which symbolizes the 33 Buddhist levels of perfection. Each tier of the roof bears a typical *chofa*, a slender, stylized bird's-head finial, and several *hang hong* (swans' tails), which represent three-headed nagas. Inside, you can still see the original throne, the **Phra Ratcha Banlang Pradap Muk**, a masterpiece of mother-of-pearl inlaid work. When a senior member of the royal family dies, the hall is used for the lying-in-state: the body, embalmed and seated in a huge sealed urn, is placed in the west transept, waiting up to two years for an auspicious day to be cremated.

To the right and behind the Dusit Maha Prasat rises a strange model mountain, decorated with fabulous animals and topped by a castle and prang. It represents **Mount Krailas**, a version of Mount Meru, the centre of the Hindu universe, and was built as the site of the royal tonsure ceremony. In former times, Thai children had shaved heads, except for a tuft on the crown, which, between the ages of five and eight, was cut in a Hindu initiation rite to welcome adolescence. For the royal children, the rite was an elaborate ceremony that sometimes lasted five days, culminating with the king's cutting of the hair knot. The child was then bathed at the model Krailas, in water representing the original river of the universe flowing down the central mountain.

Wat Phra Kaeo Museum

In the nineteenth-century Royal Mint in front of the Dusit Maha Prasat – next to a small, basic **café** and an incongruous hair salon – the **Wat Phra Kaeo Museum** houses a mildly interesting collection of artefacts associated with the Emerald Buddha along with architectural elements rescued from the Grand Palace grounds during restoration in the 1980s. Highlights include the bones of various kings' white elephants, and upstairs, the Emerald Buddha's original costumes and two useful scale models of the Grand Palace, one as it is now, the other as it was when first built. Also on the first floor stands the grey stone slab of the Manangasila Seat, where Ramkhamhaeng, the great thirteenth-century king of Sukhothai, the first Thai capital, is said to have sat and taught his subjects. It was discovered in 1833 by Rama IV during his monkhood and brought to Bangkok, where Rama VI used it as the throne for his coronation.

Wat Pho

Where Wat Phra Kaeo may seem too perfect and shrink-wrapped for some, **Wat Pho** (daily 8.30am–6pm; B20; personal guides available, charging B200/300/400 for 1, 2 or 3 visitors; ⓦwww.watpho.com), covering twenty acres to the south of the Grand Palace, is lively and shambolic, a complex arrangement of lavish structures that jostle with classrooms, basketball courts and a turtle pond. Busloads of tourists shuffle in and out of the **north entrance**, stopping only to gawp at the colossal Reclining Buddha, but you can avoid the worst of the crowds by using the **main entrance** on Soi Chetuphon to explore the huge compound, where you're likely to be approached by friendly young monks wanting to practise their English.

Wat Pho is the oldest temple in Bangkok and older than the city itself, having been founded in the seventeenth century under the name Wat Photaram. Foreigners have stuck to the contraction of this old name, even though Rama I, after enlarging the temple, changed the name in 1801 to Wat Phra Chetuphon, which is how it is generally known to Thais. The temple had another major overhaul in 1832, when Rama III built the chapel of the Reclining Buddha, and turned the temple into a public centre of learning by decorating the walls and pillars with inscriptions and diagrams on subjects such as history, literature, animal husbandry and astrology. Dubbed Thailand's first university, the wat is still an important centre for traditional medicine, notably **Thai massage**, which is used against all kinds of illnesses, from backaches to viruses. Excellent massages

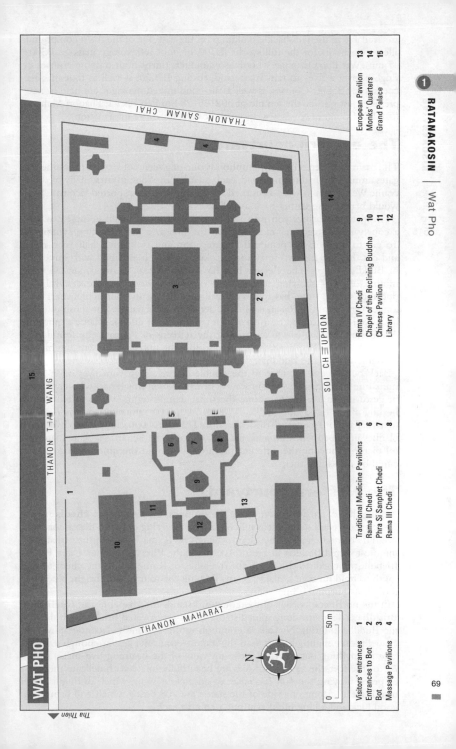

WAT PHO

Visitors' entrances	1
Entrances to Bot	2
Bot	3
Massage Pavilions	4

Traditional Medicine Pavilions	5
Rama II Chedi	6
Phra Si Sanphet Chedi	7
Rama III Chedi	8

Rama IV Chedi	9
Chapel of the Reclining Buddha	10
Chinese Pavilion	11
Library	12

European Pavilion	13
Monks' Quarters	14
Grand Palace	15

THANON SANAM CHAI

THANON TAI WANG

SOI CHETUPHON

THANON MAHARAT

Tha Thien

N

0   50 m

are available in the ramshackle buildings on the east side of the main compound; allow two hours for the full works (B300/hr; foot reflexology massage B300/ 45min). Wat Pho's massage school also conducts thirty-hour training courses in English, over a five- to ten-day period, costing B7000, as well as foot-massage courses for B5500. Courses, as well as air-conditioned massages, are held in new premises just outside the temple, at 392/25–28 Soi Pen Phat 1, Thanon Maharat (T02 221 3686 or W www.watpomassage.com for more information).

The eastern courtyard

The main entrance on Soi Chetuphon is one of a series of sixteen monumental gates around the main compound, each guarded by stone **giants**, many of them comic Westerners in wide-brimmed hats – ships which exported rice to China would bring these statues back as ballast.

The entrance brings you into the eastern half of the main complex, where a courtyard of structures radiates from the bot in a disorientating symmetry. To get to the bot, the principal congregation and ordination hall, turn right and cut through the two surrounding cloisters, which are lined with hundreds of Buddha images. The elegant **bot** has beautiful teak doors decorated with mother-of-pearl, showing stories from the *Ramayana* in minute detail. Look out also for the stone bas-reliefs around the base of the bot, which narrate a longer version of the *Ramayana* in 152 action-packed panels. The plush interior has a well-proportioned altar on which ten statues of disciples frame a graceful, Ayutthayan Buddha image containing the remains of Rama I, the founder of Bangkok (Rama IV placed them there so that the public could worship him at the same time as the Buddha).

Back outside the entrance to the double cloister, keep your eyes open for a miniature mountain covered in statues of naked men in tall hats who appear to be gesturing rudely: they are *rishis* (hermits), demonstrating various positions of healing massage. Skirting the southwestern corner of the cloisters, you'll come to two pavilions between the eastern and western courtyards, which display plaques inscribed with the precepts of traditional medicine, as well as anatomical pictures showing the different pressure points and the illnesses that can be cured by massaging them.

The western courtyard

Among the 99 chedis strewn about the grounds, the four **great chedis** in the western courtyard stand out as much for their covering of garish tiles as for their size. The central chedi is the oldest, erected by Rama I to hold the remains of the most sacred Buddha image of Ayutthaya, the Phra Si Sanphet. Later, Rama III built the chedi to the north for the ashes of Rama II and the chedi to the south to hold his own remains; Rama IV built the fourth, with bright blue tiles, though its purpose is uncertain.

In the northwest corner of the courtyard stands the chapel of the **Reclining Buddha**, a 45-metre-long gilded statue of plaster-covered brick which depicts the Buddha entering Nirvana, a common motif in Buddhist iconography. The chapel is only slightly bigger than the statue – you can't get far enough away to take in anything but a surreal close-up view of the beaming five-metre smile. As for the feet, the vast black soles are beautifully inlaid with delicate mother-of-pearl showing the 108 *lakshanas*, or auspicious signs, which distinguish the true Buddha. Along one side of the statue are 108 bowls which will bring you good luck and a long life if you put a coin in each.

△ Flying kites, Sanam Luang

Sanam Luang and around

Sprawling across thirty acres north of the Grand Palace, **Sanam Luang** is one of the last open spaces left in Bangkok, a bare field where residents of the capital gather in the early evening to meet, eat and play. The nearby pavements are the marketplace for some exotic spiritual salesmen: on the eastern side sit astrologers and palm-readers, and sellers of bizarre virility potions and

Kite-flying

Flying intricate and colourful **kites** is now done mostly for fun in Thailand, but it has its roots in more serious activities. Filled with gunpowder and fitted with long fuses, kites were deployed in the first Thai kingdom at Sukhothai (1240–1438) as machines of war. In the same era, special *ngao* kites, with heads in the shape of bamboo bows, were used in Brahmin rituals: the string of the bow would vibrate in the wind and make a noise to frighten away evil spirits (nowadays noisy kites are still used, though only by farmers, to scare the birds). By the height of the Ayutthayan period (1351–1767) kites had become largely decorative: royal ceremonies were enhanced by fantastically shaped kites, adorned with jingling bells and ornamental lamps.

In the nineteenth century, Rama V, by his enthusiastic lead, popularized kite-flying as a wholesome and fashionable recreation. **Contests** are now held all over the country between February and April, when winds are strong and farmers traditionally have free time after harvesting the rice. These contests fall into two broad categories: those involving manoeuvrable flat kites, often in the shapes of animals; and those in which the beauty of static display kites is judged. The most popular contest of all, which comes under the first category, matches two teams, one flying star-shaped *chula*s, two-metre-high "male" kites, the other flying the smaller, more agile *pakpaos*, diamond-shaped "females". Each team uses its skill and teamwork to ensnare the other's kites and drag them back across a dividing line.

contraptions; on the western side and spreading around Thammasat University and Wat Mahathat, scores of small-time hawkers sell amulets, taking advantage of the spiritually auspicious location. In the early part of the year, especially in March during the Thai Sports and Kite Festival, the sky is filled with kite-fighting contests (see box on p.71).

As it's in front of the Grand Palace, the field is also the venue for national ceremonies, such as royal funerals and the **Ploughing Ceremony**, held in May at a time selected by astrologers to bring good fortune to the rice harvest. The elaborate Brahmin ceremony is led by an official from the Ministry of Agriculture, who stands in for the king in case the royal power were to be reduced by any failure in the ritual. At the designated time, the official cuts a series of circular furrows with a plough drawn by two oxen, and scatters rice that has been sprinkled with lustral water by the Brahmin priests of the court. When the ritual is over, spectators rush in to grab handfuls of the rice, which they then plant in their own paddies for good luck.

Wat Mahathat

On Sanam Luang's western side, with its main entrance on Thanon Maharat, **Wat Mahathat** (daily 9am–5pm; free), founded in the eighteenth century, provides a welcome respite from the surrounding tourist hype, and a chance to engage with the eager monks studying at **Mahachulalongkorn Buddhist University** here. As the nation's centre for the Mahanikai monastic sect (where Rama IV spent 27 years as a monk before becoming king in 1851), and housing one of the two Buddhist universities in Bangkok, the wat buzzes with purpose. It's this activity, and the chance of interaction and participation, rather than any special architectural features, which make a visit so rewarding. The many university-attending monks at the wat are friendly and keen to practise their English, and are more than likely to approach you: diverting topics might range from the poetry of Dylan Thomas to English football results gleaned from the BBC World Service.

Situated in Section Five of the wat is its **Vipassana Meditation Centre**, where sitting and walking meditation practice is available in English (daily 7–10am, 1–4pm & 6–8pm; ☎02 222 6011 or 02 623 5613 or go to ⓦwww .section-5.org for further information). Participants generally stay in the simple surroundings of the meditation building itself (donation requested), and must wear white clothes (available to rent at the centre) and observe the eight main Buddhist precepts (see p.242). Talks in English on meditation and Buddhism are held here every evening (8–9pm), as well as at the International Buddhist Meditation Centre (Room 106 or 209; ☎02 623 5881, ⓦwww.mcu.ac.th/ibmc) in the Mahachulalongkorn University building on the second and fourth Saturdays of every month (3–5pm).

The National Museum

Near the northwest corner of Sanam Luang, the **National Museum** (Wed–Sun 9am–4pm; B40 including free leaflet with map; ⓦwww .thailandmuseum.com) houses a colossal hoard of Thailand's chief artistic riches, ranging from sculptural treasures in the north and south wings, through bizarre decorative objects in the older buildings, to outlandish funeral chariots and the exquisite Buddhaisawan Chapel, as well as occasionally staging worthwhile temporary exhibitions (details on ☎02 224 1333). It's worth making time for the free **guided tours in English** (Wed & Thurs

9.30am): they're generally entertaining and their explication of the choicest exhibits provides a good introduction to Thai religion and culture. By the ticket office are a bookshop and a pleasant, air-conditioned **café**, serving drinks, sandwiches and cakes, while the **restaurant** inside the museum grounds, by the funeral chariots building, dishes up decent, inexpensive Thai food.

The first building you'll come to near the ticket office houses an informative overview of the history of Thailand, including a small archeological gem: a black stone **inscription**, credited to King Ramkhamhaeng of Sukhothai, which became the first capital of the Thai nation (c.1278–99) under his rule. Discovered in 1833 by the future Rama IV, it's the oldest extant inscription using the Thai alphabet. This, combined with the description it records of prosperity and piety in Sukhothai's Golden Age, has made the stone a symbol of Thai nationhood.

The main collection: southern building

At the back of the compound, two large modern buildings, flanking an old converted palace, house the museum's **main collection**, kicking off on the ground floor of the **southern building**. Look out here for some historic sculptures from the rest of Asia, including one of the earliest representations of the Buddha, from Gandhara in northwest India. Alexander the Great left a garrison at Gandhara, which explains why the image is in the style of Classical Greek sculpture: for example, the *ushnisha*, the supernatural bump on the top of the head, which symbolizes the Buddha's intellectual and spiritual power, is rationalized into a bun of thick, wavy hair.

Upstairs, the **prehistory** room displays axe heads and spear points from Ban Chiang in the northeast of Thailand, one of the earliest Bronze Age cultures ever discovered. Alongside are many roughly contemporaneous metal artefacts from Kanchanaburi province, as well as some excellent examples of the developments of Ban Chiang's famous pottery. In the adjacent **Dvaravati** room (S7; sixth to eleventh centuries), the pick of the stone and terracotta Buddhas is a small head in smooth, pink clay, whose downcast eyes and faintly smiling full lips typify the serene look of this era. At the far end of the first floor, you can't miss a voluptuous Javanese statue of elephant-headed Ganesh, Hindu god of wisdom and the arts, which, being the symbol of the Fine Arts Department, is always freshly garlanded. As Ganesh is known as the clearer of obstacles, Hindus always worship him before other gods, so by tradition he has grown fat through getting first choice of the offerings – witness his trunk jammed into a bowl of food in this sculpture.

Room S9 next door contains the most famous piece of **Srivijaya** art (eighth to thirteenth centuries), a bronze Bodhisattva Avalokitesvara found at Chaiya in southern Thailand (according to Mahayana Buddhism, a *bodhisattva* is a saint who has postponed his passage into Nirvana to help ordinary believers gain enlightenment). With its pouting face and sinuous torso, this image has become the ubiquitous emblem of southern Thailand. The rough chronological order of the collection continues back downstairs with an exhibition of **Khmer** and **Lopburi** sculpture (seventh to fourteenth centuries), most notably some dynamic bronze statuettes and stone lintels. Look out for an elaborate lintel that depicts Vishnu reclining on a dragon in the sea of eternity, dreaming up a new universe after the old one has been annihilated in the Hindu cycle of creation and destruction. Out of his navel comes a lotus, and out of this emerges four-headed Brahma, who will put the dream into practice.

The main collection: northern building

The second half of the survey, in the northern building, begins upstairs with the **Sukhothai** collection (thirteenth to fifteenth centuries), which features some typically elegant and sinuous Buddha images, as well as chunky bronzes of Hindu gods and a wide range of ceramics. The **Lanna** rooms (covering the north of Thailand from roughly the thirteenth to sixteenth centuries) include a miniature set of golden regalia, among them tiny umbrellas and a cute pair of filigree flip-flops, which would have been enshrined in a chedi. An ungainly but serene Buddha head, carved from grainy, pink sandstone, represents the **Ayutthaya** style of sculpture (fourteenth to eighteenth centuries): the faintest incision of a moustache above the lips betrays the Khmer influences that came to Ayutthaya after its conquest of Angkor. A sumptuous scripture cabinet, showing a cityscape of old Ayutthaya, is a more unusual piece, one of a surviving handful of such carved and painted items of furniture.

Downstairs in the section on **Bangkok** or **Ratanakosin** art (eighteenth century onwards), a stiffly realistic standing bronze brings you full circle. In his zeal for Western naturalism, Rama V had the statue made in the Gandhara style of the earliest Buddha image displayed in the first room of the museum.

The funeral chariots

To the east of the northern building, beyond the café on the left, stands a large garage where the fantastically elaborate **funeral chariots** of the royal family are stored. Pre-eminent among these is the Vejayant Rajarot, built by Rama I in 1785 for carrying the urn at his own funeral. The thirteen-metre-high structure symbolizes heaven on Mount Meru, while the dragons and divinities around the sides – piled in five golden tiers to suggest the flames of the cremation – represent the mythological inhabitants of the mountain's forests. Each weighing around forty tonnes and requiring the pulling power of three hundred men, the teak chariots last had an outing in 1996, for the funeral of the present king's much-revered mother.

Wang Na (Palace of the Second King)

The sprawling central building of the compound was originally part of the **Wang Na**, a huge palace stretching across Sanam Luang to Khlong Lod, which housed the "second king", appointed by the reigning monarch as his heir and deputy. When Rama V did away with the office in 1887, he turned the "Palace of the Second King" into a museum, which now contains a fascinating array of Thai *objets d'art*. As you enter (room 5), the display of sumptuous rare gold pieces behind heavy iron bars includes a well-preserved armlet taken from the ruined prang of fifteenth-century Wat Ratburana in Ayutthaya. In adjacent room 6, an intricately carved ivory seat turns out, with gruesome irony, to be a *howdah*, for use on an elephant's back. Among the masks worn by *khon* actors next door (room 7), look out especially for a fierce Hanuman, the white monkey-warrior in the *Ramayana* epic, gleaming with mother-of-pearl.

The huge and varied ceramic collection in room 8 includes some sophisticated pieces from Sukhothai, while the room behind (9) holds a riot of mother-of-pearl items, whose flaming rainbow of colours comes from the shell of the turbo snail from the Gulf of Thailand. It's also worth seeking out the display of richly decorated musical instruments in room 15.

Buddhaisawan Chapel

The second holiest image in Thailand, after the Emerald Buddha, is housed in the **Buddhaisawan Chapel**, the vast hall in front of the eastern entrance to the Wang Na. Inside, the fine proportions of the hall, with its ornate coffered ceiling and lacquered window shutters, are enhanced by painted rows of divinities and converted demons, all turned to face the chubby, glowing **Phra Sihing Buddha**, which according to legend was magically created in Sri Lanka and sent to Sukhothai in the thirteenth century. Like the Emerald Buddha, the image was believed to bring good luck to its owner and was frequently snatched from one northern Thai town to another, until Rama I brought it down from Chiang Mai in 1795 and installed it here in the second king's private chapel. Two other images in Thailand (in Nakhon Si Thammarat and Chiang Mai) now claim to be the authentic Phra Sihing Buddha, but all three are in fact derived from a lost original – this one is in a fifteenth-century Sukhothai style. It's still much loved by ordinary people and at Thai New Year is carried out onto Sanam Luang, where worshippers sprinkle it with water as a merit-making gesture.

The careful detail and rich, soothing colours of the surrounding 200-year-old **murals** are surprisingly well preserved; the bottom row between the windows narrates the life of the Buddha, beginning in the far right-hand corner with his parents' wedding.

Tamnak Daeng

On the south side of the Buddhaisawan chapel, the sumptuous **Tamnak Daeng** (Red House) stands out, a large, airy Ayutthaya-style house made of rare golden teak, surmounted by a multi-tiered roof decorated with carved foliage and swan's tail finials. Originally part of the private quarters of Princess Sri Sudarak, elder sister of Rama I, it was moved from the Grand Palace to the old palace in Thonburi for Queen Sri Suriyen, wife of Rama II; when her son became second king to Rama IV, he dismantled the edifice again and shipped it here to the Wang Na compound. Inside, it's furnished in the style of the early Bangkok period, with some of the beautiful objects that once belonged to Sri Suriyen, a huge, ornately carved box bed, and the uncommon luxury of an indoor toilet and bathroom.

The National Gallery and Silpakorn University Gallery

If the National Museum hasn't finished you off, two other lesser galleries nearby might. The **National Gallery**, across from the National Theatre on the north side of Sanam Luang at 4 Thanon Chao Fa (Wed–Sun 9am–4pm; B30; ☎02 282 2639–40, ⓦwww.thailandmuseum.com), displays in its upstairs gallery some rather beautiful early-twentieth-century temple banners depicting Buddhist subjects, but houses a permanent collection of largely uninspiring and derivative twentieth-century Thai art downstairs. Its temporary exhibitions can be pretty good however. The fine old wooden building that houses the gallery is also worth more than a cursory glance – it used to be the Royal Mint, and is constructed in typical early-twentieth-century style, around a central courtyard.

The **Silpakorn University Gallery** (Mon–Fri 9am–7pm, Sat 10am–4pm; free; ☎02 623 6120 ext 1418) on Thanon Na Phra Lan, across the road from the entrance to the Grand Palace, also stages regular exhibitions, by students, teachers and artists-in-residence. The country's first art school, the university was founded in 1943 by Professor Silpa Bhirasri, the much-revered, naturalized Italian sculptor (see p.249).

Mae Toranee

In a tiny park by the hectic bus stops at the northeast corner of Sanam Luang stands the voluptuous but rather neglected figure of **Mae Toranee**, the earth goddess, wringing the water from her ponytail. Originally part of a fountain built here by Rama V's queen, Saowaba, to provide Bangkokians with fresh drinking water, the statue illustrates a Buddhist legend featured in the murals of many temples. While the Buddha was sitting in meditation at a crucial stage of his enlightenment, Mara, the force of evil, sent a host of earthly temptations and demons to try to divert him from his path. The Buddha remained cross-legged and pointed his right hand towards the ground – the most popular pose of Buddha statues in Thailand – to call the earth goddess to bear witness to his countless meritorious deeds, which had earned him an ocean of water stored in the earth. Mae Toranee obliged by wringing her hair and engulfing Mara's demons in the deluge.

The lak muang

At 6.54am on April 21, 1782 – the astrologically determined time for the auspicious founding of Bangkok – a pillar containing the city's horoscope was ceremonially driven into the ground opposite the northeast corner of the Grand Palace. This phallic pillar, the **lak muang** – all Thai cities have one, to provide a home for their guardian spirits – was made from a four-metre tree trunk carved with a lotus-shaped crown, and is now sheltered in an elegant shrine surrounded by immaculate gardens. It shares the shrine with the taller *lak muang* of Thonburi, which was recently incorporated into Greater Bangkok.

Hundreds of worshippers come every day to pray and offer flowers, particularly childless couples seeking the gift of fertility. In one corner of the gardens you can often see short performances of **classical dancing**, paid for by well-off families when they have a piece of good fortune to celebrate.

Banglamphu
and the Democracy
Monument area

Best known as the site of the travellers' mecca Thanon Khao San, the **Banglamphu** district has a couple of noteworthy temples and still boasts a good number of wooden shophouses and narrow alleyways alongside the purpose-built guest houses, travel agents and jewellery shops. But the most interesting sights in this part of the city are found in the neighbourhoods to the south and east of the huge stone **Democracy Monument**, which forms the centrepiece of an enormous roundabout that siphons traffic from the major Rajdamnoen Klang artery. Most of these areas are within walking distance of the Khao San guest houses and equally accessible from the Grand Palace, and their proximity to the royal district means they retain a traditional flavour and remain unsullied by high-rise architecture. The string of temple-supply shops around Wat Suthat and Sao Ching Cha make this a rewarding area to explore, and the amulet market in the grounds of Wat Rajnadda is also well worth seeking out.

Banglamphu

Banglamphu's primary attraction is the legendary **Thanon Khao San**, a narrow road no more than four hundred metres long that is well established as *the* backpackers' hub of Southeast Asia. Crammed with Internet cafés, guest houses and restaurants serving yoghurt shakes and muesli, its sidewalks lined with tattooists, hair-braiders and stalls piled high with travellers' fashions and bootleg CDs, it's a lively, high-energy place that's fun to visit even if you're not staying in the area. Cheap clothes, jewellery and handicrafts are all good buys here (little is top quality on Khao San, but vendors are quick to pick up on global trends) and it's also a good spot to organize onward travel – bearing in mind the innumerable Khao San scams, as outlined on p.47.

The fastest and least stressful way of getting to this area is by boat. **Public longtail boats** run along Khlong Saen Saeb from various spots in downtown Bangkok (see p.37) to the Tha Phan Fah terminus right next to the Golden Mount compound, including to and from a particularly useful stop at Saphan Huachang, which is a few minutes' walk from both the Ratchathewi and Siam Skytrain stops. (The other fast way to get on to the Skytrain system is to take a taxi from Banglamphu to the National Stadium Skytrain stop.) The Chao Phraya **express boats** (see p.35) operate an equally efficient service to three different piers in the Banglamphu area: Tha Phra Athit (sometimes referred to as Tha Banglamphu; stop N13), a few hundred metres west of Thanon Khao San; Tha Saphan Rama VIII (Rama VIII Bridge; N14) at the western end of Samsen Soi 5; and Tha Thewes (N15) at the west end of Thanon Krung Kasem. Note that if you're using the boat service in the evening to head downtown via the Central Skytrain station at Saphan Taksin, the last boat leaves N13 at about 7.15pm. If you're simply crossing the river, there's no need to wait for the Chao Phraya Express as a **cross-river shuttle boat** runs continually during daylight hours from under Pinklao bridge, beside the Bangkok Information Centre on Thanon Phra Athit, to Tha Phra Pinklao on the Thonburi bank.

For access from anywhere else you'll need to make use of the city **bus** network: Democracy Monument is served by dozens of buses from all parts of the city, and as a landmark is hard to miss; if you're coming from eastern or northern parts of the city (such as Hualamphong Station, Siam Square or Sukhumvit), get off the bus as soon as you see it rather than waiting for Rajdamnoen Klang's more westerly stop outside the *Royal Hotel*, where it's almost impossible to cross the multiple lanes of traffic. Buses running out of Banglamphu have several different pick-up points in the area: to make things simpler, we've assigned numbers to these **bus stops**, though they are not numbered on the ground. Where there are two bus stops on the same route they share a number. Bus stops are marked on the Banglamphu map on p.80. For on-the-spot advice, contact the BTB booth in front of Wat Chana Songkhram on Thanon Chakrabongse, and for a more detailed breakdown of Bangkok's bus routes see p.36.

Bus Stop 1
(Thanon Chakrabongse, near the 7–11)
#6, #9 to Pak Khlong Talat flower market

Though ultra budget-conscious world travellers are still Khao San's main customers, Banglamphu is also starting to attract higher-spending sophisticates to its growing number of stylish restaurants and lively bars and clubs. At night, young Thais from all over the city gather here to browse the fashion stalls and pavement displays set up by local art students, mingling with the crowds of foreigners and squashing into the trendy bars and clubs that have made Khao San the city's most happening place to party (see p.195 for recommendations). Banglamphu boasts a surprising range of eating places too, from guest-house cafés on Thanon Khao San to bohemian Thai restaurants on Thanon Phra Athit that are favoured by students from nearby Thammasat University; the best of these are listed on p.182. For a roundup of accommodation on Khao San and elsewhere in Banglamphu, see p.169.

Wat Chana Songkhram

Sandwiched between Thanon Khao San and the Chao Phraya River, at the heart of the Banglamphu backpackers' ghetto, stands the lusciously renovated

#6, #9, #32 to Wat Pho
#30 to the Southern Bus Terminal

Bus Stop 2
(Thanon Phra Athit, south side, near *Hemlock*; and Thanon Phra Sumen, south side, near *Banglumpoo Place* hotel)
#53 to the Grand Palace and Chinatown
#56 to Thanon Ratchasima for Vimanmek Palace and Dusit

Bus Stop 3
(Thanon Phra Athit, north side, near the cross-river ferry entrance; and Thanon Phra Sumen, north side, opposite *Banglumpoo Place* hotel)
#3 (air-con) to Chatuchak Weekend Market and Mo Chit Northern Bus Terminal
#53 to Hualamphong train station (change at Bus Stop 6, but same ticket)

Bus Stop 4
(Thanon Rajdamnoen Klang, north side, outside Lottery Building)
#2 to Ekamai Eastern Bus Terminal
#15, #47 to Jim Thompson's House, Thanon Silom and Patpong
#15, #47, #79, #79 (air-con) to Siam Square
#39, #44, #59, #503 (air-con), #509 (air-con), #157 (air con) to Chatuchak Weekend Market
#47 to Lumphini boxing stadium
#70, #201, #503 (air-con), #509 (air-con) to TAT and Ratchadamnoen boxing stadium
#70 to Dusit
#157 (air-con) to Mo Chit Northern Bus Terminal
#511 (air-con) to Ekamai Eastern Bus Terminal and Pak Nam (for Ancient City buses)

Bus Stop 5
(Thanon Rajdamnoen Klang, south side)
#44 to Sanam Luang, the Grand Palace and Wat Pho

Bus Stop 6
(Thanon Krung Kasem, north side)
#53 to Hualamphong train station (buses start from here)

eighteenth-century **Wat Chana Songkhram**. As with temple compounds throughout the country, Wat Chana Songkhram is used for all sorts of neighbourhood activities (including car parking and football games); in this instance, part of the temple yard has been appropriated by stallholders selling secondhand books and travellers' clothes, making the most of the constant stream of tourists who use the wat as a short cut between the river and Khao San. It's worth slowing down for a closer look though, as the gables of the bot roof are beautifully ornate, embossed with a golden relief of Vishnu astride Garuda, enmeshed in an intricate design of red and blue glass mosaics, and the golden finials are shaped like nagas. Peeking over the compound walls onto the guest houses and bars of Soi Ram Bhuttri are a row of *kuti*, or monks' quarters: simple but elegant wooden cabins on stilts with steeply pitched roofs.

Phra Athit

Thanon **Phra Athit**, the Banglamphu road that runs alongside the (mostly obscured) Chao Phraya River, is known for its arty atmosphere and

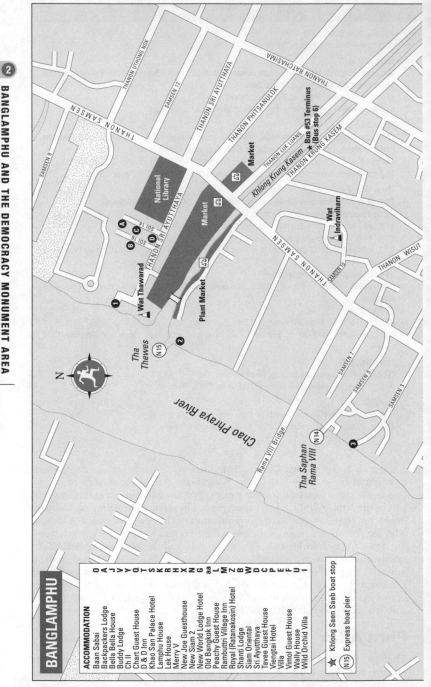

BANGLAMPHU

ACCOMMODATION

Baan Sabai	O
Backpackers Lodge	A
Bella Bella House	J
Buddy Lodge	V
Ch II	Y
Chart Guest House	Q
D & D Inn	T
Khao San Palace Hotel	S
Lamphu House	K
Lek House	R
Merry V	H
New Joe Guesthouse	X
New Siam 2	N
New World Lodge Hotel	G
Old Bangkok Inn	aa
Peachy Guest House	L
Rambuttri Village Inn	M
Royal (Ratanakosin) Hotel	Z
Shanti Lodge	B
Siam Oriental	W
Sri Ayutthaya	D
Tavee Guest House	C
Viengtai Hotel	P
Villa	E
Vimol Guest House	F
Wally House	U
Wild Orchid Villa	I

★ Khlong Saen Saeb boat stop

(N15) Express boat pier

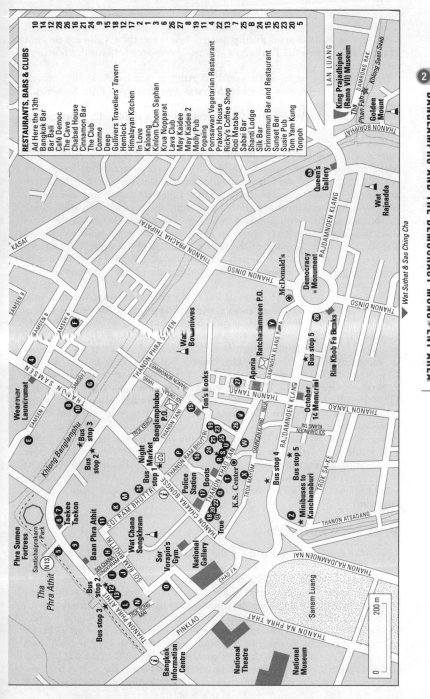

RESTAURANTS, BARS & CLUBS	
Ad Here the 13th	10
Bangkok Bar	14
Bar Bali	12
Café Democ	28
The Cave	26
Chabad House	16
Cinnamon Bar	21
The Club	24
Comme	9
Deep	15
Gullivers Travellers' Tavern	18
Hemlock	12
Himalayan Kitchen	17
In Love	2
Kaloang	1
Kinlom Chom Saphan	3
Krua Nopparat	6
Lava Club	26
May Kaidee	8
May Kaidee 2	19
Molly Pub	11
Popaing	4
Pornsawan Vegetarian Restaurant	22
Prakorb House	13
Ricky's Coffee Shop	7
Roti Mataba	25
Sabai Bar	B
Shanti Lodge	24
Silk Bar	15
Srinnmmun Bar and Restaurant	25
Sunset Bar	23
Susie Pub	20
Tom Yam Kung	5
Tonpoh	

Wat Suthat & Sao Ching Cha

81

numerous little bar-restaurants that draw crowds of students from nearby Thammasat University. Many of these places open only in the evenings, but some serve passing tourists during daylight hours and there's also a little knot of shops selling unusual Thai crafts and art-photocards towards the northern end of the road.

This northern stretch of Thanon Phra Athit is dominated by the crenellated whitewashed tower of **Phra Sumen Fortress** (aka Phra Sumeru), a renovated corner of the original eighteenth-century city walls that stands beside the river and its juncture with Khlong Banglamphu. The fortress was the northernmost of fourteen octagonal towers built by Rama I in 1783 to protect the royal island of Ratanakosin and originally contained 38 rooms for storing ammunition. (The only other surviving tower, also renovated, is Phra Mahakan Fortress, next to the Golden Mount; see p.86.) Nowadays there's nothing to see inside the Phra Sumen tower, but it makes a striking landmark and the area around it has been turned into a pleasant grassy riverside recreation area, **Santichaiprakarn Park**, with English-language signs describing the history of the fortifications. A park sign also highlights one of the area's last remaining lamphu trees (*duabanga grandiflora*), which continues to grow in a muddy pool on the edge of the river to the left of the royal *sala*. Lamphu trees were once so common in this neighbourhood that they gave the area its name – Banglamphu means "the place with lamphu trees" – though they've all but disappeared now.

The fort marks the northernmost limit of a **riverside walkway** that runs down to the Bangkok Information Centre at Phra Pinklao Bridge. As well as providing a good view of the boats and barges on the Chao Phraya, the Phra Sumen–Phra Pinklao walkway takes you past the front entrances of two very grand old buildings, both of them beautifully restored and currently occupied by international organizations. The United Nations' Food and Agriculture Organization (FAO) now uses the early-twentieth-century mansion known as **Baan Maliwan** as its library (closed to casual visitors), while the nearby UNICEF office is housed in the late-nineteenth-century palace of one of the wives of Rama IV, which also served as the headquarters of the clandestine Seri Thai resistance movement (see p.232) during World War II. Both these mansions show their most elegant faces to the river, as in those days most visitors would have arrived by boat. On the eastern side of Thanon Phra Athit, there's another fine early-twentieth-century mansion, **Baan Phra Athit**, at #201/1; most of this building is now occupied by a private company, but one wing has been turned into the café-bar *Coffee and More*, with views onto the courtyard.

Wat Indraviharn

Located in the northern reaches of the Banglamphu district on Thanon Wisut Kasat, **Wat Indraviharn** (also spelt Wat Intharawihan or Wat In) is famous for the enormous standing Buddha that dominates its precincts. Commissioned by Rama IV in the mid-nineteenth century, the 32-metre-high image is the tallest such representation – depicting the Buddha holding an alms bowl from beneath the folds of his robe – in the world, and is covered all over in gold mirror-mosaic; the topknot enshrines a Buddha relic from Sri Lanka. Though it's hardly the most elegant of statues, the beautifully pedicured foot-long toenails peep out gracefully from beneath devotees' garlands of fragrant jasmine, and you can get reasonable views of the neighbourhood by climbing the stairways of the tower supporting the statue from behind; when unlocked, the doorways in the upper part of the tower give access to the interior of the hollow image, affording vistas from shoulder level. Elsewhere in the wat's compact grounds you'll find the usual amalgam of architectural and spiritual styles, including a Chinese shrine and statues of Ramas IV and V.

Wat Indraviharn is one of an increasing number of favourite hangouts for **con-artists**, and the popular scam here is to offer tourists a tuk-tuk tour of Bangkok for a bargain B20, which invariably features a hard-sell visit to a jewellery shop – see p.218 for more on the famous Bangkok jewellery scam and p.55 for more on con-artists. Avoid all these hassles by hailing a passing metered taxi instead, or move on by **public transport**: Chao Phraya express boat stops N14 and N15 are within reach, and bus #3 runs from Thanon Samsen to Thanon Phra Athit.

Democracy Monument and around

About 300m southeast of Thanon Khao San and midway along Rajdamnoen Klang (the avenue that connects the Grand Palace and the new royal district of Dusit) looms the imposing **Democracy Monument** (*Anu Sawari Pracha Tippatai*). Begun in 1939, it was conceived as a testimony to the ideals that fuelled the 1932 revolution and the changeover to a constitutional monarchy – hence its symbolic positioning between the royal residences. Its dimensions are also significant: the four wings tower to a height of 24m, the same as the radius of the monument – allusions to June 24, the date the system was changed – and the 75 cannons around the perimeter refer to the year 2475 BE (1932 AD). The monument contains a copy of the constitution and is a focal point for public events and demonstrations and, less controversially, gets decked out with flowers every year on December 5, in honour of the king's birthday. If you're prepared to brave the traffic that streams round Democracy day and night, you can climb the steps at the base of the monument and inspect its facades at closer quarters. Each wing is carved with friezes showing heroic scenes from Thailand's history.

The monument was designed by Corrado Feroci, an Italian sculptor who'd been invited to Thailand by Rama VI in 1924 to encourage the pursuit of Western art. He changed his name to Silpa Bhirasri and stayed in Thailand until his death, producing many of Bangkok's statues and monuments – including the Rama I statue at Memorial Bridge and Victory Monument in the Phrayathai district – as well as founding Thailand's first Institute of Fine Arts.

Rajdamnoen Klang and Democracy Monument have long been the rallying point for political demonstrations, including the fateful student-led protests of October 14, 1973 (see p.234), when half a million people gathered here to demand a new constitution and an end to the autocratic regime of the so-called "Three Tyrants". The October 14 demonstration was savagely repressed: it turned into a bloody riot and culminated in the death of several hundred protesters at the hands of the police and the military. After years of procrastination, the events of this catastrophic day were finally commemorated in 2002 with the erection of the **October 14 Memorial**, a small granite amphitheatre encircling an elegant modern chedi bearing the names of some of the dead. The memorial stands in front of the former headquarters of Colonel Narong Kittikachorn, one of the Three Tyrants, 200m west of Democracy Monument, at the corner of Rajdamnoen Klang and Thanon Tanao.

The Queen's Gallery

It's an easy stroll from the long-running, rather staid National Gallery (see p.75) to the newest high-profile art museum in the area, **The Queen's Gallery** (Thurs–Tues 10am–7pm; B20; ⓦwww.queengallery.org), on the corner of Rajdamnoen Klang and Thanon Phra Sumen. This privately funded five-storey space stages temporary exhibitions of contemporary Thai art, plus the occasional show by foreign artists. Reading rooms on each floor contain a vast selection of artists' monographs, many of them with English-language texts, and the small bookshop beside the gallery entrance specializes in hard-to-find Thai art books.

King Prajadhipok (Rama VII) Museum

Appropriately located just 400m east of Democracy Monument, the **King Prajadhipok Museum** (Tues–Sun 9am–4pm; B40; ⓦwww.kpi.ac.th/museum) on Thanon Lan Luang charts the life and achievements of **Rama VII**, the king whose ten-year reign embraced Thailand's 1932 transition from rule by absolute monarchy to rule by democratic constitutional monarchy. Situated within the elegant European-style walls of an early-twentieth-century former shop, the museum is hardly an unmissable attraction, though its displays are accessible and easy to digest, and offer expansive English-language captions. The section explaining the background to the 1932 revolution is the most important, featuring browsable copies of early drafts of the Constitution and some insight into the exchanges between the king and the committed group of intellectuals behind this radical political change. When this group finally seized power in 1932, Rama VII agreed to take the compromise option, later presiding at a ceremony in which the Constitution was officially conferred. It wasn't long however, before relations between Rama VII and Thailand's new leaders soured, leading to his abdication in 1935. Rama VII was a keen amateur film-maker and he commissioned the building of Thailand's first cinema, the Sala Chalermkrung Theatre (see p.204) in 1933; the museum contains a miniature replica of this movie theatre, where old films from the Rama VII era are screened twice daily, at 10am and 2pm.

Wat Rajnadda, Loh Prasat and the amulet market

Five minutes' walk southeast of Democracy Monument, at the point where Rajdamnoen Klang meets Thanon Mahachai, stands the assortment of religious buildings known collectively as **Wat Rajnadda**. It's immediately recognizable by the multi-tiered, castle-like structure called **Loh Prasat**, or "Iron Monastery" – a reference to its 37 forbiddingly dark metal spires, which represent the 37 virtues necessary for attaining enlightenment. The only structure of its kind in Bangkok, Loh Prasat is the dominant and most bizarre of Wat Rajnadda's components. Each tier is pierced by passageways running north–south and east–west (fifteen in each direction at ground level), with small meditation cells at each point of intersection. The Sri Lankan monastery on which it is modelled contained a thousand cells; this one probably has half that number.

In the southeast (Thanon Mahachai) corner of the temple compound, Bangkok's biggest amulet market, the **Wat Rajnadda Buddha Center**, comprises at least a hundred stalls selling tiny Buddha images of all designs,

Amulets

To gain protection from malevolent spirits and physical misfortune, most Thais wear or carry at least one **amulet** at all times. These tiny charms – usually between one and four centimetres high – are generally miniature replicas of sacred images and are often encased in a small, transparent, silver-edged case worn on a necklace.

The most popular **images** are copies of sacred statues from famous wats, while others show revered holy men, kings (Rama V is a favourite), healers, or a many-armed monk depicted closing his eyes, ears and mouth so as to concentrate better on reaching Nirvana – a human version of the hear-no-evil, see-no-evil, speak-no-evil monkeys. On the reverse side a *yantra* is often inscribed, a combination of letters and figures also designed to ward off evil, sometimes of a very specific nature, such as protecting your durian orchards from gales or your tuk-tuk from oncoming traffic. Individually hand-crafted or mass-produced, amulets can be made from bronze, clay, plaster or gold, and some even have sacred ingredients added, such as the ashes of burnt holy texts. But what really determines an amulet's efficacy is its history: where and by whom it was made, who or what it represents and who consecrated it. Monks are often involved in the making of the images and are always called upon to consecrate them – the more charismatic the monk, the more powerful the amulet. In return, the proceeds from the sale of amulets contribute to wat funds.

The **belief in amulets** is thought to have originated in India, where tiny images were sold to pilgrims who visited the four holy sites associated with the Buddha's birth, enlightenment, first sermon and death. But not all amulets found in Thailand are Buddhist-related – there's a whole range of other spiritually powerful objects to wear for protection, including tigers' teeth, rose quartz, tamarind seeds, coloured threads and miniature phalluses. Worn around the waist rather than the neck, the phallus amulets provide protection for the genitals as well as being associated with fertility, and are of Hindu origin.

For some people, amulets are not only a vital form of spiritual protection, but valuable **collectors' items** as well. Amulet-collecting mania is something akin to stamp collecting – there are at least six Thai magazines for collectors, which give histories of certain types, tips on distinguishing between genuine items and fakes, and personal accounts of particularly powerful amulet experiences. The most rewarding places to watch the collectors and browse the wares yourself are at Wat Rajnadda Buddha Center (see p.84); along "Amulet Alley" on Trok Mahathat, between Wat Mahathat (see p.72) and the river; and at Chatuchak Weekend Market (see p.129).

materials and prices. Alongside these miniature charms are statues of Hindu deities, dolls and carved wooden phalluses, also bought to placate or ward off disgruntled spirits, as well as love potions and tapes of sacred music. While the amulet market at Wat Rajnadda is probably the best in Bangkok, you'll find less pricey examples from the streetside vendors who congregate daily along the pavement in front of Wat Mahathat. Prices start as low as B20 and rise into the thousands.

Wat Saket and the Golden Mount

Beautifully illuminated at night, when it seems to float unsupported above the neighbourhood, the gleaming gold chedi across the road from Wat Rajnadda actually sits atop a structure known as the Golden Mount, within the compound of the late-eighteenth-century **Wat Saket**. The main temple was built by Rama I just outside his new city walls to serve as the capital's crematorium and over the next century became the dumping ground for some sixty thousand plague victims, most of whom were too poor to afford funeral pyres and so were left to the vultures. The **Golden Mount**, or Phu Khao Tong, is a later addition and dates back to the early nineteenth century, when Rama III commissioned a huge chedi to be constructed here on ground that proved too soft to support it. The whole thing collapsed into a hill of rubble, but as Buddhist law states that a religious building can never be destroyed, however tumbledown, so fifty years later Rama V bricked in the debris and crowned it with the more sensibly sized chedi we see today, in which he placed some relics, believed by some to be the Buddha's teeth.

To reach the base of the mount, follow the renovated crenellations of the eighteenth-century Phra Mahakan Fortress and the old city wall, past the small bird and antiques market that operates from one of the recesses. Climbing to the top, you'll pass remnants of the collapsed chedi and plaques commemorating donors to the temple. The **terrace** surrounding the base of the new chedi offers an impressive panorama of landmark roofs: the gleaming gables of Wat Rajnadda and the spikes of neighbouring Loh Prasat immediately to the west, the golden spires of the Grand Palace behind them, and further beyond, the finely proportioned prangs of Wat Arun on the other side of the river.

Wat Saket hosts an enormous annual **temple fair** in the first week of November, when the mount is illuminated with coloured lanterns and the whole compound seethes with funfair rides, food-sellers and travelling performers.

Wat Suthat, Sao Ching Cha and Thanon Bamrung Muang

Located about 700m southwest of the Golden Mount, or a similar distance directly south of Democracy Monument along Thanon Dinso, **Wat Suthat** (daily 9am–9pm; B20) is one of Thailand's most important temples and contains Bangkok's tallest viharn, built in the early nineteenth century to house the eight-metre-high meditating figure of Phra Sri Sakyamuni Buddha. The statue sits on a glittering mosaic dais surrounded by surreal **murals** that depict the last 24 lives of the Buddha rather than the more usual ten. The galleries that encircle the viharn contain 156 serenely posed Buddha images, making a nice contrast to the **Chinese statues** dotted around the viharn's courtyard and that of the bot in the adjacent compound, most of which were brought over from China during Rama I's reign, as ballast in rice boats: check out the depictions of gormless Western sailors and the supercilious Chinese scholars.

The area just in front of Wat Suthat is dominated by the towering, red-painted teak posts of **Sao Ching Cha**, otherwise known as the **Giant Swing**, once the focal point of a Brahmin ceremony to honour Shiva's annual visit to earth. Teams of two or four young men would stand on the outsized seat (now missing) and swing up to a height of 25m, to grab between their teeth a bag of gold suspended on the end of a bamboo pole. The act of swinging probably symbolized the rising and setting of the sun, though legend also has it that Shiva and his consort, Uma, were banned from swinging in their heavenly abode because doing so caused cataclysmic floods on earth – prompting Shiva to demand that the practice be continued on earth as a rite to ensure moderate rains and bountiful harvests. Accidents were so common with the terrestrial version that it was outlawed in the 1930s.

The streets leading up to Wat Suthat and Sao Ching Cha are renowned as the best place in the city to buy **religious paraphernalia**, and are well worth a browse – even for tourists. **Thanon Bamrung Muang** in particular is lined

△ Sao Ching Cha (the Giant Swing)

with shops selling everything a good Buddhist could need, from household offertory tables to temple umbrellas and two-metre Buddha images. They also sell special alms packs for devotees to donate to monks; a typical pack is contained within a (holy saffron-coloured) plastic bucket (which can be used by the monk for washing his robes, or himself), and comprises such daily necessities as soap, toothpaste, soap powder, toilet roll, candles and incense.

Wat Rajabophit

From Wat Suthat, walk south down Thanon Titong for a few hundred metres before turning right (west) onto Thanon Rajabophit, on which stands **Wat Rajabophit** (see map on p.60), one of the city's prettiest temples and another example of Chinese influence. It was built by Rama V and is characteristic of this progressive king in its unusual design, with the rectangular bot and viharn connected by a circular cloister that encloses a chedi. Every external wall in the compound is covered in the pastel shades of Chinese *bencharong* ceramic tiles, creating a stunning overall effect, while the bot interior looks like a tiny banqueting hall, with gilded Gothic vaults and intricate mother-of-pearl doors.

If you now head west towards the Grand Palace from Wat Rajabophit, as you cross the canal you'll pass a gold **statue of a pig**, erected in tribute to one of Rama V's wives, born in the Chinese Year of the Pig. Alternatively, walking in a southerly direction down Thanon Fuang Nakhon to its continuation, Thanon Banmo, will lead you all the way down to the Chao Phraya River and Memorial Bridge, taking in some fine old Chinese shophouses and the exuberant flower and vegetable market, Pak Khlong Talat, along the way (see p.95 for a description of this route).

Chinatown and Pahurat

When the newly crowned Rama I decided to move his capital across to the east bank of the river in 1782, the Chinese community living on the proposed site of his palace was given no choice but to relocate downriver, to the **Sampeng** area. Two hundred years on, **Chinatown** has grown into the country's largest Chinese district, an atmospheric and enjoyably chaotic sprawl of narrow, relentlessly crowded alleyways, temples and shophouses that's chiefly of interest for its markets and its colonial-style architecture, though you'll also find a couple of characterful temples here as well as some rewarding eating experiences (see p.185). It's all packed in between Charoen Krung (New Road) and the river, separated from Ratanakosin by the Indian area of **Pahurat** – famous for its cloth and dressmakers' trimmings – and bordered to the east by Hualamphong train station. Real estate in Sampeng is said to be amongst the most valuable in the country, and there are over a hundred gold and jewellery shops along Thanon Yaowarat – Chinatown's nerve centre – alone.

Getting to and from Chinatown and Pahurat

The easiest access to Chinatown is either by **subway** to Hualamphong Station, or by Chao Phraya **express boat** to Tha Rachawongse (Rajawong; N5) at the southern end of Thanon Rajawong, which runs through the centre of Chinatown. The express boat service also stops just a few metres from Pak Khlong Talat market and the southern end of Thanon Triphet, at Tha Saphan Phut (Memorial Bridge; N6).

This part of the city is also well served by **buses** from downtown Bangkok, as well as from Banglamphu and Ratanakosin (see boxes on p.78 and p.36); from Banglamphu either take any Hualamphong-bound bus and then walk from the train station, or catch the non-air-conditioned bus #56, which runs along Thanon Tanao at the end of Thanon Khao San and then goes all the way down Mahachai and Chakraphet roads in Chinatown – get off just after the Merry King department store for Sampeng Lane. Coming from downtown Bangkok and/or the Skytrain network, either switch to the subway, or jump on a non-air-conditioned bus #25 or #40, both of which run from Thanon Sukhumvit, via Siam Square to Hualamphong, then Thanon Yaowarat and on to Pahurat. Travelling out of Chinatown, west-bound air-conditioned #507 and ordinary buses #25, #40 and #53 all go to Sanam Luang (for Wat Pho and the Grand Palace).

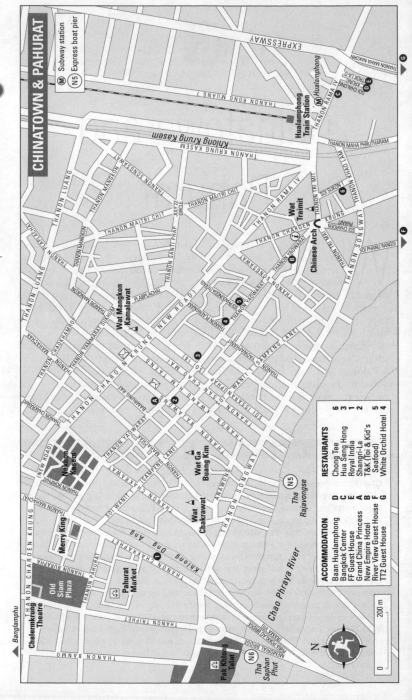

CHINATOWN & PAHURAT

M Subway station

(N5) Express boat pier

Chao Phraya River

ACCOMMODATION

Baan Hualamphong	D
Bangkok Center	C
FF Guest House	E
Grand China Princess	A
New Empire Hotel	B
River View Guest House	F
TT2 Guest House	G

RESTAURANTS

Chong Tee	6
Hua Seng Hong	3
Royal India	1
Shangri-La	2
T&K (Toi & Kid's Seafood)	5
White Orchid Hotel	4

0   200 m

Nearly all Chinatown's shops and restaurants shut down for the annual three-day holiday held to celebrate **Chinese New Year** (on the new moon of the first lunar month, sometime between late January and mid-February), but throughout this period Sampeng's main roads throng with foodstalls and the streets are enlivened by Chinese dragon parades and Chinese opera shows. During the nine-day **Vegetarian Festival** in October or November (described on p.186) most of the city's Chinese restaurants stop serving meat, flying special yellow flags to show that they're upholding the community's tradition.

Sampeng

The following fairly lengthy route takes you through **Sampeng**'s most interesting neighbourhoods and could easily take a whole day to complete on foot. For the most authentic Chinatown experience it's best to come during the week, as some shops and stalls shut at weekends; on weekdays they begin closing

The Chinese in Thailand

The **Chinese** have been a dominant force in the shaping of Thailand, and **commerce** is the foundation of their success. Chinese merchants first gained a toehold here in the mid-fourteenth century, when they contributed so much to the prosperity of the city-state of Ayutthaya that they were the only foreign community allowed to live within the city walls. Soon their compatriots were established all over the country, and when the capital was eventually moved to Bangkok in 1782 it was to an already flourishing Chinese trading post.

The start of the Bangkok era marked an end to the wars that had dogged Thailand and as the economy began to boom, both Rama I and Rama II encouraged Chinese immigration to boost the indigenous workforce. Thousands of migrants arrived from southern China, most of them young men eager to earn money that could be sent back to families impoverished by civil wars and persistently bad harvests. They saw their overseas stints as temporary measures, intending to return after a few years, though many never did. By the middle of the nineteenth century half the capital's population were of pure or mixed Chinese blood, and they were quickly becoming the masters of the new import-export trade, particularly the burgeoning tin and rubber industries. By the end of the century, the Chinese dominated Thailand's commercial and urban sector, while the Thais remained in firm control of the political domain, an arrangement that apparently satisfied both parties: as the old Chinese proverb goes, "We don't mind who holds the head of the cow, providing we can milk it".

Up until the beginning of the twentieth century, **intermarriage** between the two communities had been common, because so few Chinese women had emigrated – indeed, there is some Chinese blood in almost every Thai citizen, including the king. But in the early 1900s Chinese women started to arrive in Thailand, making Chinese society increasingly self-sufficient and enclosed. **Anti-Chinese feeling** grew and discriminatory laws ensued, including the restricting of Chinese-language education and the closing of some jobs to Chinese citizens, a movement that increased in fervour as Communism began to be perceived as a threat. Since the late 1970s, strict immigration controls have been enforced, limiting the number of new settlers to one hundred per nationality per year, a particularly harsh imposition on the Chinese. However, the established Thai-Chinese community is as crucial as ever to the nation's success and, as wealth and business interests take precedence over military influence within the political sphere, the number of Thai-Chinese businesspeople in government is growing.

around 5pm. Orientation in Chinatown can be quite tricky: the alleys (known as *trok* rather than the more usual soi) are extremely narrow, their turn-offs and other road signs often obscured by the mounds of merchandise that clutter the sidewalks and the surrounding hordes of buyers and sellers. One other point to bear in mind: Chinatown's two main arteries are one-way streets, with traffic running west along the entire length of Thanon Yaowarat, and east along Thanon Charoen Krung as far as Thanon Songsawat. For a detailed tour of the alleys and markets, use *Nancy Chandler's Map of Bangkok*; alternatively, ask for help at the BTB **tourist information** booth (Mon–Sat 9am–5pm) just northwest of the Chinese Arch on Thanon Yaowarat.

Wat Traimit and the Golden Buddha

Given the confusing layout of the district, it's worth starting your explorations at the eastern edge of Chinatown, just west of Hualamphong train and subway stations, with the triangle of land occupied by **Wat Traimit** (daily 9am–5pm; B20). Cross the khlong beside the station and walk 200m down (signed) Thanon Tri Mit to enter the temple compound. Outwardly unprepossessing, the temple boasts a quite stunning interior feature: the world's largest solid-gold Buddha is housed here, fitting for a community so closely linked with the gold trade, even if the image has nothing to do with China's spiritual heritage. Over 3m tall and weighing five and a half tons, the **Golden Buddha** gleams as if coated in liquid metal, seated amidst candles and surrounded with offerings of lotus buds and incense. A fine example of the curvaceous grace of Sukhothai art, the beautifully proportioned figure is best appreciated by comparing it with the cruder Sukhothai Buddha in the next-door bot, to the east.

Cast in the thirteenth century, the image was brought to Bangkok by Rama III, completely encased in stucco – a common ruse to conceal valuable statues from would-be thieves. The disguise was so good that no one guessed what was underneath until 1955 when the image was accidentally knocked in the process of being moved to Wat Traimit, and the stucco cracked to reveal a patch of gold. The discovery launched a country-wide craze for tapping away at plaster Buddhas in search of hidden precious metals, but Wat Traimit's is still the most valuable – it's valued, by weight alone, at over US$10 million. Sections of the stucco casing are now on display alongside the Golden Buddha.

Sampeng Lane

Leaving Wat Traimit by the Charoen Krung/Yaowarat exit (at the back of the temple compound), walk northwest along Thanon Yaowarat, and turn left onto Thanon Songsawat, to reach **Sampeng Lane** (also signposted as **Soi Wanit 1**). This area used to thrive on opium dens, gambling houses and brothels, but now sticks to a more reputable (if tacky) commercial trade. Stretching southeast–northwest for about 1km, Sampeng Lane is a fun – if exhaustingly congested – place to browse and shop, unfurling itself like a ramshackle department store selling everything from Chinese silk pyjamas to computer games at bargain-basement rates. Like goods are more or less gathered in sections, so at the eastern end you'll find mostly cheap jewellery and hair accessories, for example, before passing through stalls specializing in ceramics, Chinese lanterns and shoes, followed by clothes (west of Thanon Rajawong), a very good selection of fabrics, plus sarongs and haberdashery – see *Nancy Chandler's Map of Bangkok* for a detailed breakdown of what's sold where. To complete the shopping experience, there are food outlets every few steps to help sustain your energy.

△ Chinatown tea seller

Soi Issaranuphap

For a rather more sensuous experience, take a right about halfway down Sampeng Lane, into **Soi Issaranuphap** (also signed in places as Soi 16). Packed with people from dawn till dusk, this long, dark alleyway, which also traverses Charoen Krung (New Road), is where you come in search of ginseng roots (essential for good health), quivering fish heads, cubes of cockroach-killer chalk and pungent piles of cinnamon sticks. You'll see Chinese grandfathers discussing business in darkened shops, ancient pharmacists concocting bizarre potions to order, alleys branching off in all directions to gaudy Chinese temples and market squares. Soi Issaranuphap finally ends at the Thanon Plaplachai intersection amid a flurry of shops specializing in paper **funeral art**. Believing that the deceased should be well provided for in their afterlife, Chinese people buy miniature paper replicas of necessities to be burned with the body: especially popular are houses, cars, suits of clothing and, of course, money.

Wat Mangkon Kamalawat

If Soi Issaranuphap epitomizes traditional Chinatown commerce, then **Wat Mangkon Kamalawat** (also known as **Wat Leng Nee Yee** or, in English, "Dragon Flower Temple") stands as a superb example of the community's spiritual practices. Best approached via its dramatic multi-tiered gateway 10m up Thanon Charoen Krung (New Road) from the Soi Issaranuphap junction, Wat Mangkon receives a constant stream of devotees, who come to leave offerings at one or more of the small altars inside this important Mahayana Buddhist temple. As with the Theravada Buddhism espoused by the Thais, Mahayana Buddhism (see "Religion: Thai Buddhism" in Contexts, p.239) fuses with other ancient religious beliefs, notably Confucianism and Taoism, and the statues and shrines within Wat Mangkon cover the whole spectrum. Passing through the secondary gateway, under the glazed ceramic gables topped with undulating Chinese dragons, you're greeted by a set of four outsize statues of bearded and rather forbidding sages, each clasping a symbolic object: a parasol, a pagoda, a snake's head and a mandolin. Beyond them, a series of Buddha images swathed in saffron netting occupies the next chamber, a lovely open-sided room of gold paintwork, red-lacquered wood, lattice lanterns and pictorial wall panels inlaid with mother-of-pearl. Elsewhere in the compound are little booths selling devotional paraphernalia, a Chinese medicine stall and a fortune-teller.

Wat Ga Buang Kim

Less than 100m up Thanon Charoen Krung (New Road) from Wat Mangkon, a left turn into Thanon Rajawong, followed by a right turn into Thanon Anawong and a further right turn into the narrow, two-pronged Soi Krai brings you to the atmospheric neighbourhood temple of **Wat Ga Buang Kim**. Here, as at more typically Thai temples upcountry, local residents socialize in the shade of the tiny, enclosed courtyard and the occasional worshipper drops by to make offerings at the altar. This particular wat is remarkable for its exquisitely ornamented Chinese-style "vegetarian hall", a one-room shrine with altar centrepiece framed by intricately carved wooden tableaux – gold-painted miniatures arranged as if in sequence, with recognizable characters reappearing in new positions and in different moods. The hall's outer wall is adorned with small tableaux, too, the area around the doorway at the top of the stairs peopled with finely crafted ceramic figurines drawn from Chinese opera stories. The other building in the wat compound is a stage used for Chinese opera performances.

Wat Chakrawat

Back on Anawong, a right turn down Thanon Chakrawat leads to the quite dissimilar **Wat Chakrawat**, home to several long-suffering crocodiles, not to mention monkeys, dogs and chess-playing local residents. **Crocodiles** have lived in the tiny pond behind the bot for about fifty years, ever since one was brought here after being hauled out of the Chao Phraya, where it had been endangering the limbs of bathers. The original crocodile – stuffed – sits in a glass case overlooking the current generation in the pond.

Across the other side of the wat compound is a grotto housing two unusual Buddhist relics. The first is a black silhouette on the wall, decorated with squares of gold leaf and believed to be the Buddha's shadow. Nearby, the statue of a fat monk looks on. The story goes that this monk was so good-looking that he was forever being tempted by the attentions of women; the only way he could deter them was to make himself ugly – which he did by gorging himself into obesity.

Nakhon Kasem

Further along Thanon Chakrawat, away from the river, is the western limit of Chinatown and an odd assortment of shops in the grid of lanes known as **Nakhon Kasem** (Thieves' Market), bordered by Thanon Charoen Krung and Thanon Yaowarat to the north and south and Chakrawat and Boriphat roads to the east and west. In the sois that crisscross Nakhon Kasem, outlets once full of illicitly acquired goods now stock a vast range of metal wares, from antique gongs to modern musical instruments and machine parts.

Pahurat and Pak Khlong Talat

The ethnic emphasis changes west of Nakhon Kasem. Cross Khlong Ong Ang and you're in **Pahurat** – here, in the small square south of the intersection of Chakraphet and Pahurat roads, is where the capital's sizeable Indian community congregates. Unless you're looking for *beedi* cigarettes or Bollywood VCDs, curiosity-shopping is not as rewarding here as in Chinatown, but if you're interested in buying **fabrics** this is definitely the place: Thanon Pahurat is chock-a-block with cloth merchants specializing in everything from curtain materials through saree lengths to *lakhon* dance costumes complete with accessories.

Also here, at the Charoen Krung (New Road)/Thanon Triphet intersection, is the **Old Siam Plaza**: its mint-green and cream exterior, resplendent with shutters and balustraded balconies, is redolent of a colonial summer palace, and its airy, three-storey interior is filled with a strange combination of shops selling either upmarket gifts or hi-tech consumer goods. Most rewarding are the half-dozen shops on the ground floor that carry an excellent range of silk from north and northeast Thailand; many of them offer dressmaking services as well. But most of the ground floor is taken up by a permanent food festival and is packed with stalls selling snacks, sweets and sticky desserts. Pahurat is also renowned for its Indian restaurants, and a short stroll along Thanon Chakraphet takes you past a choice selection of curry houses and street vendors.

Pak Khlong Talat and Memorial Bridge

A stroll through the 24-hour flower and vegetable market **Pak Khlong Talat** is a fine and fitting way to round off a day in Chinatown, though if you're an early riser it's also a great place to come before dawn, when market gardeners from Thonburi boat and truck their freshly picked produce across the Chao Phraya ready for sale to the shopkeepers, restaurateurs and hoteliers. Occupying an ideal position close to the river, the market has been operating from covered halls between the southern ends of Khlong Lod, Thanon Banmo, Thanon Chakraphet and the river bank since the nineteenth century and is the biggest wholesale market in the capital. The flower stalls, selling twenty different varieties of cut orchids and myriad other tropical blooms, spill onto the streets along the riverfront as well, and, though prices are lowest in the early morning, you can still get some good bargains here in the afternoon. For the most interesting **approach** to the flower market from the Old Siam Plaza, turn west across Thanon Triphet to reach Thanon Banmo, and then follow this road south down towards the Chao Phraya River. As you near the river, notice the facing rows of traditional Chinese shophouses, still in use today, which retain their characteristic (peeling) pastel-painted facades, shutters and stucco curlicues. There's an entrance into the market on your right and just after sundown this southernmost stretch of Thanon Banmo fills with handcarts and vans unloading the most amazing quantities of fresh blooms.

The riverside end of Thanon Triphet and the area around the base of Memorial Bridge host a huge **night bazaar** (nightly 8pm–midnight) that's dominated by cheap and unusual fashions – and by throngs of teenage fashion victims. **Memorial Bridge** itself (aka **Saphan Phut**) was built in 1932 to commemorate the 150th anniversary of the foundation of the Chakri dynasty and of Bangkok, and is dedicated to Rama I (or Phra Buddha Yodfa, to give him his official title), whose bronze statue sits at the approach. The bridge carries traffic across to Thonburi and has since been supplemented by the adjacent twin-track Saphan Phra Pokklao. The Chao Phraya **express boat** service stops just a few metres from the market at Tha Saphan Phut (N6). Numerous city **buses** stop in front of the market and pier, including the northbound non-air-conditioned #3 and air-conditioned #512, which both run to Banglamphu (see box on p.36).

Thonburi

angkok really began across the river from Ratanakosin in **Thonburi**, and though you won't find any portentous ruins on this side of the Chao Phraya you will get a glimpse of an age-old way of life that has all but disappeared from Bangkok proper. For Thonburi is still crisscrossed by **canals**, or khlongs, and life here continues to revolve around the waterways. The main arteries of Khlong Bangkok Noi and Khlong Bangkok Yai are particularly important: vendors of food and household goods paddle their boats along the subsidiary canals that weave through the residential areas, and canalside factories use them to transport their wares to the Chao Phraya River. The **architecture** along the canals ranges from ramshackle, makeshift homes balanced just above the water – and prone to flooding during the monsoon season – to villa-style residences fronted by lawns and waterside verandas. Venture on to the Thonburi backroads just three or four kilometres west of the river and you find yourself surrounded by market gardens and rural homes, with no hint of the throbbing metropolis across on the other bank. Modern Thonburi, on the other hand, sprawling to each side of Thanon Phra Pinklao, consists of the prosaic line-up of department stores, cinemas, restaurants and markets found all over urbanized Thailand.

Devoid of grand ruins and isolated from central Bangkok, it's hard to imagine Thonburi as a former capital of Thailand, but so it was for fifteen years, between

---

Getting to and from Thonburi

Getting to Thonburi is simply a matter of crossing the river. You can either use one of the numerous **bridges**, of which Memorial (Saphan Phut)/Phra Pokklao and Phra Pinklao are the most central; take a **cross-river ferry** (see the map on p.98); or hop on the Chao Phraya **express ferry**, which makes stops just north of Phra Pinklao Bridge, near Thonburi train station, and near Siriraj Hospital. Useful city **buses** that cross the river into Thonburi include air-con #507 from Thanon Rama IV, Hualamphong Station and Banglamphu; air-con #511 from Thanon Sukhumvit and Banglamphu; and non-air-con #159 from Chatuchak Weekend Market, Hualamphong and Banglamphu; see the box on p.36 for details.

You might also find yourself taking a train from **Thonburi Station**, 850m west of the Tha Bangkok Noi ferry stop, as this is the departure point for trains to Kanchanaburi – not to be confused with Thonburi's other, even smaller train station, **Wongwian Yai** (for trains to Samut Sakhon), which is further south. The **Southern Bus Terminal** is also in Thonburi, at the junction of Thanon Borom Ratchonni and the Nakhon Chaisri Highway: all public and air-con buses to southern destinations leave from here, including those for Nakhon Pathom, Damnoen Saduak, Phetchaburi and Kanchanaburi. Details on all these transport terminals are given on p.137.

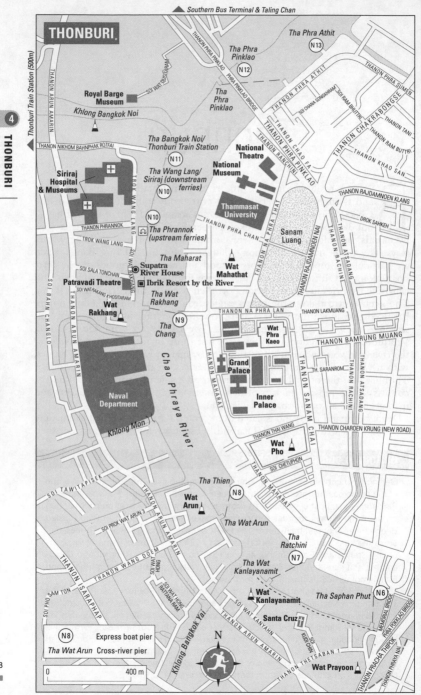

THONBURI

4

THONBURI

Thonburi Train Station (500m)

Southern Bus Terminal & Taling Chan

THANON PHRA PINKLAO

Tha Phra Athit

(N13)

Tha Phra Pinklao

(N12)

THANON PHRA ATHIT

THANON PHRA SUMEN

THANON CHAO FA

THANON CHAKRABONGSE

SOI CHANA SONGKRAM

SOI RAM BHUTRI

THANON RAM BUTTRI

THANON TANI

Tha Phra Pinklao

PHRA PINKLAO BRIDGE

THANON CHAO FA

THANON RANCHINI

THANON KHAO SAN

Royal Barge Museum

SOI WAT DUSITARAM

Khlong Bangkok Noi

THANON NIKHOM BAHNPHAK ROTFAI

Tha Bangkok Noi/ Thonburi Train Station

(N11)

National Theatre

National Museum

THANON PHRA PINKLAO

THANON RAJDAMNOEN KLANG

DROK SAHKEH

Tha Wang Lang/ Siriraj (downstream ferries)

(N10)

Siriraj Hospital & Museums

TROK WANG LANG

Thammasat University

THANON NA PHRA THAT

THANON ATSADANG

THANON RACHINI

(N10)

THANON PHRANNOK

Tha Phrannok (upstream ferries)

TROK WANG LANG

THANON PHRA CHAN

Sanam Luang

SOI WAT RAKANG

SOI SALA TONCHAN

Tha Maharat

Supatra River House

Ibrik Resort by the River

Wat Mahathat

Patravadi Theatre

SOI WAT RAKANG KHOSITARAM

Tha Wat Rakhang

THANON NA PHRA LAN

THANON LAKMUANG

Wat Rakhang

THANON ARUN AMARIN

SOI BAHN CHANGLO

Tha Chang

(N9)

THANON MAHARAT

Wat Phra Kaeo

THANON BAMRUNG MUANG

TH. SARANROM

THANON ATSADANG

THANON RACHINI

Chao Phraya River

Grand Palace

Naval Department

Inner Palace

THANON SANAM CHAI

THANON CHAROEN KRUNG (NEW ROAD)

Khlong Mon

THANON THAI WANG

Wat Pho

SOI CHETUPHON

SOI TAWITAPISE

Tha Thien

(N8)

THANON MAHARAT

SOI PROK WAT ARUN 3

Wat Arun

THANON ARUN AMARIN

Tha Wat Arun

THANON WANG DOEM

SOI WAT HONG RATTANA RAM

SOI PHO SAM TON

Tha Ratchini

(N7)

THANON ISARAPHAP

Tha Wat Kanlayanamit

Wat Kanlayanamit

Tha Saphan Phut

(N6)

MEMORIAL BRIDGE

PHRA POKKLAO BRIDGE

SOI WAT KANYAH

Santa Cruz

SOI KUDI CHIN

THANON ARUN AMARIN

Khlong Bangkok Yai

THANON THETSABAN 1

THANON PRACHA THIPOK

THANON PHAYA NAI

Wat Prayoon

N

(N8) Express boat pier

Tha Wat Arun Cross-river pier

0   400 m

98

the fall of Ayutthaya in 1767 and the establishment of Bangkok in 1782. General Phraya Taksin set up his capital here, strategically near the sea and far from the marauding Burmese, but the story of his brief reign is a chronicle of battles that left little time and few resources to devote to the building of a city worthy of its predecessor. When General Chao Phraya displaced the by-then demented Taksin to become Rama I, his first decision as founder of the Chakri dynasty was to move the capital to the more defensible site across the river. It wasn't until 1932 that Thonburi was linked to its replacement by Memorial Bridge (Saphan Phut), and Thonburi retained its separate identity for another forty years until, in 1971, it officially became part of Bangkok.

The usual way to explore Thonburi's traditional **canalside neighbourhoods** is on a longtail boat tour (see box on p.100), though it's also fun to wander through on foot. There are a number of sights to add focus to any itinerary, including the imposing riverside structure of **Wat Arun**, the **Royal Barge Museum**, the bizarre anatomical exhibits of the **Siriraj Hospital museums** and the idiosyncratic temples of **Wat Rakhang** and **Wat Prayoon**.

The lack of footbridges over canals means that **walking** between sights often involves using the heavily trafficked Thanon Arun Amarin, so for these stretches it's more comfortable to jump onto a motorbike taxi. The slower, more convoluted alternative would be to leapfrog your way up or down the river by **boat**, using the numerous cross-river ferries that sail from small piers all the way down the Thonburi bank to link up with the Chao Phraya express boat stops on the other side.

Around Khlong Bangkok Noi

Broad, busy **Khlong Bangkok Noi** is bordered by some typical stilt-house neighbourhoods and is the site of the popular **Royal Barge Museum**. The main attractions south of the khlong are gathered along the west bank of the Chao Phraya, where the sprawling Siriraj Hospital dominates a big chunk of waterfront and harbours a collection of curious **medical museums**, after which peaceful **Wat Rakhang** comes as pleasant relief.

Royal Barge Museum

Since the Ayutthaya era, kings of Thailand have been conveyed along their country's waterways in royal barges. For centuries these slender, exquisitely elegant, black-and-gold wooden vessels were used on all important royal outings, and even up until 1967 the current king used to process down the Chao Phraya River to Wat Arun in a **flotilla of royal barges** at least once a year, on the occasion of Kathin, the annual donation of robes by the laity to the temple at the end of the rainy season. But the hundred-year-old boats are becoming quite frail, so such a procession is now a rare event: the last full-scale royal processions were mounted in 1999, to mark the king's 72nd birthday, and in 2006 to celebrate his sixtieth year on the throne. A royal barge procession along the Chao Phraya is a magnificent event, all the more spectacular because it happens so infrequently. Fifty or more barges fill the width of the river and stretch for almost 1km, drifting slowly to the measured beat of a drum and the hypnotic strains of ancient boating hymns, chanted by over two thousand oarsmen dressed in luscious brocades.

The most popular way to explore the sights of Thonburi is by **boat**, taking in Wat Arun and the Royal Barge Museum, then continuing along Thonburi's network of small canals. The easiest option is to take a fixed-price trip from one of the piers on the Bangkok side of the Chao Phraya, and most of these companies also feature visits to Thonburi's two main **floating markets**, both of which are heavily touristed and rather contrived. **Wat Sai** floating market happens daily from Monday to Friday but is very commercialized, and half of it is land-based anyway, while **Taling Chan** floating market is also fairly manufactured but more fun, though it only operates on Saturdays and Sundays. Taling Chan market is held on Khlong Chak Phra and is easily woven in to a private boat tour as described below; it's held in front of Taling Chan District Office, a couple of kilometres west of Thonburi train station, and can also be reached by taking bus #79 from Democracy Monument/Ratchadamnoen Klang to Khet Taling Chan. Arguably more photogenic, and certainly a lot more genuine, are the individual **floating vendors** who continue to paddle from house to house touting anything from hot food to plastic buckets: you've a good chance of seeing some of them in action on almost any private boat tour on any day of the week, particularly in the morning. For an authentic floating-market experience, consider heading out of Bangkok to Amphawa, in Samut Songkhram province, described on p.153.

Fixed-priced trips with the Boat Tour Centre (℡02 235 3108) at Tha Si Phraya cost B800 per boat for one whistle-stop hour, B1500 for two hours, and go either to Wat Sai (for which you need to be at the pier by about 8am; Mon–Fri only), or around the Thonburi canals, taking in Wat Arun and the Royal Barge Museum (can depart any time). The Mitchaopaya Travel Service (℡02 623 6169), operating out of Tha Chang, offers trips of varying durations that all take in the Royal Barge Museum and Wat Arun: in one hour (B800), you'll go out along Khlong Bangkok Noi and back via Khlong Mon, in ninety minutes (B1000) you'll come back along Khlong Bangkok Yai, while in two hours (B1200) you'll have time to go right down the back canals on the Thonburi side and visit an orchid farm. From Monday to Friday, all of these Mitcha-opaya trips stop off at the tiny so-called "Thonburi Floating Market", which even their own staff can't recommend, but on Saturdays and Sundays they take in the livelier Taling Chan floating market. Real Asia (℡02 665 6364, ⓦwww.realasia.net) runs guided full-day walking and boat tours of the Thonburi canals for B1800 per person. For details of dinner cruises down the Chao Phraya River, see p.183.

It's also possible to **organize your own longtail boat trip** around Thonburi from other piers, including Tha Oriental (at the *Oriental Hotel*), the pier at the River City shopping centre, Tha Wang Nah (next to the Bangkok Information Centre on Thanon Phra Athit in Banglamphu), and the Tha Phra Athit pier that's across from *Ricky's Coffee Shop* on Thanon Phra Athit (200m south of the N13 Tha Phra Athit express boat pier), but bear the above prices in mind and be prepared for some heavy bargaining. An enjoyable 90-minute loop from Tha Phra Athit, via Khlong Bangkok Noi, Khlong Chak Phra and Khlong Bangkok Yai, should cost B700 for a private two-person trip and will take in a variety of different khlongside residences, temples and itinerant floating vendors, but won't include any stops.

The eight beautifully crafted vessels at the heart of the ceremony are housed in the **Royal Barge Museum** on the north bank of Khlong Bangkok Noi (daily 9am–5pm; B30; ⓦwww.thailandmuseum.com). Up to 50m long and intricately lacquered and gilded all over, they taper at the prow into imposing mythical figures after a design first used by the kings of Ayutthaya. Rama I had the boats copied and, when those fell into disrepair, Rama VI commissioned the exact reconstructions still in use today. The most important is *Sri Suphanahongse*, which bears the king and queen and is graced by a glittering five-metre-high prow representing the golden swan Hamsa, mount of the Hindu god Brahma. In front of it floats *Anantanagaraj*, fronted by a magnificent seven-headed naga and bearing a Buddha image. The newest addition to the fleet is *Narai Song Suban*, which was commissioned by the current king for his golden jubilee in 1996; it is a copy of the mid-nineteenth-century original and is crowned with a black Vishnu (Narai) astride a garuda figurehead. A display of miniaturized royal barges at the back of the museum recreates the exact formation of a traditional procession.

The museum features on most canal tours, but it's also easy to visit on your own. Just take the Chao Phraya **express boat** to Tha Phra Pinklao (N12) or, if coming from Banglamphu, take the cheaper, more frequent cross-river ferry from under Pinklao bridge, beside the Bangkok Information Centre, to Tha Phra Pinklao across the river, then walk up the road a hundred metres and take the first left down Soi Wat Dusitaram. If coming by **bus** from the Bangkok side

△ The royal barge *Sri Suphanahongse*

(air-con buses #503, #507, #509, #511and #32 all cross the river here), get off at the first stop on the Thonburi side, which is right beside the mouth of Soi Wat Dusitaram. Signs from Soi Wat Dusitaram lead you through a jumble of walkways and stilt-houses to the museum, about ten minutes' walk away.

Siriraj Hospital museums

For some unfathomable reason, a surprising number of tourists make a point of visiting the **Anatomical Museum** (Mon–Fri 9am–noon & 1–4pm; free;

Eng and Chang, the Siamese twins

Eng (In) and Chang (Chan), the "original" **Siamese twins**, were born in Samut Songkhram (74km southwest of Bangkok, see p.153) in 1811, when the town was known as Mae Khlong after the estuary on which it sits, and the country was known as Siam. The boys' bodies were joined from breastbone to navel by a short fleshy ligament, but they shared no vital organs and eventually managed to stretch their connecting tissue so that they could stand almost side by side instead of permanently facing each other.

In 1824, the boys were spotted by entrepreneurial Scottish trader Robert Hunter, who returned five years later with an American sea merchant, Captain Abel Coffin, to convince the twins' mother to let them take her sons on a world tour. Hunter and Coffin anticipated a lucrative career as producer-managers of an exotic **freak show**, and were not disappointed. They launched the twins in Boston, advertising them as "the Monster" and charging the public fifty cents to watch the boys demonstrate how they walked and ran. Though shabbily treated and poorly paid, the twins soon developed a more theatrical show, enthralling their audiences with impressive acrobatics and feats of strength, and earning the soubriquet "the eighth wonder of the world". At the age of 21, having split from their exploitative managers, the twins became self-employed, but continued to tour with other companies across the world. Wherever they went, they would always be given a thorough examination by local **medics**, partly to counter accusations of fakery, but also because this was the first time the world and its doctors had been introduced to conjoined twins. Such was the twins' international celebrity that the term "Siamese twins" has been used ever since. Chang and Eng also sought advice from these doctors on surgical separation – an issue they returned to repeatedly right up until their deaths but never acted upon, despite plenty of gruesome suggestions.

By 1840 the twins had become quite wealthy and decided to settle down. They were granted American citizenship, assumed the family name Bunker, and became slave-owning **plantation farmers** in North Carolina. Three years later they married two local sisters, Addie and Sally Yates, and between them went on to father 21 children. The families lived in separate houses and the twins shuttled between the two, keeping to a strict timetable of three days in each household; for an intriguing imagined account of this bizarre state of affairs, read Darin Strauss's novel *Chang and Eng*, reviewed on p.255. Chang and Eng had quite different personalities, and relations between the two couples soured, leading to the division of their assets, with Chang's family getting most of the land, and Eng's most of the slaves. To support their dependants, the twins were obliged to take their show back on the road several times, on occasion working with the infamous showman P.T. Barnum. Their final tour was born out of financial desperation following the 1861–65 Civil War, which had wiped out most of the twins' riches and led to the liberation of all their slaves.

In 1874, Chang succumbed to bronchitis and died; Eng, who might have survived on his own if an operation had been performed immediately, died a few hours later, possibly of shock. They were 62. The twins are buried in White Plains in North Carolina, but there's a memorial to them near their birthplace in Samut Songkhram.

@ www.si.mahidol.ac.th/eng), one of six small collections of medical curiosities housed in Thonburi's enormous Siriraj teaching hospital. The Anatomical Museum was set up to teach students how to dissect the human body, but its most notorious exhibits are the specimens of conjoined twins kept in jars in a couple of old wooden display cabinets. There is also a picture of the most famous conjoined twins in history, the genuinely Siamese twins, Chang and Eng, who were born just outside Bangkok in Samut Songkhran (see box on p.102). The collection was established in 1927 and looks very dated in comparison to modern museums; there is almost no information in English. Exit right from the back door of the Anatomical Building and take the first left to find the **Museum of History of Thai Medicine** (Mon–Fri 9am–noon & 1–4pm; free), a potentially more stimulating exhibition whose wax tableaux recreate the traditional medical practices of midwives, masseuses, pharmacists and yogis, though these also have no English-language captions.

Easiest **access** to the hospital is by Chao Phraya express boat to Tha Wang Lang/Siriraj (downstream service; N10) or nearby Tha Phrannok (upstream service; N10). From the piers walk a few metres up Thanon Phrannok and enter the hospital via its side entrance. Follow the road through the hospital compound for about 350m, turn left just before the (signed) Museum of History of Thai Medicine, and the Anatomical Museum is the first building on your left.

Wat Rakhang

The charming riverside temple of **Wat Rakhang** (Temple of the Bells) gets its name from the five large bells donated by King Rama I and is notable for the hundreds of smaller chimes that tinkle away under the eaves of the main bot and, more accessibly, in the temple courtyard, where devotees come to strike them and hope for a run of good luck. To be extra-certain of having wishes granted, visitors sometimes also buy turtles from the temple stalls outside and release them into the Chao Phraya River below. Behind the bot stands an attractive eighteenth-century wooden *ho trai* (scripture library) that still boasts some original murals on the wooden panels inside, as well as exquisitely renovated gold-leaf paintwork on the window shutters and pillars. A cross-river **ferry** shuttles between Wat Rakhang's pier and the Tha Chang (Grand Palace; N9) express-boat pier, or you can **walk** to Wat Rakhang in five minutes from the Tha Wang Lang/Siriraj and Phrannok express-boat piers (N10): turn south (left) through the Phrannok pierside market and continue until you reach the temple, passing the posh *Supatra River House* restaurant (see p.204), the tiny *Ibrik Resort by the River* boutique hotel (see p.173) and Patravadi Theatre on the way.

Around Khlong Bangkok Yai

The most visited sight in Thonburi is **Wat Arun**, whose distinctive, corncob-shaped profile dominates the area just north of Khlong Bangkok Yai. South of the khlong, a peaceful **riverside walkway** connects Wat Kanlayanamit with Memorial Bridge, where you can jump into one of the frequent cross-river shuttles to pick up the Chao Phraya express ferry at Tha Saphan Phut (N6) on the other bank, though it's worth making a detour to the unusual cemetery at **Wat Prayoon** first.

Wat Arun

Almost directly across the river from Wat Pho rises the enormous, five-pranged **Wat Arun** (daily 7am–5pm; B20; Ⓦ www.watarun.org), the Temple of Dawn, probably Bangkok's most memorable landmark and familiar as the silhouette used in the TAT logo. It looks particularly impressive from the river as you head downstream from the Grand Palace towards the *Oriental Hotel*, and it's well worth stopping off for a closer look. All boat tours include half an hour here, but Wat Arun is also easily visited by yourself, although tour operators will try to persuade you otherwise: just take a cross-river ferry from the pier adjacent to the Chao Phraya express boat pier at Tha Thien. The temple also looks great after dark, when its profile is prettily illuminated – best appreciated from on board one of the dinner cruises that glide nightly up the Chao Phraya; see p.183 for details.

A wat has occupied this site since the Ayutthaya period, but only in 1768 did it become known as the Temple of Dawn, when General Phraya Taksin reputedly reached his new capital at the break of day. The temple served as his royal chapel and housed the recaptured Emerald Buddha for several years until the image was moved to Wat Phra Kaeo in 1785 (see p.63). Despite losing its special status after the relocation, Wat Arun remained important and was reconstructed and enlarged to its present height of 81m by Rama II and Rama III.

The prang that you see today is in classic Ayutthayan style, built as a representation of Mount Meru, the home of the gods in Khmer cosmology. Climbing the two tiers of the square base that supports the **central prang**, you not only enjoy a good view of the river and beyond, but also get a chance to examine the tower's distinctive decorations. Both this main prang and the four minor ones that encircle it are studded all over with bits of broken porcelain, ceramic shards and tiny bowls that have been fashioned into an amazing array of polychromatic flowers. The statues of mythical *yaksha* demons and half-bird, half-human *kinnari* that support the different levels are similarly decorated. The crockery probably came from China, possibly from commercial shipments that were damaged at sea, but whatever its provenance, the overall effect is highly decorative and far more subtle than the dazzling glass mosaics that clad most wat buildings. On the first terrace, the mondops at each cardinal point contain statues of the Buddha at the most important stages of his life: at birth (north), in meditation (east), preaching his first sermon (south) and entering Nirvana (west). The second platform surrounds the base of the prang proper, whose closed entranceways are guarded by four statues of the Hindu god Indra on his three-headed elephant Erawan. In the niches of the smaller prangs stand statues of Phra Pai, the god of the wind, on horseback.

Santa Cruz and Wat Prayoon

About 700m downstream of Wat Arun, the bot at **Wat Kanlayanamit** stands very tall in order to accommodate its 15-metre-high, nineteenth-century, seated Buddha image, the largest in Bangkok, but is chiefly of interest because it marks the start of the riverside walkway to Memorial Bridge. En route, you'll pass the distinctive pastel facade and pretty stained-glass windows of **Santa Cruz** (also known as **Wat Kudi Jeen**), a Catholic church that sits at the heart of what used to be Thonburi's Portuguese quarter. The Portuguese came to Thailand both to trade and to proselytize, and by 1856 had made the largest of the European communities in Bangkok: four thousand Portuguese Christians lived in and around Thonburi at this time, about one percent of the total population. The

Portuguese ghetto is a thing of the distant past, but plenty of local residents still have Portuguese blood in them and the church and its adjacent school continue to be well attended.

The walkway stops at the base of **Memorial Bridge** (Saphan Phut), where cross-river ferries shuttle back and forth to Tha Saphan Phut (N6) across the water. Before leaving Thonburi, however, it's worth stopping off at nearby **Wat Prayoon** (officially Wat Prayurawongsawat) for a wander around the temple's **Khao Mor cemetery**, which is located in a separate compound to the southeast side of the wat, just off Thanon Pracha Thipok, three minutes' walk from the bridge. The cemetery's unusual collection of miniature chedis and shrines is set on an artificial hill, which was constructed on a whim of Rama III's, after he'd noticed the pleasing shapes made by dripping candle wax. Wedged in among the grottoes, caverns and ledges of this uneven mass are numerous shrines to departed devotees, forming a phenomenal gallery of different styles, from traditionally Thai chedis, bots or prangs to such obviously foreign designs as the tiny Wild West house complete with cactuses at the front door. Turtles fill the pond surrounding the mound – you can feed them with the bags of banana and papaya sold nearby. At the edge of the pond stands a memorial to the unfortunate people who lost their lives when one of the saluting cannons exploded at the temple's dedication ceremony in 1836.

Dusit

Connected to Ratanakosin via the boulevards of Rajdamnoen Klang and Rajdamnoen Nok, the unusually spacious, leafy area known as **Dusit** has been a royal district since the reign of Rama V, King Chulalongkorn (1868–1910). Almost a century and a half later, it maintains a dignified ambience with its broad tree-lined avenues, grand, widely spaced government buildings and almost total absence of shops, restaurants and residential developments. It's one of the calmer Bangkok neighbourhoods – save for the inevitable thundering traffic – and makes an agreeably uncluttered contrast to the livelier streets of Ratanakosin and Chinatown. However, be prepared to do a fair bit of walking, as the main sights are quite spread out.

Rama V was the first Thai monarch to visit Europe and he returned with radical plans for the modernization of his capital, the fruits of which are most visible in Dusit – notably at **Vimanmek Palace** and **Wat Benjamabophit**, the so-called "Marble Temple". Even now, Rama V still commands a loyal following and his statue, which stands at the Thanon U-Thong–Thanon Sri Ayutthaya crossroads, is presented with offerings every week and is also the focus of celebrations on Chulalongkorn Day (Oct 23).

Today, the peaceful Dusit area retains its European feel, and much of the country's decision-making goes on behind the high fences and impressive

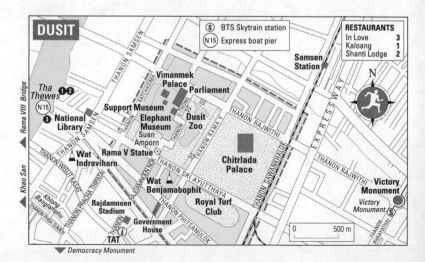

facades: the building that houses the National Parliament is here, as is Government House (which is used mainly for official functions), and the king's official residence, Chitrlada Palace, occupies the eastern edge of the area. On December 2 Dusit is also the venue for the spectacular annual **Trooping the Colour**, when hundreds of magnificently uniformed Royal Guards demonstrate their allegiance to the king by parading around Suan Amporn, across the road from the Rama V statue. Across from Chitrlada Palace, **Dusit Zoo** makes a pleasant enough place to take the kids. The **restaurants** and guest houses of Thewes are within walking distance of Dusit; they are marked on the Banglamphu map on p.80 and reviewed under Banglamphu on p.183 and p.171.

The Vimanmek Palace compound and Dusit Zoo

The ticket price for Vimanmek Palace (daily 9.30am–4pm; compulsory free guided tours every 30min, last tour 3.15pm; B100, or free with a Grand Palace ticket, which remains valid for one week; ⑩ www.palaces.thai.net) also covers entry to half a dozen other small museums in the extensive palace grounds, including the Support Museum and Elephant Museum. Note that the same **dress rules** apply to Vimanmek Palace as to the Grand Palace (see p.61). All visitors to the **Vimanmek compound** are treated to free outdoor performances of traditional Thai dance daily at 10.30am and 2pm. The main entrance to the compound is on Thanon Rajwithi, but there are also ticket gates on Thanon Ratchasima, and opposite Dusit Zoo on Thanon U-Thong.

Vimanmek Palace

Constructed almost entirely of golden teak, without a single nail, breezy, elegant **Vimanmek Palace** is a beautiful coffee-coloured colonial-style mansion, designed in an L-shape to accommodate 81 rooms and encircled by delicate latticework verandas that look out onto carefully tended lawns, flower gardens and lotus ponds. It was originally built in 1868 by Rama V as a summer retreat on the tiny east-coast island of Ko Si Chang, but he had it transported bit by bit to Dusit in 1901, where the "Celestial Residence" soon became his favourite palace. The king and his enormous retinue of officials, concubines and children stayed here for lengthy periods between 1902 and 1906. All of Vimanmek's 81 rooms were out of bounds to male visitors, except for the king's own apartments, in the octagonal tower, which were entered by a separate staircase.

On display inside the palace is Rama V's collection of artefacts from all over the world, including *bencharong* ceramics, European furniture and bejewelled Thai betel-nut sets. Considered progressive in his day, Rama V introduced

△ Vimanmek Palace veranda

many newfangled ideas to Thailand: the country's first indoor bathroom is here, as is the earliest typewriter with Thai characters, and some of the first portrait paintings – portraiture had until then been seen as a way of stealing part of the sitter's soul.

The Support Museum

Elsewhere in the Vimanmek grounds several small throne halls have been converted into tiny, specialist interest museums, including collections of antique textiles, photographs taken by the king, royal ceremonial paraphernalia and antique clocks. The most interesting of these is the **Support Museum Abhisek Dusit Throne Hall**, which is housed in another very pretty building of complementary design, formerly used for meetings and banquets, immediately behind (to the east of) Vimanmek. The Support Museum showcases the exquisite handicrafts produced under Queen Sirikit's charity project, Support, which works to revitalize traditional Thai arts and crafts. Outstanding exhibits include a collection of handbags, baskets and pots woven from the *lipao* fern that grows wild in southern Thailand; jewellery and figurines inlaid with the iridescent wings of beetles; gold and silver nielloware; and lengths of intricately woven silk from the northeast.

The royal white elephants

In Thailand the most revered of all elephants are the so-called **white elephants** – actually tawny brown albinos – which are considered so sacred that they all, whether wild or captive, belong to the king by law. Their special status originates from Buddhist mythology, which tells how the previously barren Queen Maya became pregnant with the future Buddha after dreaming one night that a white elephant had entered her womb. The thirteenth-century King Ramkhamhaeng of Sukhothai adopted the beast as a symbol of the great and the divine, and ever since, a Thai king's greatness is said to be measured by the number of white elephants he owns. The present monarch, King Bhumibol, has twelve, the largest royal collection to date.

Before an elephant can be granted official "white elephant" status, it has to pass a stringent assessment of its physical and behavioural **characteristics**. Key qualities include a paleness of six or seven crucial areas – eyes, nails, palate, hair, outer edges of the ears, tail and (if male) testicles – and an all-round genteel demeanour, manifested, for instance, in the way in which it cleans its food before eating, or in a tendency to sleep in a kneeling position. The most recent addition to King Bhumibol's stables was first spotted in Lampang in 1992, but experts from the Royal Household had to spend a year watching its every move before it was finally given the all-clear. Tradition holds that an elaborate ceremony should take place every time a new white elephant is presented to the king: the animal is paraded with great pomp from its place of capture to Dusit, where it's anointed with holy water in front of an audience of the kingdom's most important priests and dignitaries, before being housed in the royal stables. Recently though, the king has decreed that as a cost-cutting measure there should be no more ceremonies for new acquisitions, and only one of the royal white elephants is now kept inside the royal palace; the others live in less luxurious rural accommodation.

The expression "white elephant" to describe an unwanted gift probably derives from the legend that the kings used to present certain enemies with one of these exotic creatures. The animal required expensive attention but, being royal, could not be put to work in order to pay for its upkeep – the recipient thus went bust trying to keep it.

Chang Ton Royal Elephant National Museum

Just behind (to the east of) the Support Museum, inside the Thanon U-Thong entrance to the Vimanmek compound, stand two whitewashed buildings that once served as the stables for the king's white elephants. Now that the sacred pachyderms have been relocated, the stables have been turned into the **Royal Elephant National Museum** (ⓦ www.thailandmuseum.com). Inside you'll find some interesting pieces of elephant paraphernalia, including sacred ropes, mahouts' amulets and magic formulae, as well as photos of the all-important ceremony in which a white elephant is granted royal status (see box on p.109).

Dusit Zoo (Khao Din)

Across Thanon U-Thong from the Elephant Museum is the side entrance into **Dusit Zoo**, also known as **Khao Din** (daily 8am–6pm; B30, children B5), which was once part of the Chitrlada Palace gardens, but is now a public park; the main entrance is on Thanon Rajwithi, and there's a third gate on Thanon Rama V, within walking distance of Wat Benjamabophit. All the usual suspects are here in the zoo, including big cats, elephants, orang-utans, chimpanzees and a reptile house, but the enclosures are pretty basic. However, it's a reasonable place for kids to let off steam, with plenty of shade, a full complement of English-language signs, a lake with pedalos and lots of foodstalls.

Wat Benjamabophit

Commissioned by Rama V in 1899, **Wat Benjamabophit** (aka Wat Bencha; daily 7am–5pm; B20) is the last major temple to have been built in Bangkok. It lies a two-hundred-metre walk south of the zoo's Thanon Rama V entrance, or about 600m from Vimanmek's U-Thong gate (coming by bus #70 from Banglamphu, get off at the crossroads in front of the Rama V statue and walk east along Thanon Sri Ayutthaya).

The temple is an interesting fusion of classical Thai and nineteenth-century European design, with its Carrara marble walls – hence the touristic tag "The Marble Temple" – complemented by the bot's unusual stained-glass windows, Victorian in style but depicting figures from Thai mythology. Inside, a fine replica of the highly revered Phra Buddha Chinnarat image that resides in the northern Thai city of Phitsanulok presides over the small room containing Rama V's ashes. The courtyard behind the bot houses a gallery of Buddha images from all over Asia, established by Rama V as an overview of different representations of the Buddha.

Wat Benjamabophit is one of the best temples in Bangkok to see religious **festivals** and rituals. Whereas monks elsewhere tend to go out on the streets every morning in search of alms, at the Marble Temple the ritual is reversed, and merit-makers come to them. Between about 6 and 7.30am, the monks line up on Thanon Nakhon Pathom, their bowls ready to receive donations of curry and rice, lotus buds, incense, even toilet paper and Coca-Cola; the demure row of saffron-robed monks is a sight that's well worth getting up early for. The monks' evening candlelight processions around the bot during the Buddhist festivals of Maha Puja (in Feb) and Visakha Puja (in May) are among the most entrancing in the country.

6

Downtown Bangkok

Extending east from the rail line and south to Thanon Sathorn, **down-town Bangkok** is central to the colossal expanse of Bangkok as a whole, but rather peripheral in a sightseer's perception of the city. This is where you'll find the main financial district, around Thanon Silom, and the chief shopping centres, around Siam Square and Thanon Ploenchit, in addition to the smart hotels and restaurants, the embassies and airline offices. Scattered widely across the downtown area are four attractive museums housed in traditional teak buildings: **Jim Thompson's House** near Siam Square, the **Suan Pakkad Palace Museum** to the north, M.R. Kukrit's Heritage Home in southern downtown, and the **Ban Kamthieng** off Thanon Sukhumvit.

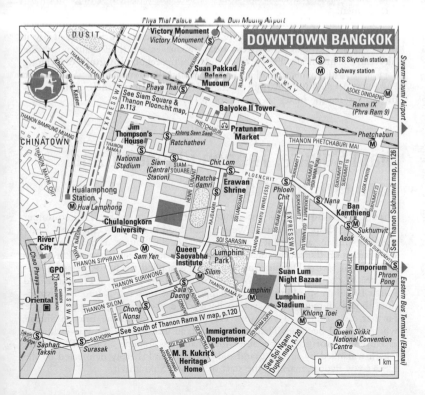

Downtown's other tourist attractions are far more diverse: **Siam Ocean World**, a hi-tech aquarium that both kids and adults can enjoy; the noisy and glittering **Erawan Shrine**; and the Art Nouveau Phya Thai Palace, a quirky, half-restored royal dwelling. The infamous **Patpong** district hardly shines as a tourist sight, yet, lamentably, its sex bars still represent a huge draw for foreign men.

If you're heading downtown from Banglamphu, allow at least an hour to get to any of the places mentioned here by **bus**. Depending on the time of day, it may be quicker to take an **express boat** downriver, and then change onto the **Skytrain**. It might also be worth considering the regular **longtails** on Khlong Saen Saeb, which runs parallel to Thanon Phetchaburi and Thanon Sukhumvit. For more detailed information on transport to each of the three main downtown areas, see the boxes above and on p.119 and p.127.

Siam Square, Thanon Ploenchit and northern downtown

Though **Siam Square** has just about everything to satisfy the Thai consumer boom – big shopping centres, Western fast-food restaurants, cinemas – don't come looking for an elegant commercial piazza: the "square" is in fact a grid of small streets on the south side of Thanon Rama I, between Thanon Phrayathai and Thanon Henri Dunant, and the name is applied freely to the surrounding area. Just to the northwest of Siam Square, at the corner of Phrayathai and Rama I roads, a spanking new contemporary art museum is under construction, though agreement has yet to be reached about what to display inside. Further east, you'll find yet more shopping malls around the Erawan Shrine, where Rama I becomes Thanon Ploenchit, an intersection sometimes known as **Ratchaprasong**. Life becomes marginally less frenetic around **Ploenchit**, which is flanked by several grand old embassies and sharply delineated by the Expressway flyover, marking the start of Thanon Sukhumvit.

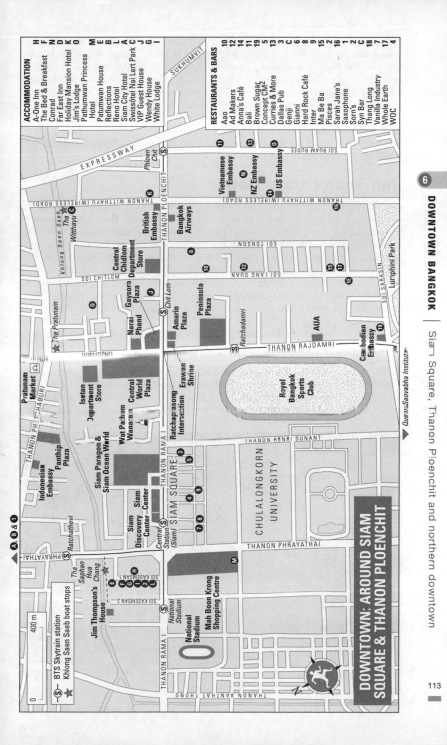

DOWNTOWN: AROUND SIAM SQUARE & THANON PLOENCHIT

ACCOMMODATION
A-One Inn	H
The Bed & Breakfast	F
Conrad	N
Far East Inn	D
Holiday Mansion Hotel	X
Jim's Lodge	O
Pathumwan Princess Hotel	M
Patumwan House	E
Reflections	B
Reno Hotel	L
Siam City Hotel	A
Swissôtel Nai Lert Park	C
VIP Guest House	J
Wendy House	G
White Lodge	I

RESTAURANTS & BARS
Aao	10
Ad Makers	12
Anna's Café	14
Bali	11
Brown Sugar	19
Concept CM2	5
Curries & More	13
Dallas Pub	3
Genji	C
Gianni	6
Hard Rock Café	8
Inter	9
Ma Be Ba	15
Pisces	2
Sarah Jane's	16
Saxophone	1
Sorn's	2
Syn Bar	C
Thang Long	18
Vanilla Industry	7
Whole Earth	17
WOC	4

Things also quieten down a little in the **northern part of downtown**, where besides Suan Pakkad, only the Baiyoke II Tower, Bangkok's tallest building, and the Pratunam covered market in its shadow might draw you into the area. One other landmark you're likely to spot here is the stone obelisk of **Victory Monument** (*Anu Sawari Chaisamoraphum*, or just *Anu Sawari*), which can be seen most spectacularly from Skytrains as they snake their way round it. It was erected after the Indo-Chinese War of 1940–41, when Thailand took back some territory in Laos and Cambodia while the French government was otherwise occupied in World War II, but nowadays it commemorates all of Thailand's past military glories.

Jim Thompson's House

Just off Siam Square at the north end of Soi Kasemsan 2, Thanon Rama I, and served by the National Stadium Skytrain station, **Jim Thompson's House** (daily from 9am, viewing on frequent 30–40min guided tours in several languages, last tour 5pm; B100, students & under-25s B50; Ⓦwww .jimthompsonhouse.org) is a kind of Ideal Home in elegant Thai style, and a peaceful refuge from downtown chaos. The house was the residence of the legendary American adventurer, entrepreneur, art collector and all-round character whose mysterious disappearance in the jungles of Malaysia in 1967 has made him even more of a legend among Thailand's farang community.

Apart from putting together this beautiful home, Thompson's most concrete contribution was to turn traditional silk-weaving from a dying art into the highly successful international industry it is today. The complex now includes a **shop** (closes 6pm), part of the Jim Thompson Thai Silk Company chain (see p.214), above which a new **gallery** hosts temporary exhibitions on textiles and the arts, such as royal maps of Siam in the nineteenth century. There's also an excellent **bar-restaurant** (last food orders 4.30pm), which serves a similar menu to *Jim Thompson's Saladaeng Café* (see p.189). Ignore any conmen at the

△ Jim Thompson's House

entrance to the soi looking for mugs to escort on rip-off shopping trips; they'll tell you that the house is closed when it isn't.

The grand, rambling **house** is in fact a combination of six teak houses, some from as far afield as Ayutthaya and most more than two hundred years old. Like all traditional houses, they were built in wall sections hung together without nails on a frame of wooden pillars, which made it easy to dismantle them, pile them onto a barge and float them to their new location. Although he had trained as an architect, Thompson had more difficulty in putting them back together again; in the end, he had to go back to Ayutthaya to hunt down

The legend of Jim Thompson

Thai silk-weavers, art-dealers and conspiracy theorists all owe a debt to **Jim Thompson**, who even now, forty years after his disappearance, remains Thailand's most famous farang. An architect by trade, Thompson left his New York practice in 1940 to join the Office of Strategic Services (later to become the CIA), a tour of duty that was to see him involved in clandestine operations in North Africa, Europe and, in 1945, the Far East, where he was detailed to a unit preparing for the invasion of Thailand. When the mission was pre-empted by the Japanese surrender, he served for a year as OSS station chief in Bangkok, forming links that were later to provide grist for endless speculation.

After an unhappy and short-lived stint as part-owner of the *Oriental Hotel*, Thompson found his calling in the struggling **silk-weavers** of the area near the present Jim Thompson House, whose traditional product was unknown in the West and had been all but abandoned by Thais in favour of less costly imported textiles. Encouragement from society friends and an enthusiastic write-up in *Vogue* convinced him there was a foreign market for Thai silk, and by 1948 he had founded the Thai Silk Company. Success was assured when, two years later, the company was commissioned to make the costumes for the Broadway run of *The King and I*. Thompson's celebrated eye for colour combinations and his tireless promotion – in the early days, he could often be seen in the lobby of the *Oriental* with bolts of silk slung over his shoulder, waiting to pounce on any remotely curious tourist – quickly made his name synonymous with Thai silk.

Like a character in a Somerset Maugham novel, Thompson played the role of Western exile to the hilt. Though he spoke no Thai, he made it his personal mission to preserve traditional arts and architecture (at a time when most Thais were more keen to emulate the West), assembling his famous Thai house and stuffing it with all manner of Oriental *objets d'art*. At the same time he held firmly to his farang roots and society connections: no foreign gathering in Bangkok was complete without Jim Thompson, and virtually every Western luminary passing through Bangkok – from Truman Capote to Ethel Merman – dined at his table.

If Thompson's life was the stuff of legend, his disappearance and presumed death only added to the mystique. On Easter Sunday, 1967, Thompson, while staying with friends in a cottage in Malaysia's Cameron Highlands, went out for a stroll and never came back. A massive search of the area, employing local guides, tracker dogs and even shamans, turned up no clues, provoking a rash of fascinating but entirely unsubstantiated theories. The grandfather of them all, advanced by a Dutch psychic, held that Thompson had been lured into an ambush by the disgraced former prime minister of Thailand, Pridi Panyonyong, and spirited off to Cambodia for indeterminate purposes; later versions, supposing that Thompson had remained a covert CIA operative all his life, proposed that he was abducted by Vietnamese Communists and brainwashed to be displayed as a high-profile defector to Communism. More recently, an amateur sleuth claims to have found evidence that Thompson met a more mundane fate, having been killed by a careless truck driver and hastily buried.

a group of carpenters who still practised the old house-building methods. Thompson added a few unconventional touches of his own, incorporating the elaborately carved front wall of a Chinese pawnshop between the drawing room and the bedroom, and reversing the other walls in the drawing room so that their carvings faced into the room.

The impeccably tasteful **interior** has been left as it was during Thompson's life, even down to the cutlery on the dining table. Complementing the fine artefacts from throughout Southeast Asia is a stunning array of Thai arts and crafts, including one of the best collections of traditional Thai paintings in the world. Thompson picked up plenty of bargains from the Thieves' Market (Nakhon Kasem) in Chinatown, before collecting Thai art became fashionable and expensive. Other pieces were liberated from decay and destruction in upcountry temples, while many of the Buddha images were turned over by ploughs, especially around Ayutthaya. Some of the exhibits are very rare, such as a headless but elegant seventh-century Dvaravati Buddha and a seventeenth-century Ayutthayan teak Buddha, but Thompson also bought pieces of little value and fakes simply for their looks – a shopping strategy that's all the more sensible in the jungle of today's Thai antiques trade.

After the guided tour, you're free to wander round the former rice barn and gardener's and maid's houses in the small **garden**, which display some gorgeous traditional Thai paintings and drawings, as well as small-scale statues and Chinese ceramics.

Siam Ocean World

Spreading over two spacious basement floors of the Siam Paragon shopping centre on Thanon Rama I, **Siam Ocean World** is a highly impressive, Australian-built aquarium (daily 9am–10pm, last admission 9pm; B450, children between 80cm and 120cm tall B280; audioguide B100; Ⓦ www.siamoceanworld.com). Despite the relatively high admission price, it gets packed at weekends and during holidays, and there are often long queues for the twenty-minute glass-bottomed boat rides (B150), which give a behind-the-scenes look at the aquarium's workings. Among other outstanding features of this US$30-million development are an eight-metre-deep glass-walled tank, which displays the multi-coloured variety of a coral reef drop-off to great effect, touch tanks for handling starfish, and a long, under-ocean tunnel where you can watch sharks and rays swimming over your head. In this global piscatorial display of around 400 species, locals such as the Mekong giant catfish and the Siamese tigerfish are not forgotten, while regularly spaced touch-screen terminals allow you to glean further information in English about the creatures on view. Popular daily highlights include shark feeds, currently at 1.30pm and 5.30pm, and it's even possible, by arrangement with Planet Scuba, to dive with the sharks here, costing from B5300 for an experienced diver to B6600 for a first-timer (Ⓦ www.sharkdive.org).

Erawan Shrine

For a glimpse of the variety and ubiquity of Thai religion, drop in on the **Erawan Shrine** (*Saan Phra Prom* in Thai), at the corner of Thanon Ploenchit and Thanon Rajdamri underneath Chit Lom Skytrain station. Remarkable as much for its setting as anything else, this shrine to Brahma, the ancient Hindu creation god, and Erawan, his elephant, squeezes in on one of the busiest and noisiest corners of modern Bangkok, in the shadow of the *Grand Hyatt Erawan*

Hotel – whose existence is the reason for the shrine. When a string of calamities held up the building of the original hotel in the 1950s, spirit doctors were called in, who instructed the owners to build a new home for the offended local spirits: the hotel was then finished without further mishap. Ill fortune struck the shrine itself, however, in early 2006, when a young, mentally disturbed Muslim man smashed the Brahma statue to pieces with a hammer – and was then brutally beaten to death by an angry mob. It's expected that an exact replica of the statue will quickly be installed, incorporating the remains of the old statue to preserve the spirit of the deity.

Be prepared for sensory overload here: the main structure shines with lurid glass of all colours and the overcrowded precinct around it is almost buried under scented garlands and incense candles. You might also catch a lacklustre group of traditional dancers performing here to the strains of a small classical orchestra – worshippers hire them to give thanks for a stroke of good fortune. To increase their future chances of such good fortune, visitors buy a bird or two from the flocks incarcerated in cages here; the bird-seller transfers the requested number of captives to a tiny hand-held cage, from which the customer duly liberates the animals, thereby accruing merit. People set on less abstract rewards will invest in a lottery ticket from one of the disabled sellers: they're thought to be the luckiest you can buy.

Pratunam Market and Baiyoke II Tower

Ten minutes' walk north of the Erawan Shrine and extending northwest from the corner of Rajaprarop and Phetchaburi roads, **Pratunam Market** is famous for its low-cost, low-quality casual clothes. The vast, dark warren of stalls is becoming touristy near the hotels on its north side, but there are still bargains to be had elsewhere, especially along the market's western side. On the north side of the market rises Bangkok's tallest building, **Baiyoke II Tower**, where high-speed lifts whisk you to the revolving observation deck on the 84th floor (daily 10am–10pm; B200, including one drink at the bar on the 83rd floor), for breathtaking views of the city.

Suan Pakkad Palace Museum

The **Suan Pakkad Palace Museum** (daily 9am–4pm; B100; ⓦwww .suanpakkad.com), five minutes' walk from Phaya Thai Skytrain station, at 352–4 Thanon Sri Ayutthaya, stands on what was once a cabbage patch but is now one of the finest gardens in Bangkok. Most of this private collection of beautiful Thai objects from all periods is displayed in four groups of traditional wooden houses, which were transported to Bangkok from various parts of the country. You can either take a guided tour in English (free) or explore the loosely arranged collection yourself. A leaflet and bamboo fan are handed out at the ticket office, and some of the exhibits are labelled. The attached **Marsi Gallery**, in the modern Chumbhot-Pantip Center of Arts on the east side of the garden, displays some interesting temporary exhibitions of contemporary art (ⓣ02 246 1775–6 for details).

The highlight of Suan Pakkad is the renovated **Lacquer Pavilion**, across the reedy pond at the back of the grounds. Set on stilts, the pavilion is actually an amalgam of two eighteenth- or late-seventeenth-century temple buildings, a *ho trai* (library) and a *ho khien* (writing room), one inside the other, which were found between Ayutthaya and Bang Pa-In. The interior walls are beautifully decorated with gilt on black lacquer: the upper panels depict the life of the Buddha while the lower ones show scenes from the *Ramayana*. Look out especially for the grisly details in the tableau on the back wall, showing the earth goddess drowning the evil forces of Mara. Underneath are depicted some European dandies on horseback, probably merchants, whose presence suggests that the work was executed before the fall of Ayutthaya in 1767.

The carefully observed details of daily life and nature are skilful and lively, especially considering the restraints which the **lacquering technique** places on the artist, who has no opportunity for corrections or touching up. The design has to be punched into a piece of paper, which is then laid on the panel of black lacquer (a kind of plant resin); a small bag of chalk dust is pressed on top so that the dust penetrates the minute holes in the paper, leaving a line of dots on the lacquer to mark the pattern; a gummy substance is then applied to any background areas that are to remain black, before the whole surface is covered in microscopically thin squares of gold leaf; thin sheets of blotting paper, sprinkled with water, are then laid over the panel, which when pulled off bring away the gummy substance and the unwanted pieces of gold leaf. This leaves the rest of the gold decoration in high relief against the black background.

Divided between House no. 8 and the Ban Chiang Gallery in the Chumbhot-Pantip Center of Arts is a very good collection of elegant, whorled pottery and bronze jewellery, which the former owner of Suan Pakkad Palace, Princess Chumbhot, excavated from tombs at Ban Chiang, the major Bronze Age settlement in northeastern Thailand. Scattered around the rest of the museum are some attractive Thai and Khmer religious sculptures among an eclectic jumble of artefacts, including fine ceramics and some intriguing kiln-wasters, failed pots which have melted together in the kiln to form weird, almost rubbery pieces of sculpture; an extensive collection of colourful papier-mâché *khon* masks; monks' elegant ceremonial fans; and some rich teak carvings, including a 200-year-old temple door showing episodes from *Sang Thong*, a folk tale about a childless king and queen who discover a handsome son in a conch shell.

Phya Thai Palace

An intriguing way to spend a Saturday in Bangkok is to explore **Phya Thai Palace**, a grandiose and eccentric relic of the early twentieth century on Thanon Rajwithi, about ten minutes' walk west of Victory Monument and its Skytrain station. Built mostly by **Vajiravudh**, Rama VI, who lived here from 1919 for the last six years of his reign, it initially became the most luxurious hotel in Southeast Asia after his death, incorporating Thailand's first radio station, then after the 1932 coup, a military hospital. Parts of the airy, rambling complex have been splendidly restored by the Palace Fan Club, while others show nearly a century's worth of wear and tear, and one building is still used as offices by Phra Mongkutklao Army Hospital; you're quite likely to come across a musical performance or rehearsal as you're being guided round the otherwise empty rooms. Engaging **tours** in English (90min–2hr; free), led by volunteer guides, usually kick off at 9.30am and 1.30pm on Saturdays. It is also possible to visit on weekdays, as long as you make an appointment and pay B500. For further information, contact Miss Pisadaporn Rupramarn on ☏02 354 7660 (Mon–Fri ext. 93646 or 93694, Sat ext. 93698). It's well worth buying the excellent guidebook, not only to help the palace restoration fund, but also to read the extraordinary story of **Dusit Thani**: this miniature utopian city was set up by King Vajiravudh on an acre of the palace grounds (now dismantled), as a political experiment complete with two daily newspapers, elections and a constitution – only a decade or so before a real constitution was forcibly imposed on the monarchy after the coup of 1932.

Most of the central building, the **Phiman Chakri Hall**, is in a sumptuous, English, Art Nouveau style, featuring silk wallpaper, ornate murals, Italian marble – and an extravagant but unusable fireplace that reminded Vajiravudh of his schooling in England. The king's first bedroom, decorated in royal red and appointed with a huge, step-down, marble bath, later went for B120 a night as a hotel suite. Outside in the grounds, between a pond used for bathing and the canal which gave access to Khlong Samsen, Vajiravudh first constructed for himself a simple wooden house so that he could keep an eye on the builders, the **Mekhala Ruchi Pavilion**, which later became the king's barber's. In front of the Phiman Chakri Hall, the **Thewarat Sapharom Hall**, a neo-Byzantine teak audience hall, is still used for occasional **classical concerts**. Don't leave without sampling the lovely, Art Nouveau **coffee shop**, a former waiting room covered in ornate teak carving.

Southern downtown

South of Thanon Rama I, commercial development gives way to a dispersed assortment of large institutions, dominated by Thailand's most prestigious centre of higher learning, Chulalongkorn University, and the green expanse of **Lumphini Park**. Thanon Rama IV marks another change of character: downtown proper, centring on the high-rise, American-style boulevard of Thanon Silom, heart of the financial district, extends from here to the river. Alongside the smoked-glass banks and offices, the plush hotels and tourist shops, and opposite Bangkok's Carmelite convent, lies the dark heart of Bangkok nightlife, **Patpong**. Further west along Silom, at the corner of Thanon Pan, lies the colourful landmark of the Maha Uma Devi Temple (aka Sri Mahamariamman or Wat Khaek), a gaudy South Indian, Hindu shrine built in 1895 in honour of Uma Devi. Carrying on to the river, the strip west of Charoen Krung (New Road) reveals some of the history of Bangkok's early

Getting to and from the southern downtown area

The Silom Line of the **Skytrain** runs through this area, flying over much of Thanon Silom, before veering down Thanon Narathiwat Ratchanakharin then along Thanon Sathorn to the river. The big advantage of staying at the western edge of this area is that you'll be handily placed for Chao Phraya **express boats**, with piers at Si Phraya, Wat Muang Kae, the Oriental and Sathorn. Indeed, if you're staying anywhere in this area and travelling by public transport to Ratanakosin, you're best off catching a bus to the nearest express-boat stop, or the Skytrain to Saphan Taksin station, and finishing your journey on the water.

At the other side of this area, the **subway** runs from Hualamphong Station under Thanon Rama IV, with stations at Sam Yan (for the Snake Farm), Silom and Lumphini (for the budget accommodation area of Soi Ngam Duphli and Suan Lum Night Bazaar). The most useful **bus** for Soi Ngam Duphli is likely to be air-con #507, which connects you with Hualamphong Station, Chinatown, Ratanakosin, Banglamphu and the Southern Bus Terminal, while countless buses run along Thanon Silom.

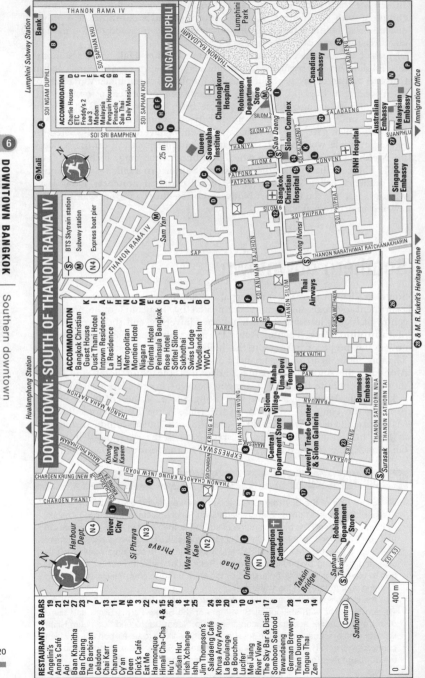

dealings with foreigners in the fading grandeur of the old trading quarter. Here you'll find the only place in Bangkok where you might be able to eke out an architectural walk, though it's hardly compelling. Incongruous churches and "colonial" buildings (the best of these is the Authors' Wing of the *Oriental Hotel*, where nostalgic afternoon teas are served) are hemmed in by the spice shops and *halal* canteens of the growing Muslim area around Thanon Charoen Krung.

The Queen Saovabha Memorial Institute (Snake Farm)

The **Queen Saovabha Memorial Institute** (*Sathan Saovabha*), often simply known as the **Snake Farm**, at the corner of Thanon Rama IV and Thanon Henri Dunant (a 10min walk from Sala Daeng Skytrain station or Sam Yan or Si Lom subway stations), is a bit of a circus act, but an entertaining, informative and worthy one at that. Run by the Thai Red Cross, it has a double function: to produce snake-bite serums and to educate the public on the dangers of Thai snakes. The latter mission involves putting on displays (Mon–Fri 10.30am & 2pm, Sat, Sun & hols 10.30am; B70; ☎02 252 0161–4, ⓦwww.redcross.or.th) that begin with a slick half-hour slide-show illustrating, among other things, how to apply a tourniquet and immobilize a bitten limb. Things warm up with a live, half-hour demonstration of snake-handling, snake-feeding and venom extraction, which is well presented and safe, and gains a perverse fascination from the knowledge that the strongest venoms of the snakes on show can kill in only three minutes. If you're still not herpetologically sated, a wide range of Thai snakes can be seen live in cages around the grounds, as well as preserved and bottled in a small snake museum.

Lumphini Park

If you're sick of cars and concrete, head for **Lumphini Park** (*Suan Lum*; daily 5am–7pm), at the east end of Thanon Silom, where the air is almost fresh and the traffic noise dies down to a low murmur. Named after the town in Nepal where the Buddha was born, it was the country's first public park, donated by Rama VI, whose statue by Silpa Bhirasri (see p.249) stands at the main, southwest entrance. The park is arrayed around two lakes, where you can join the locals in feeding the turtles and fish with bread or take out a pedalo or rowing boat, and is landscaped with a wide variety of local trees and numerous pagodas and pavilions, usually occupied by chess-players. In the early morning and at dusk, exercise freaks hit the outdoor gym on the southwest side of the park, or en masse do some jogging along the yellow-marked circuit or some balletic t'ai chi, stopping for the twice-daily broadcast of the national anthem. On Sunday afternoons in the cool season, free classical concerts draw in scores of urban picnickers. The park is a popular area for gay cruising, and you might be offered dope, though the police patrol regularly – for all that, it's not at all an intimidating place. To recharge your batteries, make for the inexpensive garden restaurant in the northwest corner, or the pavement foodstalls at the northern edge of the park.

Patpong

Concentrated into a small area between the eastern ends of Thanon Silom and Thanon Suriwong, the neon-lit go-go bars of the **Patpong** district

△ Victory Monument

loom like rides in a tawdry sexual Disneyland. In front of each bar, girls cajole passers-by with a lifeless sensuality while insistent touts proffer printed menus and photographs detailing the degradations on show. Inside, bikini-clad women gyrate to Western music and play hostess to the (almost exclusively male) spectators; upstairs, live shows feature women who, to use Spalding Gray's phrase in *Swimming to Cambodia*, "do everything with their vaginas except have babies".

Patpong was no more than a sea of mud when the capital was founded on the marshy river bank to the west, but by the 1960s it had grown into a flash district of nightclubs and dance halls for rich Thais, owned by a Chinese millionaire godfather who gave his name to the area. In 1969, an American entrepreneur turned an existing teahouse into a luxurious nightclub to satisfy the tastes of soldiers on R&R trips from Vietnam, and so Patpong's transformation into a Western sex reservation began. At first, the area was rough and violent, but over the years it has wised up to the desires of the affluent farang, and now markets itself as a packaged concept of Oriental decadence. The centre of the skin trade lies along the interconnected sois of **Patpong 1 and 2**, where lines of go-go bars share their patch with respectable restaurants, a 24-hour supermarket and an overabundance of pharmacies. By night, it's a thumping theme park, whose blazing neon promises tend towards self-parody, with names like *Thigh Bar* and *Chicken Divine*. Budget travellers, purposeful besuited businessmen and noisy lager louts throng the streets, and even the most demure tourists – of both sexes – turn out to do some shopping at the night market down the middle of Patpong 1, where hawkers sell fake watches, bags and designer T-shirts. By day, a relaxed hangover descends on the place. Bar-girls hang out at foodstalls and cafés in respectable dress, often recognizable by faces that are pinched and strained from the continuous use of antibiotics and heroin in an attempt to ward off sexually transmitted diseases and boredom. Farang men slump at the bars on Patpong 2, drinking and watching videos, unable to find anything else to do in the whole of Bangkok.

The small dead-end alley to the east of Patpong 2, **Silom 4** (ie Soi 4, Thanon Silom), hosts some of Bangkok's hippest nightlife, its bars, clubs and pavements heaving at weekends with the capital's bright young things. Several gay venues can be found on Silom 4, but the focus of the scene has shifted to **Silom 2**, while in between, **Thanon Thaniya**'s hostess bars and restaurants cater to Japanese tourists.

M.R. Kukrit's Heritage Home

Ten minutes' walk south of Thanon Sathorn and twenty minutes from Chong Nonsi Skytrain station, at 19 Soi Phra Pinit (Soi 7, Thanon Narathiwat Ratchanakharin), lies **M.R. Kukrit's Heritage Home**, the beautiful traditional house and gardens of one of Thailand's leading figures of the twentieth century (*Baan Mom Kukrit*; Sat, Sun & public hols 10am–5pm; B50). M.R. (*Mom Rajawongse*, a princely title) **Kukrit Pramoj** (1911–95) was a remarkable all-rounder, descended from Rama II on his father's side and, on his mother's side, from the influential ministerial family, the Bunnags. Kukrit graduated in Philosophy, Politics and Economics from Oxford University and went on to become a university lecturer back in Thailand, but his greatest claim to fame is probably as a writer: he founded, owned and penned a daily column for *Siam Rath*, the most influential Thai-language newspaper, and wrote short stories, novels, plays and poetry. He was also a respected performer in classical dance-drama (*khon*), and he starred as an Asian prime minister in the Hollywood film *The Ugly American*,

Bangkok owes its reputation as the carnal capital of the world to a highly efficient sex industry adept at peddling fantasies of cheap sex on tap. More than a thousand sex-related businesses operate in the city, but the gaudy neon fleshpots of Patpong give a misleading impression of an activity that is deeply rooted in Thai culture – the overwhelming majority of Thailand's prostitutes of both sexes (estimated at anywhere between 200,000 and 700,000) work with Thai men, not farangs.

Prostitution and polygamy have long been intrinsic to the Thai way of life. Until Rama VI broke with the custom in 1910, Thai kings had always kept a retinue of concubines around them, a select few of whom would be elevated to the status of wife and royal mother, the rest forming a harem of ladies-in-waiting and sexual play-things. The practice was aped by the status-hungry nobility and, from the early nine-teenth century, by newly rich merchants keen to have lots of sons and heirs. Though the monarch is now monogamous, many men of all classes still keep mistresses, known as *mia noi* (minor wives), a tradition bolstered by the popular philosophy that an official wife (*mia luang*) should be treated like the temple's main Buddha image – respected and elevated upon the altar – whereas the minor wife is an amulet, to be taken along wherever you go. For those not wealthy enough to take on *mia noi*, prostitution is a far less costly and equally accepted option. Statistics indicate that at least two-fifths of sexually active Thai men are thought to use the services of prostitutes twice a month on average, and it's common practice for a night out with the boys to wind up in a brothel or massage parlour.

The **farang sex industry** is a relatively new development, having had its start during the Vietnam War, when the American military set up seven bases around Thailand. The GIs' appetite for "entertainment" fuelled the creation of instant red-light districts near the bases, attracting women from surrounding rural areas to cash in on the boom; Bangkok joined the fray in 1967, when the US secured the right to ferry soldiers in from Vietnam for R&R breaks. By the mid-1970s, the bases had been evacuated, but the sex infrastructure remained and tourists moved in to fill the vacuum, lured by advertising that diverted most of the traffic to Bangkok and the beach resort of Pattaya. Sex tourism has since grown to become an established part of the Thai economy.

The majority of the women who work in the Patpong bars come from the poorest rural areas of north and northeast Thailand. **Economic refugees** in search of a better life, they're easily drawn into an industry in which they can make in a single night what it takes a month to earn in the rice fields. In some northeastern villages, money sent home by prostitutes in Bangkok far exceeds financial aid given by the government. Women from rural communities have always been expected to contribute an equal share to the family income, and many opt for a couple of lucra-tive years in the sex bars and brothels as the most effective way of helping to pay off family debts and improve the living conditions of parents stuck in the poverty trap. Reinforcing this social obligation is the pervasive Buddhist notion of karma,

opposite Marlon Brando. In 1974, during an especially turbulent period for Thailand, life imitated art, when Kukrit was called on to become Thailand's PM at the head of a coalition of seventeen parties. However, just four hundred days into his premiership, the Thai military leadership dismissed him for being too anti-American.

The **residence**, which has been left just as it was when Kukrit was alive, reflects his complex character. In the large, open-sided *sala* (pavilion) for public functions near the entrance is an attractive display of *khon* masks, including a gold one which Kukrit wore when he played the demon king, Totsagan (Ravana). In and around the adjoining Khmer-styled garden, keep which holds that your lot, however unhappy, is the product of past-life misdeeds and can only be improved by making sufficient merit to ensure a better life next time round.

While most women enter the racket presumably knowing at least something of what lies ahead, younger girls definitely do not. **Child prostitution** is rife: an estimated ten percent of prostitutes are under 14, some are as young as 9. They are valuable property: a prepubescent virgin can be rented to her first customer for US$1000, as sex with someone so young is believed by some to have rejuvenating properties. Most child prostitutes have been sold by desperate parents as **bonded slaves** to pimps or agents, and are kept locked up until they have fully repaid the money given to their parents, which may take two or more years.

Despite its ubiquity, prostitution has been **illegal** in Thailand since 1960, but sex-industry bosses easily circumvent the law by registering their establishments as bars, restaurants, barbers, nightclubs or massage parlours, and making payoffs to the police. Sex workers, on the other hand, often endure exploitation and violence from employers, pimps and customers rather than face fines and long rehabilitation sentences in prison-like reform centres. Life is made even more difficult by the fact that abortion is illegal in Thailand. A 1996 amendment to the **anti-prostitution law** attempts to treat sex workers as victims rather than criminals, penalizing parents who sell their children to the flesh trade and punishing owners, managers and customers of any place of prostitution with a jail sentence or a heavy fine, but this has reportedly been haphazardly enforced, owing to the number of influential police and politicians allegedly involved in the sex industry. Under this amendment anyone caught having sex with an under-15 is charged with rape, though this has apparently resulted in an increase in trafficking of young children from neighbouring countries as they are less likely to seek help.

In recent years, the spectre of **AIDS** has put the problems of the sex industry into sharp focus: UN AIDS statistics from 2003 reported that about one in five sex workers in Thailand was infected with HIV/AIDS and about one in 75 of the general adult Thai population; in the same year there were 58,000 AIDS-related deaths in the country. However, the rate of new HIV infections is in decline – down from 143,000 in 1991 to 21,000 in 2003 – thanks to an aggressive, World Health Organization-approved AIDS awareness campaign conducted by the government and the Population and Community Development Association (PDA), a Bangkok-based NGO. A vital component of the campaign was to send health officials into brothels to administer blood tests and give out condoms. Though the government no longer funds many AIDS-awareness initiatives, the high-profile PDA (Ⓦwww.pda.or.th/eng), which also runs the famous *Cabbages and Condoms* restaurant on Thanon Sukhumvit (reviewed on p.191), continues to campaign and educate the public, spurred on by fears that young Thais are too complacent about the virus, and by recent reports of a worrying rise in new infections.

your eyes peeled for the the *mai dut*, sculpted miniature trees similar to bonsai, some of which Kukrit worked on for decades. The living quarters beyond are made up of five teak houses on stilts, assembled from various parts of central Thailand and joined by an open veranda. The bedroom, study and various sitting rooms are decked out with beautiful *objets d'art*; look out especially for the carved bed that belonged to Rama II and the very delicate, 200-year-old nielloware (gold inlay) from Nakhon Si Thammarat in southern Thailand in the formal reception room. In the small family prayer room, Kukrit Pramoj's ashes are enshrined in the base of a reproduction of the Emerald Buddha.

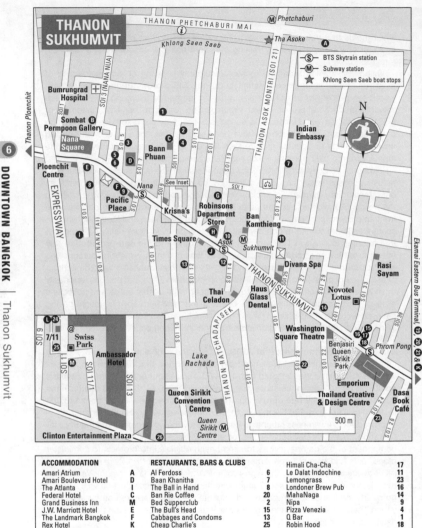

THANON SUKHUMVIT

ACCOMMODATION		RESTAURANTS, BARS & CLUBS			
Amari Atrium	A	Al Ferdoss	6	Himali Cha-Cha	17
Amari Boulevard Hotel	D	Baan Khanitha	7	Le Dalat Indochine	11
The Atlanta	I	The Ball in Hand	8	Lemongrass	23
Federal Hotel	C	Ban Rie Coffee	20	Londoner Brew Pub	16
Grand Business Inn	M	Bed Supperclub	2	MahaNaga	14
J.W. Marriott Hotel	E	The Bull's Head	15	Nipa	9
The Landmark Bangkok	F	Cabbages and Condoms	10	Pizza Venezia	4
Rex Hotel	K	Cheap Charlie's	25	Q Bar	1
Sheraton Grande Sukhumvit	J	Dosa King	13	Robin Hood	18
Suk 11	L	Face Bangkok (La Na Thai & Hazara)	21	Suda Restaurant	12
SV Guest House	G	Gaeng Pa Lerd Rod	17	Tamarind Café	22
Westin Grande Sukhumvit	H	Gallery 11	24	Took Lae Dee	5
Zenith Hotel	B	Gullivers Traveler's Tavern	3	Vientiane Kitchen (Khrua Vientiane)	19
				Yong Lee	26

Thanon Sukhumvit

Thanon Sukhumvit is Bangkok's longest road – it keeps going east all the way to Cambodia – but for such an important artery it's way too narrow for the volume of traffic that needs to use it, and is further hemmed in by the overhead Skytrain line. Packed with high-rise hotels and office blocks, an amazing array

The **Skytrain** (see p.38) has stops all the way along Thanon Sukhumvit, making journeys to places such as Siam Square and Chatuchak Weekend Market a fast and hassle-free undertaking, and giving you the chance to link up with the Chao Phraya express boats at Saphan Taksin/Tha Sathorn (for a calmish ride to Ratanakosin, for example). Similarly, the Sukhumvit **subway** stop at the mouth of Soi 21 (Thanon Asok Montri) makes it easy to get to Hualamphong Station and Chinatown.

The volume of traffic on Sukhumvit means that travelling by **bus** across town – to Ratanakosin or Banglamphu, for example – can take an age. If possible, try to travel to and from Thanon Sukhumvit outside rush hour (7–9am & 3–7pm); it's almost as bad in a taxi, which will often take at least an hour to reach Ratanakosin. Useful buses for getting to Ratanakosin include #508 (air-con) and #25 (ordinary) – both of which run via Siam Square, so you could also take the Skytrain to Siam Square and then change on to the bus; full details of bus routes are given on p.36.

A much faster way of getting across town is to hop on one of the **longtail boats** that ply Khlong Saen Saeb; the canal service begins at Tha Phan Fah near Democracy Monument in the west of the city, runs parallel with part of Thanon Sukhumvit and has stops at the northern ends of Soi Nana Nua (Soi 3) and Thanon Asok Montri (Soi 21), from where you can either walk down to Thanon Sukhumvit, hop on a bus, or take a motorbike taxi. This reduces the journey between Thanon Sukhumvit and the Banglamphu/Ratanakosin area to about thirty minutes; for more details on boat routes, see p.38.

of specialist restaurants (from Lebanese to Laotian), tailors, bookstores and stall after stall selling cheap souvenirs and T-shirts, it's a lively part of town that also attracts a high proportion of single male tourists to its enclaves of girlie bars on Soi Nana Tai, Soi Cowboy and the Clinton Entertainment Plaza. But for the most part it's not a seedy area, and is home to many expats and middle-class Thais. Shops (see p.211), restaurants (see p.191) and bars (see p.197) are Sukhumvit's main attractions, though the museum-like northern Thai house **Ban Kamthieng** offers a refreshing alternative to the area's pervasive consumer culture, while the **Thailand Creative and Design Centre** aims to give you an insight into the nation's style and aesthetic.

Ban Kamthieng (Kamthieng House)

Another reconstructed traditional Thai residence, **Ban Kamthieng** (Tues–Sat 9am–5pm; B100; @www.siam-society.org) was moved in the 1960s from the northern province of Chiang Mai to 131 Thanon Asok Montri (Soi 21), off Thanon Sukhumvit, and set up as an ethnological museum by the Siam Society. The delightful complex of polished teak buildings makes a pleasing oasis beneath the towering glass skyscrapers that dominate the rest of Sukhumvit, and is easily reached from the Asok Skytrain and Sukhumvit subway stops. It differs from Suan Pakkad, Jim Thompson's House and M.R. Kukrit's Heritage Home in being the home of a rural family, and the objects on display give a fair insight into country life for the well-heeled in northern Thailand, though unless you've already visited the north you may find the 21st-century metropolitan context unhelpfully anomalous.

The house was built on the banks of the Ping River in the mid-nineteenth century, and the **ground-level** display of farming tools and fish traps evokes the upcountry custom of fishing in flooded rice paddies to supplement the supply from the rivers. **Upstairs**, the main display focuses on the ritual life of a typical northern Thai household, explaining the role of the spirits, the practice of making offerings, and the belief in talismans, magic shirts and male tattoos. The rectangular lintel above the door is a *hum yon*, carved in floral patterns that represent testicles and designed to ward off evil spirits. Walk along the open veranda to the authentically equipped kitchen to see a video lesson in making spicy frog soup, and to the granary to find an interesting exhibition on the rituals associated with rice-farming. Elsewhere in the Siam Society compound you'll find an esoteric bookshop (see p.218) and an antiques outlet.

Thailand Creative and Design Centre (TCDC)

Appropriately located on the sixth floor of the Emporium, one of Bangkok's most fashion-conscious shopping plazas, the **Thailand Creative and Design Centre** (Tues–Sun 10.30am–10pm; Ⓦwww.tcdc.or.th) seeks to celebrate, promote and inspire the nation's design innovations through its permanent display on international design and society, and via its programme of national and international exhibitions and talks. As well as its sleekly functional exhibition spaces, there's a resource centre, café and shop. The Emporium Shopping Centre is on Thanon Sukhumvit between sois 22 and 24, right alongside BTS Phrom Pong station.

7

Chatuchak
and the outskirts

The amorphous clutter of Greater Bangkok doesn't harbour many attractions, but there are a handful of places on the outskirts of the city which make pleasant half-day outings. Nearly all the places described in this chapter can be reached fairly painlessly by some sort of city transport, either by ferry up the Chao Phraya River or by Skytrain, subway or city bus.

If you're in Bangkok on a Saturday or Sunday it's well worth making the effort to visit the enormous **Chatuchak Weekend Market**, where you could browse away an entire day among the thousands of stalls selling everything from handmade paper to bargain-priced sarongs. The open-air **Prasart Museum** boasts many finely crafted replicas of traditional Thai buildings and is recommended for anyone who hasn't got the time to go upcountry and admire Thailand's temples and palaces in situ. Taking a boat ride up the Chao Phraya River makes a nice change to sitting in city-centre traffic, and the upstream town of **Nonthaburi** and the tranquil but less easily accessible island of **Ko Kred** provide the ideal excuse for doing just that.

Chatuchak Weekend Market ("JJ")

With over eight thousand open-air stalls to peruse, and wares as diverse as Lao silk, Siamese kittens and designer lamps to choose from, the enormous **Chatuchak Weekend Market**, or "**JJ**" as it's usually abbreviated, from "Jatu Jak" (Sat & Sun 7am–6pm), is Bangkok's most enjoyable – and exhausting – shopping experience. It occupies a huge patch of ground between the Northern Bus Terminal and Mo Chit Skytrain (N8)/Chatuchak Park subway stations, and is best reached by Skytrain or subway if you're coming from downtown areas; Kamphaeng Phet subway station is the most convenient as it exits right into the most interesting, southwestern, corner of the market. Coming from Banglamphu, you can either get a bus to the nearest Skytrain stop (probably National Stadium or Ratchathewi) and then take the train, or take the #503 or #509 bus all the way from Rajdamnoen Klang (about 1hr); see p.37 for details.

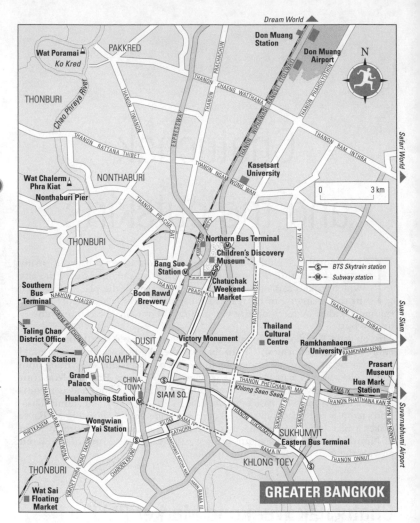

Aside from trendy one-off clothes and accessories, best buys include antique lacquerware, unusual sarongs, traditional cotton clothing and crafts from the north, jeans, silver jewellery, and ceramics, particularly the five-coloured *bencharong*. The market is divided into 26 numbered **sections**, plus a dozen unnumbered ones, each of them more or less dedicated to a particular genre, for example household items, young fashions, plants, secondhand books, or crafts. If you have several hours to spare, it's fun just to browse at whim, but if you're looking for souvenirs, handicrafts or traditional textiles you should start with sections 22, 24, 25 and 26, which are all in a cluster at the southwest (Kamphaeng Phet subway) end of the market; sections A, B and C, behind the market's head office and information centre are also full of interesting artefacts. *Nancy Chandler's Map of Bangkok* has a fabulously detailed and informatively annotated **map** of all the sections in the market: it's best bought before you arrive but is available at Teak

House Art in Section 2, near Kamphaeng Phet subway's exit 2. Maps are also posted at various points around the market and for specific help you can also ask at the market office near Gate 1 off Thanon Kamphaeng Phet 2.

The market also contains a controversial **wildlife** section that has long doubled as a clearing-house for protected and endangered species such as gibbons, palm cockatoos and Indian pied hornbills, many of them smuggled in from Laos and Cambodia and sold to private animal collectors and foreign zoos. The illegal trade goes on beneath the counter, and may be in decline following a spate of crackdowns, but you're bound to come across fighting cocks around the back (demonstrations are almost continuous), miniature flying squirrels being fed milk through pipettes, and iridescent red and blue Siamese fighting fish, kept in individual jars and shielded from each other's aggressive stares by sheets of cardboard.

There's no shortage of **foodstalls** inside the market compound, particularly at the southern end, where you'll find plenty of places serving inexpensive *phat thai* and Isaan snacks. Close by these stalls is a classy little juice bar called *Viva* where you can rest your feet while listening to the manager's jazz tapes. The biggest restaurant here is *Toh Plue*, whose main branch is on the edge of the block containing the market office and makes a good rendezvous point (there's a second branch beside Kamphaeng Phet subway station's exit 1). For veggie food, head for *Chamlong's* (also known as *Asoke*), an ultra-cheap food-court-style restaurant just outside the market on Thanon Kamphaeng Phet (across Thanon Kamphaeng Phet 2; five minutes' walk from Kamphaeng Phet subway's exit 1; Sat & Sun 8am–noon). You can **change money** (Sat & Sun 8am–6pm) in the market building at the south end of the market, and there are several ATMs here too. A few very small electric **trams** circulate around the market's main inner ringroad, transporting weary shoppers for free, though they always seem to be full.

The Prasart Museum

Located right out on the eastern edge of the city (and still surrounded by fields), the **Prasart Museum** at 9 Soi 4A, Soi Krungthep Kreetha, Thanon Krungthep Kreetha (Tues–Sun 10am–3pm; B1000 for one or two people; call ☏02 379 3601 to book the compulsory tour) is an unusual open-air exhibition of traditional Asian buildings, collected and reassembled by wealthy entrepreneur and art lover Khun Prasart. The museum is rarely visited by independent tourists – partly because of the intentionally limited opening hours and inflated admission price, and partly because it takes a long time to get there by public transport – but it makes a pleasant day out and is worth the effort.

Set in a gorgeously lush tropical garden, the museum comprises about a dozen replicas of **traditional buildings**, including a golden teak palace inspired by the royal residence now housed at the National Museum, a Chinese temple and water garden, a Khmer shrine, a Sukhothai-era teak library set over a lotus pond, and a European-style mansion, fashionable with Bangkok royalty in the late nineteenth century. Some of these structures have been assembled from the ruins of buildings found all over Asia, but there's no attempt at purist authenticity – the aim is to give a flavour of architectural styles, not an exact reproduction. Many of the other buildings, including the Thai wat and the Chinese temple, were constructed from scratch, using designs dreamt up by Khun Prasart and his team. Whatever their origins, all the buildings are beautifully crafted, with great attention paid to carvings and decorations, and many are filled with antique **artefacts**, including Burmese woodcarvings, prehistoric pottery from Ban Chiang and Lopburi-era statuettes. There are also some unusual pieces of royal memorabilia and an exquisite collection of *bencharong* ceramics. Khun Prasart also owns a ceramics workshop, which produces reproductions of famous designs; they can be bought either at the museum, or at his showroom, the Prasart Collection, on the second floor of the Peninsula Plaza shopping centre on Thanon Rajdamri.

Non-air-con **bus** #93 runs almost to the door: pick it up near its downtown starting point on Thanon Si Phraya near the River City shopping complex and the GPO, or anywhere along its route on Phetchaburi and Phetchaburi Mai roads (both the Khlong Saen Saeb canal boats and the subway have potentially useful stops at the Thanon Asok Montri/Sukhumvit Soi 21 junction with Thanon Phetchaburi Mai). The #93 terminates on Thanon Krungthep Kreetha, but you should get off a couple of stops before the terminus, at the first stop on Thanon Krungthep Kreetha, as soon as you see the sign for the Prasart Museum (about 1hr 15min by bus from Thanon Si Phraya). Follow the sign down Soi Krungthep Kreetha, go past the golf course and, after about a fifteen-minute walk, turn off down Soi 4A.

Nonthaburi

A trip to **NONTHABURI**, the first town beyond the northern boundary of Bangkok, is the easiest excursion you can make from the centre of the city and affords a perfect opportunity to recharge your batteries. Nonthaburi is the last

△ Wat Chalerm Phra Kiat, Nonthaburi

Durians

The naturalist Alfred Russel Wallace, eulogizing the taste of the **durian**, compared it to "rich butter-like custard highly flavoured with almonds, but intermingled with wafts of flavour that call to mind cream cheese, onion sauce, brown sherry and other incongruities". He neglected to discuss the smell of the fruit's skin, which is so bad – somewhere between detergent and dogshit – that durians are barred from Thai hotels and aeroplanes. The different **varieties** bear strange names which do nothing to make them more appetizing: "frog", "golden pillow", "gibbon" and so on. However, the durian has fervent admirers, perhaps because it's such an acquired taste, and because it's considered a strong aphrodisiac. Aficionados discuss the varieties with as much subtlety as if they were vintage champagnes, and they treat the durian as a social fruit, to be shared around, despite a price tag of up to B3000 each.

Durian season is roughly April to June and the most famous durian orchards are around Nonthaburi, where the fruits are said to have an incomparably rich and nutty flavour due to the fine clay soil. If you don't smell them first, you can recognize durians by their sci-fi appearance: the shape and size of a rugby ball, but slightly deflated, they're covered in a thick, pale-green shell which is heavily armoured with short, sharp spikes (*duri* means "thorn" in Malay). By cutting along one of the faint seams with a good knife, you'll reveal a white pith in which are set a handful of yellow blobs with the texture of a wrinkled soufflé: this is what you eat. The taste is best when the smell is at its highest, about three days after the fruit has dropped. Be careful when out walking near the trees: because of its great weight and sharp spikes, a falling durian can lead to serious injury, or even an ignominious death.

stop upriver for express boats, around one hour fifteen minutes from Central Pier (Sathorn) on a "standard" boat, under an hour if you catch a "special express". The ride itself is most of the fun, weaving round huge, crawling sand barges and tiny canoes, and the slow pace of the boat gives you plenty of time to take in the sights on the way. On the north side of Banglamphu, beyond Thewes flower market, the Art Nouveau Bangkhunprom Palace and the elegant, new Rama VIII Bridge, you'll pass the royal boathouse in front of the National Library on the east bank, where you can glimpse the minor ceremonial boats that escort the grand royal barges. Further out are dazzling Buddhist temples and drably painted mosques, catering for Bangkok's growing Muslim population, as well as a few remaining communities who still live in houses on stilts or houseboats – around Krungthon Bridge, for example, you'll see people living on the huge teak vessels used to carry rice, sand and charcoal.

Disembarking at suburban Nonthaburi, on the east bank of the river, you won't find a great deal to do, in truth. There's a market that's famous for the quality of its fruit, while the attractive, old Provincial Office across the road is covered in rickety wooden latticework. To break up your trip with a slow, scenic drink or lunch, you'll find a floating seafood restaurant, *Rim Fang*, to the right at the end of the prom which, though a bit overpriced, is quiet and breezy.

Set in relaxing grounds about 1km north of Nonthaburi pier on the west bank of the river, elegant **Wat Chalerm Phra Kiat** injects a splash of urban refinement among a grove of breadfruit trees. You can get there from the express-boat pier by taking the ferry straight across the Chao Phraya and then catching a motorbike taxi. The beautifully proportioned temple, which has been lavishly restored, was built by Rama III in memory of his mother, whose family lived and presided over vast orchards in the area. Entering the walls of the temple compound, you feel as if you're coming upon a stately folly in a secret garden, and a strong Chinese influence shows itself in the unusual ribbed roofs and elegantly curved gables, decorated with pastel ceramics. The restorers have done their best work inside: look out especially for the simple, delicate landscapes on the shutters.

Ko Kred

About 7km north of Nonthaburi, the tiny island of **KO KRED** lies in a particularly sharp bend in the Chao Phraya, cut off from the east bank by a waterway created to make the cargo route from Ayutthaya to the Gulf of Thailand just that little bit faster. Although it's slowly being discovered by day-trippers from Bangkok, this artificial island remains something of a time capsule, a little oasis of village life completely at odds with the metropolitan chaos downriver. Roughly ten square kilometres in all, Ko Kred has no roads, just a concrete path that follows its circumference, with a few arterial walkways branching off towards the interior. Villagers, the majority of whom are Mon (see box below), use a small fleet of motorbike taxis to cross their island, but as a sightseer you're much better off on foot: a round-island walk takes less than an hour and a half.

There are few sights as such on Ko Kred, but its lushness and comparative emptiness make it a perfect place in which to wander. You'll no doubt come across one of the island's potteries and kilns, which churn out the regionally famous earthenware flowerpots and small water-storage jars and employ a large percentage of the village workforce; several shops dotted around the island sell Ko Kred terracotta, including what's styled as the Ancient Mon Pottery Centre near the island's northeast corner, which also displays delicate and venerable

The Mon

Dubbed by some "the Palestinians of Asia", the **Mon** people – numbering around one million in Burma and 100,000 in Thailand – have endured centuries of persecution, displacement and forced assimilation, and to this day suffer beatings, gang rapes and press-ganging as porters and human land-mine detectors at the hands of Burma's repressive military regime. Ethnologists speculate that the Mon originated either in India or Mongolia, travelling south to settle on the western banks of Thailand's Chao Phraya valley in the first century BC. Here they founded the **Dvaravati kingdom** (sixth to eleventh centuries AD), building centres at U Thong, Lopburi and Nakhon Pathom and later consolidating a northern kingdom in Haripunchai (modern-day Lamphun). They probably introduced **Theravada Buddhism** to the region, and produced some of the earliest Buddhist monuments, particularly Wheels of Law and Buddha footprints.

Like Thais, the Mon are a predominantly Buddhist, rice-growing people, but they also have strong animist beliefs. All Mon families have totemic **house spirits**, such as the turtle, snake, chicken or pig, which carry certain taboos; if you're of the chicken-spirit family, for example, the lungs and head of every chicken that you cook have to be offered to the spirits, and although you're allowed to raise and kill chickens, you must never give one away. Guests belonging to a different spirit group from their host are not allowed to stay overnight. Mon **festivals** also differ slightly from Thai ones – at Songkhran (Thai New Year), the Mon spice up the usual water-throwing and parades with a special courtship ritual in which teams of men and women play each other at bowling, throwing flirtatious banter along with their wooden discs.

museum pieces and Mon-style Buddha shrines. The island's clay is very rich in nutrients and therefore excellent for fruit-growing, and banana trees, coconut palms, pomelo, papaya, mango and durian trees all grow in abundance on Ko Kred, fed by an intricate network of irrigation channels that crisscrosses the interior. In among the orchards, the Mon have built their wooden houses, mostly in traditional style and raised high above the marshy ground on stilts. A handful of attractive riverside wats complete the picture, most notably **Wat Paramaiyikawat** (aka Wat Poramai), at the main pier at the northeast tip of the island. This engagingly ramshackle eighteenth-century temple was restored by Rama V in honour of his grandmother, with a Buddha relic placed in its white, riverside chedi, which is a replica of the Mutao Pagoda in Hanthawadi, capital of the Mon kingdom in Burma. Among an open-air scattering of Burmese-style alabaster Buddha images, the tall bot shelters some fascinating nineteenth-century murals, depicting scenes from temple life at ground level and the life of the Buddha above, all set in delicate imaginary landscapes.

Practicalities

The best time to go to Ko Kred is the weekend, when the Chao Phraya Express Boat Company (Sun only; B300; ☎02 623 6001–3, ⓦwww.chaophrayaboat .co.th) and Mitchaopaya Travel Service (Sat & Sun; B250; ☎02 623 6169) run **tours** there from central Bangkok. They both head upriver at 9am (Chao Phraya Express Boat Company from Tha Sathorn via Tha Maharat, Mitchao-paya from Tha Chang), taking in Wat Poramai and the Ancient Mon Pottery Centre, before circling the island via Ban Khanom Thai, where you can buy traditional sweets and watch them being made. Chao Phraya Express Boat Company arrives back, via Wat Sangsiritham floating market, at Tha Maharat at about 3pm (Tha Sathorn at 3.30pm), while Mitchaopaya also takes in the Royal Barge Museum (see p.99) and Wat Chalerm Phra Kiat in Nonthaburi (see p.133), returning to Tha Chang at around 4.30pm.

At other times, the main drawback of a day-trip to Ko Kred is the difficulty of **getting there**. Your best option is to take a Chao Phraya express boat to Nonthaburi, then bus #32 to Pakkred pier – or, if you're feeling flush, a char-tered longtail boat direct to Ko Kred (about B200–300). From Pakkred, the easiest way of getting across to the island is to hire a longtail boat, although shuttle boats cross at the river's narrowest point to Wat Poramai from Wat Sanam Nua, about a kilometre's walk or a short samlor or motorbike-taxi ride south of the Pakkred pier.

Excursions from Bangkok

Regular bus and train services from Bangkok give access to a number of enjoyable **excursions**, all of which are perfectly feasible as day-trips, though some also merit an overnight stay. The fertile plain to the north of the capital is bisected by the country's main artery, the Chao Phraya River, which carries boat tours to supplement the area's trains and buses. The monumental kitsch of the nineteenth-century palace at **Bang Pa-In** provides a sharp contrast with the atmospheric ruins further upriver at the former capital of **Ayutthaya**, where ancient temples, some crumbling and overgrown, others alive and kicking, are arrayed in a leafy setting. You could visit the two sites on a long day-trip from Bangkok, but separate outings or an

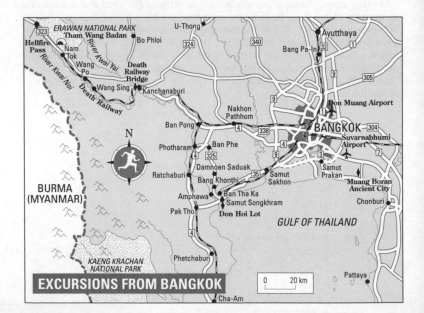

EXCURSIONS FROM BANGKOK

0   20 km

overnight stay in Ayutthaya will let you make the most of the former capital's many attractions.

To the west of the capital, the enormous nineteenth-century stupa at **Nakhon Pathom** is undeniably impressive and well worth the short journey from Bangkok; it's often visited in conjunction with an early-morning outing to the floating markets of **Damnoen Saduak**, though these are so popular with tourists that they seem staged and contrived. Better to venture a few kilometres further south to the more authentic floating markets around **Amphawa**, near **Samut Songkhram**, whose quaint canalside neighbourhoods are complemented by a stylish riverside resort that makes this a perfect overnight break from Bangkok. Tradition is also central to the untouristed town of **Phetchaburi**, with its many charming temples and wooden shophouses.

Northwest of the capital, **Kanchanaburi** has long attracted visitors to the notorious **Bridge over the River Kwai**, but the town harbours many, much more affecting World War II memorials and occupies a gloriously scenic riverside location, best savoured by spending a night in a raft house moored to the

Travelling out of Bangkok

By train

Nearly all trains depart from **Hualamphong Station**. Exceptions are the service to Kanchanaburi and Nam Tok via Nakhon Pathom, which leaves from **Thonburi Station** (sometimes still referred to by its former name, **Bangkok Noi Station**), across the river from Banglamphu in Thonburi, about an 850m walk west of the Railway Station N11 express boat stop; and the service to Samut Sakhon (aka Mahachai), for connections to Samut Songkhram, that leaves from **Wongwian Yai Station**, also in Thonburi. The 24-hour "Information" booth at Hualamphong Station keeps English-language timetables, detailing types of trains and classes available on each route, as well as fares and supplementary charges; a third-class ticket in a non-air-con carriage on an Ordinary train (the slowest) from Hualamphong to Ayutthaya, for example, will set you back just B15. Otherwise you can try phoning the Train Information Hotline on ☎1690, while the State Railway of Thailand website (🌐 www.railway.co.th) carries a timetable and fare chart for major destinations. For details on city transport to and from Hualamphong and left-luggage facilities at the station, see p.31.

By bus

Destinations in this chapter are served by air-conditioned buses (*rot air*) from two major terminals in Bangkok, both on the outskirts of the city. As regards fares, a one-way ticket to Ayutthaya, for example, typically costs B52.

The **Southern Bus Terminal**, or **Sathaanii Sai Tai Mai** (☎02 435 1199), is at the junction of Thanon Borom Ratchonni and the Nakhon Chaisri Highway, west of the Chao Phraya River in Thonburi. It handles departures to destinations west of Bangkok, such as Nakhon Pathom, Damnoen Saduak, Samut Songkhran, Phetchaburi and Kanchanaburi, and to all points south of the capital. To reach the terminal, take city bus #507 (air-con) from Banglamphu or Hualamphong Station, or air-con #511 from Banglamphu or Thanon Sukhumvit; see box on p.37 for bus route details.

The **Northern Bus Terminal**, or **Sathaanii Mo Chit** (☎02 936 2852–66), is the departure point for buses to Bang Pa-In, Ayutthaya and all northern and northeastern towns. It's on Thanon Kamphaeng Phet 2, near Chatuchak Weekend Market in the far north of the city; Skytrain's Mo Chit station and Kampaeng Phet subway station are within a short motorbike taxi or tuk-tuk ride, or take a city bus direct to the bus terminal: air-con #503, #512 and #157 run from Banglamphu and non-air-con #159 runs from the Southern Bus Terminal; see box on p.37 for bus route details.

riverbank. Finally, for a taste of Thailand's finest monuments and temples in just one rewarding bite, there's the well-designed open-air museum at **Muang Boran Ancient City**, which contains beautifully crafted replicas of the country's top buildings and is just 33km southeast of the capital.

Muang Boran Ancient City

A day-trip out to the **MUANG BORAN ANCIENT CITY** open-air museum (daily 8am–5pm; B300, children B200 including bicycle rental or tram ticket; Ⓦ www.ancientcity.com), 33km southeast of Bangkok in Samut Prakan province, is a great way to enjoy the best of Thailand's architectural heritage in relative peace and without much effort. Occupying a huge park shaped like Thailand itself, the museum comprises more than 115 traditional Thai buildings scattered around pleasantly landscaped grounds and is best toured by rented **bicycle** (B50; B150/tandem; B200/three-seater), though you can also make use of the circulating **tram** (B150 round trip, kids B75), and doing it on foot is just about possible. Many of the buildings are copies of the country's most famous monuments, and are located in the appropriate "region" of the park, with everything from Bangkok's Grand Palace (central region) to the spectacularly sited hilltop Khmer Khao Phra Viharn sanctuary (northeast) represented here. There are also some original structures, including a rare scripture repository (library) rescued from Samut Songkhram (south), as well as some painstaking reconstructions from contemporary documents of long-vanished gems, of which the Ayutthaya-period Sanphet Prasat palace (central) is a particularly fine example. A sizeable team of restorers and skilled craftspeople maintains the buildings and helps keep some of the traditional techniques alive; if you come here during the week you can watch them at work.

To get to Muang Boran from Bangkok, take air-conditioned **bus** #511 to **Samut Prakan** on the edge of built-up Greater Bangkok, then change onto songthaew (pickup bus) #36, which passes the entrance to Muang Boran. Although bus #511 runs from Banglamphu via Thanon Rama I and Thanon Sukhumvit (see p.37 for the route), wherever you're starting from, the journey is likely to be much faster if you cover downtown Bangkok by Skytrain (and boat and/or subway if necessary) and pick up the #511 at the Ekamai Skytrain stop.

Bang Pa-In

Little more than a roadside market, the village of **BANG PA-IN**, 60km north of Bangkok, has been put on the tourist map by its extravagant and rather surreal **Royal Palace** (daily 8.30am–4.30pm; ticket office closes 3.30pm; visitors are asked to dress respectfully, so no vests, shorts or mini-skirts; B100; Ⓦ www.palaces.thai.net), even though most of the buildings can be seen only from the outside. King Prasat Thong of Ayutthaya first built a palace on this site, 20km down the Chao Phraya River from his capital, in the middle of the seventeenth century. It remained a popular royal country residence until it was abandoned a century later, when the Thai capital was moved from Ayutthaya to Bangkok. In the middle of the nineteenth century, however, the advent of steamboats shortened the journey time upriver, and the palace enjoyed a revival: King Mongkut (Rama IV) built a modest residence here, which his son King Chulalongkorn (Rama V), in his passion for Westernization, knocked down to make room for the eccentric melange of European, Thai and Chinese architectural styles visible today.

Set in manicured grounds on an island in the Chao Phraya River, and ranged around an ornamental lake, the palace complex is flat and compact – a free brochure from the ticket office gives a diagram of the layout. On the north side of the lake stand a two-storey, colonial-style residence for the royal relatives and the Italianate **Warophat Phiman** (Excellent and Shining Heavenly Abode), which housed Chulalongkorn's throne hall and still contains private apartments where the present royal family sometimes stays. A covered bridge links this outer part of the palace to the **Pratu Thewarat Khanlai** (The King of the Gods Goes Forth Gate), the main entrance to the inner palace, which was reserved for the king and his immediate family. The high fence which encloses half of the bridge allowed the women of the harem to cross without being seen by male courtiers. You can't miss the photogenic **Aisawan Thiphya-art** (Divine Seat of Personal Freedom) in the middle of the lake: named after King Prasat Thong's original palace, it's the only example of pure Thai architecture at Bang Pa-In. The elegant tiers of the pavilion's roof shelter a bronze statue of Chulalongkorn.

In the inner palace, the **Uthayan Phumisathian** (Garden of the Secured Land), recently rebuilt by Queen Sirikit in grand, neo-colonial style, was Chulalongkorn's favourite house. After passing the **Ho Withun Thasana** (Sage's Lookout Tower), built so that the king could survey the surrounding countryside, you'll come to the main attraction of Bang Pa-In, the **Phra Thinang Wehart Chamrun** (Palace of Heavenly Light). A masterpiece of Chinese design, the mansion and its contents were shipped from China and presented as a gift to Chulalongkorn in 1889 by the Chinese Chamber of Commerce in Bangkok. You're allowed to take off your shoes and feast your eyes on the interior, which drips with fine porcelain and embroidery, ebony furniture inlaid with mother-of-pearl and fantastically intricate woodcarving. This residence was the favourite of Rama VI, whose carved and lacquered writing table can be seen on the ground floor.

The simple marble **obelisk** behind the Uthayan Phumisathian was erected by Chulalongkorn to hold the ashes of Queen Sunandakumariratana, his favourite wife. In 1881, Sunanda, who was then 21 and expecting a child, was taking a trip on the river here when her boat capsized. She could have been rescued quite easily, but the laws concerning the sanctity of the royal family left those around her no option: "If a boat founders, the boatmen must swim away; if they remain near the boat [or] if they lay hold of him [the royal person] to rescue him, they are to be executed." Following the tragedy, King Chulalongkorn became a zealous reformer of Thai customs and strove to make the monarchy more accessible.

Turn right out of the main entrance to the palace grounds and cross the river on the small cable car, and you'll come to the greatest oddity of all: **Wat Nivet Dhamapravat**. A grey Buddhist viharn in the style of a Gothic church, it was built by Chulalongkorn in 1878, complete with wooden pews and stained-glass windows.

Practicalities

Bang Pa-In can easily be visited on a day-trip from Bangkok. At a pinch, you could also take in a visit to Ayutthaya (see overleaf) on the same day, although this doesn't really leave enough time to get the most out of the extensive remains of the former capital. The best way of getting to Bang Pa-In from Bangkok is by **train** from Hualamphong station. The journey takes just over an hour, and all trains continue to Ayutthaya (30 daily; 30min). From Bang Pa-In station (notice the separate station hall built by Chulalongkorn for the royal family) it's a two-kilometre hike to the palace, or you can take a motorbike taxi for about B30. Slow **buses** leave Bangkok's Northern Terminal roughly every half an hour and stop at Bang Pa-In market after about two hours, a motorbike-taxi ride from the palace.

Every Sunday, the Chao Phraya Express Boat company (☏02 623 6001–3, ⓦ www.chaophrayaboat.co.th) runs **river tours** to Bang Pa-In, taking in Wat Phailom, a breeding ground for open-billed storks escaping the cold in Siberia, from November to June (during the rest of the year they visit Wat Chalerm Phra Kiat in Nonthaburi instead – see p.133), plus a shopping stop at Bang Sai folk arts and handicrafts centre. The boats leave Tha Sathorn at 7.30am, calling at Tha Maharat at 8am, and return to Maharat at 6pm, Sathorn at 6.30pm; tickets, available from the piers, are B430 (B350 one-way), not including lunch and admission to the palace and the handicrafts centre (B200). The Mitchaopaya company, based at Tha Chang (☏02 623 6169), also runs similar cruises on certain Sundays, and luxury cruises to Ayutthaya (see p.141) also stop at Bang Pa-In.

Ayutthaya

In its heyday as the capital of the Thai kingdom (from the fourteenth to the eighteenth centuries), **AYUTTHAYA** was so well endowed with temples that

The golden age of Ayutthaya

Ayutthaya takes its name from the Indian city of Ayodhya ("invincible"), legendary birthplace of Rama, hero of the *Ramayana* epic (see p.65). Founded in 1351 by U Thong, later **King Ramathibodi I**, it rose rapidly by exploiting the expanding trade routes between India and China, and by the mid-fifteenth century its empire covered most of what is now Thailand. Ayutthaya grew into a vast amphibious city built on a 140-kilometre network of canals (few of which survive); by 1685 a million people – roughly double the population of London at the time – lived on its waterways, mostly in houseboats.

By the seventeenth century, Ayutthaya's wealth had attracted **traders** of forty different nationalities, including Chinese, Portuguese, Dutch, English and French. Many lived in their own ghettos, with their own docks for the export of rice, spices, timber and hides. The kings of Ayutthaya deftly maintained their independence from outside powers, while embracing the benefits of contact: they employed foreign architects and navigators, and Japanese samurai as bodyguards; even their prime ministers were often outsiders, who could look after foreign trade without getting embroiled in court intrigues.

This four-hundred-year **golden age** came to an abrupt end in 1767 when the Burmese sacked Ayutthaya, taking tens of thousands of prisoners. The ruined city was abandoned to the jungle, but its memory endured: the architects of the new capital on Ratanakosin island in Bangkok perpetuated Ayutthaya's layout in every possible way.

sunlight reflecting off their gilt decoration was said to dazzle from three miles away. Wide, grassy spaces today occupy much of the atmospheric site 80km north of Bangkok, which now resembles a graveyard for temples: grand, brooding red-brick ruins rise out of the fields, evoking the city's bygone grandeur. A few intact buildings help form an image of what the capital must have looked like, while three fine museums flesh out the picture.

The core of the ancient capital was a four-kilometre-wide **island** at the confluence of the Lopburi, Pasak and Chao Phraya rivers, which was once encircled by a twelve-kilometre wall, crumbling parts of which can be seen at the **Phom Phet fortress** in the southeast corner. A grid of broad roads now crosses the island, known as Ko Muang, with recent buildings jostling uneasily with the ancient remains; the hub of the modern town rests on the northeast bank of the island around the corner of Thanon U Thong and Thanon Naresuan, although the newest development is off the island to the east.

Ayutthaya comes alive each year for a week in mid-December, when a **festival** is organized to commemorate the town's listing as a **World Heritage Site** by UNESCO on December 13, 1991. The highlight of the celebrations is the nightly *son et lumière* show, a grand historical romp featuring fireworks, elephant-back fights and the like, staged at Wat Phra Si Sanphet, Wat Phra Ram or one of the other ancient sites.

Arrival, information and transport

Ayutthaya can easily be visited on a day-trip from Bangkok, though dedicated ruin-baggers might want to stay overnight (see p.148). The best way of getting there is **by train** – there are about thirty a day from the capital, via Bang Pa-In (see p.140), concentrated in the early morning and evening (1hr 30min). To get to the centre of town from the station on the east bank of the Pasak, take the ferry (2B) from the jetty 100m west of the station across and upriver to Chao Phrom pier; it's then a five-minute walk to the junction of U Thong and Naresuan roads (if you're going to eat or stay at *Bann Kun Pra*, take the other ferry from the neighbouring jetty which runs directly across the river and back).

Though frequent, **buses** to Ayutthaya are slower, as they depart from Bangkok's inconvenient Northern Terminal (every 20min; 2hr). Most buses from Bangkok pull in at the bus stop on Thanon Naresuan just west of the centre of Ayutthaya, though some (mainly those on long-distance runs) only stop at Ayutthaya's Northern Bus Terminal, 2km to the east of the centre. Private aircon minibuses from Bangkok's Victory Monument and Southern Bus Terminal finish their routes opposite the Thanon Naresuan bus stop (both about every 20min during daylight hours; 1–2hr depending on traffic).

It's also possible to get here by scenic **boat tour** on the Chao Phraya River from Bangkok via Bang Pa-In Palace: River Sun Cruises (☎02 266 9125–6 or 02 266 9316) based at River City, for example, runs swanky day-trips for B1800 per person, including buffet lunch, with one leg of the journey – either up to Ayutthaya or back to Bangkok – completed in a coach or air-con minibus. A couple of plushly converted teak rice barges do luxury overnight **cruises** to Bang Pa-In and Ayutthaya: the *Manohra 2* (☎02 477 0770, ⊛www .manohracruises.com) takes three leisurely days and two nights over the trip, while the *Mekhala* (⊛www.mekhalacruise.com) does it in one and a half days and one night, with one leg between Bangkok and Ayutthaya by air-con minibus and one leg between Ayutthaya and Bang Pa-In by longtail boat.

Once in Ayutthaya, the helpful **TAT** office (daily 8.30am–4.30pm; ☎035 246076–7 or 035 322730–1, ⊜tatyutya@tat.or.th) can be found in the former city hall on the west side of Thanon Si Sanphet, opposite the Chao Sam Phraya National Museum. It's well worth heading upstairs here to the smartly presented multimedia **exhibition** on Ayutthaya (daily except Wed 8.30am–4.30pm; free), which provides an engaging introduction to the city's history, an overview of all the sights including a scale-model reconstruction of Wat Phra Si Sanphet, and insights into local traditional ways of life. The **tourist police** (☎035 242352 or 1155) have their office just to the north of TAT on Thanon Si Sanphet.

For **transport** around Ayutthaya's widespread sights, **bicycles** (B30–50 per day) can be rented at the guest houses, a few shops in front of the train station

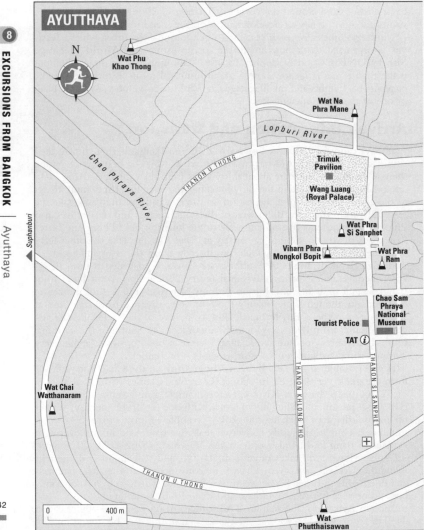

or from the tourist police; if even that sounds too much like hard work, some of the guest houses and a few cheaper outlets in front of the station have small **motorbikes** (B150–250 a day). Otherwise there are plenty of **tuk-tuks** around: their set routes for sharing passengers are more useful for locals than tourists, but a typical journey in town on your own should only cost B30–40. **Motorbike taxis** charge around B30 for medium-range journeys. If you're pushed for time you could hire a tuk-tuk for a whistle-stop tour of the old city for B200 an hour (the current going rate set by the tourist police), either from the train station or from Chao Phrom market. There's also a **tourist train**, actually an open-sided bus on wheels (every 15 or 20min; B20), which connects

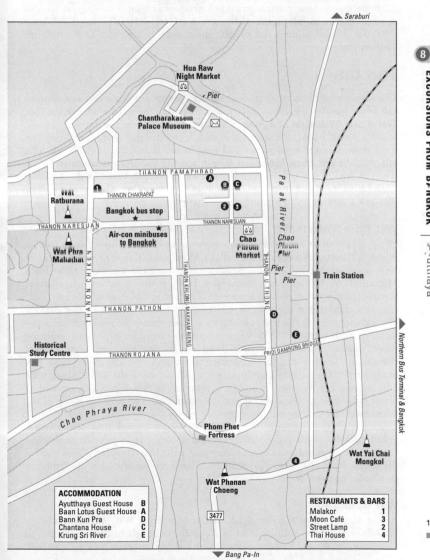

▲ Saraburi

Hua Raw
Night Market

◄ Pier

Chantharakasem
Palace Museum

THANON RAMAPHRAO

Ⓐ Ⓑ Ⓒ

Wat
Ratburana

THANON CHAKRAPAT

Bangkok bus stop

Ⓞ Ⓞ

THANON NARESUAN

THANON NARESUAN

Air-con minibuses
to Bangkok

Chao
Phrom
Market

Chao
Phrom
Pier

P a a k R i v e r

Wat Phra
Mahathat

Pier

Train Station

THANON CHIKUN

THANON KHLONG MAKHAM RIENG

THANON U THONG

Pier

THANON PATHON

Ⓓ

Historical
Study Centre

THANON ROJANA

Ⓔ

PRIDI DAMRONG BRIDGE

Chao Phraya River

Phom Phet
Fortress

Wat Yai Chai
Mongkol

Ⓞ

Wat Phanan
Choeng

3477

▲ Bang Pa-In

ACCOMMODATION
Ayutthaya Guest House	B
Baan Lotus Guest House	A
Bann Kun Pra	D
Chantana House	C
Krung Sri River	E

RESTAURANTS & BARS
Malakor	1
Moon Café	3
Street Lamp	2
Thai House	4

▶ Northern Bus Terminal & Bangkok

143

the Historical Study Centre, Wat Phanan Choeng, Wat Yai Chai Mongkol, Wat Phra Mahathat, Wat Ratburana and Viharn Phra Mongkok Bopit, spending five or ten minutes in each place.

Tour **boats**, generally accommodating up to eight passengers and charging around B700 for a two-hour trip, can be chartered from the pier outside the Chantharakasem Palace, from Wat Phanan Choeng or through guest houses. A typical tour takes in **Wat Phutthaisawan**, built around a gleaming white prang by Ramathibodi I in 1353, only two years after the city's foundation, and the recently restored **Wat Chai Watthanaram**, which was built by King Prasat Thong in 1630 to commemorate his victory over Cambodia, taking as its model the imposing symmetry of the Baphuon temple at Angkor. It's also possible to take an **elephant ride** (T035 211001; B400/person for 20min, B500 for 30min) around the central ruins from behind the TAT office off Thanon Pathon.

The City

The majority of Ayutthaya's ancient remains are spread out across the western half of the island in a patchwork of parkland: two of the most evocative temples, **Wat Phra Mahathat** and **Wat Ratburana**, stand near the modern centre, while a broad band runs down the middle of the parkland, containing the scant vestiges of the royal palace and temple, the town's most revered Buddha image at **Viharn Phra Mongkol Bopit**, and the two main **museums**. To the north of the island you'll find the best-preserved temple, **Wat Na Phra Mane**, while to the southeast lie the giant chedi of **Wat Yai Chai Mongkol** and **Wat Phanan Choeng**, still a vibrant place of worship.

Wat Phra Mahathat

Heading west out of the new town centre along Thanon Chao Phrom (which becomes Thanon Naresuan), after about 1km you'll come to the first set of ruins, a pair of temples on opposite sides of the road. The overgrown **Wat Phra Mahathat**, on the left (daily 8am–5pm; B30), is the epitome of Ayutthaya's nostalgic atmosphere of faded majesty. The name "Mahathat" (Great Relic Chedi) indicates that the temple was built to house remains of the Buddha himself: according to the royal chronicles – never renowned for historical accuracy – King Ramesuan (1388–95) was looking out of his palace one morning when ashes of the Buddha materialized out of thin air here. A gold casket containing the ashes was duly enshrined in a grand 38-metre-high prang. The prang later collapsed, but the reliquary was unearthed in the 1950s, along with a hoard of other treasures including a gorgeous marble fish which opened to reveal gold, amber, crystal and porcelain ornaments – all now on show in the Chao Sam Phraya National Museum (see p.145).

You can climb what remains of the prang to get a good view of the broad, grassy complex, with dozens of brick spires tilting at impossible angles and headless Buddhas scattered around like spare parts in a scrapyard – look out for the serene head of a stone Buddha which has become nestled in the embrace of a bodhi tree's roots.

Wat Ratburana

Across the road from Wat Phra Mahathat, the towering **Wat Ratburana** (daily 8am–5pm; B30) was built in 1424 by King Boromraja II to commemorate his elder brothers Ay and Yi, who managed to kill each other in an elephant-back duel over the succession to the throne, thus leaving it vacant for him. Four elegant Sri Lankan chedis lean outwards as if in deference to the main prang, on which some of the original stucco work can still be seen, including fine statues of garudas swooping down on nagas.

It's possible to go down steep steps inside the prang to the crypt, where on two levels you can make out fragmentary murals of the early Ayutthaya period. Several hundred Buddha images were buried down here, most of which were snatched by grave robbers, although some can be seen in the Chao Sam Phraya Museum. They're in the earliest style that can be said to be distinctly Ayutthayan – an unsmiling Khmer expression, but on an oval face and elongated body that show the strong influence of Sukhothai.

Wat Phra Si Sanphet

Nearly a kilometre west of Wat Ratburana is **Wat Phra Si Sanphet** (daily 8am–5pm; B30), built in 1448 by King Boromatrailokanat as his private chapel. Formerly the grandest of Ayutthaya's temples, and still one of the best preserved, it took its name from one of the largest standing metal images of the Buddha ever known, the **Phra Si Sanphet**, erected here in 1503. Towering 16m high and covered in 173kg of gold, it was smashed to pieces when the Burmese sacked the city, though Rama I rescued the fragments and placed them inside a chedi at Wat Pho in Bangkok. The three remaining grey chedis were built to house the ashes of three kings; their style is characteristic of the old capital, and they have now become the most hackneyed image of Ayutthaya.

The vast **Wang Luang** (Royal Palace) to the north of Wat Phra Si Sanphet was destroyed by the Burmese in 1767 and then plundered for bricks by Rama I to build Bangkok. Now you can only trace the outlines of a few walls in the grass – the only way to form a picture of this huge complex is to consult the model in the Historical Study Centre (see p.146).

Viharn Phra Mongkol Bopit

Viharn Phra Mongkol Bopit (Mon–Fri 8.30am–4.30pm, Sat & Sun 8.30am–5.30pm; free), on the south side of Wat Phra Si Sanphet, attracts tourists and Thai pilgrims in about equal measure. The pristine hall – a replica of a typical Ayutthayan viharn with its characteristic chunky lotus-capped columns around the outside – was built in 1956 (with help from the Burmese to atone for their flattening of the city two centuries earlier) in order to shelter the revered **Phra Mongkol Bopit**, one of the largest bronze Buddhas in Thailand. The powerfully austere image, with its flashing mother-of-pearl eyes, was cast in the fifteenth century, then sat exposed to the elements from the time of the Burmese invasion until its new home was built. During restoration, the hollow image was found to contain hundreds of Buddha statuettes, some of which were later buried around the shrine to protect it.

Chao Sam Phraya National Museum

A ten-minute walk south of the viharn brings you to the largest of the town's three museums, the **Chao Sam Phraya National Museum** (Wed–Sun 9am–4pm; B30; Ⓦ www.thailandmuseum.com), where most of the movable remains of Ayutthaya's glory – those which weren't plundered by treasure hunters or taken to the National Museum in Bangkok – are exhibited. The museum itself was funded by a Fine Arts Department sale of the Buddhist votive tablets excavated from Wat Ratburana in the late 1950s, and given the original name (Chao Sam Phraya) of King Boromraja II, who built the wat. Apart from numerous Buddhas and some fine woodcarving, the museum is bursting with **gold treasures** of all shapes and sizes – the original relic casket from Wat Mahathat, betel-nut sets and model chedis, a royal wimple in gold filigree, a royal sword and scabbard and a fifteenth-century crouching elephant, both dripping with gems and both found in the crypt of the main prang of Wat Ratburana.

Historical Study Centre

The **Historical Study Centre** (Mon–Fri 9am–4.30pm, Sat & Sun 9am–5pm; B100), five minutes' walk from the national museum along Thanon Rotchana, is a more modern showpiece museum. The visitors' exhibition upstairs puts the ruins in context, dramatically presenting a wealth of background detail through videos, sound effects and reconstructions – temple murals and model ships, a peasant's wooden house and a small-scale model of the Royal Palace – to build up a broad social history of Ayutthaya.

Chantharakasem Palace

In the northeast corner of the island, the museum of the **Chantharakasem Palace** (Wed–Sun 8.30am–4.30pm; B30; ⓦ www.thailandmuseum.com) was traditionally the home of the heir to the Ayutthayan throne. The Black Prince, Naresuan, built the first *wang na* (palace of the front) here in about 1577 so that he could guard the area of the city wall which was most vulnerable to enemy attack. Rama IV had the palace rebuilt in the mid-nineteenth century, and it now displays many of his possessions, including a throne platform overhung by a white *chat*, a ceremonial nine-tiered parasol which is a vital part of a king's insignia. The rest of the museum features some beautiful ceramics and Buddha images, and a small arsenal of cannon and musketry from the late Ayutthaya and early Bangkok periods.

Wat Na Phra Mane

Wat Na Phra Mane (Mon–Fri 8am–5pm, Sat & Sun 8am–6pm; B20), on the north bank of the Lopburi River opposite the Wang Luang, is Ayutthaya's most immediately rewarding temple, as it's the only one from the town's golden age which survived the ravages of the Burmese. The story goes that when the Burmese were on the brink of capturing Ayutthaya in 1760, a siege gun positioned here burst, mortally wounding their king and prompting their retreat; out of superstition, they left the temple standing when they came back to devastate the city in 1767.

The main **bot**, built in 1503, shows the distinctive features of Ayutthayan architecture: outside columns topped with lotus cups, and slits in the walls instead of windows to let the wind pass through. Inside, underneath a rich red and gold coffered ceiling representing the stars around the moon, sits a powerful six-metre-high Buddha in the disdainful, overdecorated royal style characteristic of the later Ayutthaya period.

In sharp contrast is the dark green **Phra Khan Thavaraj** Buddha which dominates the tiny viharn behind to the right. Seated in the "European position", with its robe delicately pleated and its feet up on a large lotus leaf, the gentle figure conveys a reassuring serenity. It's advertised as being from Sri Lanka, the source of Thai Buddhism, but is more likely to be a Mon image from Wat Phra Mane at Nakhon Pathom, dating from the seventh to ninth centuries.

Wat Phu Khao Thong

Head 2km northwest of Wat Na Phra Mane and you're in open country, where the fifty-metre chedi of **Wat Phu Khao Thong** rises steeply out of the fields. In 1569, after a temporary occupation of Ayutthaya, the Burmese erected a Mon-style chedi here to commemorate their victory. Forbidden by Buddhist law from pulling down a sacred monument, the Thais had to put up with this

△ Statue of King Naresuan, Ayutthaya

galling reminder of the enemy's success until it collapsed nearly two hundred years later, when King Borommakot promptly built a truly Ayutthayan chedi on the old Burmese base – just in time for the Burmese to return in 1767 and flatten the town. This "Golden Mount" has recently been restored and painted toothpaste-white, with a colossal equestrian statue of King Naresuan, conqueror of the Burmese, to keep it company. You can climb 25m of steps up the side of the chedi to look out over the countryside and the town, with glimpses of Wat Phra Si Sanphet and Viharn Phra Mongkol Bopit in the distance. In 1956, to celebrate 2500 years of Buddhism, the government placed on the tip of the spire a ball of solid gold weighing 2500g, of which there is now no trace.

Wat Yai Chai Mongkol

To the southeast of the island, if you cross the suspension bridge over the Pasak River and the rail line, then turn right at the major roundabout, you'll pass through Ayutthaya's new business zone and some rustic suburbia before reaching the ancient but still functioning **Wat Yai Chai Mongkol**, about 2km from the bridge (daily 8am–5pm; B20). Surrounded by formal lawns and flower beds, the wat was established by Ramathibodi I in 1357 as a meditation site for monks returning from study in Sri Lanka. King Naresuan put up the celebrated **chedi** to mark the decisive victory over the Burmese at Suphanburi in 1593, when he himself had sent the enemy packing by slaying the Burmese crown prince in a duel. Built on a colossal scale to outshine the huge Burmese-built chedi of Wat Phu Khao Thong on the northwest side of Ayutthaya, the chedi has come to symbolize the prowess and devotion of Naresuan and, by implication, his descendants down to the present king. By the entrance, a **reclining Buddha**, now gleamingly restored in toothpaste white, was also constructed by Naresuan.

Wat Phanan Choeng

In Ayutthaya's most prosperous period the docks and main trading area were located near the confluence of the Chao Phraya and Pasak rivers, to the west of Wat Yai Chai Mongkol. This is where you'll find the oldest and liveliest working temple in town, **Wat Phanan Choeng** (daily 8am–5pm; B20). The main viharn is often filled with the sights, sounds and smells of an incredible variety of merit-making activities, as devotees burn huge pink Chinese incense candles, offer food and rattle fortune sticks. It's even possible to buy tiny golden statues of the Buddha to be placed in one of the hundreds of niches which line the walls, a form of votive offering peculiar to this temple. If you can get here during a festival, especially Chinese New Year, you're in for an overpowering experience.

The nineteen-metre-high Buddha, which almost fills the hall, has survived since 1324, shortly before the founding of the capital, and tears are said to have flowed from its eyes when Ayutthaya was sacked by the Burmese. However, the reason for the temple's popularity with the Chinese is to be found in the early eighteenth-century shrine by the pier, with its image of a beautiful Chinese princess who drowned herself here because of the infidelity of the local ruler to whom she was betrothed: his remorse led him to build the shrine at the place where she had walked into the river.

Accommodation and eating

Although Ayutthaya is usually visited on a day-trip, for those who want to make a little more of it there is a good choice of **accommodation**. Many of the budget guest houses are ghettoized on an unnamed lane, running north from Chao Phrom market to Thanon Pamaphrao, which has earned the ironic nickname "Little Khao San Road". For details of the accommodation price codes used in the listings below, see p.167.

Ayutthaya Guest House 12/34 Thanon Naresuan ☎035 232658, ✉ayutthaya_guesthouse@yahoo.com. Large, modern, friendly establishment, with all manner of useful services including Internet access, bike and motorbike rental, and minibuses and tours to Kanchanaburi. Accommodation is in clean, wooden-floored rooms with hot showers available, either shared or en suite, fan-cooled or air-con. ❶–❸

Baan Lotus Guest House Thanon Pamaphrao ☎035 251988. Large, tranquil traditional house with polished teak floorboards and balconies, at the end of a long garden with a lotus pond at the back; rooms are clean, simple and en suite. ❷

Bann Kun Pra Thanon U Thong, just north of Pridi Damrong Bridge ☎035 241978, ⓦwww.bannkunpra.com. Airy, attractive rooms spread across two buildings: a rambling, hundred-year-old riverside teak house with a large, comfy chillout terrace, where some rooms have river-view balconies; and a newer block near the road, where all rooms have en-suite cold-water bathrooms and some have air-con; all have access to smart, shared, hot showers. Internet access, bike rental, healthy breakfasts and a warm welcome. Fan ❸, air-con ❺, dorms B250.

Chantana House 12/22 Thanon Naresuan ☎035 323200 or 089 885 0257, ✉chantanahouse@yahoo.com. Smart, welcoming guest house in an attractive building with garden, opposite *Ayutthaya Guest House*. Its large, spotlessly clean, en-suite rooms come with hot water and either fan or air-con. Fan ❸, air-con ❹

Krung Sri River 27/2 Moo 11, Thanon Rojana ☎035 244333–7, ⓦwww .krungsririver.com. Luxury hotel with swanky lobby, gym and attractive pool, occupying a prime, but noisy, position at the eastern end of the Pridi Damrong Bridge. ❼

Eating

The main travellers' hangout in the evening is the small, laid-back *Moon Café* on the same lane as the *Ayutthaya Guest House*, which has regular live music and serves good Western and Thai **food**; under the same ownership, *Street Lamp* across the road is a congenial restaurant, with good espressos and Internet access. Many riverside restaurants in Ayutthaya are slightly expensive and disappointing; a worthy exception is the atmospheric terrace at *Bann Kun Pra* (see above), which specializes in reasonably priced fish and seafood, notably prawns. Around the central ruins, your best bet is *Malakor*, a simple, wooden house with covered balconies on Thanon Chaikun, offering tasty Thai and Western food and views of Wat Ratburana (floodlit at night). On the road between Wat Yai Chai Mongkol and Wat Phanan Choeng, *Thai House* serves a huge variety of excellent Thai food, including delicious deep-fried banana flowers, and a choice of Thai desserts; prices are reasonable and tables are arrayed around several stilted, wooden, traditional-style houses.

Nakhon Pathom

NAKHON PATHOM is probably Thailand's oldest town, and is thought to be the point at which Buddhism first entered the region over two thousand years ago. The modern city's star attraction is the enormous Phra Pathom Chedi, an imposing stupa that dominates the skyline from every direction; everything described below is within ten minutes' walk of this landmark.

The town is 56km west of Bangkok and easily reached from the capital by train or bus.

Phra Pathom Chedi

Measuring a phenomenal 120m high, **Phra Pathom Chedi** (daily dawn–dusk; B20) stands as tall as St Paul's Cathedral in London, and is a popular place of

△ Phra Pathom Chedi, Nakhon Pathom

pilgrimage for Thais from all parts of the kingdom. Although the Buddha never actually came to Thailand, legend has it that he rested here after wandering the country, and the original 39-metre-high Indian-style chedi may have been erected to commemorate this. Since then, the chedi has been rebuilt twice; its earliest fragments are entombed within the later layers, and its origin has become indistinguishable from folklore.

Approaching the chedi from the main (northern) staircase, you're greeted by the eight-metre-high Buddha image known as **Phra Ruang Rojanarit**, standing in front of the north viharn. Each of the viharns – there's one at each of the cardinal points – has an inner and an outer chamber containing tableaux of the life of the Buddha. Proceeding clockwise around the monument – as is the custom at all Buddhist chedis – you can weave between the outer promenade and the inner cloister via ornate doors that punctuate the dividing wall; the promenade is dotted with trees, many of which have religious significance, such as the **bodhi tree** (*ficus religiosa*) under which the Buddha was meditating when he achieved enlightenment.

The museums

There are two museums within the chedi compound and, confusingly, they have similar names. The newer, more formal setup, the **Phra Pathom Chedi National Museum** (Wed–Sun 9am–noon & 1–4pm; B30; Ⓦ www.thailandmuseum.com), is clearly signposted from the bottom of the chedi's south staircase. It displays a good collection of Dvaravati-era (sixth to eleventh centuries) artefacts excavated nearby, including Wheels of Law – an emblem introduced by Theravada Buddhists before naturalistic images were permitted – and Buddha statuary with the U-shaped robe and thick facial features characteristic of Dvaravati sculpture. More a curiosity shop than a museum, the **Phra Pathom Chedi Museum** (Wed–Sun 9am–noon & 1–4pm; free), halfway up the steps near the east viharn, is an Aladdin's cave of Buddhist amulets, seashells, Chinese ceramics, Thai musical instruments and ancient statues.

Practicalities

Trains leave Bangkok's Hualamphong Station twelve times a day and take about eighty minutes; there are also a couple of trains a day from Bangkok's Thonburi Station (about 1hr). A 200-metre walk south from Nakhon Pathom's train station across the khlong and through the market will get you to the chedi. **Buses** leave Bangkok's Southern Bus Terminal every ten minutes and take about an hour; try to avoid being dumped at Nakhon Pathom's bus terminal, which is about 1km east of the town centre – most buses circle the chedi first, so get off there instead. Buses heading for Kanchanaburi, Damnoen Saduak and Phetchaburi collect passengers from stops outside the police station across the road from the chedi's southern gate, and further west along Thanon Rajvithee, near the *Nakorn Inn Hotel*. Buses bound for Bangkok pick up from Thanon Phaya Pan on the north bank of the khlong, across from the *Mitpaisal Hotel*.

You can **change money** at the exchange booth (banking hours only) on Thanon Phaya Pan, beside the bridge over the khlong, one block south of the train station; several nearby banks also have ATMs.

For **accommodation**, the *Mitpaisal Hotel*, less than 200m from the chedi's north gateway (Ⓣ 034 242422, Ⓔ mitpaisal@hotmail.com; ❷–❸), offers large, en-suite fan and air-con rooms; the hotel has one entrance just to the right of the train station exit, and another across from the north bank of the khlong (near the stop for buses to Bangkok), at 120/30 Thanon Phaya Pan. *Nakorn*

Inn Hotel (☎034 251152, ☎034 254998; ❸) on Thanon Rajvithee Soi 3, a few hundred metres from the southwest corner of the chedi compound, is the town's best hotel and offers decent air-con rooms.

For inexpensive Thai and Chinese **food** head for any of the restaurants along the eastern arm of Thanon Phraya Gong, which runs along the south (chedi) side of the canal; the place with the "Thai Food" sign is used to serving foreigners. Or try one of the garden restaurants along Thanon Rajdamnoen, which runs west from the chedi's west gate. Night-time foodstalls on Thanon Rajvithee are another good bet, and during the day the market in front of the station serves the usual takeaway goodies, including reputedly the tastiest *khao laam* (bamboo cylinders filled with steamed rice and coconut) in Thailand.

Damnoen Saduak floating markets

To get an idea of what shopping in Bangkok used to be like before all the canals were concreted over, many people take an early-morning trip to the **floating markets** (*talat khlong*) of **DAMNOEN SADUAK**, 109km southwest of Bangkok. Vineyards and orchards here back onto a labyrinth of narrow canals, and every morning between 6 and 11am local market gardeners ply these waterways in paddle boats full of fresh fruit and vegetables, and tourist-tempting soft drinks and souvenirs. As most of the vendors dress in the deep-blue jacket and high-topped straw hat traditionally favoured by Thai farmers, it's all richly atmospheric, but the setup feels increasingly manufactured, and some visitors have complained of seeing more tourists than vendors, however early they arrive.

The target for most tourists is the main **Talat Khlong Ton Kem**, 2km west of Damnoen Saduak's tiny town centre at the intersection of Khlong Damnoen Saduak and Khlong Thong Lang. Many of the wooden houses here have been converted into warehouse-style souvenir shops and tourist restaurants, diverting trade away from the khlong vendors and into the hands of large commercial enterprises. But, for the moment at least, a semblance of the traditional water trade continues, and the two bridges between Ton Kem and **Talat Khlong Hia Kui** (a little further south down Khlong Thong Lang) make decent vantage points. Touts invariably congregate at the Ton Kem pier to hassle you into taking a **boat trip** around the khlong network (asking an hourly rate of around B150–200 per person), but there are distinct disadvantages in being propelled between markets at top speed in a noisy motorized boat. For a less hectic and more sensitive look at the markets, explore via the walkways beside the canals.

Practicalities

To reach the market in good time you have to catch one of the earliest **buses** from Bangkok's Southern Bus Terminal (from 6am; 2hr 30min). Or join one of the numerous half- or full-day trips (from B250, or B360 including Nakhon Pathom and the River Kwai). Damnoen Saduak's bus terminal is just north of Thanarat Bridge and Khlong Damnoen Saduak, on the main Bangkok/Nakhon Pathom–Samut Songkhram road, Highway 325. Frequent yellow **songthaews** (pickup buses) cover the 2km to Ton Kem, but walk if you've got the time: a walkway follows the canal, which you can get to from Thanarat Bridge, or you can cross the bridge and take the road to the right (west), Thanon Sukhaphiban 1, through the orchards. Drivers on the earliest buses from Bangkok sometimes do not terminate at the bus station but instead cross Thanarat Bridge and then drop tourists at a pier a few hundred metres along Thanon Sukhaphiban 1.

The best way to see the markets is to stay overnight in Damnoen Saduak and get up at dawn, well before the buses and coach tours from Bangkok arrive. There's decent budget **accommodation** at the *Little Bird Hotel*, also known as *Noknoi* (☎032 254382; ❷–❸), whose sign is clearly visible from the main road and Thanarat Bridge. Rooms here are good value: enormous, clean and all with en-suite bathrooms, and there's air-con if you want it. The staff at *Little Bird* can also arrange floating market boat trips.

Samut Songkhram and Amphawa

Rarely visited by foreign tourists and yet within easy reach of Bangkok, the tiny estuarine province of **Samut Songkhram** is nourished by the Mae Khlong River as it meanders through on the last leg of its route to the Gulf. Fishing is an important industry round here, as is market gardening, but for visitors it is the network of three hundred canals woven around the river, and the traditional way of life the waterways still support, that is most intriguing. As well as some of the most genuine floating markets in Thailand, there are chances to witness traditional cottage industries such as palm-sugar production and *bencharong* ceramic painting, plus more than a hundred historic temples to admire, a number of them dating back to the reign of Rama II, who was born in the province. The other famous sons of the region are Eng and Chang, the "original" Siamese twins (see box on p.102), who grew up in Samut Songkhram and are commemorated at the tiny In-Chan Museum (Mon–Fri 8.30am–4.30pm; free), 4km north of the town centre on Thanon Ekachai (Route 3092).

If you're dependent on public transport, your first stop will be the provincial capital of Samut Songkhram, also commonly known as **Mae Khlong**, after the river that cuts through it, but there's little reason to linger here as the sights and most of the accommodation are out of town, mainly in the **Amphawa** district a few kilometres upriver.

Amphawa

The district town of **Amphawa** retains much traditional charm alongside its modern development. Its old neighbourhoods hug the banks of the Mae Khlong River and the Khlong Amphawa tributary, the wooden homes and shops facing the water and accessed either by boat or on foot along one of the waterfront walkways. Frequent songthaews (pickup buses) and local buses (both approximately every 30min; 15min) connect Samut Songkhram market with Amphawa market, which sets up beside the khlong, just back from its confluence with the river.

King Rama II Memorial Park and Wat Amphawan

King Rama II was born in Amphawa (his mother's home town) in 1767 and is honoured with a memorial park and temple erected on the site of his probable birthplace, beside the Mae Khlong River on the western edge of Amphawa town, five-minutes' walk west of Amphawa market and khlong. It's accessible both by boat and by road, 6km from Samut Songkhram on the Amphawa–Bang Khonthi road.

Rama II, or Phra Buddhalertla Naphalai as he is known in Thai, was a famously cultured king and a respected poet and playwright, and the **museum** (Wed–Sun 9am–4pm; B10) at the heart of the **King Rama II Memorial Park** (daily 9am–6pm) displays lots of rather esoteric Rama II memorabilia, including a big collection of nineteenth-century musical instruments and a gallery of *khon* masks used in traditional theatre. On the edge of the park, **Wat Amphawan** is graced with a statue of the king and decorated with murals that depict scenes from his life, including a behind-the-altar panorama of nineteenth-century Bangkok, with Ratanakosin Island's Grand Palace, Wat Pho and Sanam Luang still recognizable to modern eyes.

Wat Chulamani and Ban Pinsuwan bencharong workshop

The canalside **Wat Chulamani** was until the late 1980s the domain of the locally famous abbot Luang Pho Nuang, a man believed by many to be able to perform miracles, and followers still come to the temple to pay respects to his body, which is preserved in a glass-sided coffin in the main viharn. The breathtakingly detailed decor inside the viharn is testament to the devotion he inspired: the intricate black-and-gold lacquered artwork that covers every surface has taken years and cost millions of baht to complete. Across the temple compound, the bot's modern, pastel-toned murals tell the story of the Buddha's life, beginning inside the door on the right with a scene showing the young Buddha emerging from a tent (his birth) and being able to walk on lilypads straightaway. The death of the Buddha and his entry into nirvana is depicted on the wall behind the altar. Wat Chulamani is located beside Khlong Amphawa, a twenty-minute walk east of Amphawa market, or a five-minute boat-ride. It is also signed off Highway 325, so any bus going to Damnoen Saduak from Samut Songkhram will drop you within reach.

A few hundred metres down the road from Wat Chulamani, and also accessible on foot, by bus and by canal, the Ban Pinsuwan **bencharong workshop** specializes in reproductions of famous antique *bencharong* ceramics, the exquisite five-coloured pottery that used to be the tableware of choice for the Thai aristocracy and is now a prized collector's item. A *bencharong* museum, exhibiting the chronology of styles, is planned.

Tha Ka Floating Market and the palm-sugar centres

Unlike at the over-touristed markets of nearby Damnoen Saduak, the **floating market at Tha Ka** is still the province of local residents, with market gardeners either paddling up here in their small wooden sampans, or motoring along in their noisy longtails, the boats piled high with whatever is in season, be it pomelos or betel nuts, rambutans or okra, or with perennially popular snacks like hot noodle soup and freshly cooked satay. The Tha Ka market operates only six times a month, on a **timetable** that's dependent on the tides (for boat access) and is therefore dictated by the moon; thus market days are restricted to the second, seventh and twelfth mornings of every fifteen-day lunar cycle, from around 7am to 11am (contact any TAT office for exact dates). The market takes place on Khlong Phanla in the village of Ban Tha Ka, a half-hour **boat ride** from Amphawa's *Baan Tai Had Resort*, or about an hour from Damnoen Saduak; it's usually incorporated into a day-trip (about B200 per person). The boat ride to the market is half the fun, but you can also get there by **road**, following Highway 325 out of Samut Songkhram for 10km, then taking a five-kilometre access road to Ban Tha Ka.

Most boat trips to Tha Ka also make a stop at one of the nearby **palm-sugar-making centres**. The sap of the coconut palm is a crucial ingredient in many Thai sweets and the fertile soil of Samut Songkhram province supports many small-scale sugar-palm plantations. There are several palm-sugar cottage industries between Amphawa and Ban Tha Ka, off Highway 325, accessible by car, by Damnoen Saduak-bound bus or by longtail boat.

Practicalities

The traditional way of travelling to Samut Songkhram from Bangkok – by **train** – is still the most scenic, albeit rather convoluted. It's a very unusual line, being single track and for much of its route literally squeezed in between homes, palms and mangroves, and, most memorably, between market stalls, so that at both the Samut Sakhon and Samut Songkhram termini the train really does chug to a standstill amidst the trays of seafood. Trains leave from tiny Wongwian Yai station, just south of the Wongwian Yai roundabout on Thanon Somdet Phra Chao Taksin in southern Thonburi (take non-air-con bus #6 from Ratchadamnoen Klang in Banglamphu to the roundabout, or travel on the cross-river ferry from River City to Khlong San and then walk) and arrive in **Samut Sakhon**, also known as **Mahachai**, about an hour later (approximately hourly, but for the fastest onward connections catch the 5.30am, 8.35am, 12.15pm or 3.25pm). At Samut Sakhon you take a ferry across the Tha Chin River (there's no rail bridge) and then wait for the departure of the connecting train from **Ban Laem** on the other bank to Samut Songkhram at the end of the line (4 daily; 1hr). The **bus** ride to Samut Songkhram from Bangkok's Southern Bus Terminal (every 20min; 1hr 30min) is faster, but the views are dominated by urban sprawl. Buses also run direct to **Amphawa** from Bangkok's Southern Bus Terminal (every 20min; 2hr).

Once in Samut Songkhram, you have various options for getting around, though the public transport network is limited and doesn't encompass all the sights. **Taxi-boats** and other chartered river transport operate from the Mae Khlong River pier, which is close to the train station and market in the town centre. **Songthaews** to Amphawa and **local buses** to Amphawa and Damnoen Saduak, via Highway 325, leave from the central market, between the train and bus stations. A big part of this area's appeal is that it's best explored by boat, most rewardingly on a **tour** from *Baan Tai Had Resort* (B150–200 per person), though it's also possible to charter a boat from the town-centre pier in Samut Songkhram. Independent exploration is possible if you have your own vehicle, and *Baan Tai Had* rents out bicycles, kayaks and jetskis. Alternatively, you could join a one-day **cycling tour** from Bangkok: both Spice Roads (☏02 712 5305, ⓦwww.spiceroads.com) and Bike and Travel (☏02 990 0274, ⓦwww.cyclingthailand.com) run day-trips to Amphawa from the capital, with minibus transport from Bangkok and bicycle rental included in the US$50 price.

With its contemporary, comfortable **bungalows** set around a Bali-style garden, swimming pool and restaurant, luxurious but good-value *Baan Tai Had Resort* (☏034 767220, ⓦwww.hotelthailand.com/samutsongkram/baantaihad; ⑥) makes a great escape from Bangkok, not least because of its local tour programmes and English-speaking guides. It's located beside the Mae Khlong River in the Amphawa district, about 6km upstream from Samut Songkhram; taxi-boats from Samut Songkhram's pier cost B60 and take about fifteen minutes. There's cheaper fan and air-con accommodation in Samut Songkhram town centre, at the welcoming *Maeklong Hotel* (☏034 711150; ❷–❸), about 150m due north of the train station at 526/10-13 Thanon Si Jumpa.

Seafood is the obvious regional speciality and the most famous local dish is *hoi lot pat cha*, a spicy stir-fry that centres on the tubular molluscs – *hoi lot* – that are harvested in their sackloads at low tide from a muddy sandbank known as Don Hoi Lot at the mouth of the Mae Khlong estuary. A dozen restaurants occupy the area around the Don Hoi Lot pier, many offering views out over the gulf and its abundant sandbar; the pier is 5km south of Highway 35 and served by songthaews from Samut Songkhram market. In Samut Songkhram itself, the foodstalls alongside the pier make a pleasant spot for a lunch of cheap seafood *phat thai*.

Phetchaburi

Straddling the Phet River about 120km south of Bangkok, **PHETCHABURI** has long had a reputation as a cultural centre and became a favourite country retreat of Rama IV, who had a hilltop palace built here in the 1850s. Modern Phetchaburi has lost relatively little of the ambience that so attracted the king: the central riverside area is hemmed in by historic wats in varying states of disrepair, and wooden rather than concrete shophouses still line the river bank. Many Bangkok tour operators combine the floating markets of Damnoen Saduak (see p.152) with Phetchaburi as a day-trip package, but the town is also served by frequent buses from the capital.

The Town

The pinnacles and rooftops of the town's thirty-odd wats are visible in every direction, but only a few are worth stopping off to investigate; the following

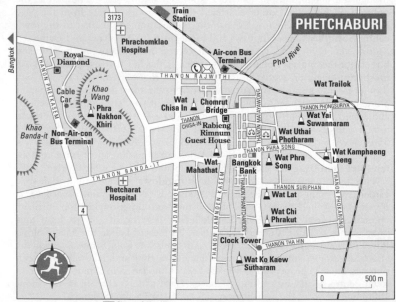

description takes in the three most interesting, and can be done as a leisurely two-hour circular walk beginning from Chomrut Bridge, which is centrally located close to the market, about ten minutes' walk south of the air-con bus terminal. Alternatively, hop on one of the public **songthaews** (pickup buses) that circulate round the town, hire a samlor (cycle rickshaw) or rent a **bicycle** from *Rabieng Rimnum Guest House*.

Wat Yai Suwannaram

Of all Phetchaburi's temples, the most attractive is the still-functioning seventeenth-century **Wat Yai Suwannaram** on Thanon Phongsuriya, about 700m east of Chomrut Bridge. The temple's fine old teak hall has elaborately carved doors and stands near a traditional scripture library built on stilts in the middle of a pond to prevent ants destroying the precious documents.

Across from the pond and hidden behind high whitewashed walls stands the windowless Ayutthayan-style bot. Enter the walled compound from the south and pass through the statue-filled cloisters into the bot itself, which is supported by intricately patterned red and gold pillars and contains a remarkable, if rather faded, set of murals, depicting Indra, Brahma and other lower-ranking divinities ranged in five rows of ascending importance. If you climb the steps in front of the Buddha image seated against the far back wall you'll get a close-up of the left foot, which for some reason was cast with six toes.

Wat Kamphaeng Laeng

Fifteen minutes' walk east and then south of Wat Yai, the five tumbledown prangs of **Wat Kamphaeng Laeng** on Thanon Phra Song mark out Phetchaburi as the probable southernmost outpost of the Khmer empire. Built to enshrine Hindu deities and set out in a cruciform arrangement facing east, the laterite corncob-style prangs were later adapted for Buddhist use, as you can see from the two which now house Buddha images. There has been some attempt to restore a few of the carvings and false balustraded windows, but these days worshippers congregate in the modern whitewashed wat behind these shrines, leaving the atmospheric and appealingly quaint collection of decaying prangs and casuarina topiary to chickens, stray dogs and the occasional tourist.

Wat Mahathat and the market

Continuing west along Thanon Phra Song from Wat Kamphaeng Laeng, across the river, you can see the prangs of Phetchaburi's most fully restored and important temple, **Wat Mahathat**, long before you reach them. The five landmark prangs at its heart are adorned with stucco figures of mythical creatures, though these are nothing compared with those on the roofs of the main viharn and the bot. Instead of tapering off into the usual serpentine *chofa*, the gables are studded with miniature figures of angels and gods, which add an almost mischievous vitality to the place. In a similar vein, a couple of gold-embossed crocodiles snarl above the entrance to the bot, and a caricature carving of a bespectacled man rubs shoulders with mythical giants in a relief around the base of the gold Buddha, housed in a separate mondop nearby.

Leaving Wat Mahathat, it's a five-minute walk north up Thanon Damnoen Kasem to Thanon Phongsuriya and another few minutes east to Chomrut Bridge, but if you have the time, backtrack a little and return via the **market**, which lines Thanon Matayawong and spills over into the alleyways on either side – there are enough stalls selling the locally famous *khanom* (palm-sugar sweets) to make it worth your while. The most famous local speciality is *khanom* *maw kaeng*, a baked sweet egg custard made with mung beans and coconut and sometimes flavoured with lotus seeds, durian or taro.

Khao Wang

Scattered over the crest of the hill known as **Khao Wang**, about thirty minutes' walk from Wat Mahathat on the western outskirts of town, the assorted structures that make up Rama IV's palace are a strange medley of mid-nineteenth-century Thai and European styles. Whenever the king came on an excursion here, he stayed in the airy summerhouse on the summit, **Phra Nakhon Khiri** (daily 9am–4pm; B40, children B10; Ⓦwww.thailandmuseum.com), with its Mediterranean-style shutters and verandas. Now a museum, it houses a moderately interesting collection of ceramics, furniture and other artefacts given to the royal family by foreign friends.

A **cable car** (daily 8.15am–5.15pm; B50, children under 90cm tall go free) runs to the summit from a spot at the base of the western flank of the hill that's just off Highway 4, quite near the non-air-con bus terminal. To get to the base of the hill from the town centre, take a white local songthaew from Thanon Phongsuriya and ask for Khao Wang. If you want to walk to the summit, get off as soon as you see the pathway on the eastern flank of the hill, just across from the junction with Thanon Rajwithi; for the cable car, stay put until you've passed the last of the souvenir stalls on Highway 4, then walk south about 700m.

Practicalities

Air-con **buses** from Bangkok's Southern Bus Terminal (every 30min; 2hr) arrive at Phetchaburi's air-con bus terminal just off Thanon Rajwithi, from where it's about ten minutes' walk south to the town centre and Chomrut Bridge. The main station for non-air-con buses is on the southwest edge of Khao Wang, about thirty minutes' walk or a ten-minute songthaew ride from the town centre. Ten **trains** a day run from Bangkok's Hualamphong Station (about 3hr) to Phetchaburi train station, which is on the northern outskirts of town, not far from Khao Wang, but about 1500m from the town centre.

There is no TAT office in town, but *Rabieng Rimnum Guest House* is a good source of local **information**. The branch of Bangkok Bank 150m east of Wat Mahathat on Thanon Phra Song does **currency exchange** and has an ATM.

Phetchaburi's plushest **accommodation** is the *Royal Diamond* (Ⓣ032 411061, Ⓦwww.royaldiamondhotel.com; ❺), which has comfortable air-con rooms and is located west of Khao Wang, on the outskirts of town, on Soi Sam Chao Phet, which is just off the Phetkasem Highway. Most travellers, however, stay at the *Rabieng Rimnum (Rim Nam) Guest House*, centrally located at 1 Thanon Chisa-in, on the southwest corner of Chomrut Bridge (Ⓣ032 425707; ❷). Occupying a century-old house next to the Phet River, it has nine simple rooms with shared bathrooms and the best restaurant in town, boasting an interesting menu of inexpensive Thai dishes, from banana blossom salad to spicy crab soup.

Kanchanaburi and the River Kwai

Set in a landscape of limestone hills 121km northwest of Bangkok, **KANCHANABURI** is most famous as the location of the Bridge over the

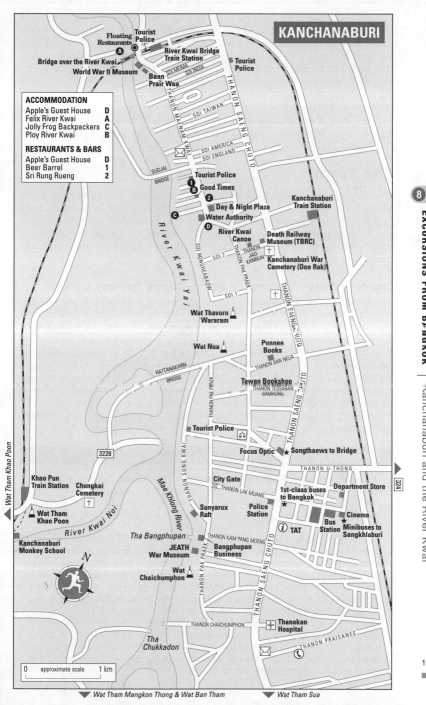

KANCHANABURI

Floating Restaurants
Tourist Police
Bridge over the River Kwai
River Kwai Bridge Train Station
Tourist Police
World War II Museum
Baan Prair Waa
SOI MEIMA
SOI INDIA
THANON MAENAM KWAI
SOI TAIWAN
THANON SAENG CHUTO

ACCOMMODATION
Apple's Guest House	D
Felix River Kwai	A
Jolly Frog Backpackers	C
Ploy River Kwai	B

RESTAURANTS & BARS
Apple's Guest House	D
Beer Barrel	1
Sri Rung Rueng	2

SOI AMERICA
SOI ENGLAND
SUDJAI BRIDGE
Tourist Police
Good Times
Day & Night Plaza
Water Authority
River Kwai Canoe
Kanchanaburi Train Station
Death Railway Museum (TBRC)
Kanchanaburi War Cemetery (Don Rak)
River Kwai Yai
SOI PONGHEABKON
SOI 2
THANON JAO KANNUN
THANON PAK PRAEK
SOI 1
Wat Thavorn Wararam
Wat Nua
Punnee Books
THANON BAN NEUA
THANON SAENG CHUTO
Tawan Bookshop
THANON TESSABAN BAMHUNG
RATTANAKARN BRIDGE
THANON PAK PRAEK
Tourist Police
Focus Optic
Songthaews to Bridge
3228
THANON U-THONG
324
Khao Pun Train Station
Chungkai Cemetery
City Gate
THANON LAK MUANG
1st-class buses to Bangkok
Department Store
Wat Tham Khao Poon
THANON SONG KWAI
Sunyarux Raft
Police Station
Cinema
Bus Station
Minibuses to Sangkhlaburi
River Kwai Noi
Mae Khlong River
TAT
Kanchanaburi Monkey School
Tha Bangphupan
THANON KAM PANG MOENG
Bangphupan Business
JEATH War Museum
Wat Chaichumphon
THANON PAK PRAEK
N
Tha Chukkadon
THANON CHAICHUMPHON
Thanakan Hospital
THANON PRAISANEE
THANON SAENG CHUTO

0 approximate scale 1 km

159

Wat Tham Mangkon Thong & Wat Ban Tham   Wat Tham Sua

River Kwai. However, it has a lot more to offer, including fine riverine scenery and some moving relics from World War II, when the town served as a POW camp and base for construction work on the notorious Thailand–Burma Death Railway. It's possible to see the Bridge and ride the railway on a day-trip from Bangkok, but if you have the time, the town makes a pleasant spot for an overnight stay; there are many guest houses and hotels prettily set alongside the river, including some with accommodation in raft houses moored beside the river bank. The Bridge forms the dramatic centrepiece of the annual *son-et-lumière* **River Kwai Bridge Festival**, which is held over ten nights from the end of November to commemorate the first Allied bombing of the Bridge on November 28, 1944.

The Town

Strung out along the east bank of the River Kwai and its continuation, as the Mae Khlong River, south of the Kwai Noi confluence, Kanchanaburi is a long, narrow ribbon of a town. The **war sights** are sandwiched between the river and the busy main drag, Thanon Saeng Chuto, with the Bridge over the River Kwai marking the northern limit, and the JEATH War Museum towards the town's southern edge.

Death Railway Museum (Thailand–Burma Railway Centre)

The **Death Railway Museum** (formerly known as the Thailand–Burma Railway Centre; daily 9am–5pm; B60, kids B30; Ⓦ www.tbrconline.com) is the best place to start any tour of Kanchanaburi's World War II memorials. Located on Thanon Jaokannun, across the road from the train station and next to the Don Rak Kanchanaburi War Cemetery, it aims to provide an informed context for the thousands of people who visit the POW graves every week, presenting a sophisticated history of the Death Railway line itself, with the help of original artefacts, illustrations and scale models. The human stories are well documented too, notably via some unique original photographs and video footage shot by Japanese engineers, as well as through interviews with surviving Asian labourers on the railway.

The Death Railway

Shortly after entering World War II in December 1941, Japan began looking for a supply route to connect its newly acquired territories that now stretched from Singapore to the Burma-India border. In spite of the almost impenetrable terrain, the River Kwai basin was chosen as the route for a new 415-kilometre-long **Thailand–Burma Railway**.

About 60,000 Allied POWs were shipped up from captured Southeast Asian territories to work on the link, their numbers later augmented by as many as 200,000 conscripted Asian labourers. Work began at both ends in June 1942. Three million cubic metres of rock were shifted and 14km of bridges built with little else but picks and shovels, dynamite and pulleys. By the time the line was completed fifteen months later it had more than earned its nickname, the **Death Railway**: an estimated 16,000 POWs and 100,000 Asian labourers died while working on it.

Food rations were completely inadequate for men forced into backbreaking eighteen-hour shifts, often followed by night-long marches to the next camp. Many suffered from beri-beri, many more died of dysentery-induced starvation, but the biggest killers were cholera and malaria, particularly during the monsoon. It is said that one man died for every sleeper laid on the track.

Kanchanaburi War Cemetery (Don Rak)

Many of the Allied POWs who died during the construction of the Thailand–Burma Railway are buried in the **Kanchanaburi War Cemetery**, also called **Don Rak** (daily 8am–4pm; free), opposite the train station on Thanon Saeng Chuto. The 6982 POW graves are laid out in straight lines amid immaculate lawns and flowering shrubs. Many of the identical stone memorial slabs state simply "A man who died for his country" – at the upcountry camps, bodies were thrown onto mass funeral pyres, making identification impossible. Others, inscribed with names, dates and regiments, indicate that the overwhelming majority of the dead were under 25 years old.

The Bridge over the River Kwai

For many people the plain steel arches of the **Bridge over the River Kwai** come as a disappointment: lacks drama and looks nothing like as hard to construct as it does in David Lean's famous 1957 film *Bridge on the River Kwai* (which was in fact shot in Sri Lanka). But it is the film, of course, that draws tour buses here by the dozen, and makes the Bridge approach seethe with trinket-sellers and touts. To get here, either take any songthaew heading north up Thanon Saeng Chuto and then walk the 850m from the junction, hire a samlor (cycle rickshaw), or cycle – it's 5km from the bus station.

The fording of the Kwai Yai at this point was one of the first major obstacles in the construction of the Thailand–Burma Railway. Sections of a steel bridge were brought up from Java and reassembled by POWs using only pulleys and derricks. A temporary **wooden bridge** was built alongside it, taking its first train in February 1943; three months later the steel bridge was finished. Both bridges were severely damaged by Allied bombers (rather than commando-saboteurs as in the film) in 1944 and 1945, but the steel bridge was repaired after the war and is still in use today. In fact the best way to see the Bridge is by taking the **train** over it: the Kanchanaburi Nam Tok train crosses it three times a day in each direction, stopping briefly at the River Kwai Bridge station on the

△ The Bridge over the River Kwai

east bank of the river (see below for details); or you can take the yellow **tourist tram** that shuttles the 1km back and forth across the Bridge (daily 8–10am & 12–2pm; 15min return; B20 return), departing from River Kwai Bridge station. You can also walk over the Bridge to the souvenir stalls on the west bank.

World War II Museum

Not to be confused with the original JEATH War Museum, the **World War II Museum** (daily 8am–6pm; B30), 30m south of the Bridge on Thanon Maenam Kwai, is a privately owned collection of inappropriately juxtaposed curiosities that lack the human interest of the town's other museums. The war section comprises a mixture of memorabilia (a rusted bombshell, the carpet used by the local Japanese commander) and reconstructed tableaux featuring emaciated POWs, while other displays include stamp and banknote collections and a gallery of selected "Miss Thailand" portraits from 1934 onwards.

JEATH War Museum

Founded by the chief abbot of Wat Chaichumpon and housed within the temple grounds in a reconstructed Allied POW hut of thatched palm, the ramshackle and unashamedly low-tech **JEATH War Museum** (daily 8.30am–6pm; B30) was the town's first public repository for the photographs, letters and memorabilia of the POWs who worked on the Death Railway. These items are now rather faded and seem poorly presented when compared to the slicker, more informative exhibitions at the Death Railway Museum, but the JEATH Museum is still an inevitable stop on any organized tour of the town. JEATH is an acronym of six of the countries involved in the railway: Japan, England, Australia, America, Thailand and Holland. The museum is located beside the Mae Khlong on Thanon Pak Praek, at the southern end of town. It's about 700m from the TAT office, or 5km from the Bridge.

Riding the Death Railway

The two-hour rail journey along the notorious Thailand–Burma **Death Railway** from Kanchanaburi to Nam Tok is one of Thailand's most scenic. Leaving Kanchanaburi via the Bridge over the River Kwai, the train chugs through the Kwai Noi valley, stopping frequently at pretty flower-decked country stations.

The most hair-raising section of track begins shortly after Tha Kilen at **Wang Sing**, also known as Arrow Hill, when the train squeezes through thirty-metre solid rock cuttings, dug at the cost of numerous POW lives. Six kilometres further, it slows to a crawl at the approach to the **Wang Po viaduct**, where a 300-metre-long trestle bridge clings to the cliff face as it curves with the Kwai Noi – almost every man who worked on this part of the railway died. Half an hour later, the train reaches its terminus at the small town of **Nam Tok**.

There are three **Kanchanaburi–Nam Tok trains** daily in both directions (currently departing Kanchanaburi at 6.07am, 10.30am and 4.30pm and returning from Nam Tok at 5.25am, 1pm and 3.15pm), so a day return is feasible; Kanchanaburi TAT has timetables. Many Kanchanaburi tour operators offer a day-trip that includes other war sights and waterfalls as well as a ride on the railway. Though it's possible to do the **Bangkok–Kanchanaburi–Nam Tok round trip** in one day, bear in mind that this leaves no time for exploring, and that only third class, hard seats are available. The 7.45am train from Bangkok's Thonburi station arrives in Nam Tok at 12.40pm, then departs for Bangkok at 1pm, returning to the capital at 5.40pm.

Practicalities

The most enjoyable way to get to Kanchanaburi is by **train** from Thonburi station in Bangkok (about 2hr 30min) or Nakhon Pathom (about 1hr 30min); they depart from the capital twice a day at approximately 7.45am and 1.50pm, stopping at Nakhon Pathom around 8.45am and 2.55pm. The main Kanchanaburi train station is on Thanon Saeng Chuto, about 2km north of the town centre, but if you're doing a day-trip and want to see the Bridge, get off at River Kwai Bridge train station, five minutes further on. Nonstop air-conditioned **buses** from Bangkok's Southern Bus Terminal are faster (about 2hr) and more frequent (every 15min), arriving at the bus station off Thanon Saeng Chuto. The speediest transport option from Bangkok is to take one of the **tourist minibuses** from Thanon Khao San, which take two hours.

Kanchanaburi is best explored by **bicycle**, since the town measures about 5km from north to south and all the war sights are sandwiched between the River Kwai and the busy Thanon Saeng Chuto. Bikes can be rented for around B30 per day from most guest houses and some tour agents. Alternatively, you can use the orange **public songthaew** (pickup bus) service that runs from outside the Focus Optic optician's on Thanon Saeng Chuto (one block north of the bus station), goes north via the Kanchanaburi War Cemetery, Death Railway Museum, train station and access road to the Bridge (every 15min; 15min to the Bridge turn-off; B8). Failing that, there are plenty of **samlor** (cycle rickshaws) available for hire, or you could charter a **longtail boat** from the Bridge (around B600/two hours).

The **TAT** office (daily 8.30am–4.30pm, ☏034 511200, ✉tatkan@tat.or.th) is on Thanon Saeng Chuto, a few hundred metres south of the bus station. Several banks on Thanon Saeng Chuto have ATMs and offer money changing facilities.

Accommodation

Most people make the most of the inspiring scenery by **staying** on or near the river, in either a raft house or a guest house, though noise from the longtail boats, the bankside bars and the karaoke rafts, which are towed up and down the river until the early hours, can be a problem. Popular options on the riverside include *Jolly Frog Backpackers*, just off the southern end of Thanon Maenam Kwai, the heart of the travellers' area, at 28 Soi China (☏034 514579; **①–②**), which has comfortable en-suite bamboo huts (some with air-con) ranged around a riverside garden plus a few cheaper floating rafts with shared facilities. A short distance inland, at 52 Soi Rongheabaow 3, 朮 *Apple's Guest House* (☏034 512017, ⊛www.applenoi-kanchanaburi.com; **②–④**) is a small, welcoming outfit with twenty spotless en-suite rooms (fan and air-con) set round a lawn. *Ploy River Kwai*, further north up Thanon Maenam Kwai (☏034 515804, ⊛www.ploygh.com; **④–⑤**), offers chic, contemporary-styled air-con rooms, though you only get river views from the restaurant. For riverside luxury, the best option is *Felix River Kwai* (☏034 515061, ⊛www.felixriverkwai.co.th; **⑦–⑧**) which occupies a lovely spot on the west bank of the Kwai Yai within walking distance of the Bridge and has over two hundred large air-con rooms and two swimming pools; reservations are essential for weekends.

Eating and drinking

Among the most popular **places to eat** is the cluster of floating restaurants beside the Bridge, serving authentic if rather pricey seafood to accompany the river views. A cheaper place to enjoy genuine local food is the night market, which sets up at around dusk on Thanon Saeng Chuto in front of the bus station. For more tourist-oriented dishes, head for ⚔ *Apple's Guest House*, 52 Soi Rongheabaow 3, whose exceptionally good mid-priced menu includes mouthwatering meat and veggie *matsaman* curries. Bamboo-roofed *Sri Rung Rueng*, nearby on Thanon Maenam Kwai, is another popular, well-priced spot, offering a huge menu that includes *tom kha*, curries, steaks and cocktails. Across the road, the rustic-styled outdoor beer garden at *Beer Barrel* (nightly from 4pm) makes a pleasant place for an ice-cold draught beer.

Listings

Listings

Accommodation

Bearing in mind Bangkok's appalling traffic jams, you should think carefully about what you want to do in the city before deciding which part of town to stay in: easy access to relevant train networks and river transport can be crucial.

For double rooms under B400, the widest choice lies with the **guest houses** of Banglamphu and the smaller, dingier travellers' ghetto that has grown up around Soi Ngam Duphli, off the south side of Thanon Rama IV. Bangkok guest houses are tailored to the independent traveller's needs and range from cramped, windowless, no-frills crash pads to airier places with private Western-style bathrooms; rooms are generally fan-cooled, though air-conditioning is an increasingly common option. Many Bangkok guest houses offer very good facilities, including cheap cafés, safes or lockers for valuables, luggage storage, Internet access and travel and tour operator desks. They rarely accept bookings unless you pay a cash deposit in advance, though it's often useful to phone ahead and establish whether a place is full already – during peak season (July, Aug and Nov–Feb) you may have difficulty getting a room after noon.

Banglamphu is also starting to cater for the slightly better-off tourist, and you'll find some good mid-priced options along and around its hub, Thanon Khao San. But the majority of the city's **moderate and expensive** rooms are concentrated downtown around Siam Square and Thanon Ploenchit and in the area between Thanon Rama IV and Thanon Charoen Krung (New Road); along Thanon Sukhumvit, where the eastern suburbs start; and to a lesser extent in Chinatown. Air-conditioned rooms with hot-water bathrooms can be had for around B500 in these areas, but for that you're looking at a rather basic cubicle. You'll probably have to pay more like B800 for smart furnishings and a swimming pool.

Accommodation prices

Throughout this guide, accommodation has been categorized according to the **price codes** given below. These categories represent the **minimum** you can expect to pay in the **high season** (roughly July, Aug and Nov–Feb) for a **double room**. If travelling on your own, expect to pay anything between sixty and one hundred percent of the rates quoted for a double room. All top-whack and some mid-range hotels will add **seven percent tax** and a **ten percent service charge** to your bill – the price codes below are based on net rates after taxes have been added.

❶ Under B200
❷ B200–350
❸ B350–500
❹ B500–700
❺ B700–1000
❻ B1000–1500
❼ B1500–2500
❽ B2500–4000
❾ Over B4000

Many hotels offer discounts to customers who book through their own websites, but you can often get even bigger discounts (up to sixty percent off published prices) if you use a commercial online hotel-booking service such as those listed below.

Asia Hotels Ⓦwww.asia-hotels.com
Hotel Thailand Ⓦhotelthailand.com
Passion Asia Ⓦwww.passionasia.com
Sawadee Ⓦwww.sawadee.com
Thai Focus Ⓦwww.thaifocus.com

Bangkok boasts an increasing number of exceptionally stylish **super-deluxe** hotels, many of them designed as intimate, small-scale **boutique** hotels, with chic minimalist decor and excellent facilities that often include a **spa** (see p.207 for more on spas). The cream of this accommodation, with rates starting from B4000, is scenically sited along the banks of the Chao Phraya River, though there are a few top-notch hotels in the downtown area too, which is also where you'll find the best business hotels. Many luxury hotels quote rates in US dollars, though you can always pay in baht.

Many of the expensive hotels listed in this guide offer special deals for **families**, usually allowing one or two under-12s to share their parents' room for free, so long as no extra bedding is required. It's also often possible to cram two adults and two children into the double rooms in inexpensive and mid-priced hotels (as opposed to guest houses), as beds in these places are usually big enough for two. A number of guest houses offer three-person rooms.

For **long-stay accommodation**, the most economical option is usually a room with a bathroom in an apartment building, which is likely to set you back at least B5000 a month. Many foreigners end up living in apartments off Thanon Sukhumvit, around Victory Monument and Pratunam, or on Soi Boonprarop, off Thanon Rajaprarop just north of Pratunam. Visit the Teaching in Thailand website, Ⓦwww.ajarn.com, for links to a room-finder website and tips on living in Bangkok, or try Ⓦwww.sabaai.com for serviced apartments. The *Bangkok Post* (Ⓦwww.bangkokpost.com) carries rental ads in its Thursday property section, as well as online, as does the monthly listings magazine *Metro*; vacancies are also sometimes advertised on the noticeboards in the AUA Language Centre on Thanon Rajdamri.

Banglamphu

Nearly all backpackers head straight for **Banglamphu**, Bangkok's long-established travellers' ghetto and arguably the most enjoyable area to base yourself in the city. Here you'll find the cheapest accommodation and some of the best nightlife in Bangkok, with enough bars, restaurants and shops to keep any visitor happy for a week or more, though some people find this insularity tiresome after just a few hours. It's also within easy reach of the Grand Palace and other major sights in **Ratanakosin** (which has only one, very plush, accommodation option of its own).

The increasingly sophisticated nightlife scene has enticed more moneyed travellers into Banglamphu and a growing number of **Khao San** guest houses are reinventing themselves as good-value mini-hotels boasting chic decor, swimming pools and even views from the windows – a remarkable facelift from the cardboard cells of old. The cheap sleeps are still there though – in the darker corners of Khao San itself, as well as on the smaller, quieter roads off and around it. Rooms overlooking Thanon Khao San are noisy late into the night, and the same is increasingly true of accommodation on parallel **Thanon Ram Bhuttri**, where a plethora of bars keeps the street busy at all hours. Things are a little quieter on the roads that encircle the nearby temple, Wat Chana Songkhram, namely **Soi Ram Bhuttri** and its feeder alley, **Soi Chana Songkhram**; along **Phra Athit**, which runs parallel to the Chao Phraya River and is packed with trendy Thai café-bars and restaurants (and also has a useful express-boat stop, N13); and in the residential alleyways that parallel Thanon Khao San to the south: **Trok Mayom** and **Damnoen Klang Neua**. About ten minutes' walk north from Thanon Khao San, the handful of guest houses scattered amongst the neighbourhood shophouses of the **Thanon Samsen sois** offer a more authentically Thai atmosphere. A further fifteen minutes' walk in the same direction will take you to **Thanon Sri Ayutthaya**, behind the National Library in **Thewes** (a few minutes' walk from express-boat stop N15), the calmest area in Banglamphu, where rooms are larger and guest houses smaller. We've listed only the cream of what's on offer in each small enclave of Banglamphu: if your first choice is full there'll almost certainly be a vacancy somewhere just along the soi, if not right next door. **Theft** is a problem in Banglamphu, particularly at the cheaper guest houses, so don't leave anything valuable in your room and heed the guest houses' notices about padlocks and safety lockers.

Traveller-oriented facilities in Banglamphu are second to none. The **Bangkok Information Centre is on Thanon Phra Athit** (see p.27), and there's a **tourist information booth** (Mon–Sat 9am–5pm) in front of Wat Chana Songkhram on Thanon Chakrabongse, near the Soi Ram Bhuttri junction (see the lively neighbourhood website Ⓦ www.khaosanroad.com for further useful information and links). Almost every alternate building on Thanon Khao San, Thanon Ram Bhuttri and Soi Ram Bhuttri offers **Internet access**, as do many of the guest houses; intense competition keeps the rates very low (B40/hour or less) and there's an especially enticing cyber lounge, *True*, on Khao San (details on p.42). There are also Catnet Internet terminals (see Basics, p.42) at the Ratchadamnoen Post Office. As well as numerous money **exchange** places on Thanon Khao San, you'll find two branches of national banks, several ATMs, an outlet for Boots the Chemist and a couple of self-service **laundries**; at the Wearever laundromat on Thanon Samsen, between sois 1 and 3, you can also lounge on sofas, drink coffee, and enjoy free wi-fi acess. Several places will download your digital pictures on to a CD. Banglamphu is well served by **public transport**, details of which can be found in the box on p.78. Banglamphu accommodation is marked on the **map** on p.80.

Thanon Khao San, Thanon Ram Bhuttri and Soi Damnoen Klang Neua

🏃 **Buddy Lodge** 265 Thanon Khao San ☏ 02 629 4477, Ⓦ www.buddylodge.com. The most stylish and expensive hotel on Khao San and right in the thick of the action. The charming, colonial-style rooms are done out in cream, with louvred shutters, balconies, air-con and polished dark-wood floors, though they are not as pristine as you might

expect for the price. There's a beautiful rooftop pool, a spa (see p.209), and several bars and restaurants downstairs in the Buddy Village complex. Specify an upper-floor location away from Khao San to ensure a quieter night's sleep. ⓐ

Chart Guest House 62 Thanon Khao San ☏ 02 282 0171, Ⓔ chartguesthouse@hotmail.com. Clean, comfortable enough hotel in the heart of the road; the cheapest rooms have no view and share a bathroom; the priciest have air-con and windows. Rooms in all categories are no-frills and a little cramped. Fan ❷, fan and bathroom ❸, air-con ❹

Ch II 85 Soi Damnoen Klang Neua ☎02 282 1596. Shabby but cheap rooms, some with windows and some en suite, in a fairly quiet location, though you may be woken by the 5am prayer calls at the local mosque. There are only a couple of other guest houses on this road, so it has a local feel to it, even though Khao San is less than 200m away. Fan ❶, fan and bathroom ❷

D & D Inn 68–70 Thanon Khao San ☎02 629 0526, ⓦ www.khaosanby.com. The delightful rooftop pool, with expansive views, is the clincher at this good-value, mid-sized hotel located in the midst of the throng. Rooms all have air-con and satellite TV and are comfortably furnished and perfectly fine, if not immaculate. The cheapest single rooms have no window. ❺

Khao San Palace Hotel 139 Thanon Khao San ☎02 282 0578. Clean and well-appointed hotel with a rooftop pool. All rooms have bathrooms and windows and some also have air-con and TV. The best rooms are in the new wing – they're nicely tiled and some have panoramic views. Fan ❸, air-con ❸–❹

Lek House 125 Thanon Khao San ☎02 281 8441. Classic old-style Khao San guest house, with 20 small, basic rooms and shared facilities, but less shabby than many others in the same price bracket and a lot friendlier than most. Could get noisy at night as it's right next to the popular *Silk Bar*. ❷

New Joe Guesthouse 81 Trok Mayom ☎02 281 2948, ⓦ www.newjoe.com. Very basic rooms in a block just behind Khao San, but they all have fans and private bathrooms. ❷

Royal (Ratanakosin) Hotel 2 Thanon Rajdamnoen Klang ☎02 222 9111. Determinedly old-fashioned hotel that's used mainly by older Thai tourists and for conferences. Air-con rooms in the new wing are decent enough if unexciting and there's a pool and a restaurant, but the chief attraction is the location, just a 5min stroll from Sanam Luang (or a further 10min to the Grand Palace) – though getting to Thanon Khao San entails a life-endangering leap across 12 lanes of traffic. Old wing ❻, new wing ❼

Siam Oriental 190 Thanon Khao San ☎02 629 0312, ⓔ siam_oriental@hotmail.com. Small hotel right in the middle of Thanon Khao San, offering spartan but clean rooms,

all with attached bathrooms and most with windows. Some rooms have air-con and a few also have balconies. Fan ❸ air-con ❸–❺

Viengtai Hotel 42 Thanon Ram Bhuttri ☎02 280 5392, ⓦ www.viengtai.co.th. The second best of the options in Banglamphu's upper price bracket, with a good location just a few metres from the shops and restaurants of Thanon Khao San, though street-facing rooms get noise from the burgeoning number of Ram Bhuttri bars. Rooms are a decent size if not especially stylish, they all have air-con and TV, and there's a big pool. ❼

Wally House 189/1–2 Thanon Khao San ☎02 282 7067. Small guest house behind the restaurant and Internet café of the same name, with a range of very cheap, simple rooms, some of them en suite, the nicest of which are in a big, old, wooden-floored teak house set back from Khao San above a small courtyard. Fan ❶, fan and bathroom ❷

Soi Ram Bhuttri, Soi Chana Songkhram and Thanon Phra Athit

Baan Sabai 12 Soi Rong Mai, between Soi Ram Bhuttri and Thanon Chao Fa ☎02 629 1599, ⓔ baansabai@hotmail.com. Built round a courtyard, this large, upbeat, hotel-style guest house has a range of bright, fresh and decent-sized en-suite rooms, some of them air-con, though the cheapest have no windows. Fan ❷, air-con ❹

Bella Bella House Soi Ram Bhuttri ☎02 629 3090. The pale-pink rooms in this guest house are decently priced and some boast lovely views over Wat Chana Songkhram. The cheapest share bathrooms, and the most expensive have air-con. Fan ❷, air-con ❸

Lamphu House 75 Soi Ram Bhuttri ☎02 629 5861, ⓦ www.lamphuhouse.com. With smart bamboo beds, coconut-wood clothes rails and elegant rattan lamps in even its cheapest rooms, this travellers' hotel has a cheery, modern feel. Cheapest rooms share facilities and have no outside view; the pricier ones have air-con and balconies overlooking the courtyard. Fan ❷, fan and bathroom ❸, air-con ❹

Merry V Soi Ram Bhuttri ☎02 282 9267. Large, efficiently run guest house offering some of the cheapest accommodation in

Banglamphu. Rooms are basic and small, many share bathrooms and it's pot luck whether you get a window or not. Useful noticeboard in the downstairs restaurant. Fan ❶ fan and bathroom ❸

🏃 **New Siam 2 50 Trok Rong Mai** ☏ 02 282 2795, ⓦ www.newsiamguesthouse.com. Very pleasant and well run small hotel whose en-suite fan and air-con rooms stand out for their thoughtfully designed extras such as in-room safes, cable TV and drying rails on the balconies. Occupies a quiet but convenient location and has a small street-side pool. Popular with families and triple rooms are also available. Fan ❹, air-con ❹

Peachy Guest House 10 Thanon Phra Athit ☏ 02 281 6471. Popular, good value, very cheap place set round a small courtyard, with lots of clean, simple rooms, most with shared bathrooms but some with air-con. Fan and shared bathroom ❶, air-con and shared bathroom ❷, air-con and bathroom ❸

Rambuttri Village Inn 95 Soi Ram Bhuttri ☏ 02 282 9162, ⓦ www.khaosan-hotels.com. The draw at this otherwise rather characterless six-storey hotel is the good-sized rooftop swimming pool. Rooms are plain and unadorned, either with or without bathroom and air-con, and the plaza out front is full of tailors' shops – and their touts. Book online only, and at least five days ahead. Fan and shared bathroom ❸, air-con and bathroom ❺

Wild Orchid Villa 8 Soi Chana Songkhram ☏ 02 629 4378, ⓔ wild_orchid_villa@hotmail.com. Painted in an appropriately wild colour scheme of lemon, aqua and blackberry, this hotel features some cosily furnished air-con rooms at the top of its price range (though their bathrooms are inconveniently accessed via the balcony), and some much less interesting windowless options, with shared bathrooms, at the bottom end. Has a very pleasant seating area out front. Fan and shared bathroom ❷, air-con and bathroom ❹

Samsen sois, Thewes and the fringes

Backpackers Lodge 85 Soi 14, Thanon Sri Ayutthaya ☏ 02 282 3231. Quiet, family-run place in the peaceful Thewes quarter of north Banglamphu. Just 12 simple partition-walled rooms, all with shared bathroom, and a communal area downstairs. ❷

New World Lodge Hotel Samsen Soi 2 ☏ 02 281 5596, ⓦ www.newworldlodge.com. Friendly, well-run Muslim hotel in an interesting traditional neighbourhood. Rooms are large, smartly outfitted and have air-con, TV and tiny balconies; some have khlong views. There's also a pleasant canalside seating area and café. The cheapest rooms in the much less appealing guest-house wing are shabby and share bathrooms. Guest house ❷, hotel ❻

🏃 **Old Bangkok Inn 609 Thanon Phra Sumen** ☏ 02 629 1785, ⓦ www .oldbangkokinn.com. This chic little boutique guest house has just ten air-con rooms, each of them styled in dark wood, with antique north-Thai partitions and antique Burmese doors, beds and ironwork lamps, plus elegant contemporary-accented bathrooms. All rooms have a PC with free broadband acess and DVD player. Some also have a tiny private garden. Very convenient for the Khlong Saen Saeb canal-boat service and 15min walk from Tha Phra Athit express-boat pier or 10min walk from Khao San. ❽

🏃 **Shanti Lodge 37 Soi 16, Thanon Sri Ayutthaya** ☏ 02 281 2497, ⓦ www .shantilodge.com. Quiet place with an appealingly laid-back, whole-earth vibe and a variety of small but characterful rooms – some have rattan walls, others are decorated with Indian motifs. The cheapest share bathrooms, the most expensive have air-con. Has a very good, predominantly vegetarian restaurant downstairs (see p.185). Fan ❷, fan and bathroom ❸, air-con ❹

Sri Ayutthaya 23/11 Soi 14, Thanon Sri Ayutthaya ☏ 02 282 5942. The most attractive guest house in Thewes, where the good-sized rooms (choose between fan rooms with or without private bathroom and en suites with air-con) are elegantly done out with beautiful wood-panelled walls and polished wood floors. Fan ❸, air-con ❹

Tavee Guest House 83 Soi 14, Thanon Sri Ayutthaya ☏ 02 282 5983. Decent-sized rooms; quiet and friendly and one of the cheaper places in the Thewes quarter. Offers rooms with shared bathroom plus some en-suite ones with air-con. Fan ❷, air-con ❹

Villa 230 Samsen Soi 1 ☏ 02 281 7009. One of Banglamphu's more therapeutic guest houses, in a lovely old Thai home and garden with just ten large rooms, each idiosyncratically furnished in simple, semi-traditional style; bathrooms are shared and rooms are priced according to their size. Just 5min walk from Khao San. ❸–❹

Vimol Guest House 358 Samsen Soi 4 ☎02 281 4615. Old-style, family-run guest house in a quiet but interesting neighbourhood that has just a smattering of other tourist places. The simple, cramped, hardboard-walled rooms are ultra basic and have shared bathrooms but are possibly the cheapest in Banglamphu. ❶

Chakrabongse Villas 396 Thanon Maharat ☎02 224 6686, ⓦwww.thaivillas.com; see Ratanakosin map on p.60. Riverside luxury accommodation with a difference: in the luxuriant gardens of hundred-year-old Chakrabongse House, overlooking Wat Arun and within walking distance of Wat Pho, three tranquil villas beautifully furnished in dark wood and silk, with polished teak floors. All have aircon and cable TV, and there's a small, attractive swimming pool and an open-sided riverfront pavilion for relaxing or dining (if ordered in advance). ❾

Chinatown and Hualamphong Station area

Not far from the Ratanakosin sights, **Chinatown** (**Sampeng**) is one of the most frenetic and quintessentially Asian parts of Bangkok. Staying here, or in one of the sois around the conveniently close **Hualamphong Station**, can be noisy, but there's always plenty to look at, and some people choose to base themselves in this area in order to get away from the travellers' scene in Banglamphu.

Hualamphong is on the **subway** system, and Chinatown is served by a number of useful **bus** routes: for details see the box on p.89. Accommodation in this area is marked on the **map** on p.90.

Baan Hualamphong 336/20 Soi Chalong Krung ☎02 639 8054, ⓦwww .baanhualampong.com. Custom-built wooden guest house that's attractively designed, has a stylish modern decor and is fitted with contemporary bathrooms and furnishings. There are big, bright, double rooms plus five-person dorms at B200 per bed, but all rooms share bathrooms. Has kitchen facilities, inviting lounging areas and a roof terrace, and provides a left-luggage service. ❹

Bangkok Center 328 Thanon Rama IV ☎02 238 4848, ⓦwww.bangkokcentrehotel.com. Handily placed upper-mid-range option with efficient service right by the subway station and just across the road from the train station. Rooms are smartly furnished if a little old-fashioned, and all have air-con and TV; there's a pool, restaurant and Internet access on the premises. ❻

FF Guest House 338/10 Trok La-O, off Thanon Rama IV ☎02 233 4168.Tiny, family-run guest house offering ten cheap, basic rooms with shared bathrooms. Located at the end of an alley just a 5min walk from the train and subway stations. ❷

Grand China Princess 215 Thanon Yaowarat ☎02 224 9977, ⓦwww.grandchina.com. The

poshest hotel in Chinatown boasts fairly luxurious accommodation in its 27-storey-high tower close to the heart of the bustle, with stunning views over all the city landmarks, a small rooftop swimming pool, revolving panoramic restaurant and several other food outlets. ❼

New Empire Hotel 572 Thanon Yaowarat ☎02 234 6990, ⓦwww.newempirehotel.com. Medium-sized hotel right in the thick of the Chinatown bustle, offering pretty decent superior (renovated) rooms with air-con and TV and some slightly cheaper, rather faded versions. In either category, it's worth requesting a room on the seventh floor to get panoramic views towards the river. ❹–❺

River View Guest House 768 Soi Panurangsri, Thanon Songvad ☎02 235 8501, ⓔriverview_ bkk@hotmail.com. Large, plain, old-style rooms, with fans at the lower end of the range, air-con and TVs at the top. Great views over the bend in the river from upper-floor rooms, some of which have balconies, and especially from the top-floor restaurant. Located in a lively if hard-to-find spot right next to the Chinese temple San Jao Sien Khong: head north for 400m from River City shopping centre (on the express-boat line) along Soi Wanit 2, before following signs to the guest house to the left. Fan ❸, air-con ❹

TT2 Guest House 516 Soi Kaeo Fa (formerly Soi Sawang and known to taxi drivers as such), off Thanon Maha Nakorn ☎02 236 2946, ✉ttguesthouse@hotmail.com. A long-running, traveller-friendly budget place, this guest house is clean, friendly and well run, keeps good bulletin boards, has Internet access and a small library and stores left luggage

at B10 a day. All rooms share bathrooms. During high season, there are B100 beds in a three-person dorm. Roughly a 15min walk from either the station or the N3 Si Phraya express-boat stop; to get here from the train station, cross Thanon Rama IV, then walk left for 250m, cross Thanon Maha Nakorn and walk down it (following signs for *TT2*) for 275m as far as Soi Kaeo Fa, where you turn left and then first right. The guest house is opposite Wat Kaeo Jam Fa. ❷

Thonburi

Few tourists stay on the **Thonburi** side of the river (not least because accommodation is very thin on the ground), though many daytrippers visit its canals and temples. Staying here is surprisingly convenient, with express boats and cross-river shuttles serving Banglamphu and Ratanakosin across on the other bank; see p.97 for transport details.

Ibrik Resort by the River 256 Soi Wat Rakang ☎02 848 9220, ⊛www .ibrikresort.com; see map on p.98. With just three rooms, this is the most bijou of boutique resorts. Each room is beautifully appointed in boho-chic style, with traditional wood floors, modernist white walls and sparkling silk accessories – and two of them have balconies right over the Chao Phraya

River. It's just like staying at a trendy friend's in a neighbourhood that sees hardly any other tourists and is famous for its great streetfood market at nearby Tha Wang Lang. It's right next door to *Supatra River House* restaurant and 5min walk from express-boat stop Tha Wang Lang/ Phrannok, just one ferry stop from the Grand Palace across the river. ❶

Siam Square, Thanon Ploenchit and northern downtown

Siam Square – not really a square, but a grid of shops and restaurants between Thanon Phrayathai and Thanon Henri Dunant – and nearby **Thanon Ploenchit** are as central as Bangkok gets, at the heart of the Skytrain system and with all kinds of shopping on hand. There's no ultra-cheap accommodation here, but a few scaled-up guest houses have sprung up alongside the expensive hotels. Concentrated in their own small "ghetto" on **Soi Kasemsan 1**, which runs north off Thanon Rama I just west of Thanon Phrayathai and is the next soi along from Jim Thompson's House (see p.114), these offer an informal guest-house atmosphere, with hotel comforts – air-conditioning and en-suite hot-water bathrooms – at moderate prices. Several luxury hotels have set up on **Thanon Witthayu**, aka **Wireless Road**, home of the American and British embassies (among others).

Accommodation in this area is marked on the **map** on p.113 or on the main colour map at the back of the book. For details of the area's **public transport**, see the box on p.112.

Inexpensive and moderate

A-One Inn 25/13 Soi Kasemsan 1, Thanon Rama I ☎02 215 3029, ⊛www.aoneinn.com.

The original upscale guest house, and still justifiably popular, with Internet access and a reliable left-luggage room. Bedrooms all have satellite TV and come in a variety of sizes, including family rooms (but no singles). **④**

The Bed & Breakfast 36/42 Soi Kasemsan 1, Thanon Rama I ⓣ 02 215 3004, ⓕ 02 215 2493. Bright, clean and family-run, though the rooms – carpeted, en suite and with telephones – are a bit cramped. As the name suggests, a simple breakfast – coffee, toast and fruit – is included. **④**

Far East Inn 20/8–11 Soi Bangkok Bazaar, Soi Chitlom ⓣ 02 255 4041–5, ⓦ www.geocities .com/fareastinn or www.tyha.org. The large rooms here are unexceptional but well equipped – air-con, cable TV, mini-bars and baths with hot water – and the place is friendly, very central and reasonably quiet. Discounts for YHA members. **⑥**

Patumwan House 22 Soi Kasemsan 1, Thanon Rama I ⓣ 02 612 3580–99, ⓦ www .patumwanhouse.com. Around the corner at the far end of the soi, with very large, though rather bare rooms with satellite TV, fridges and wardrobes; facilities include a café and Internet access. At the lower end of this price code. Discounted weekly and monthly rates. **⑥**

Reno Hotel 40 Soi Kasemsan 1, Thanon Rama I ⓣ 02 215 0026, ⓔ renohotel@bblife.com. Friendly hotel, boasting large, comfortable, en-suite rooms with air-con, hot water and TV, a small swimming pool and a stylishly refurbished bar-restaurant where breakfast is served (included in the price). Internet access; small discounts for stays of a fortnight or a month. **⑤**

VIP Guest House 1025/5–9 Thanon Ploenchit ⓣ 02 252 9535–8, ⓔ ghouse_g@hotmail.com. Very clean, self-styled "boutique" hotel in a peerless location. In the attractive, parquet-floored rooms (all with air-con and hot water), large beds leave just enough space for a couple of armchairs and a dressing table, as well as cable TV, mini-bar and tea- and coffee-making facilities. Breakfast included. **⑥**

🏃 **Wendy House** 36/2 Soi Kasemsan 1, Thanon Rama I ⓣ 02 214 1149–50, ⓦ www.wendyguesthouse.com. Friendly and well-run guest house, with smart, clean and comfortable rooms, some with fridge and cable TV. Internet and wireless access in the ground-floor café, where breakfast (included in the price) is served. Discounted weekly rates. **⑤**

White Lodge 36/8 Soi Kasemsan 1, Thanon Rama I ⓣ 02 216 8867 or 215 3041, ⓕ 02 216 8228.

Cheapest guest house on the soi, with well-maintained, shining white cubicles, a welcoming atmosphere, and good breakfasts at *Sorn's* next door. **③**

Expensive

Conrad All Seasons Place, 87 Thanon Witthayu ⓣ 02 690 9999, ⓦ www.conradhotels.com. A recent addition to the city's luxury hotel scene, which places a high premium on design, aiming to add a cutting edge to traditional Thai style. Bathroom fittings include free-standing baths, glass walls and huge shower heads, and there's an enticing pool, spa, gym and two floodlit tennis courts. Eating options include the modern Chinese *Liu*, a branch of Beijing's hottest restaurant. **⑨**

Holiday Mansion Hotel 53 Thanon Witthayu ⓣ 02 255 0099, ⓔ hmtel@ksc.th.com. Handily placed opposite the British Embassy, this hotel's main selling point is its large, attractive swimming pool. The bright and spacious bedrooms are nothing to write home about, but come with cable TV, air-con and hot water. Rates include breakfast. **⑦**

🏃 **Jim's Lodge** 125/7 Soi Ruam Rudee, Thanon Ploenchit ⓣ 02 255 3100, ⓦ www.jimslodge.com. In a relatively peaceful residential area, convenient for the British and American embassies, with friendly and helpful staff; offers international standards, including satellite TV and mini-bars, on a smaller scale and at bargain prices (towards the lower end of this price code); no swimming pool, but there is a roof garden with outdoor Jacuzzi. **⑦**

Pathumwan Princess Hotel 444 Thanon Phrayathai ⓣ 02 216 3700, ⓦ www.pprincess.com. At the southern end of the Mah Boon Krong (MBK) Shopping Centre, affordable luxury that's recently been refurbished in a crisp, modern style and is popular with families and businessmen. Facilities run to Korean and Japanese restaurants, a large, saltwater swimming pool with hot and cold Jacuzzis, a health spa and a huge fitness club (including jogging track and squash and tennis courts). **⑧**

🏃 **Reflections** 81 Soi Ari (aka Thanon Phaholyothin Soi 7), between sois 2 and 3 ⓣ 02 270 3344, ⓦ www.reflections-thai.com. An oasis of kitsch in a neighbourhood busy with foodstalls and office workers, the *Reflections* compound is centred an intriguingly camp-pop hotel plus a similarly styled gift shop and restaurant. The 28 rooms in the hotel come in two sizes and all have air-con, but otherwise each is entirely individual as every room was designed by a different artist. You might choose, for example, to stay in the all-pink "princess" room, in the one that evokes beachfront life, or in the one influenced by Parisian boho style (browse the website to see the full range). Though it's outside main shopping and entertainment districts, the hotel is just 5min walk from BTS Ari, five stops north of Siam Square and three stops south of Chatuchak Weekend Market; see the main colour map at the end of the book. Has a spa and pool. ❽

Siam City Hotel 477 Thanon Sri Ayutthaya ☎02 247 0123, ⓦwww.siamhotels.com. Elegant, welcoming luxury hotel on the northern side of downtown (next to Phaya Thai Skytrain station and opposite Suan Pakkad). Rooms are tastefully done out in dark wood and subdued colours, and there's a spa, health club, swimming pool and a comprehensive array of restaurants: Thai, Chinese, Japanese, Italian, international and a bakery. ❽

🏃 **Swissôtel Nai Lert Park** 2 Thanon Witthayu ☎02 253 0123, ⓦwww.nailertpark .swissotel.com. The main distinguishing feature of this welcoming, low-rise hotel is its lushly beautiful gardens, overlooked by many of the chic and spacious, balconied bedrooms; set into the grounds are a landscaped swimming pool, tennis courts, squash court and popular spa and health club. Good deli-café, cool bar (Syn Bar, see p.196) and Japanese (Genji, see p.186), French and Chinese restaurants. ❾

Downtown: south of Thanon Rama IV

South of Thanon Rama IV, the left bank of the river contains a full cross-section of places to stay. Tucked away at the eastern edge of this area is **Soi Ngam Duphli**, a small ghetto of cheap guest houses that is often choked with traffic escaping the jams on Thanon Rama IV. The neighbourhood is generally on the slide, but is close to Lumphini subway station and a lot handier for the downtown areas and the new airport than Banglamphu.

Some medium-range places are scattered between Thanon Rama IV and the river, ranging from the notorious (the *Malaysia*) to the sedate (the *Bangkok Christian Guest House*). The area also lays claim to the capital's biggest selection of top hotels, which are among the most opulent in the world. Traversed by the Skytrain, this area is especially good for eating and nightlife. Staying by the river itself off **Thanon Charoen Krung**, aka **New Road**, has the added advantage of easy access to express boats, which will ferry you upstream to view the treasures of Ratanakosin.

Accommodation in this area is marked on the **map** on p.120. For advice on **public transport** in southern downtown, see the box on p.119.

△ The Authors' Wing at the *Oriental Hotel*

Inexpensive

ETC Guest House 5/3 Soi Ngam Duphli ☎02 287 1477–8, ✉etc@etc.co.th. Above a branch of the recommended travel agent of the same name, and very handy for Thanon Rama IV, though consequently a little noisy. Friendly, helpful and very clean, catering mainly to Japanese travellers. Rooms come with fans and are further cooled by air-conditioning in the corridors; hot-water bathrooms are either shared or en suite. Breakfast is included and Internet access is available. ❷

Freddy's 2 27/40 Soi Sri Bamphen ☎02 286 7826, 🖷02 213 2097. Popular, clean, well-organized guest house with a variety of rooms with shared bathrooms and plenty of comfortable common areas, including a small café and beer garden at the rear. Rather noisy. ❶

Lee 3 Guest House 13 Soi Saphan Khu ☎02 679 7045. In an old wooden house, the best of the Lee family of guest houses spread around this and adjoining sois. Decent, quiet and very cheap, with shared cold-water bathrooms. ❶

Madam Guest House 11 Soi Saphan Khu ☎02 286 9289, 🖷02 213 2087. Cleanish, often cramped, but characterful bedrooms, some with their own cold-water bathrooms, in a warren-like, balconied wooden house. ❶

🏃 **Sala Thai Daily Mansion 15 Soi Saphan Khu** ☎02 287 1436, 🖷02 677 6880. The pick of the area. A clean and efficiently run place at the end of this quiet, shaded alley, with bright, modern rooms with wall fans, sharing hot-water bathrooms. Especially good for lone travellers, as singles are half the price of doubles. ❸

Moderate

Charlie House 1034/36–37 Soi Saphan Khu ☎02 679 8330–1, 🖷www.charliehousethailand .com. Good mid-range alternative to the crash-pads of Soi Ngam Duphli: bright, clean lobby restaurant, serving good, reasonably priced food, and small, non-smoking carpeted bedrooms with hot-water bathrooms, air-con and TV, close to Thanon Rama IV. Internet access. ❹

Intown Residence 1086/6 Thanon Charoen Krung ☎02 639 0960–2, ✉intownbkk@hotmail .com. Clean, welcoming, rather old-fashioned and very good-value hotel sandwiched between shops on the noisy main road (ask for a room away from the street). Slightly chintzy but comfortable rooms, at the lower end of their price code, come with air-con, hot-water bathrooms, mini-bars, satellite TVs and phones. Weekly and monthly discounts available. ❹

Malaysia Hotel 54 Soi Ngam Duphli ☎02 679 7127–36, 🖷www.malaysiahotelbkk.com. Once a travellers' legend famous for its compendious noticeboard, now better known for its seedy 24hr coffeeshop and massage parlour. The accommodation itself is reasonable value though: the rooms are large and have air-con, mini-bars and hot-water bathrooms; some have cable TV. There's a swimming pool (B50/day for non-guests) and Internet access. ❹

Niagara 26 Soi Suksa Witthaya, off the south side of Thanon Silom ☎02 233 5783, 🖷02 233 6563. No facilities other than a coffeeshop, but the clean bedrooms, with air-con, hot-water bathrooms, TV, telephones and rates at the lower end of this price code, are a snip. ❺

Penguin House 27/23 Soi Sri Bamphen ☎02 679 9991–2, 🖷www.geocities.com/penguinhouse. New, modern block with a ground-floor café and large, reasonably attractive rooms above, featuring air-con, hot water, cable TV and fridges; ask for one away from the busy road. Discounted monthly rates available. ❺

Pinnacle 17 Soi Ngam Duphli ☎02 287 0111–31, 🖷www.pinnaclehotels.com. Bland but reliable international-standard place, with rooftop Jacuzzi and fitness centre; rates include breakfast. ❻

Woodlands Inn 1158/5–7 Soi 32, Thanon Charoen Krung ☎02 235 3894, 🖷www .woodlandsinn.org. Simple but well-run hotel next to the GPO, under South Indian management and popular with travellers from the subcontinent. All rooms have air-con, cable TV and hot-water bathrooms, and there's a good-value South Indian restaurant on the ground floor. ❹

YWCA 13 Thanon Sathorn Tai ☎02 287 3136, 🖷www.ywcabangkok.com. Reliable, low-rise accommodation for women in neat standard or spacious deluxe rooms, all with air-con and hot water. Breakfast included. Deeply discounted monthly rates. ❻

Expensive

Bangkok Christian Guest House 123 Soi 2, Saladaeng, off the eastern end of Thanon Silom

☎02 233 2206, Ⓦwww.bcgh.org. Well-run, orderly missionary house in a shiny, modern building, where plain but immaculately kept rooms come with air-con and hot-water bathrooms. At the lower end of this price code, with breakfast included. ❼

Bangkok Marriott Resort & Spa 257 Thanon Charoennakorn ☎02 476 0022, Ⓦwww.marriott.com. A luxury retreat from the frenetic city centre, well to the south on the Thonburi bank, but connected to Taksin Bridge (for the Skytrain and Chao Phraya express boats), 10min away, by hotel ferries every 15min. Arrayed around a highly appealing swimming pool, the tranquil, riverside gardens are filled with vegetation and birdsong, while the stylish and spacious bedrooms come with polished hardwood floors and balconies. There's a fitness centre, a branch of the classy Mandara Spas, and among a wide choice of eateries, a good Japanese teppanyaki house and a bakery-café. Good value, at the lower end of this price code. ❾

Dusit Thani Hotel 946 Thanon Rama IV, on the corner of Thanon Silom ☎02 236 9999, Ⓦwww.dusit.com. Elegant, centrally placed top-class hotel, geared for both business and leisure, with very high standards of service. Many of the elegant rooms enjoy views of Lumphini Park and the sleek downtown high-rises. The hotel is famous for its restaurants, including *Thien Duong* (see p.190) and the French *D'Sens*, which has some spectacular top-floor views. ❾

La Residence 173/8–9 Thanon Suriwong ☎02 266 5400–1, Ⓦwww.laresidencebangkok.com. A small, intimate boutique hotel where the tasteful, individually decorated rooms stretch to mini-bars, safes and cable TV. Continental breakfast included. ❼

Luxx 6/11 Thanon Decho ☎02 635 8800, Ⓦwww.staywithluxx.com. Welcoming boutique hotel offering a good dose of contemporary style at reasonable prices. Decorated in white, grey and plain, unvarnished teak, the rooms feature DVD players, safes, dressing gowns and cute wooden baths surmounted by outsized shower heads. Continental or American breakfast included. ❽

Metropolitan 27 Thanon Sathorn Tai ☎02 625 3333, Ⓦwww.metropolitan.como.bz. The height of chic, minimalist urban living, where the largest standard hotel rooms in the city

(the "Metropolitan" rooms) are stylishly decorated in dark wood, creamy Portuguese limestone and lotus-themed contemporary artworks, while Yohji Yamamoto outfits adorn all the staff. There's a very seductive pool, a fine spa (see p.208), a well-equipped fitness centre with a daily schedule of complimentary classes, ranging from t'ai chi to Pilates, an excellent restaurant, *Cy'an* (see p.188), and a fiercely hip private bar. ❾

Montien Hotel 54 Thanon Surawongse, on the corner of Rama IV ☎02 233 7060, Ⓦwww.montien.com. Grand, airy and solicitous luxury hotel, with a strongly Thai character, very handily placed for business and nightlife. ❾

Oriental Hotel 48 Oriental Avenue, off Thanon Charoen Krung ☎02 659 9000, Ⓦwww.mandarinoriental.com. One of the world's best hotels, this effortlessly stylish riverside establishment boasts immaculate standards of service (1200 staff to around 400 rooms, and a neat little trick with matchsticks so they can make up your room every time you're out). It's long outgrown the original premises, an atmospheric, colonial-style wooden building, now dubbed the Authors' Wing – many famous scribes have stayed here, including Joseph Conrad and Graham Greene. ❿

Peninsula Bangkok 333 Thanon Charoennakorn, Klongsan ☎02 861 2888, Ⓦwww.peninsula.com. Superb top-class hotel which self-consciously aims to rival the *Oriental* across the river. Service is flawless, the decor stylishly blends traditional and modern Asian design, and every room has a panoramic view of the Chao Phraya. Although it's on the Thonburi side of the river, the hotel operates a shuttle boat across to a pier and reception area by the *Shangri-La Hotel* off Thanon Charoen Krung. ❾

Rose Hotel 118 Thanon Suriwong ☎02 266 8268–72, Ⓦwww.rosehotelbkk.com. Set back from the main road but very handy for the city's nightlife, this thirty-year-old hotel has just been cleverly refurbished: the simple, compact rooms now boast a stylish, retro look, in keeping with the age of the place. The ground-floor public rooms, where breakfast (included in the price) is served, are more elegant again, and a swimming pool is planned. Internet access. Towards the lower end of this price code. ❼

Sofitel Silom 188 Thanon Silom ☎02 238 1991, ⊛www.sofitel.com. Towards the quieter end of Thanon Silom, a clever renovation combines contemporary Asian artworks and furnishings with understated French elegance. A wine bar and Mediterranean, Japanese and rooftop Chinese restaurants, as well as a fitness club and small pool, complete the picture. ❾

Sukhothai 13/3 Thanon Sathorn Tai ☎02 287 0222, ⊛www.sukhothai.com. The most elegant of Bangkok's top hotels, its decor inspired by the walled city of Sukhothai: low-rise accommodation coolly furnished in silks, teak and granite, around six acres of gardens and lotus ponds. Excellent restaurants including the Thai *Celadon* (see p.188). ❾

Swiss Lodge 3 Thanon Convent ☎02 233 5345, ⊛www.swisslodge.com. Swish, friendly, good-value, boutique hotel, with high standards of service, just off Thanon Silom and ideally placed for business and nightlife. *Café Swiss* serves fondue, raclette and all your other Swiss favourites, while the tiny terrace swimming pool confirms the national stereotypes of neatness and clever design. ❽

Thanon Sukhumvit

Staying on **Thanon Sukhumvit** puts you within walking distance of a huge choice of restaurants, bars, clubs and shops, but you're a long way from the main Ratanakosin sights, and the sheer volume of traffic on Sukhumvit itself means that travelling by bus or taxi across town can take an age; access to downtown areas, however, is made easy by Sukhumvit's Skytrain and subway stops.

Although this is not the place to come if you're on a tight budget, Sukhumvit has one exceptional mid-priced guest house (*Suk 11*); the area's four- and five-star hotels tend to be oriented towards business travellers, but facilities are good and the downtown views from the high-rise rooms are a real plus. The best accommodation here is between and along sois (side-roads) 1 to 21; many of the sois are surprisingly quiet, even leafy, and offer a welcome breather from the congested frenzy of Thanon Sukhumvit itself – transport down the longer sois is provided by motorbike – taxi drivers who wait at the soi's mouth, clad in numbered waistcoats. Advance reservations are recommended during high season.

For details of **public transport** in the Sukhumvit area see the box on p.127. Sukhumvit accommodation is marked on the **map** on p.126.

Inexpensive and moderate

The Atlanta At the far southern end of Soi 2 ☎02 252 1650, ⊛www.theatlantahotel.bizland .com. Classic old-style, five-storey hotel with lots of colonial-era character and some of the cheapest accommodation on Sukhumvit. However, rooms are simple and some are fairly scruffy, though they are all en suite and some have air-con while others have small balconies. There are two swimming pools, Internet access and a left-luggage facility. The hotel restaurant serves an extensive Thai menu, including lots of vegetarian dishes, and shows classic movies set in Asia. Fan ❹, air-con ❹–❺

Federal Hotel 27 Soi 11 ☎02 253 0175, ⊛www .federalbangkok.com. Efficiently run, mid-sized, old-style hotel at the far end of Soi 11 so there's a feeling of space and a relatively uncluttered skyline; many rooms look out on the poolside seating area, though the cheapest have no window. All rooms have air-con and cable TV; the upstairs ones are smart and good value and worth paying a little extra for. ❺–❻

Rex Hotel Between sois 32 and 34 (opposite Soi 49), about 300m west from Thong Lo Skytrain station Exit 2 ☎02 259 0106, ℻02 258 6635. The best-value accommodation close to the Eastern Bus Terminal (one stop on the BTS), this old-fashioned hotel is comfortable and well maintained and has a pool and a restaurant to complement its sizeable air-con rooms, but is too isolated from the best of Sukhumvit for a longer stay. ❺–❻

Suk 11 Behind the 7-11 store at 1/3 Soi 11 ☎02 253 5927, ⊛www.suk11.com.

One of the most unusual and characterful little hotels in Bangkok, this is also the most backpacker-oriented guest house in the area. The interior of the apparently ordinary apartment-style building has been transformed to resemble a village of traditional wooden houses, accessed by a dimly lit plankway that winds past a variety of guest rooms, terraces and lounging areas. The rooms themselves are simple but comfortable and very clean, they're all air-conditioned and some are en suite. In high season, B250 beds in five-person air-con dorms are also available. It's friendly, well run and thoughtfully appointed, keeps informative noticeboards, provides free breakfast, has wi-fi Internet capability and washing machines, stores left luggage (B20/day), and accepts advance reservations via the website. Shared bathroom ④ en-suite ⑤

SV Guest House Soi 19 ☎02 253 1747, ⓕ02 255 7174. Some of the least expensive beds in the area in this long-running, clean and well-maintained guest house. All double rooms have air-con, the cheapest share bathrooms and have no outside window, the best are very good value and have private bathrooms, air-con and cable TV. Shared bathroom ③ en-suite ④

Expensive

Amari Atrium 1880 Thanon Phetchaburi Mai ☎02 718 2000–1, ⓦwww.amari.com. Welcoming, efficiently run and environmentally friendly luxury hotel, earning the government's highest seal of eco-approval. There's a lively range of restaurants and bars, a small but attractive outdoor pool, a well-equipped gym, steam room, sauna and Jacuzzi. Many rooms have been adapted for the disabled and elderly. The hotel's a little out on a limb, but is handy for the subway, boats on Khlong Saen Saeb and TAT's main office, and there's a free shuttle bus to the major shopping centres. ⑨

Amari Boulevard Hotel Soi 5 ☎02 255 2930, ⓦwww.amari.com. Medium-sized, unpretentious and friendly upmarket tourist hotel. Rooms are comfortably furnished and all enjoy fine views of the Bangkok skyline from their balcony or terrace. There's an attractive rooftop swimming pool and garden terrace which becomes the Thai-food restaurant Season in the evenings. ⑧

Grand Business Inn 2/4-2/11 Soi 11 ☎02 254 7981, ⓦwww.awgroup.com. Good-value mid-range hotel offering 66 large, comfortable, standard-issue air-con rooms, all with bathtubs and cable TV. In a very central location just a few metres from BTS Nana. ⑦

J.W. Marriott Hotel Soi 2 ☎02 656 7700, ⓦwww.marriotthotels.com. Deluxe hotel, offering comfortable rooms geared towards business travellers, six restaurants (including the *Marriott Café*, known for its exceptionally good all-day buffets), a swimming pool, spa and fitness centre. ⑨

Landmark Bangkok Between sois 4 and 6 ☎02 254 0404, ⓦwww.landmarkbangkok.com. Although many of its customers are business people, the *Landmark's* welcoming atmosphere also makes it a favourite with tourists and families. Rooms are of a very high standard without being offputtingly plush, facilities include a rooftop pool, squash court and health club, and there's broadband access in every room. ⑨

Sheraton Grande Sukhumvit Between sois 12 and 14 ☎02 649 8888, ⓦwww.sheratongrandesukhumvit.com. Deluxe accommodation in stylishly understated rooms, all of which offer fine views of the cityscape (the honeymoon suites have their own rooftop plunge pools). Facilities include a gorgeous free form swimming pool and tropical garden on the ninth floor, a spa with a range of treatment plans, the trendy *Basil* Thai restaurant (see p.191) and the *Living Room* bar, which is famous for its jazz singers. Those aged 17 and under stay for free if sharing adults' room. ⑨

Westin Grande Sukhumvit Above Robinson's Department Store, between sois 17 and 19 ☎02 651 1000, ⓦwww.westin.com/bangkok. Conveniently located four-star hotel that's aimed at the fashion-conscious business traveller but would suit holidaymakers too. The decor is modish but cheerful, with groovy pale-wood desks, flat-screen TVs and Westin's trademark super-deluxe "heavenly" mattresses. Facilities include several restaurants, a swimming pool, gym and spa, a kids' club and a business centre. Good value for its class. ⑨

Zenith Hotel 29 Soi 3 ☎02 655 4999, ⓦwww.zenith-hotel.com. Central and reasonably smart if fairly bland upper-mid-range option, where the high-rise rooms are large and sleek (all have air-con and TV) and there's a rooftop swimming pool. ⑧

10

Eating

Bangkok boasts an astonishing fifty thousand places to eat – that's almost one for every hundred citizens – ranging from grubby street-side noodle shops to the most elegant of restaurants. Despite this glut, an awful lot of tourists venture no further than the front doorstep of their guest house, preferring the dining-room's ersatz Thai or Western dishes to the more adventurous fare to be found in even the most touristy accommodation areas.

Thai restaurants of all types are found all over the city. The best **gourmet Thai** restaurants operate from the downtown districts around Thanon Sukhumvit and Thanon Silom, proffering wonderful royal, traditional and regional cuisines that definitely merit an occasional splurge – though even here, you'd have to push the boat out to spend more than B500 per person. Over in Banglamphu, Thanon Phra Athit has become famous for its dozen or so trendy little restaurant-bars, each with distinctive decor and a contemporary Thai menu aimed at young Thai diners. At the other end of the scale there are the **night markets** and **street stalls**, where you can generally get a lip-smacking feast for under B100. These are so numerous in Bangkok that we can only flag the most promising areas – but wherever you're staying, you'll hardly have to walk a block in any direction before encountering something appealing.

For the non-Thai cuisines, Chinatown naturally rates as the most authentic district for pure **Chinese** food; likewise neighbouring Pahurat, the capital's Indian enclave, is best for unadulterated **Indian** dishes; and good, comparatively cheap **Japanese** restaurants are concentrated on and around Soi Thaniya, at the east end of Thanon Silom. The place to head for Western, **travellers' food** – from herbal teas and hamburgers to muesli – as well as a hearty range of veggie options, is Thanon Khao San, packed with small, inexpensive tourist restaurants; standards vary, but there are some definite gems among the blander establishments.

Besides the night markets and street stalls, **fast food** comes in two main forms: the Thai version is the upper-floor **food courts** of shopping centres and department stores all over the city, serving up mostly one-dish meals from around the country, while the old Western favourites like *McDonald's* and *KFC* mainly congregate around Thanon Sukhumvit and Siam Square. In addition, downtown Bangkok has a good quota of **coffee shops**, including several

---

The glorious range and flavours of **Thai cuisine** are discussed in our colour insert. For a detailed **food and drink glossary**, turn to p.264. Information about Thai **cookery courses** is given on p.52.

Thai food is eaten with a **fork** (left hand) and a **spoon** (right hand); there is no need for a knife as food is served in bite-sized chunks, which are forked onto the spoon and fed into the mouth. Steamed **rice** (*khao*) is served with most meals, and indeed the most commonly heard phrase for "to eat" is *kin khao* (literally, "eat rice"). **Chopsticks** are provided only for noodle dishes.

Instead of being divided into courses, a Thai meal – even the soup – is served all at once, and shared communally, so that complementary taste combinations can be enjoyed. The more people, the more taste and texture sensations; if there are only two of you, it's best to order at least three dishes, plus your own individual plates of steamed rice, while three diners would order at least four dishes and so on. Only put a serving of one dish on your rice plate at each time, and then only one or two spoonfuls.

Bland food is anathema to Thais, and restaurant tables usually come decked out with a **condiment** set featuring the four basic flavours, salty, sour, sweet and spicy: fish sauce with chopped chillies; vinegar with chopped chillies; sugar; and dried and ground red chillies – and often extra ground peanuts and a bottle of chilli ketchup as well. If you do bite into a chilli, the way to combat the searing heat is to take a mouthful of plain rice – swigging water just exacerbates the sensation.

branches of local company Black Canyon and Starbucks, the latter expensive but usually graced with armchairs and free newspapers.

Few Thais are **vegetarian**, but in the capital it's fairly easy to find specially concocted Thai and Western veggie dishes, usually at tourist-oriented eateries. Even at the plainest street stall, it's usually possible to persuade the cook to rustle up a vegetable-only fried rice or noodle dish. If you're **vegan** you'll need to stress that you don't want egg when you order, as eggs get used a lot; cheese and other dairy produce, however, don't feature at all in Thai cuisine.

Hygiene is a consideration when eating anywhere in Bangkok, but being too cautious means you'll end up spending a lot of money and missing out on some real treats – you can be pretty sure that any noodle stall or curry shop that's permanently packed with customers is a safe bet. Foods that are generally considered high risk include salads, raw or undercooked meat, fish or eggs, ice and ice cream. If you're really concerned about health standards you could stick to restaurants and foodstalls displaying a "Clean Food Good Taste" sign, part of a food sanitation project set up by the Ministry of Public Health, TAT and the Ministry of Interior. Thais don't drink **water** straight from the tap and nor should you: plastic bottles of drinking water (*nam plao*) are sold everywhere for around B5–10, as well as the full multinational panoply of soft drinks.

In the more expensive restaurants listed below you may have to pay a ten percent service charge and seven percent government tax. Phone numbers are given for the more popular or out-of-the-way establishments, where booking may be advisable. Most restaurants in Bangkok are open every day for lunch and dinner; we've noted exceptions in the listings below.

Banglamphu and the Democracy Monument area

Banglamphu is a great area for eating. **Khao San** is stacked full of guest-house restaurants serving the whole range of cheap and familiar travellers' fare; there are also some good Thai places here, as well as veggie, Indian, Israeli and Italian joints. For a complete contrast you need only walk a few hundred metres down to riverside **Thanon Phra Athit**, where the pavement heaves with arty little café-restaurants; these are patronized mainly by students from Thammasat University up the road, but most offer English-language menus to any interested tourists. The food in these places is generally modern Thai, nearly always very good and reasonably priced. There are also some recommended trendy Thai places on the Banglamphu **fringes**, plus a few traditional options too. Hot-food stalls serving very cheap **night-market** fare pop up nightly all over the Khao San area, so there's always something available to soak up the beer. For restaurant locations see the map on p.80 and for details of public transport to this area see the box on p.78.

Around Khao San

Chabad House 96 Thanon Ram Bhuttri Ⓦ www .jewishthailand.com. A little piece of Israel, run by the Bangkok branch of the Jewish Chabad-Lubavitch movement. Serves a well-priced kosher menu (B75–130) of falafel, baba ganoush, schnitzels, hummus, salads and Jewish breads in air-conditioned calm, on the ground floor of a long-established community centre and guest house. Sun–Thurs 10am–10pm, Fri 10am–3pm.

Himalayan Kitchen 1 Thanon Khao San. One of only a handful of places serving South Asian food in the area, this first-floor restaurant – which gives good bird's-eye views of Khao San action – is decorated with Nepalese thanka paintings and dishes out decent Nepalese veg and non-veg thalis (from B160).

🏃 **May Kaidee 117/1 Thanon Tanao, though actually on the parallel soi to the west; easiest access is to take first left on Soi Damnoen Klang Neua;** Ⓦ www.maykaidee.com. Simple, neighbourhood restaurant serving the best vegetarian food in Banglamphu. Try the tasty green curry with coconut, the Vietnamese-style veggie spring rolls or the sticky black-rice pudding. May Kaidee herself also runs veggie cookery classes, detailed on p.52. Most dishes B50–60.

Popaing Soi Ram Bhuttri. Popular place for cheap seafood: mussels and cockles cost just B50 per plate, squid B70, or you can get a large helping of seafood noodles for B100. Eat in the low-rent restaurant area or on the street beneath the temple wall.

Prakorb House Thanon Khao San. Archetypal travellers' haven, with only a few tables, and an emphasis on wholesome ingredients. Inexpensive herbal teas, mango shakes, delicious pumpkin curry, and lots more besides (B40–60).

🏃 **Srinnmmun Bar and Restaurant 335 Thanon Ram Bhuttri.** This funky little cabin of a place with just a handful of tables and a penchant for soft country music serves delicious Thai food (cooked on the street), especially shrimps drizzled with coconut sauce, spicy *yam* salads and stir-fried veg with pineapple, cashews and tofu. Most dishes B40–60.

Sunset Bar Sunset Street, 197–201 Thanon Khao San. Turning off Khao San at the Sunset Street sign, ignore the street-view tables of *Sabai Bar* and follow the narrow passageway as it opens out into a tranquil, shrub-filled courtyard, occupied by the *Sunset Bar* coffee-shop and restaurant – the perfect place to escape the Khao San hustle with a mid-priced juice or snack. The courtyard's handsome, mango-coloured, 1907 villa is another enticement: a discreet branch of Starbucks, complete with sofas, occupies its ground floor, while the upper floor is given over to the Kraichitti Gallery, a commercial art outlet.

Tom Yam Kung Thanon Khao San. Occasionally mouth-blastingly authentic Thai food served in the courtyard of a beautiful early-twentieth-century villa that's hidden behind Khao San's modern clutter. The menu (B60–150) includes spicy fried catfish, coconut-palm curry with tofu and shrimps in sugar cane. Well-priced cocktails, draught beer and a small wine list. Open 24hr.

Phra Athit area

🏃 **Hemlock 56 Thanon Phra Athit, next door but one from Pra Arthit Mansion; the sign is visible from the road but not from the pavement** ☎ 02 282 7507. Small, stylish, highly recommended air-con restaurant that's very popular with students and young Thai couples. Offers a long and interesting menu

The **Chao Phraya River** looks fabulous at night, when most of the noisy longtails have stopped terrorizing the ferries, and the riverside temples and other grand monuments – including the Grand Palace and Wat Arun – are elegantly illuminated. Joining one of the nightly **dinner cruises** along the river is a great way to appreciate it all. Call ahead to reserve a table and check departure details – some places offer free transport from hotels, and some cruises may not run during the rainy season (May to October). If you have other plans for dinner, it's now possible to take a cruise at other times of the day: the *Manohra* (see below) runs **cocktail cruises** between 6 and 7pm (B750), while the *Shangri-La Horizon* (see below) sails off on a **lunch cruise** at noon (international buffet; B1850), returning to the hotel pier around 2.30pm, with optional drop-offs at the Grand Palace or Wat Arun.

Loy Nava ☏02 235 3108. Departs Si Phraya pier at 8pm (returning 10pm). Thai set meal. B1200.

Maeyanang Run by the *Oriental Hotel* ☏02 236 0400. Departs *Oriental* at 7.30pm (not Mon), returning at 9.30pm. Thai buffet. B1600.

Manohra Beautiful converted rice barge operated by the *Bangkok Marriott Resort*, south of Taksin Bridge in Thonburi ☏02 477 0770, ⊛www.manohracruises.com. Departs hotel at 7.30pm, returning 10pm, with pick-ups at Tha Sathorn and Tha Oriental possible. Thai set dinner, accompanied by live traditional music. B1500.

Pearl of Siam ☏02 225 6179. Departs River City at 7.30pm, returning at 9.30pm. Thai and international buffet. B1200.

Shangri-La Horizon ☏02 236 7777. Departs *Shangri-La Hotel* pier, north of Taksin Bridge, at 7.30pm, returning at 9.30pm. International buffet. B2200.

Wan Fah ☏02 222 8679, ⊛www.wanfah.com. Departs River City at 7pm, returning at 9pm. Thai or seafood set menu. B1200.

(10)

of unusual Thai dishes (mostly about B60), including banana-flower salad (*yam hua plee*), coconut and mushroom curry, grand lotus rice and various *laap* and fish dishes. The traditional *miang* starters (shiny green wild tea leaves filled with chopped vegetables, fish and meat) are also very tasty, and there's a good vegetarian selection. Mon–Sat 5pm–midnight; worth reserving a table on Friday and Saturday nights.

Krua Nopparat 130–132 Thanon Phra Athit. The decor in this unassuming air-con restaurant is noticeably plain compared to all the arty joints on this road, but the Thai food (B60–100) is good, especially the eggplant wing-bean salad and the battered crab.

Ricky's Coffee Shop 22 Thanon Phra Athit. With its atmospherically dark woodwork, red lanterns and marble-top tables, this contemporary take on a traditional Chinese coffee house is an enjoyable spot to idle over fresh coffee (choose from several blends: B50) and feast on the deli-style offerings – pastrami,

imported cheeses – served over baguettes and croissants, not to mention the all-day breakfasts and veggie lunch menu (most dishes B70–120). Daily 7.30am–8pm.

Roti Mataba 136 Thanon Phra Athit. Famous outlet for the ever-popular fried Indian breads, or rotis, served here in lots of sweet and savoury varieties, including with vegetable and meat curries, and with bananas and condensed milk (from B20). Closed Sun.

Tonpoh Thanon Phra Athit, next to Tha Phra Athit express-boat pier. Sizeable, good-value seafood menu (B60–220) and a relatively scenic riverside location; good place for a beer and a snack at the end of a long day's sightseeing.

Thanon Samsen, Thewes and the fringes

In Love Beside the Tha Thewes express-boat pier at 2/1 Thanon Krung Kasem. Popular place for seafood – and riverine breezes – with decent Chao Phraya views, an airy upstairs terrace, and a huge menu including baked cottonfish in mango sauce, steamed

One of the most refreshing snacks in Bangkok is **fruit** (*phonlamai*), and you'll find it offered everywhere – neatly sliced in glass boxes on hawker carts, blended into delicious shakes at night market stalls and guest houses, and served as a dessert in restaurants. The more familiar Thai fruits are not listed below, but include forty varieties of banana (*kluay*), dozens of different mangoes (*mamuang*), three types of pineapple (*sapparot*), coconuts (*maprao*), oranges (*som*), lemons (*manao*) and watermelons (*taeng moh*). To avoid stomach trouble, peel all fruit before eating it, and use common sense if you're tempted to buy it pre-peeled on the street, avoiding anything that looks fly-blown or seems to have been sitting in the sun for hours.

Custard apple (soursop; *noina*; July–Sept). Inside the knobbly, muddy-green skin you'll find creamy, almond-coloured blancmange-like flesh, having a strong flavour of strawberries and pears, with a hint of cinnamon, and many seeds.

Durian (*thurian*; April–June). Thailand's most prized, and expensive, fruit (see also p.133) has a greeny-yellow, spiky exterior and grows to roughly the size of a rugby ball. Inside, it divides into segments of thick, yellow-white flesh which gives off a disgustingly strong stink that's been compared to a mixture of mature cheese and caramel. Not surprisingly, many airlines and hotels ban the eating of this smelly delicacy on their premises. Most Thais consider it the king of fruits, while most foreigners find it utterly foul in both taste and smell.

Guava (*farang*; year-round). The apple of the tropics has green textured skin and sweet, crisp flesh that can be pink or white and is studded with tiny edible seeds. It has five times the vitamin C content of an orange, and is sometimes eaten cut into strips and sprinkled with sugar and chilli.

Jackfruit (*khanun*; year-round). This large, pear-shaped fruit can weigh up to twenty kilograms and has a thick, bobbly, greeny-yellow shell protecting sweet yellow flesh. Green, unripe jackfruit is sometimes cooked as a vegetable in curries.

Longan (*lamyai*; July–Oct). A close relative of the lychee, with succulent white flesh covered in thin, brittle skin.

Lychee (*linjii*; April–May). Under rough, reddish-brown skin, the lychee has sweet, richly flavoured white flesh, rose-scented and with plenty of vitamin C, surrounding a brown, egg-shaped pit.

Mangosteen (*mangkut*; April–Sept). The size of a small apple, with smooth, purple skin and a fleshy inside that divides into succulent white segments that are sweet though slightly acidic.

Papaya (paw-paw; *malakaw*; year-round). Looks like an elongated watermelon, with smooth green skin and yellowy-orange flesh that's a rich source of vitamins A and C. It's a favourite in fruit salads and shakes, and sometimes appears in its green, unripe form in salads, notably *som tam*.

Pomelo (*som oh*; Oct–Dec). The largest of all the citrus fruits, it looks rather like a grapefruit, though it is slightly drier and has less flavour.

Rambutan (*ngaw*; May–Sept). The bright red rambutan's soft, spiny exterior has given it its name – *rambut* means "hair" in Malay. Usually about the size of a golf ball, it has a white, opaque flesh of delicate flavour, similar to a lychee.

Rose apple (*chomphuu*; year-round). Linked in myth with the golden fruit of immortality, the rose apple is small and egg-shaped, with white, rose-scented flesh.

Sapodilla (sapota; *lamut*; Sept–Dec). These small, brown, rough-skinned ovals look a bit like kiwi fruit and conceal a grainy, yellowish pulp that tastes almost honey-sweet.

Tamarind (*makhaam*; Dec–Jan). A Thai favourite and a pricey delicacy – carrying the seeds is said to make you safe from wounding by knives or bullets. Comes in rough, brown pods containing up to ten seeds, each surrounded by a sticky, dry pulp which has a sour, lemony taste.

sea bass with lime and chilli, and *tom yam kung*. Most dishes B160–190.

Isaan restaurants Behind the Rajdamnoen Boxing Stadium on Thanon Rajdamnoen Nok. A cluster of restaurants serving cheapish northeastern (Isaan) fare (from B60) to hungry boxing fans: take your pick for hearty plates of *kai yaang* and *khao niaw*.

Kaloang Beside the river at the far western end of Thanon Sri Ayutthaya. Flamboyant service and excellent seafood attracts an almost exclusively Thai clientele to this open-air riverside restaurant. Dishes (from B120–250) well worth shelling out for include the fried rolled shrimps served with a sweet dip, the roast squid cooked in a piquant sauce and the steamed butter fish.

Kinlom Chom Saphan Riverside end of Thanon Samsen Soi 3. This sprawling, waterside seafood restaurant boasts close-up views of the lyre-like Rama VIII Bridge and is always busy with a youngish Thai crowd. The predominantly seafood menu (from B120–250) features everything from crab to grouper cooked in multiple ways, including with curry, garlic or sweet basil sauces. As well as the usual complement of *tom yam* and *tom kha* soups, there are *yam* salads and meat options including stir-fried ostrich with herbs. Daily 11am–2am.

May Kaidee 2 33 Thanon Samsen, between the klhong and Sol 1 @www.maykaidee.com This air-con branch of Banglamphu's best-loved Thai veggie restaurant may lack the ad-hoc character of the original (see p.190), but the menu is the same – pumpkin soup, banana flower salad, curry-fried tofu with vegetables – and equally cheap (most dishes B50–60). See p.52 for details of owner May Kaidee's veggie cookery classes.

Na Pralan Café Almost opposite the main entrance to the Grand Palace, Thanon Na Phra Lan. Technically in Ratanakosin (it's marked on the map on p.60) but very close to Banglamphu, this small, cheap café, only a couple of doors up the street from the Silpakorn University Art College, is ideally placed for refreshment after your tour of the Grand Palace. Popular with students, it occupies a quaint old air-con shophouse with battered, artsy decor. The menu, well thought out with some unusual twists, offers mostly one-dish meals with rice, and a range of ice creams, coffees, teas and beers. Mon–Sat 10am–midnight, Sun 10am–6pm.

Pornsawan Vegetarian Restaurant 80 Thanon Samsen, between sois 4 and 6. Cheap, no-frills Thai veggie café that uses soya products instead of meat in its curries and stir-fries. Daily 7am–6.30pm.

Shanti Lodge 37 Soi 16, Thanon Sri Ayutthaya. The restaurant attached to the famously chilled-out guest house serves an exceptionally innovative menu of predominantly vegetarian dishes, including tofu stuffed with brown rice, assorted curries and vegetables; and mushroom laap. Most dishes around B75.

Chinatown and Pahurat

In the evenings, night-time hot-food stalls open up all along Thanon Yaowarat and Soi Phadungdao: the Bangkok Tourist Bureau information booth (Mon–Sat 9am–5pm), at the east (Chinese Arch) end of Thanon Yaowarat, has a brochure detailing some of the specialist stalls. The places listed below are marked on the map on p.90; for details of public transport to this area see the box on p.89.

Chong Tee 84 Soi Sukon 1, Thanon Trimit, between Hualamphong Station and Wat Traimit. Delicious and moreishly cheap pork satay and sweet toast.

Hua Seng Hong 371 Thanon Yaowarat. Thai bird's-nest soup is one of the specialities here, but locals tend to go for the tasty wonton noodle soup or the stir-fried crab noodles (dishes from B160).

T&K (Toi & Kid's Seafood) 49 Soi Phadungdao, just off Thanon Yaowarat. Highly rated barbecued seafood, with everything from prawns (B150 a serving) to oysters (B30 each) on offer. Daily 4.30pm–2am.

Royal India Just off Thanon Chakraphet at 392/1. Famously good curries (from B60) served in the heart of Bangkok's most Indian of neighbourhoods to an almost exclusively South Asian clientele. Especially renowned for its choice Indian breads.

Shangri-La 306 Thanon Yaowarat (cnr of Thanon Rajawong). Cavernous place serving Chinese classics (B80–300), including lots of seafood, and lunchtime dim sum. Very popular, especially for family outings.

White Orchid Hotel 409–421 Thanon Yaowarat. Recommended for its dim sum, with bamboo baskets of prawn dumplings, spicy spare ribs, stuffed beancurd and the like, served in three different portion sizes at fairly high prices. Dim sum 11am–2pm & 5–10pm. All-you-can-eat lunchtime buffets also worth stopping by for.

Downtown: Around Siam Square and Thanon Ploenchit

The map on p.113 shows the places listed below; for details of public transport to this area, see the box on p.114. In this area, there are also branches of *Anna's Café* (see p.188), in Diethelm Tower B, Thanon Witthayu (☎02 252 0864), and *Aoi* (see p.188), in the Siam Paragon shopping centre on Thanon Rama I (☎02 129 4348).

Aao 45/4–8 Soi Lang Suan, Thanon Ploenchit ☎02 254 5699. Bright, almost unnerving retro-Sixties decor is the setting for friendly service and very tasty Thai dishes – notably *kaeng phanaeng kai* (B90) and wing-bean salad – most of which are available spiced to order and/or in vegetarian versions. Closed Sun.

Bali 15/3 Soi Ruam Rudee ☎02 250 0711. Top-notch authentic Indonesian food at moderate prices and homely, efficient service in a cosy old house just off Thanon Ploenchit. Blow out on seven-course rijsttafel for B340. Closed Sun.

Curries & More 63/3 Soi Ruam Rudee ☎02 253 5408–9. And a whole lot more… This offshoot of Baan Khanitha (see p.190) offers something for everyone, including European-style fish, steaks and pasta, as well as curries from around the country (from around B300). Try the delicious *chu chi khung nang*, deep-fried freshwater prawns with mild, Indian-style curry, or the prawn and pomelo salad. The modern, white-painted interior is hung with contemporary paintings, but the garden, surrounded by waterfalls and with water flowing over the transparent roof, is the place to be.

Food for Fun Floor 4, Siam Center. Highly enjoyable, inexpensive, new food court, decorated in startling primary colours. Lots of traditional Thai drinks and all manner of tasty one-dish meals – *khao man kai*, *khanom jiin* and laap and som tam from the Isaan counter – as well as pizza, pastas, Vietnamese and Korean food.

Food Loft Floor 7, Central Chidlom, Thanon Ploenchit. Bangkok's top department store lays on a suitably upscale food court of all hues – Thai, Vietnamese, Malay, Chinese, Japanese, Indian, Italian. Choose your own ingredients and watch them cooked in front of you, eat in the stylish, minimalist seating areas and then ponder whether you have room for a Thai or Western dessert.

Genji Swissôtel Nai Lert Park, 2 Thanon Witthayu ☎02 253 0123. Excellent, genteel Japanese restaurant overlooking the hotel's beautiful gardens, with a sushi bar, teppanyaki grill tables and private dining rooms. The sushi and tempura set (B900) is especially delicious.

Gianni 34/1 Soi Tonson, Thanon Ploenchit ☎02 252 1619. One of Bangkok's best independent Italian restaurants, successfully blending traditional and modern in both its decor and food. Offerings include a belt- (and bank-) busting tasting menu for B1190 and innovative pastas.

Inter 432/1–2 Soi 9, Siam Square. Honest, efficient Thai restaurant that's popular with students and shoppers, serving good one-dish meals for around B50, as well as curries, salads and Isaan food, in a no-frills, fluorescent-lit canteen atmosphere.

Ma Be Ba 93 Soi Lang Suan ☎02 254 9595. Lively, spacious and extravagantly decorated Italian restaurant dishing up a good variety of antipasti, excellent pastas (around B300 and upwards) and pizzas (in two sizes), and traditional main courses strong on seafood. Live music nightly, mostly pop covers, country and Latin, plus jazz piano early evenings Wed–Fri.

Mah Boon Krong Food Centre North end of Floor 6, MBK shopping centre, corner of Thanon Rama I and Thanon Phrayathai. Increase your knowledge of Thai food here: ingredients, names and pictures of a wide variety of tasty, cheap one-dish meals from all over the country are displayed at the various stalls, as well as fresh juices and a wide range of desserts. Other cuisines, such as Vietnamese, Chinese, Indian, Japanese and Italian are now also represented, charging slightly higher prices.

Pisces 36/6 Soi Kasemsan 1, Thanon Rama I. Drawing plenty of custom from the local guest houses, a friendly, family-run restaurant, neat and colourful, serving a wide variety of breakfasts and cheap, tasty Thai food, with lots of vegetarian options. Daily 8am–1pm & 5–10.30pm.

Sarah Jane's Ground Floor, Sindhorn Tower 1, 130–132 Thanon Witthayu ☎02 650 9992–3. Long-standing, moderately priced restaurant,

popular with Bangkok residents from Isaan (the northeast of Thailand), serving excellent, simple northeastern dishes, as well as Italian food. It's in slick but unfussy modern premises that can be slightly tricky to find at night, towards the rear of a modern office block.

Sorn's 36/8 Soi Kasemsan 1, Thanon Rama I. In this quiet lane of superior guest houses, a laid-back, moderately priced hangout decorated with black-and-white prints of Thailand by the photographer owner. Delicious versions of standard Thai dishes – the *tom kha kai* is especially good – as well as Western meals, a huge breakfast menu including reasonably priced set meals, and good teas and coffees. Daily 7am–noon & 5–11pm.

Thang Long 82/5 Soi Lang Suan ☎02 251 3504. Excellent Vietnamese food such as lemongrass fish (B175) in this stylish, minimalist and popular restaurant, all stone floors, plants and whitewashed walls.

Vanilla Industry Soi 11, Siam Square. Small, sophisticated, good-value, first-floor restaurant that's a shrine to Western gourmet delights (backed up by a cookery school on the floor above): smoked salmon finger sandwiches, spot-on desserts such as strawberry panna cotta, pastas, salads and other main courses, and excellent teas and coffees.

Whole Earth 93/3 Soi Lang Suan ☎02 252 5574. Long-standing veggie-oriented restaurant, serving interesting and varied Thai and Indian-style dishes (B100 and under) for both vegetarians and omnivores in a relaxing atmosphere.

Zen Floor 6, Central World Plaza, corner of Thanon Ploenchit and Thanon Rajdamri ☎02 255 6462; **Floor 3, MBK shopping centre, corner of Thanon Rama I and Thanon Phrayathai** ☎02 620 9007–8; **and Floor 4, Siam Center, Thanon Rama I** ☎02 658 1183–4. Good-value Japanese restaurant with wacky modern wooden design and seductive booths. Among a huge range of dishes, the complete meal sets (with pictures to help you choose) are filling and particularly good.

Downtown: south of Thanon Rama IV

The places listed below are marked on the map on p.120 or on the colour map at the back of the book; for details of public transport to this area, see the box on p.119. In this area, there are also branches of *Baan Khanitha* (see p.190) at 67

△ *Harmonique* restaurant.

Thanon Sathorn Tai, at the corner of Soi Suan Phlu (☎02 675 4200), and *Zen* (see 187), at 1/1 Thanon Convent (☎02 266 7150–1).

Angelini's Shangri-La Hotel, 89 Soi Wat Suan Plu, Thanon Charoen Krung ☎02 236 7777. One of the capital's best Italians, pricey but not too extravagant. The setting is lively and relaxed, with open-plan kitchen and big picture windows onto the pool and river. There are some unusual main courses as well as old favourites like ossobucco, or you can invent your own wood-oven-baked pizza.

Anna's Café 118 Thanon Saladaeng ☎02 632 0619–20. In a large, elegant villa between Silom and Sathorn roads, reliable, varied and very reasonably priced Thai and Western dishes and desserts, including a very good *som tam*, *kai yaang* and sticky rice combo.

Aoi 132/10–11 Soi 6, Thanon Silom ☎02 235 2321–2. The best place in town for a Japanese blowout, justifiably popular with the expat community. Excellent authentic food and elegant decor. Good-value lunch sets (from B250) available and a superb sushi bar.

Ban Chiang 14 Soi Srivieng, off Thanon Surasak, between Thanon Silom and Thanon Sathorn ☎02 236 7045. Fine central and northeastern Thai cuisine at reasonable prices. The restaurant can be difficult to find, off the western end of Thanon Silom down towards Thanon Sathorn, but rewards persistence with an elegant, surprisingly quiet setting in an old wooden house with garden tables.

Celadon Sukhothai Hotel, 13/3 Thanon Sathorn Tai ☎02 287 0222. Consistently rated as one of the best hotel restaurants in Bangkok and a favourite with locals, serving outstanding traditional and contemporary Thai food in an elegant setting surrounded by lotus ponds.

Chai Karr 312/3 Thanon Silom, opposite Holiday Inn ☎02 233 2549. Folksy, traditional-style wooden decor is the welcoming setting for a wide variety of well-prepared, modestly priced Thai and Chinese dishes, followed by home-made coconut ice cream. Closed Sun.

Charuvan 70–2 Thanon Silom, near the entrance to Soi 4. Cheap but lackadaisical place to refuel, with an air-con room, specializing in tasty duck on rice; the beer's a bargain too.

Cy'an Metropolitan Hotel, 27 Thanon Sathorn Tai ☎02 625 3333. Highly inventive cooking, fusing Asian and Mediterranean elements to produce strong, clean flavours, with great attention to detail. Charming service to go with it, in a stylish room with the best tables on a terrace overlooking the pool.

Deen 786 Thanon Silom. Small, basic, air-con Muslim café (so no alcohol), almost opposite Silom Village. It draws most of its clientele from the Islamic south of Thailand, serving Thai and Chinese standard dishes with a southern twist, as well as spicy Indian-style curries and southern Thai specialities such as *grupuk* (crispy fish) and *roti kaeng* (Muslim pancakes with curry).

Eat Me 1/6 Soi Phiphat 2, Thanon Convent ☎02 238 0931. Highly fashionable art gallery and restaurant in a striking, white, modernist building, with changing exhibitions on the walls and a temptingly relaxing balcony. The pricey, far-reaching menu is more international – tenderloin steak fillet with Dijon sauce, pancetta-wrapped chicken breast with grape salad – than fusion, though the lemon-grass crème brûlée is not to be missed. Daily 3pm–1am.

Harmonique 22 Soi 34, Thanon Charoen Krung, on the lane between Wat Muang Kae express-boat pier and the GPO ☎02 237 8175. A relaxing, welcoming, moderately priced restaurant that's well worth a trip: tables are scattered throughout several converted shophouses, decorated with antiques, and a quiet, leafy courtyard, and the Thai food is varied and excellent – among the seafood specialities, try the crab or red shrimp curries. Closed Sun.

Himali Cha-Cha 1229/11 Soi 47/1, Thanon Charoen Krung, south of GPO ☎02 235 1569 **(plus a branch down a short alley off the north end of Thanon Convent, opposite Irish Xchange).** Fine North Indian restaurant, founded by a character who was chef to numerous Indian ambassadors, and now run by his son. Moderate prices, homely atmosphere, attentive service and a good vegetarian selection.

Indian Hut 311/2–5 Thanon Suriwong, ☎02 237 8812. Bright, white-tablecloth, North Indian restaurant – look out for the Pizza Hut-style sign – that's reasonably priced and justly popular with local Indians. For carnivores, tandoori's the thing, with an especially good kastoori chicken kebab with saffron and cumin. There's a huge selection of mostly vegetarian pakoras as appetizers, as well as plenty of veggie main courses and breads, and a hard-to-resist house dahl.

Ishq 142 Thanon Sathorn Nua ☎02 634 5398–9. A beautiful Portuguese colonial-style

mansion, with especially opulent bathrooms, set back from the main road and Surasak BTS station amidst fountains. Pricey but very good food from all over southeast Asia, including tasty Lao mushroom soup and Vietnamese beef balls.

🏃 **Jim Thompson's Saladaeng Café 120/1 Soi 1, Thanon Saladaeng** ☎02 266 9167. A civilized, moderately priced haven with tables in the elegantly informal air-con interior or out in the leafy garden. Thai food stretches to some unusual dishes such as deep-fried morning glory with spicy shrimp and minced pork. There's pasta, salads and other Western dishes, plus a few stabs at fusion including delicious spaghetti sai ua (with northern Thai sausage and tomato sauce) and linguini tom yam kung. The array of desserts is mouthwatering, rounded off by good coffee and a wide choice of teas.

🏃 **Khrua Aroy Aroy 3/1 Thanon Pan.** In a fruitful area for cheap food (including a night market across Silom on Soi 20), this simple shophouse restaurant stands out for its choice of tasty, well-prepared dishes from all around the kingdom, notably northern *khao soi* (curried broth with egg noodles and meat) and southern *kaeng matsaman* (rich Muslim-style curry with meat and potatoes). Lunchtimes only.

La Boulange 2–2/1 Thanon Convent. A fine choice for breakfast with great croissants and all sorts of tempting patisserie made on the premises. For savoury lunches and dinners, choose from a variety of quiches, sandwiches, salads and typical brasserie fare such as gigot d'agneau.

Le Bouchon 37/17 Patpong 2, near Thanon Suriwong ☎02 234 9109. Cosy, welcoming bar-bistro that's frequented by the city's French expats, offering French home-cooking, such as lamb shank in a white bean sauce (B490); booking is strongly recommended. Closed Sun lunchtime.

🏃 **Le Café Siam 4 Soi Sri Akson, Thanon Chua Ploeng** ☎02 671 0030, ⓦwww .lecafesiam.com. An early-twentieth-century Sino-Thai mansion in a tranquil garden that's difficult to find off the eastern end of Soi Sri Bamphen, but well worth the effort (the restaurant suggests the number of a taxi company – ☎02 611 6499 – or you can download a map from their website). The French and Thai food, with main courses starting at B200, is superb, served in a relaxing ambience that subtly blends Chinese and French styles, with an especially seductive bar area upstairs. Evenings only.

Mali Soi Jusmag, just off Soi Ngam Duphli. Cosy, low-lit, moderately priced restaurant, mostly air-con with a few cramped tables out front. The Thai menu specializes in salads and northeastern food, with plenty of veggie options, while Western options run as far as burgers, potato salad, all-day breakfasts, delicious banana pancakes and a few Mexican dishes.

Mei Jiang Peninsula Hotel, 333 Thanon Charoennakorn, Klongsan ☎ 02 861 2888. Probably Bangkok's best Chinese restaurant, with beautiful views of the hotel gardens and the river night and day. It's designed like an elegant teak box, and staff are very attentive and graceful. Specialities include duck smoked with tea and excellent lunchtime dim sum – a bargain, starting at B80 a dish.

River View Floor 2, River City shopping centre, off Thanon Charoen Krung ☎ 02 237 0077–8, **ext 233.** A bit cheesy – waiters with jazzy waistcoats and truly awful muzak – but the views of the river are great and the food's very tasty, including lots of fish dishes, salads and a vegetarian selection; the deep-fried chicken with cashew nuts (B150)

and deep-fried pompanos fish with mango salad are recommended.

Somboon Seafood Thanon Suriwong, corner of Thanon Narathiwat Ratchanakharin ☎ 02 234 **4499.** Highly favoured seafood restaurant, known for its crab curry (B250) and soy-steamed sea bass, with simple, smart decor and an array of marine life lined up in tanks outside awaiting its gastronomic fate.

🏃 **Thien Duong Dusit Thani Hotel, cnr Silom and Rama IV roads** ☎ 02 236 9999. Probably Bangkok's finest Vietnamese, a classy and expensive restaurant serving beautifully prepared dishes such as succulent salat cua, deep-fried soft-shell crab salad with cashew nuts and herb dressing, and zesty goi ngo sen, lotus-stem salad with shrimp and pork.

🏃 **Tongue Thai 18–20 Soi 38, Thanon Charoen Krung** ☎ 02 630 9918–9. Excellent Thai restaurant in front of the Oriental Place shopping mall. Very high standards of food and cleanliness, with charming, unpretentious service, in a 100-year-old shophouse elegantly decorated with Thai and Chinese antiques and contemporary art. Veggies are very well catered for with delicious dishes such as tofu in black bean sauce and deep-fried banana-flower and corn cakes, while carnivores should try the fantastic beef curry (phanaeng neua; B170).

Thanon Sukhumvit

See the map on p.126 for locations of the places listed below. In this area, there are also branches of *Aoi* (see p.196), Floor 4, Emporium shopping centre (☎ 02 664 8590–2), and *Himali Cha-Cha* (see p.189), 2 Soi 35, Thanon Sukhumvit (☎ 02 258 8846). For those restaurants east of sois 39 and 26 that are not shown on the map, we've given directions from the nearest Skytrain station. For details of public transport to the Sukhumvit area, see the box on p.127.

Al Ferdoss Soi 3/1. Long-running Lebanese and Turkish restaurant in the heart of Sukhumvit's Middle Eastern soi, where you can smoke hookah pipes on the streetside terrace and choose from a menu (B70–150) that encompasses shish, hummus, tabouleh and the rest.

Baan Khanitha 36/1 Soi 23 ☎ 02 258 4128. The big attraction at this long-running favourite haunt of Sukhumvit expats is the setting in a traditional Thai house. The food is upmarket Thai and fairly pricey, and includes lots of fiery salads (*yam*), and a good range of

tom yam soups, green curries and seafood curries.

Bangkok Baking Company Ground Floor, J.W. Marriott Hotel, between sois 2 and 4. Exceptionally delicious cakes, pastries and breads: everything from rosemary focaccia to tiramisu cheesecake (B65–100).

Ban Rie Coffee Opposite Ekamai Eastern Bus Terminal and beside the Ekamai Skytrain station on the corner of Soi 63. A wistful little haven of incongruity at one of Sukhumvit's many congested junctions, this chic teakwood pavilion welcomes you via a wooden walkway across a narrow fringe of rice-fields and works hard to create a soothing ambience inside. It serves a decent selection of mid-priced hot and iced coffees, as well as Thai desserts, and also offers Internet access and terrace seating.

Basil Sheraton Grande Hotel, between sois 12 and 14. Mouthwateringly fine traditional Thai food with a modern twist is the order of the day at this trendy, relatively informal though high-priced restaurant in the super-deluxe five-star *Sheraton*. Recommendations include the grilled river prawns with chilli, the *matsaman* curry (both served with red and green rice) and the surprisingly delicious durian cheesecake. Vegetarian menu on request. Also offers cooking classes (see p.52).

Cabbages and Condoms 6–8 Soi 12 Ⓦwww .pda.or.th/restaurant. Run by the Population and Community Development Association of Thailand (PDA; see p.125) – "our food is guaranteed not to cause pregnancy" – so diners are treated to authentic Thai food in the Condom Room, and relaxed scoffing of barbecued seafood in the beer garden. Try the spicy catfish salad (B130) or the prawns steamed in a whole coconut (B250). All proceeds go to the PDA, and there's an adjacent shop selling double-entendre T-shirts, cards, key rings and of course, condoms.

Dosa King Mouth of Soi 19. Informal, all-vegetarian Indian café serving good, unpretentious food from both north and south, including twenty different dosa (southern pancake) dishes, tandooris, etc. An alcohol-free zone so you'll have to make do with sweet lassi instead. Most dishes B120–180.

Face Bangkok: La Na Thai and Hazara 29 Soi 38; about 150m walk from BTS Thong Lo Exit 4 ☏02 713 6048, Ⓦwww.facebars .com. Two restaurants, a bar, a bakery and a spa occupy this attractive compound of traditional, steeply gabled wooden Thai houses. Each restaurant is tastefully styled with appropriate artefacts and fabrics, and the adjacent *Face Bar* makes a chic 'n' funky place for a pre- or post-dinner drink. All venues offer an extensive list of imported wines. The very upmarket *Lan Na Thai* restaurant (daily 11.30am–2.30pm & 6.30–11.30pm) serves quality Thai food, such as northern-Thai-style pork curry (B390) and deep-fried grouper with tamarind sauce (B460), while the *Hazara* (daily

6.30–11.30pm) specializes in Afghani and north-Indian tandoor cuisine, including murgh Peshwar chicken (B390) and the signature cardamon–marinated lamb (B590).

Gaeng Pa Lerd Rod Soi 33/1; no English sign but it's just before the Bull's Head. Hugely popular outdoor restaurant whose tables are clustered under trees in a streetside yard and get packed with office workers at lunchtime. Thai curries (from B40) are the speciality here, with dishes ranging from conventional versions, like catfish and beef curries, to more adventurous offerings like fried cobra with chilli, and curried frog. Inexpensive.

Gallery 11 Soi 11. Sharing the traffic-free sub-soi with the idiosyncratic *Suk 11* guest house, this restaurant fosters a similarly laid-back rustic atmosphere, with its wooden building, plentiful foliage and moody lighting. The food is good, authentic, mid-priced Thai, with plenty of spicy *yam* salads, seafood and curries, mostly B100–200. Also serves lots of cocktails and imported wines by the glass (B150).

Le Dalat Indochine 14 Soi 23 ☏02 661 7967. There's Indochinese romance aplenty at this delightfully atmospheric restaurant, which is housed in an early-twentieth-century villa decked out in homely style with plenty of photos, pot plants at every turn and eclectic curiosities in the male and female toilets. The extensive, Vietnamese menu features favourites such as a goi ca salad of aromatic herbs and shredded pork, chao tom shrimp sticks and ga sa gung, chicken curry with caramelized ginger. Set dinners from B1000.

Lemongrass 5/1 Soi 24 ☏02 258 8637. Known for its delicious Thai nouvelle cuisine (B120–500), including a particularly good minced chicken with ginger, and for its pleasant setting in a converted traditional house. A vegetarian menu is available on request. Advance reservations recommended. Daily 6–11pm.

MahaNaga 2 Soi 29, Ⓦwww.mahanaga .com. The dining experience at this tranquil enclave is best appreciated after dark, when the fountain-courtyard tables are romantically lit and the air-con interior seduces with its burgundy velvet drapes. Cuisine is fusion fine-dining, though some east-west combos work better than others and the vegetarian selection is underwhelming. Grilled salmon in red curry is a winner (B350), or you might brave the rack of lamb served with spicy vegetables, egg noodles and mango sauce (B450).

Nipa 3rd Floor, Landmark Plaza, between sois 4 and 6. Tasteful traditional Thai-style place, run by the adjacent hotel, the *Landmark Bangkok*, whose classy menu features an adventurous range of dishes, including spicy fish curry (B180), several *matsaman* and green curries (B220), excellent som tam and mouthwatering braised spare ribs. Also offers a sizeable vegetarian selection. Regular cookery classes are held here – see p.52 for details.

Pizza Venezia Soi 11 Ⓦ www.veneziabangkok .com. Fairly formal Italian place that's a favourite with Sukhumvit expats for its pizzas (B180–360). Also offers a diverse roster of daily specials, plus classic pasta, meat and fish dishes, including a good oven-baked sea bass in white-wine sauce (B590).

Suda Restaurant Soi 14. Unpretentious shop-house restaurant whose formica tables and plastic chairs spill out onto the soi and are mainly patronized by budget-conscious expats and their Thai friends. The friendly proprietor serves a good, long menu of Thai standards (from B40), including deep-fried chicken in banana leaves, battered shrimps, fried tuna with cashews and chilli, and sticky rice with mango.

🏃 **Tamarind Café 300m down Soi 20** Ⓦ www.tamarind-cafe.com. This stylish vegetarian café and photo gallery serves an eclectic menu that fuses flavours from Korea, Malaysia, Thailand, Japan and the Mediterranean in a refreshingly innovative

menu. Wild mushroom steak (B280), Malaysian-style quesadilla (B95) and triple-bean salad (B110) all feature, as does all-day brunch. There are changing photo exhibitions, lounge-style seating, free wi-fi Internet access, and a roof terrace. Mon–Fri 11am–11pm, Sat & Sun 9am–11pm.

Took Lae Dee Inside the Foodland supermarket on Soi 5. The place to come for very cheap breakfasts: hearty American breakfasts eaten at the counter cost just B55.

🏃 **Vientiane Kitchen (Khrua Vientiane) 8 Soi 36, about 50m south off Thanon Sukhumvit.** Just a 3min walk west then south from Thong Lo Skytrain station (Exit 2) and you're transported into a little piece of rural northeastern Thailand, where the menu's stocked full of delicacies from the northeast (Isaan), a live band sets the mood with heart-felt folk songs, and there are even occasional performances by a troupe of upcountry dancers. The Lao- and Isaan-accented menu (B120–250) includes vegetable curry with ants' eggs, spicy-fried frog, jackfruit curry, and farm chicken with cashews, plus there's a decent range of veggie options such as meat-free laap and sweet-and-sour dishes. With its airy, barn-like interior and a mixed clientele of Thais and expats, it all adds up to a very enjoyable dining experience.

Yong Lee Corner of Soi 15. One of the few refreshingly basic – and brusque – rice-and-noodle shops on Sukhumvit; dishes cost from just B40. Daily 11.30am–2.30pm & 5.30–9.30pm.

Thai cuisine

Thai food is now hugely popular in the West, but nothing, of course, beats coming to Thailand to experience the full range of subtle and fiery flavours, constructed from the freshest ingredients.

▲ Colourful Thai desserts at MBK Food Centre

Four fundamental tastes are identified in Thai cuisine – spiciness, sourness, saltiness and sweetness – and diners aim to share a variety of dishes that impart a balance of these flavours, along with complementary textures. Lemon grass, basil, coriander, galangal, chilli, garlic, lime juice, coconut milk and fermented fish sauce (used instead of salt) are some of the distinctive components that bring these tastes to life.

In Bangkok, alongside the repertoire of standard Thai dishes described below, you'll find plenty of Chinese-style stir-fries such as sweet-and-sour and chicken with cashew nuts, as well as the distinctively spicy and ever-popular cuisine of northeastern Thailand.

Curries

Thai curries (**kaeng**) have as their foundation a variety of curry pastes, elaborate and subtle blends of herbs, spices, garlic, shallots and chilli peppers that are traditionally ground together with a pestle and mortar. The use of some of these spices, as well as of coconut cream, was imported from India long ago; curries that don't use coconut cream are naturally less sweet and thinner, with the consistency of soups.

▲ Fish awaiting their fate at *Somboon Seafood Restaurant*

While some curries, such as *kaeng karii* (mild and yellow) and *kaeng matsaman* (literally "Muslim curry", with potatoes, peanuts and usually beef), still show their roots, others have been adapted into quintessentially Thai dishes, notably *kaeng khiaw wan* (sweet and green), *kaeng phet* (red and hot) and *kaeng phanaeng* (thick and savoury, with peanuts). *Kaeng som* generally contains vegetables and fish and takes its distinctive sourness from the addition of tamarind or, in the northeast, okra leaves. Traditionally eaten during the cool season, *kaeng*

▼ Vats of curries at *Khrua Aroy Aroy*

liang uses up gourds or other bland vegetables, but is made aromatic by the heat of peppercorns and shallots and the fragrance of basil leaves.

Soups

Thai soups (**tom**), an essential component of most shared meals, are eaten simultaneously with other dishes, not as a starter. They are often flavoured with the distinctive tang of lemon grass, kaffir lime leaves and galangal, and garnished with fresh

▲ Street café

coriander – and can be extremely hot, if the cook adds liberal handfuls of chillies to the pot. Two favourites are *tom kha kai*, a creamy coconut chicken soup; and *tom yam kung*, a hot and sour prawn soup without coconut milk. *Khao tom*, a starchy rice soup that's generally eaten for breakfast, meets the approval of few Westerners, except as a traditional hangover cure.

Salads

One of the lesser-known delights of Thai cuisine is the **yam** or salad, which can often impart all four of the fundamental flavours in an unusual and refreshing harmony. *Yam* can be made in many permutations – with noodles, meat, seafood or vegetables, for example – but at the heart of every variety is a liberal squirt of fresh lime juice and a fiery sprinkling of chopped chillies. As well as *som tam*, *laap* and *nam tok* (described overleaf in the box on northeastern cuisine), salads to look out for include *yam som oh* (pomelo), *yam hua plee* (banana flowers) and *yam plaa duk foo* (crispy fried catfish).

Noodle and rice dishes

▲ Chilies

Thais eat **noodles** when Westerners would dig into a sandwich – for lunch, as a late-night snack or just to pass the time. Sold on street stalls everywhere, they come in assorted varieties – including *kway tiaw* (made with rice flour) and *ba mii* (egg noodles), *sen yai* (wide) and *sen lek* (thin) – and get boiled up as soups (*nam*), doused in gravy (*rat na*) or stir-fried (*haeng*, "dry", or *phat*, "fried"). Most famous of noodle dishes is *kway tiaw phat thai* – usually abbreviated to **phat thai**, meaning "Thai fry-up" – a delicious combination of fried noodles, bean sprouts, egg, tofu and spring onions, sprinkled with ground peanuts and the juice of half a lime, and often spiked with tiny dried shrimps.

Fried **rice** (*khao phat*) is the other faithful standby that's guaranteed to feature on menus right across the country. Also popular are cheap, one-dish meals served on a bed of steamed rice, notably *khao kaeng* (with curry), *khao na pet* (with roast duck) and *khao muu daeng* (with red-roasted pork).

▲ *Tom yam kung* and *kaeng matsaman*

Desserts

Desserts (**khanom**) don't really figure on most restaurant menus, but a few places offer bowls of *luk taan cheum*, a jellied concoction of lotus or palm seeds floating in a syrup scented with jasmine or other aromatic flowers. Coconut milk is a feature of most other desserts, notably delicious coconut ice cream, *khao niaw mamuang* (sticky rice with mango), and a royal Thai cuisine special of coconut custard (*sangkhayaa*) cooked inside a small pumpkin, whose flesh you can also eat.

▲ Street vendor pounding *som tam*

Northeastern Thai food

In Bangkok, northeastern food is the most prevalent of Thailand's several regional cuisines, partly due to the large numbers of migrants from the northeast (or Isaan) who work in the capital. Their staple food is **sticky rice** (*khao niaw*), which is more suited to the infertile lands of Isaan than the standard grain. Served in its own special rattan basket, it's usually eaten with the fingers – rolled up into small balls and dipped into chilli sauces. A classic combination is sticky rice with **som tam**, a spicy green-papaya salad with garlic, raw chillies, green beans, tomatoes, peanuts and dried shrimps (or fresh crab), and **kai yaang**, basted and barbecued chicken on a stick. Raw minced pork, beef or chicken is the basis of another popular Isaan dish, **laap**, a salad that's subtly flavoured with mint and lime. A similar northeastern salad is **nam tok**, featuring grilled beef or pork and roasted rice powder, which takes its name, "waterfall", from its refreshing blend of complex tastes.

Nightlife

For many of Bangkok's male visitors, nightfall is the signal to hit the city's sex bars, most notoriously in the area off Thanon Silom known as Patpong (see p.121). Fortunately, Bangkok's **nightlife** has thoroughly grown up and left these neon sumps behind in the last ten years, offering everything from microbreweries and vertiginous, rooftop cocktail bars to fiercely chic clubs and dance bars, hosting top-class DJs: within spitting distance of the beer bellies flopped onto Patpong's bars, for example, lies Soi 4, Thanon Silom, one of the city's most happening after-dark haunts. Though Silom 4 started out as a purely gay area (for details of Bangkok's gay nightlife, see p.200), it now offers a range of styles in gay, mixed and straight pubs, DJ bars and clubs. Along with Silom 4, the high-concept clubs and bars of Sukhumvit and the lively, teeming venues of Banglamphu pull in the style-conscious cream of Thai youth and are tempting an increasing number of travellers to stuff their party gear into their rucksacks.

Most bars and clubs operate nightly until 1am, while clubs on Silom 4 can stay open until 2am, with closing time strictly enforced under the current

---

Drink

Beer (*bia*) is one of the few consumer items in Thailand that's not a bargain due to the heavy taxes levied on the beverage – at around B50 for a 330ml bottle in the shops, it works out roughly the same as what you'd pay in the West (larger, 660ml bottles, when available, are always slightly better value). The two most famous local beers are Singha, which now has six percent alcohol content and an improved taste (ask for "*bia sing*"), and the cheaper Chang, which weighs in at a head-banging seven percent alcohol. All manner of foreign beers are now brewed in Thailand, including Heineken and Asahi, and in Bangkok you'll find imported bottles from all over the world.

Wine attracts even higher taxation than beer. It's now found on plenty of upmarket and tourist-oriented restaurant menus, but expect to be disappointed both by the quality and by the price. At about B75 for a hip-flask-sized 375ml bottle, the local **whisky** is a lot better value, and Thais think nothing of consuming a bottle a night, heavily diluted with ice and soda or Coke. The most palatable and widely available of these is Mekong, which is very pleasant once you've stopped expecting it to taste like Scotch; distilled from rice, Mekong is 35 percent proof, deep gold in colour and tastes slightly sweet. If that's not to your taste, a pricier Thai **rum** is also available, Sang Thip, made from sugar cane, and even stronger than the whisky at forty percent proof. Check the menu carefully when ordering a bottle of Mekong from a bar in a tourist area, as they often ask up to five times more than you'd pay in a guest house or shop.

△ *Bed Supperclub*, Thanon Sukhumvit

government's Social Order Policy. This has also involved occasional clampdowns on illegal drugs, including urine testing of bar customers, and more widespread ID checks to curb under-age drinking (you have to be 21 or over to drink in bars and clubs) – it's worth bringing your passport out with you, as ID is often requested however old you are.

For convenient drinking and dancing, we've split the most recommended of the city's bars and clubs into four central areas. The travellers' enclave of **Banglamphu** takes on a new personality after dark, when its hub, Thanon Khao San, becomes a "walking street", closed to all traffic but open to almost any kind of makeshift stall, selling everything from fried bananas and cheap beer to bargain fashions and idiosyncratic art works. Young Thais crowd the area to browse and snack before piling in to Banglamphu's countless bars and clubs, most of which host a good mix of local and foreign drinkers and ravers. Venues here tend to be low-key, with free entry (though some places ask you to show ID first), reasonably priced drinks and up-to-date sounds, or there's always plenty of kerbside restaurant tables, which make great places to nurse a few beers and watch the parade. Away from Khao San and nearby Soi Ram Bhuttri, Thanon Phra Athit is famous for its style-conscious little restaurant-bars where tables spill over onto the pavement, and the live music is likely to be a lone piano-player or guitarist.

Downtown bars, which tend to attract both foreign and Thai drinkers, are concentrated on adjoining Soi Lang Suan and Soi Sarasin (between Thanon Ploenchit and Lumphini Park), and in studenty Siam Square, as well as around the east end of Thanon Silom. Lang Suan and Sarasin boast several live-music bars, while the western end of the latter (between the jazz bar *Brown Sugar* and Thanon Rajdamri) supports a gaggle of good-time, gay and straight, DJ bars that are very popular with young Thais at weekends. On Silom 4, while most of the gay venues have been around for some years now, other bars and clubs have opened and closed with bewildering speed. All the same – once you've passed through the ID check at the entrance – on a short, slow bar-crawl around this wide, traffic-free alley lined with pavement tables, it would be hard not to find somewhere to enjoy yourself. If, among all the choice of nightlife around Silom, you do end up in one of Patpong's sex shows, watch out for hyper-inflated bar bills and other cons – plenty of customers get ripped off in some way, and stories of menacing bouncers are legion. **Thanon Sukhumvit** also has its share of girlie bars and bar-beers (open-sided drinking halls with huge circular bars) packed full of hostesses, but it's also garnering quite a reputation for high-concept "destination bars" (where the decor is as important as the drinks menu), as well as being the home of several long-established British-style pubs.

During the cool season (Nov–Feb), an evening out at one of the seasonal **beer gardens** is a pleasant way of soaking up the urban atmosphere (and the traffic fumes). You'll find them in hotel forecourts or sprawled in front of dozens of shopping centres all over the city.

Banglamphu and Ratanakosin

Except where indicated, all bars listed below are marked on the map on p.80. For advice on getting public transport to this area see the box on p.78.

Ad Here the 13th 13 Thanon Samsen. Friendly, intimate little jazz bar where half a dozen tables of Thai and expat musos congregate to listen to nightly sets from the in-house blues 'n' jazz quartet (about 10pm onwards). Well-priced beer and plenty of cocktails. Nightly 6pm–midnight.

Bangkok Bar Next to *Sawasdee* Inn at 149 Soi Ram Bhuttri. This skinny two-storey dance bar is fronted by a different DJ every night whose pop and house beats draw capacity crowds nightly. Nightly 6pm–1am.

Bar Bali 58 Thanon Phra Athit. Typical Phra Athit bar-restaurant, with just a half-dozen tables, a small menu of salads and drinking foods and a decent selection of well-priced cocktails. Nightly 6pm–1am.

Café Democ 78 Thanon Rajdamnoen Klang. Fashionable, dark and dinky bar that overlooks Democracy Monument and is spread over one and a half cosy floors, with extra seating on the semi-circular mezzanine. Lots of cocktails, nightly sessions from up-and-coming Thai DJs, and regular hip-hop evenings. Tues–Sun 4pm–2am.

The Cave Thanon Khao San. Feel like climbing the walls after your tenth bottle of Singha? This bar comes complete with indoor climbing wall, charging B100 per climb or B200/hour. Also sells climbing shoes and gear. Nightly 5pm–midnight.

Cinnamon Bar 106 Thanon Ram Bhuttri. Drink at little tables on the narrow outside terrace, beneath the waterfall wall and plastic bamboo trees, or join the fashionable,

well-behaved student crowd around the pool table inside. Nightly 6pm–1am.

The Club Thanon Khao San. The kitsch, pseudo-Italianate interior – designed to evoke a classical courtyard garden, complete with central fountain and statue of a chubby child hugging a fish – is unlikely to appeal to many Western clubbers, but Thais love this place, putting up with the ID checks at the door and making the most of the two bars and resident DJs. Also serves food. Daily 11am–1am.

Comme Thanon Phra Athit. Live music from enthusiastic cover bands, easy chairs and an open frontage mean that this inviting bar-restaurant, one of the largest on Phra Athit, nearly always gets a good crowd. Also serves some food (mostly Thai standards). 6pm–1am.

Deep 329/1–2 Thanon Ram Bhuttri. Get here early if you want a table on a Friday or Saturday night as the bands draw eager crowds that pack out the tiny bar. 6pm–1am.

Gulliver's Traveler's Tavern Thanon Khao San, ⓦwww.gulliverbangkok.com. Infamous, long-established backpacker-oriented air-con pub with pool tables, sports TV and reasonably priced beer (happy hours 3–9pm). Also does international food and has another branch on Thanon Sukhumvit. Daily 11am–1am.

Lava Club Basement, Bayon Building, 209 Thanon Khao San. Self-consciously sophisticated basement lounge bar done out in "volcanic" red and black with laser displays to enhance the look. DJs play mainly house and rave. Nightly 8pm–1am; ID sometimes required.

Molly Pub Thanon Ram Bhuttri. The attractive, colonial-style facade, complete with pastel-coloured shutters, makes a pleasant backdrop for the outdoor tables and low-slung wooden chairs that are perfectly located for people-watching over a Beer Chang or two. Also serves food. Daily 11am–1am.

Po 230 Tha Thien, Thanon Maharat (see map on p.60). When the Chao Phraya express boats start to wind down around 6pm, this bar takes over the rustic wooden pier and the balcony above with their great sunset views across the river. Beer and Thai whisky with accompanying Thai food and loud Thai and Western pop music – very popular with local students.

Sabai Bar Mouth of Sunset Street, 197 Thanon Khao San. Open-sided, three-storey, streetside bar that's the perfect spot for watching the Khao San parade. Nightly 6pm–1am.

Silk Bar 129–131 Thanon Khao San. The tiered outdoor decks are a popular spot for sipping cocktails while watching the nightly Khao San hustle; inside there's air-con, a pool table, a DJ and a small menu of standard Thai fare. Daily 6am–1am.

Susie Pub Next to *Marco Polo Guest House* on the soi between Thanon Khao San and Thanon Ram Bhuttri. Big, dark, phenomenally popular pub that's usually standing-room-only after 9pm. Has a pool table, decent music, resident DJs and cheapish beer. Packed with young Thais. Daily 11am–1am; ID sometimes required.

Siam Square, Thanon Ploenchit and northern downtown

The venues listed below are marked on the map on p.113; for the lowdown on public transport to this area, see the box on p.112.

Ad Makers 51/51 Soi Lang Suan ☎02 652 0168. Friendly, spacious bar with Wild West-style wooden decor and good food, attracting a cross-section of Thais and foreigners and featuring nightly folk and rock bands.

Brown Sugar 231/19–20 Soi Sarasin ☎02 250 1826. Chic, pricey, lively bar, acknowledged as the capital's top jazz venue.

Concept CM2 *Novotel*, Soi 6, Siam Square ☎02 209 8888. More theme park than nightclub, with live bands and various, barely distinct entertainment zones, including karaoke, an Italian restaurant and everything from bhangra to hip-hop in the Boom Room. Admission B550 (including two drinks) Fri & Sat, B220 (including one drink) Sun–Thurs.

Dallas Pub Soi 6, Siam Square ☎02 255 3276. Typical dark, noisy hangout playing *pleng pua chiwit*, "songs for life" – Thai folk music blended with Western prog and folk rock – bedecked with buffalo skulls, Indian heads, American flags. A lot of fun: singalongs to decent live bands, dancing round the tables, cheap beer and friendly, casual staff.

WOC 264/4–6 Soi 3, Siam Square. Smart, modernist but easy-going hangout for students and twenty-somethings, with reasonably priced drinks, a good choice of accompanying snacks and some interesting Thai/Italian pastas for main dishes. A little hard to find up some stairs by Siam Square's Centerpoint.

Hard Rock Café Soi 11, Siam Square. Genuine outlet of the famous chain, better for drink than food. Brash enthusiasm and big sounds, with predictable live bands nightly.

Saxophone 3/8 Victory Monument (southeast corner), Thanon Phrayathai ☎02 246 5472. Lively, spacious venue that hosts nightly jazz, blues, folk and rock bands and attracts a good mix of Thais and farangs; decent food, relaxed drinking atmosphere and, all things considered, reasonable prices.

Syn Bar Swissôtel Nai Lert Park, 2 Thanon Witthayu. Hip hotel bar, popular at weekends, decorated retro style with bubble chairs and sparkling fibreoptic carpet. Excellent cocktails and nightly DJs playing house and Latin; happy hour Mon–Fri 5–9pm.

Southern downtown: south of Thanon Rama IV

See the map on p.120 for locations of the venues listed below; for the lowdown on public transport to this area, see p.119.

Barbican 9/4–5 Soi Thaniya, east end of Thanon Silom ☎02 234 3590. Stylishly modern fortress-like decor to match the name: dark woods, metal and undressed stone. With Guinness on tap and the financial pages posted above the urinals, it could almost be a smart City of London pub – until you look out of the windows onto the soi's incongruous Japanese hostess bars. Good food, DJ sessions and happy hours Mon–Fri 5–7pm.

Hu'u Ascott Building, 187 Thanon Sathorn Tai. Moody, elegant and dimly lit bar in Asian minimalist style, playing hot or cool sounds according to the time of night and serving excellent cocktails, alongside snacks and tapas; be prepared for a stylish surprise at the toilet washbasins.

Irish Xchange 1/5 Thanon Convent, off the east end of Thanon Silom ☎02 266 7160. Blarney Bangkok-style: a warm, relaxing Irish pub, tastefully done out in dark wood and familiar Irish knick-knacks and packed with expats, especially on Fri night. Guinness and Kilkenny Bitter on tap, expensive food such as Irish stew and beef and Guinness pie, and a rota of house bands.

Lucifer 76/1–3 Patpong 1. Popular dance club in the dark heart of Patpong, largely untouched by the sleaze around it. Done out with mosaics and stalactites like a satanic grotto, with balconies to look down on the dance-floor action. Free entry, except Fri & Sat, B150 including one drink. *Radio City*, the interconnected bar downstairs, is only slightly less raucous, with jumping live bands, including famous Elvis and Tom Jones impersonators, and tables out on the sweaty pavement.

Noriega's Soi 4, Thanon Silom. Unpretentious, good-time bar at the end of the alley, with nightly live bands playing jazz, blues and rock; salsa lessons followed by big Latin sounds on Sun evenings.

🏃 **The Sky Bar & Distil** Floor 63, State Tower, 1055 Thanon Silom, cnr of Thanon Charoen Krung ☎02 624 9555. Thrill-seekers and view addicts shouldn't miss forking out for an al fresco drink here, 275 metres above the city's pavements – come around 6pm to enjoy the stunning panoramas in both the light and the dark. It's standing only at *The Sky Bar*, a circular restaurant-bar on the edge of the building with almost 360° views, but for the sunset itself, you're better off on the outside terrace of *Distil* on the other side of the building (where bookings are accepted), which has a wider choice of drinks, charming service and huge couches to recline on.

Speed Soi 4, Thanon Silom. Dance bar with an industrial feel in black and silver, popular at the weekend, playing hip-hop and R&B. Fri & Sat B100, including one drink.

Tapas Bar Soi 4, Thanon Silom ⊛www .tapasroom.com. Vaguely Spanish-oriented, pricey bar (but no tapas) with Moorish-style decor, whose outside tables are probably the best spot for checking out the comings and goings on the soi; inside, music ranges from house and hip-hop to Latin jazz and funk, often with an accompanying percussionist (Fri & Sat admission B100).

🏃 **Tawandaeng German Brewery** 462/61 Thanon Rama III ☎02 678 1114–5. A taxi-ride south of Thanon Sathorn down Thanon Narathiwat Ratchanakharin, and best to book a table in advance – this vast all-rounder is well worth the effort. Under a huge dome, up to 1600 revellers enjoy good food and great micro-brewed beer every night, but the main attraction is the mercurial cabaret (not Sun), featuring Fong Naam, led by Bruce Gaston, who blend Thai classical and popular with Western styles of music.

Thanon Sukhumvit

The places listed below are marked on the map on p.126. For advice on getting public transport to this area, see the box on p.127.

The Ball in Hand First floor of the Sin building, behind 7–11 on Soi 4 ⓦwww.theballinhand .com. In notoriously sleazy Soi 4, better known as Soi Nana, this vast pool hall and bar stands out from all the other places with pool tables because of its dozen or so high-quality imported tables, its strict no-hustle policy and its regular competitions. Daily from about 1pm to 1am.

Bed Supperclub 26 Soi 11 ☏02 651 3537, ⓦwww.bedsupperclub.com. Worth visiting for the futuristic visuals alone, this seductively curvaceous spacepod bar squats self-consciously in an otherwise quite ordinary soi. Inside, the all-white interior is dimly lit and surprisingly cosy, with deep couches inviting drinkers to recline around the edges of the upstairs gallery, getting a good view of the downstairs bar and DJ. The vibe is always welcoming and a lot less pretentious than you might expect; some nights are themed, including a weekly gay night (check listings mags or website for details), when a B500 cover charge is redeemble against two drinks of the equivalent price. The restaurant section is starker, lit with glacial ultraviolet, and serving a Pacific Rim fusion menu 7.30–9pm (reservations essential). Bar opens nightly 8pm–2am; ID required.

The Bull's Head Soi 33/1. A Sukhumvit institution that takes pride in being Bangkok's most authentic British pub, right down to the horse brasses, jukebox and typical pub food. Famous for its Sunday evening "toss the boss" happy hours (5–7pm), when a flip of a coin determines whether or not you have to pay for your round. Daily 11am–1.30am.

Cheap Charlie's Soi 11. Idiosyncratic, long-running pavement bar that's famous for its cheap beer and lack of tables and chairs. A few lucky punters get to occupy the bar-stools but otherwise it's standing-room only. Daily 3pm–2am.

Gulliver's Traveler's Tavern 6 Soi 5 ⓦwww .gulliverbangkok.com. An offshoot of the original Khao San sports bar, this cavernous branch has tables inside and out at which it serves draught Guinness and the rest (happy hour lasts from midday–9pm), as well as an international menu. Shows live sporting fixtures on TV and has table football, pool tables and Internet access. Daily 11am–1am.

Londoner Brew Pub Mouth of Soi 33 ⓦwww .the-londoner.com. Aside from the pool table, darts board, big-screen sports TV and live music (nightly from about 9pm), it's the specially brewed pints of Londoner's Pride Cream Bitter and London Pilsner 33 that draw in the punters. Happy hours 4–7pm & 11pm–1am. Also has free wi-fi Internet access. Daily 11am–1am.

Q Bar 34 Soi 11 ⓦwww.qbarbangkok.com. Very dark, very trendy, New York-style bar occupying two floors and a terrace. Famous for its wide choice of chilled vodkas, and for its music, *Q Bar* appeals to a mixed crowd of fashionable people, particularly on Friday and Saturday nights when the DJs fill the dance floor. Arrive before 11pm if you want a seat, and don't turn up in shorts, singlets or sandals if you're male. Mon–Thurs B400 including two free drinks, Fri–Sun B600. Daily 8pm–1am; ID required.

Robin Hood Mouth of Soi 33/1. Another popular British pub, with pool table, sports TV and English food, plus an all-day breakfast for B280. Daily 11am–1am.

Gay and lesbian Bangkok

B uddhist tolerance and a national abhorrence of confrontation and victimization combine to make Thai society relatively tolerant of **homosexuality**, if not exactly positive about same-sex relationships. Most Thais are extremely private and discreet about being gay, generally pursuing a "don't ask, don't tell" understanding with their family. Hardly any public figures are out, yet the predilections of several respected social, political and entertainment figures are widely known and accepted. There is no mention of homosexuality at all in Thai law, which means that the age of consent for gay sex is fifteen, the same as for heterosexuals. This also means that gay rights are not protected under Thai law. However, most Thais are horrified by the idea of gay-bashing and generally regard it as unthinkable to spurn a child or relative for being gay. Although excessively physical displays of affection are frowned upon for both heterosexuals and homosexuals, Western **gay couples** should get no hassle about being seen together in public – it's more common, in fact, for friends of the same sex (gay or not) to walk hand-in-hand, than for heterosexual couples to do so.

Information and contacts for gay travellers

Anjaree PO Box 322, Rajdamnoen PO, Bangkok 10200 ©anjaree@loxinfo.com. General information on the lesbian community in Thailand.

Dreaded Ned's Ⓦwww.dreadedned.com. Events listings and information on almost every gay venue in the country.

Lesla Ⓦwww.lesla.com. Thailand's largest lesbian organization hosts regular events and runs a web-board.

Long Yang Club Ⓦwww.longyangclub.org/thailand. This international organization was founded to promote friendship between men of Western and Eastern origin and runs regular socials.

Utopia Ⓦwww.utopia-asia.com & Ⓦwww.utopia-asia.com/womthai.htm. Asia's best gay and lesbian website lists clubs, events, accommodation and organizations for gays and lesbians and has useful links to other sites in Asia and the rest of the world. Its offshoot, Utopia Tours, is a gay-oriented travel agency offering trips and guides within Thailand and the rest of Asia; tours can be booked through Door East, *Tarntawan Palace Hotel*, 119/5–10 Thanon Suriwong (℡02 238 3227, Ⓦwww.utopia-tours.com).

Transvestites (known as *katoey* or "ladyboys") and transsexuals are a lot more visible in Thailand than in the west. You'll find cross-dressers doing quite ordinary jobs and there are a number of transvestites and transsexuals in the public eye too – including national volleyball stars and champion *muay thai* boxers. The government tourist office vigorously promotes the transvestite cabarets in Bangkok (see p.205), all of which are advertised as family entertainment. *Katoey* also regularly appear as characters in soap operas, TV comedies and films, where they are depicted as harmless figures of fun. Richard Totman's *The Third Sex* offers an interesting insight into Thai *katoey*, their experiences in society and public attitudes towards them; see "Books" on p.252 for a review.

The gay scene

Bangkok's **gay scene** is mainly focused on mainstream venues like karaoke bars, restaurants, massage parlours, gyms, saunas and escort agencies. Most of the action happens on Silom 4 (near Patpong), on the more exclusive Silom 2 (towards Thanon Rama IV), and at the rougher, mostly Thai bars of Thanon Sutthisarn near the Chatuchak Weekend Market. As in the straight scene, venues reflect class and status differences. Expensive international-style places are very popular, attracting upper- and middle-class gays, many of whom have travelled or been educated abroad and developed Western tastes, as well as a contingent of Thais seeking foreign sugar daddies.

The farang-oriented gay **sex industry** is a tiny but highly visible part of Bangkok's gay scene and, with its tawdry floor shows and host services, it bears a dispiriting resemblance to the straight sex trade. Like their female counterparts in the heterosexual fleshpots, many of the boys working in the gay sex bars that dominate these districts are underage (anyone caught having sex with a prostitute below the age of 18 faces imprisonment). A significant number of gay prostitutes are gay by economic necessity rather than by inclination. As with the straight sex scene, we do not list the commercial gay sex bars.

The gay scene is heavily male, and there are hardly any **lesbian**-only venues, though quite a few gay bars are mixed. Thai lesbians generally eschew the word lesbian, which in Thailand is associated with male fantasies, instead referring to themselves as either *tom* (for tomboy) or *dee* (for lady).

Every year in mid-November, the capital's gay community puts on a big show for **Bangkok Pride** (Ⓦ www.bangkokpride.org), strutting its stuff around Thanon Silom in a week of parades, cabarets, fancy-dress competitions and sports contests that culminates with a jamboree in Lumphini Park on the Saturday.

Gay bars and clubs

The bars, clubs and bar-restaurants listed here are the most notable of Bangkok's gay nightlife venues; *Bed Supperclub* (see p.200) also hosts a regular gay night.

The Balcony Soi 4, Thanon Silom. Unpretentious, fun bar-restaurant with a large, popular terrace, reasonably priced drinks, karaoke and decent Thai and Western food.

Dick's Café Duangthawee Plaza, 894/7–8 Soi Pratuchai, Thanon Suriwong. Stylish day-and-night café-restaurant (daily 10.30am–2am), hung with exhibitions by gay artists, on a traffic-free soi opposite the prominent Wall St Tower, ideal for drinking, eating decent Thai and Western food or just chilling out.

Disgo Disgo Soi 2, Thanon Silom. Small, well-designed bar-disco with a retro feel, playing good dance music to a fun young crowd.

DJ Station Soi 2, Thanon Silom. Highly fashionable but unpretentious disco, packed at weekends, attracting a mix of Thais and farangs; cabaret show nightly at 11.30pm. B100 including one drink (B200 including two drinks Fri & Sat).

Expresso Soi 2, Thanon Silom. Immaculately designed bar-lounge with cool water features and subtle lighting.

Freeman Dance Arena 60/18–21 Soi 2/1, Thanon Silom (in a small soi between Soi Thaniya and Soi 2). Busy disco, somewhat more Thai-oriented than *DJ Station*, with slick cabaret shows at 11.30pm and 1am. B150 including one drink (B250 including two drinks

Fri & Sat). Under the same management is *Richard's*, a smart, pre-club bar-restaurant next door.

JJ Park 8/3 Soi 2, Thanon Silom. Classy, Thai-oriented bar-restaurant, for relaxed socializing rather than raving, with nightly singers, comedy shows and good food.

Sphinx 98–104 Soi 4, Thanon Silom. Chic decor, terrace seating and very good Thai and Western food attract a sophisticated crowd to this ground-floor bar and restaurant; karaoke and live music upstairs at *Pharaoh's*.

Telephone Pub 114/11–13 Soi 4, Thanon Silom. Cruisey, dimly lit, long-standing eating and drinking venue with a terrace on the alley and telephones on the tables inside.

Vega Soi 39, Thanon Sukhumvit. Trendy bar-restaurant run by a group of lesbians. The live music, karaoke and dance floor attract a mixed, fashionable crowd. Mon–Sat 11am–1am.

Entertainment

The most accessible of the capital's performing arts are **Thai dancing**, particularly when served up in bite-size portions at tourist-oriented venues, and the graceful and humorous **puppet shows** at the Traditional Thai Puppet Theatre on Thanon Rama IV. **Thai boxing** is also well worth watching: the live experience at either of Bangkok's two main national stadia far outshines the TV coverage.

(13) Traditional and contemporary drama, dance and music

Drama pretty much equals dance in classical Thai theatre, and many of the **traditional dance-dramas** are based on the Hindu epic the *Ramayana* (in Thai, *Ramakien*), a classic adventure tale of good versus evil which is taught in all the schools (see p.65 for an outline of the story). Not understanding the plots can be a major disadvantage, so try reading an abridged version beforehand (see

Traditional dance-drama

The most spectacular form of traditional Thai theatre is **khon**, a stylized drama performed in masks and elaborate costumes by a troupe of highly trained classical dancers. There's little room for individual interpretation in these dances, as all the movements follow a strict choreography that's been passed down through generations: each graceful, angular gesture depicts a precise event, action or emotion which will be familiar to educated *khon* audiences. The dancers don't speak, and the story is chanted and sung by a chorus who stand at the side of the stage, accompanied by a classical *phipat* orchestra.

A typical *khon* performance features several of the best-known **Ramayana** episodes, in which the main characters are recognized by their masks, headdresses and heavily brocaded costumes. Gods and humans don't wear masks, but it's generally easy enough to distinguish the hero Rama and heroine Sita from the action; they always wear tall gilded headdresses and often appear in a threesome with Rama's brother Lakshaman. Monkey **masks** are always open-mouthed, almost laughing, and come in several colours: monkey army chief Hanuman always wears white, and his two right-hand men – Nilanol, the god of fire, and Nilapat, the god of death – wear red and black respectively. In contrast, the demons have grim mouths, clamped shut or snarling out of usually green faces; Totsagan, king of the demons, wears a green face in battle and a gold one during peace, but always sports a two-tier headdress carved with two rows of faces. Even if you don't see a show, you're bound to come across copies of the masks worn by the main *khon* characters, which are sold as souvenirs and constitute an art form in their own right.

△ *Lakhon chatri* dancers, Erawan Shrine

"Books" p.254) and check out the wonderfully imaginative murals at Wat Phra Kaeo (see p.64), after which you'll certainly be able to sort the goodies from the baddies, if little else.

The best way to experience the traditional performing arts is usually at a show designed for tourists, where background knowledge and stoic concentration are not essential. The easiest place to get a glimpse of the variety and spectacle intrinsic to traditional Thai theatre is at the unashamedly tourist-oriented Siam Niramit cultural extravaganza, described below. Several tourist restaurants offer low-tech versions of the Siam Niramit experience, in the form of nightly **culture shows** that usually feature a medley of Thai dancing and classical music, perhaps with a martial-arts demonstration thrown in. In some cases there's a set fee for dinner and show, in others the performance is free but the à la carte prices are slightly inflated; it's always worth calling ahead to reserve, especially if you want a vegetarian version of the set menu.

Thai dancing is performed for its original ritual purpose, usually several times a day, at the Lak Muang Shrine behind the Grand Palace (see the map on p.60) and the Erawan Shrine on the corner of Thanon Ploenchit (see the map on p.112). Both shrines have resident troupes of dancers who are hired by worshippers to perform *lakhon chatri*, a sort of *khon* dance-drama, to thank benevolent spirits for answered prayers. The dancers are always dressed up in full gear and accompanied by musicians, but the length and complexity of the dance and the number of dancers depend on the amount of money paid by the supplicant: a price list is posted near the dance area. The musicians at the Erawan Shrine are particularly highly rated, though the almost comic apathy of the dancers there doesn't do them justice.

Non-Thai-speaking audiences are likely to struggle with much of the contemporary **Thai theatre** performed in the city, though all the venues listed below occasionally stage shows that will appeal to visitors, be that experimental drama, **classical concerts** or performances by visiting international dance and theatre companies. Consult the monthly listings magazine *Bangkok Metro* for details of current programmes.

Culture shows

Siam Niramit Ratchada theatre, 19 Thanon Tiam Ruammit, a 5-min walk from the Thailand Culture Centre subway, following signs for the South Korean embassy (see colour map) ☏02 649 9222, ⓦwww.siamniramit .com. Nightly from 6pm, show starts at 8pm; B1500; tickets can be bought on the spot or through most travel agents. Staged in a purpose-built 2000-seat theatre, this eighty-minute show presents a history of regional Thailand's culture and beliefs in a hi-tech spectacular of fantastic costumes and huge chorus numbers, enlivened by acrobatics and flashy special effects. The theatre complex also includes crafts outlets and a buffet restaurant (dinner costs B500).

Silom Village Thanon Silom (see map on p.120) ☏02 234 4581. Nightly at 8.30pm; B600. This complex of tourist shops hosts a nightly fifty-minute indoor show to accompany a set menu of Thai food, as well as a rather desultory free show at 7.45pm at its outdoor restaurant.

Supatra River House 266 Soi Wat Rakhang, Thonburi (see map on p.98) ☏02 411 0305. Fri & Sat at 8.30pm; B650–850 including food. Free shuttle boat transport from Tha Maharat in front of Wat Mahathat. Twice a week, diners at this upmarket, riverside restaurant are entertained with traditional-style dance-dramas staged by performers from the nearby Patravadi Theatre.

Other venues

National Theatre Next to the National Museum on the northwest corner of Sanam Luang

(see map on p.60) ☏02 224 1342 or 02 222 1012. Stages roughly weekly shows of *lakhon* (classical dance-drama) and *likay* (folk drama) – a programme in English is posted up in the theatre foyer, or contact the nearby Bangkok Information Centre (see p.27), who keep a copy of the programme in Thai; plus outdoor shows of classical music and dancing at the National Museum in the dry season (Dec–April Sat & Sun 5pm; B20).

Patravadi Theatre 69/1 Soi Wat Rakhang, Thonburi (see map on p.98) ☏02 412 7287, ⓦwww.patravaditheatre.com; free shuttle boat transport from Tha Maharat in front of Wat Mahathat. The city's most famous venue for experimental, contemporary theatre. Also runs open-to-all mostly hour-long classes (B150) in *khon* dance (Fri 5pm), drumming (Sat 2pm, Sun 2.30pm) and Thai classical dance (kids Sat 2.30pm, adults 4.30–6pm), whose participants stage free shows here every Sun 6pm.

Sala Chalermkrung Theatre 66 Thanon Charoen Krung (New Road), on the intersection with Thanon Triphet in Pahurat, next to Old Siam Plaza (see map on p.91) ☏02 225 8757. See p.89 for transport info. This renovated historical theatre shows contemporary Thai drama and comedy most of the week, but occasionally stages tourist-friendly performances of traditional dance-dramas.

Thailand Cultural Centre Thanon Ratchadapisek ☏02 247 0028, ext 4280, ⓦwww .thaiculturalcenter.com; subway to Thailand Cultural Centre. The country's most prominent performing arts space puts on traditional and contemporary theatre, mainstream classical concerts, and visiting international dance and theatre shows.

Puppet theatre

The **Traditional Thai Puppet Theatre** (℡02 252 9683–4, ⓦwww.thaipuppet
.com), at Suan Lum Night Bazaar on Thanon Rama IV, stages entertaining
tourist-oriented performances, which, though pricey, are well worth it for both
adults and children. The puppets in question are jointed stick-puppets (*hun lakhon
lek*), an art form that was developed in the early twentieth century and had all
but died out before the owner of the theatre, Sakorn Yangkeowsod (aka Joe
Louis), came to its rescue in the 1980s. Each 60cm-tall puppet is manipulated by
three puppeteers, who are accomplished Thai classical dancers in their own right,
complementing their charges' elegant and precise gestures with graceful movements in a harmonious ensemble. Hour-long shows (B900, kids B300) are put on
daily at the theatre at 7.30pm, preceded by a video documentary in English at 7pm.
The puppets perform mostly stories from the *Ramakien*, accompanied by surtitles
or synopses in English and live traditional music of a high standard.

Cabaret

Glitzy and occasionally ribald entertainment is the order of the day at the capital's two **ladyboy cabaret shows**, where a bevy of luscious transvestites dons
glamorous outfits and performs over-the-top song and dance routines. Mambo
Cabaret plays at the theatre in Washington Square, between Sukhumvit sois 22
and 24 (℡02 259 5715; nightly 8pm; Nov–Feb also at 10pm; B600–800; see
map on p.126), and New Calypso Cabaret performs inside the *Asia Hotel*, close
by Ratchathevi Skytrain station at 296 Thanon Phrayathai (℡02 216 8937,
ⓦwww.calypsocabaret.com; nightly 8.15 & 9.45pm; B1000 or half-price if
booked online five days ahead).

Thai boxing

The violence of the average **Thai boxing** (*muay thai*) match may be offputting
to some, but spending a couple of hours at one of Bangkok's two main stadia
can be immensely entertaining, not least for the enthusiasm of the spectators
and the ritualistic aspects of the fights. Bouts, advertised in the English-language
newspapers, are held in the capital every night of the week at the **Rajdamnoen
Stadium**, next to the TAT office on Rajdamnoen Nok (℡02 281 4205; Mon,
Wed & Sun 6pm, Thurs 5pm), and at **Lumphini Stadium** on Thanon Rama
IV (℡02 252 8765; Tues & Fri 6.30pm, Sat 2pm & 6.30pm); see the colour
map at the back of the book for venue locations. Tickets cost B1000–2000 (at
Rajdamnoen the view from the B1000 seats is partially obscured). Sessions
usually feature ten bouts, each consisting of five three-minute rounds (with
two-minute rests in between each round), so if you're not a big fan it may
be worth turning up an hour late, as the better fights tend to happen later in
the billing. It's more fun if you buy one of the less expensive standing tickets,
enabling you to witness the wild gesticulations of the betting aficionados at
close range.

To engage in a little *muay thai* yourself, visit Sor Vorapin's Gym at 13 Trok
Kasap off Thanon Chakrabongse in Banglamphu, which holds **classes** twice
daily (B400/session, B2500/7 sessions; ℡02 282 3551, ⓦwww.thaiboxings.com).
Jitti's Gym on Soi Amon off Sukhumvit Soi 49 also offers well-regarded training

Thai boxing (*muay thai*) enjoys a following similar to football in Europe. Every province has a stadium and whenever a fight is shown on TV large noisy crowds gather round the sets in streetside restaurants and noodle shops.

There's a strong spiritual and **ritualistic** dimension to *muay thai*, adding grace to an otherwise brutal sport. Each boxer enters the ring to the wailing music of a three-piece *phipat* orchestra, often flamboyantly attired in a lurid silk robe over the statutory red or blue boxer shorts. The fighter then bows, first in the direction of his birthplace and then to the north, south, east and west, honouring both his teachers and the spirit of the ring. Next he performs a slow dance, claiming the audience's attention and demonstrating his prowess as a performer.

Any part of the body except the head may be used as an **offensive weapon** in *muay thai*, and all parts except the groin are fair targets; most knockouts are caused by kicks to the head. As the action hots up, so the orchestra speeds up its tempo and the betting in the audience becomes more frenetic. It can be a gruesome business, but it was far bloodier before modern boxing gloves were made compulsory in the 1930s – combatants used to wrap their fists with hemp impregnated with a face-lacerating dosage of ground glass.

sessions for foreigners (☎02 392 5890, Ⓦwww.thailandroad.com/jittigym). For more in-depth training and further information about Thai boxing, contact the Muay Thai Institute on the far northern outskirts of Bangkok (☎02 992 0096, Ⓦwww.muaythai-institute.net), which runs training courses for foreigners (B6400 for 40hr), including practical instruction, as well as history and theory.

Cinemas

Central Bangkok has more than forty **cinemas**, many of which show recent American and European releases with their original dialogue and Thai subtitles. Most cinemas screen shows around four times a day: rough programme details are given every day in the *Nation* but your best bet is to go to Ⓦwww.movieseer.com, which allows you to search by movie or by area in Bangkok, up to a week ahead; cinema locations are printed on *Nancy Chandler's Map of Bangkok*. Seats cost around B100; whatever cinema you're in, you're expected to stand for the king's anthem, which is played before every performance. See below for information about Bangkok's annual film festival.

There are half a dozen cinemas in and around Siam Square, and nearly every major downtown shopping plaza has two or three screens on its top floor. Movies at the French and German cultural centres, the Alliance Française, 29 Thanon Sathorn Tai (☎02 670 4200, Ⓦwww.alliance-francaise.or.th), and the Goethe Institut, 18/1 Soi Goethe, between Thanon Sathorn Tai and Soi Ngam Duphli (☎02 287 0942, Ⓦwww.goethe.de), are often subtitled in English. And if it's been a while since you've caught up on the new releases, check out the dozens of video-showing restaurants along Banglamphu's Thanon Khao San, where recent blockbusters are screened back-to-back every day and night of the year, all for the price of a banana smoothie or a cheese sandwich.

For ten days a year, usually in February, many downtown cinemas participate in the **Bangkok International Film Festival**, which provides the chance to preview new and unusual Thai films alongside some 150 features and documentaries from around the world. Check Ⓦwww.bangkokfilm.org for details.

Mind and Body

T he last few years have seen an explosion in the number of spas opening in Bangkok – mainly inside the poshest hotels, but also as small, afford-able walk-in centres around the city. With their focus on indulgent self-pampering, spas are usually associated with high-spending tourists, but the treatments on offer at Bangkok's five-star hotels are often little different from those used by traditional medical practitioners, who have long held that massage and herbs are the best way to restore physical and mental well-being. Even in the heart of the city, it's also possible to undergo a bit of highly tradi-tional mental self-help by practising meditation.

Traditional massage and spas

Thai massage is based on the principle that many physical and emotional problems are caused by the blocking of vital energy channels within the body. The masseur uses his or her feet, heels, knees and elbows, as well as hands, to exert a gentle pressure on these channels, supplementing this acupressure style technique by pulling and pushing the limbs into yogic stretches. This distinguishes Thai massage from most other massage styles, which are more concerned with tissue manipulation. One is supposed to emerge from a Thai massage feeling both relaxed and energized, and it is said that regular massages produce long-term benefits in muscles as well as stimulating the circulation and aiding natural detoxification. Thais visit a masseur for many conditions, including fevers, colds and muscle strain, but bodies that are not sick are also considered to benefit from the restorative powers of a massage, and nearly every hotel and guest house will be able to put you in touch with a masseur. Thai masseurs do not use oils or lotions and the client is treated on a mat or mattress; you'll often be given a pair of loose-fitting trousers and perhaps a loose top to change into. A session should ideally last two hours and will cost from around B300–1500, or a lot more in the most exclusive spas.

The **science** behind Thai massage has its roots in Indian Ayurvedic medicine, which classifies each component of the body according to one of the four elements (earth, water, fire and air), and holds that balancing these elements within the body is crucial to good health. Many of the stretches and manipu-lations fundamental to Thai massage are thought to have derived from yogic practices introduced to Thailand from India by Buddhist missionaries in about the second century BC; Chinese acupuncture and reflexology have also had a strong influence. In the nineteenth century, King Rama III ordered a series of murals illustrating the principles of Thai massage to be painted around the courtyard of Bangkok's Wat Pho (see p.69), and they are still in place today, along

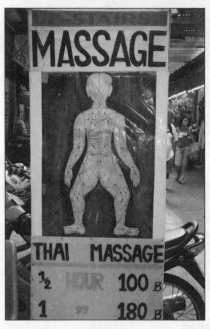

△ Pian's Massage Center, Banglamphu

with statues of ascetics depicted in typical massage poses. **Wat Pho** has been the leading school of Thai massage for hundreds of years, and it's possible to take courses there as well as to receive a massage. Masseurs who trained at Wat Pho are considered to be the best in the country and masseurs all across the city advertise this as a credential, whether it's true or not. Many Thais consider blind masseurs to be especially sensitive practitioners.

The same Indian missionaries who introduced yogic practices to Thailand are also credited with spreading the word about the therapeutic effects of herbal saunas and heated **herbal** compresses, though the **herbs** themselves are resolutely Thai and feature in Thai cuisine as well as herbal treatments. Among these the most popular are tamarind, whose acidic content makes it a useful skin exfoliant, and turmeric, which is known for its disinfectant and healing properties; both are a common component of the scrubs and body wraps offered at many spas. The same places will also use lemon grass, probably Thailand's most distinctive herb, and the ubiquitous jasmine as soothing agents in aromatherapy treatments.

Spas and massage centres

All **spas** in Bangkok feature traditional Thai massage and herbal therapies in their programmes, but most also offer dozens of other international treatments, including facials, aromatherapy, Swedish massage and various body wraps. Spa centres in upmarket hotels are usually open to non-guests but generally need to be booked in advance; day spas that are not attached to hotels may not require reservations. We've listed a selection of Bangkok's most famous spas and massage centres, but cheaper traditional massage sessions and courses are also held at dozens of guest houses in Banglamphu.

Bann Phuan Sukhumvit Soi 11. Good, inexpensive Thai massage (B200/hr). Daily noon–2am.

Banyan Tree Spa Banyan Tree Hotel, 21/100 Thanon Sathorn Tai ☎02 679 1054, ⓦwww .banyantreespa.com. Internationally famous spa hotel boasting six floors of spa treatment rooms with panoramic views of the city (including some hotel suites with their own private spa rooms). Extensive and very expensive programme of massage, body wraps and beauty treatments. Reservations essential. Daily 10am–10pm.

Como Shambhala Metropolitan, 27 Thanon Sathorn Tai ☎02 625 3333, ⓦwww .metropolitan.como.bz. Elegant, carefully designed contemporary spa, offering a short, accessible menu of expensive treatments that touch all the bases. Non-guests have access to the steam room and bubbling hydro pool (good for the circulation) and can continue their good works at *Glow*, the adjacent, healthy, organic café-restaurant. Daily 8.30am–9.30pm.

Divana Massage and Spa 7, Sukhumvit Soi 25 ☎02 661 6784, ⓦwww.divanaspa.com. Tranquil little garden-haven day spa, with a range of own-product treatments, including spas from B2350 and Thai massage from B1150/100mins. Mon–Fri 11am–11pm, Sat & Sun 10am–11pm.

Mandara Spa Bangkok Marriott Resort and Spa, 257/1–3 Thanon Charoen Nakorn, beside the Krungthep Bridge in southern Thonburi ☎02 476 0021, ⓦwww.mandaraspa.com. The famous chain of classy Asian spas has several outlets in Bangkok, including this one set within the extensive tropical gardens of the riverside *Bangkok Marriott Resort*, which offers all the trademark Mandara Spa treatments and massages, at fairly high prices. Phone the spa for complimentary ferry transport from the Saphan Taksin Skytrain station. Reservations essential. Daily 10am–10pm.

The Oriental Spa Thai Health and Beauty Center Oriental Hotel, 48 Oriental Avenue, off Thanon Charoen Krung ☎02 439 7613, ⓦwww.mandarinoriental.com. This was Bangkok's first hotel spa and, as you'd expect from the city's most famous lodging, it's a superior establishment, housed in a restored hundred-year-old teakwood home across the river from the *Oriental* and accessed by the hotel ferry. Huge

range of very expensive treatments and hydrotherapy facilities. Reservations essential. Daily 7am–10pm.

Pian's Massage Center Soi Susie Pub, off Thanon Khao San, Banglamphu ☎02 629 0924, ⓦwww.piangroup.com. Well-regarded walk-in city massage centre offering inexpensive traditional Thai massage (B180/hr), foot massages, Swedish and herbal massages. Also runs courses in Thai, Swedish, herbal and foot massage (about B30,000 for a 30-hour course, or B250 for a one-hour introduction). Daily 8am–10pm.

Ruen Nuad 42 Thanon Convent, off Thanon Silom ☎02 632 2662–3. Excellent Thai massages (B550 for 2hr), as well as aromatherapy and herbal massages, in an air-conditioned, characterful wooden house, down an alley opposite the BNH Hospital and behind *Naj* restaurant. Daily 10am–9pm.

Sikhara Spa Buddy Lodge Hotel, 265 Thanon Khao San, Banglamphu ☎02 629 4477, ⓦwww.buddylodge.com. Luxurious but refreshingly mid-priced hotel spa with a full range of treatments and massages, including aromatherapy massage in chic minimalist surroundings. Thai massage B800/60min; aromatic scrub B1500. Daily 9am–10pm.

Wat Pho Ratanakosin ⓦwww.watpho.com. See p.69.

Meditation

Most of Thailand's retreats are, naturally enough, out in the provinces, but a few temples and centres in Bangkok cater specifically for foreigners by holding **meditation sessions** in English; novices and practised meditators alike are generally welcome. The meditation taught is mostly Vipassana, or "insight", which emphasizes the minute observation of internal sensations; to join a one-off class, call to check times and then just turn up.

Though a little out of date, *A Guide to Buddhist Monasteries and Meditation Centres in Thailand* contains plenty of useful general information; originally published by the World Fellowship of Buddhists, it's now accessible online at ⓦwww.dharmanet.org/thai_94.html. An even more useful Internet resource is ⓦwww.dhammathai.org, which provides lots of general background, practical advice and details of meditation temples and centres.

House of Dhamma Insight Meditation Centre 26/9 Soi Lardprao 15, Chatuchak, Bangkok ☎02 511 0439, ⓦwww.houseofdhamma.com. Vipassana meditation classes in English on the second and third Sunday of the month, plus regular introductory two-day courses, and day, weekend and

week-long retreats. Courses in reiki and other subjects available.

International Meditation Club 138 Soi 53, Thanon Sukhumvit, Bangkok ☎081 622 4507, ⓦwww.intlmedclub.org. Regular, two-day, meditation workshops in Bangkok and three-day retreats in Pattaya and Cha-am.

Wat Mahathat Thanon Maharat, Ratanakosin. See p.72.

World Fellowship of Buddhists (WFB) 616 Benjasiri Park, Soi Medhinivet off Soi 24, Thanon Sukhumvit, Bangkok ⊤02 661 1284–7, ⓦ www.wfb-hq.org. The main information centre for advice on English-speaking retreats in Thailand. Holds a Buddhist discussion group and meditation session in English on the first Sunday of every month, with Dharma lectures and discussions on the second Sunday.

Shopping

Bangkok is a fabulous place to shop, offering varied, temptingly priced and enjoyable browsing at countless market stalls, craft outlets, chic boutiques and glitzy shopping plazas. Silk, gems and fashions are famously good buys, while the city's English-language bookshops carry an exceptional range of Southeast Asian titles. Antiques and handicrafts are also popular purchases, though watch out for old, damaged goods being passed off as antiques: if you're concerned about the quality or authenticity of your purchases, stick to TAT-approved shops (contact TAT for a list). Department stores and tourist-oriented shops in the city keep late hours, opening daily at around 10am and closing at about 9pm; many small, upmarket boutiques, for example along Thanon Charoen Krung and Thanon Silom, close on Sundays.

Downtown Bangkok is full of smart, multi-storeyed **shopping plazas** like the adjacent Siam Paragon, Siam Discovery Centre and Siam Centre on Thanon Rama I, Emporium on Thanon Sukhumvit and the Gaysorn Plaza on Thanon Ploenchit, which is where you'll find the majority of the city's fashion stores, as well as designer lifestyle goods and bookshops. The plazas tend to be pleasantly air-conditioned and thronging with trendy young Thais, but are chiefly of interest if you happen to be looking for a new outfit. You're more likely to find useful items in one of the city's numerous **department stores**, most of which are also scattered about the downtown areas. Seven-storey Central Chidlom on Thanon Ploenchit, which boasts handy services like watch-, garment- and shoe-repair booths as well as a huge product selection (including large sizes), is probably the city's best (with other Central branches on Thanon Silom

Counterfeit culture

Faking it is big business in Bangkok, a city whose copyright regulations carry about as much weight as its anti-prostitution laws. Forged **designer clothes** and accessories are the biggest sellers; street vendors along Patpong, Silom, Sukhumvit and Khao San roads will flog you a whole range of inexpensive lookalikes, including Burberry shirts, Diesel jeans, Calvin Klein wallets, Prada bags, Hermes scarves and Rolex watches. At the stalls concentrated on Thanon Khao San, pirated **DVDs and music and video CDs** and **software and games CD-ROMs** are sold at a fraction of their normal price. Quality is usually fairly high but the choice is often less than brilliant, with a concentration on mainstream pop and rock albums. Finally, several stallholders along Thanon Khao San even make up passable international **student and press cards** as well as international driver's licences – though travel agencies and other organizations in Bangkok aren't easily fooled.

and around town), but the Siam Paragon department store (which also offers garment and shoe repairs), in the shopping centre of the same name on Thanon Rama I, and Robinson's (on Sukhumvit Soi 19, at the Silom/Rama IV junction, and on Thanon Charoen Krung near Thanon Sathorn) are also good. The British chain of **pharmacies**, Boots the Chemist, has lots of branches across the city, including on Thanon Khao San, in the Siam Centre opposite Siam Square, on Patpong, in the Times Square complex between Sukhumvit sois 12 and 14, and in Emporium on Sukhumvit; Boots is the easiest place in the city to buy tampons.

The best place to buy anything to do with **mobile phones**, including rechargeable Thai SIM cards with a local phone number (see p.41), is the scores of small booths on Floor 4 of Mah Boon Krong (MBK) Shopping Centre at the Rama I/Phrayathai intersection. For **computer** hardware and software, the undisputed mecca is Panthip Plaza, across from Pratunam Market at 604/3 Thanon Phetchaburi (BTS Ratchathewi or canal stop Tha Pratunam), crammed with new and used, genuine and pirated hardware and software.

Markets

For travellers, spectating, not shopping, is apt to be the main draw of Bangkok's neighbourhood **markets** – notably the bazaars of Chinatown (see p.89) and the blooms and scents of Pak Khlong Talat, the flower and vegetable market just west of Memorial Bridge (see p.95). The massive Chatuchak Weekend Market is an exception, being both a tourist attraction and a marvellous shopping experience (see p.129 for details). If you're planning on some serious market exploration, get hold of *Nancy Chandler's Map of Bangkok*, an enthusiastically annotated creation with special sections on the main areas of interest. With the chief exception of Chatuchak, most markets operate daily from dawn till early afternoon; early morning is often the best time to go to beat the heat and crowds.

The Patpong **night market**, which also spills out onto Thanon Silom and Thanon Suriwong, is *the* place to stock up on fake designer goods; the stalls stay open from about 5pm until late into the evening. A recent arrival on the evening shopping scene is the **Suan Lum Night Bazaar**, opposite Lumphini Park at the corner of Thanon Rama IV and Thanon Witthayu (Wireless Road; ⓦ www.thainightbazaar.com), a huge development of more than three thousand booths, which is at its best between 6pm and 10pm. Down the narrow alleys of tiny booths, you'll find colourful street fashions, jewellery and lots of soaps, candles and beauty products, as well as some interesting contemporary decor: lighting, paintings, ceramics and woodcarving. At the centre stands the Traditional Thai Puppet Theatre (see p.205), with a popular Thai terrace-restaurant in front, and the attractive women's clothes and furnishings, notably rugs, of the Doi Tung at Mae Fah Luang shop (see p.214), with a hip Doi Tung coffee house attached. Other options for eating and drinking are uninspiring – your best bet is probably the open-air food court and beer garden, with a stage for nightly live music, by Thanon Witthayu.

Handicrafts, textiles and contemporary interior design

Samples of nearly all regionally produced **handicrafts** end up in Bangkok, so the selection is phenomenal. Many of the shopping plazas have at least one classy handicraft outlet, and competition keeps prices in the city at upcountry

Axe pillows

Traditional triangular pillows (*mawn*) – so named because their shape supposedly resembles an axe head (*khwaan*) – are a lot more comfortable than they look and come in a range of sizes, fabrics and colours, both traditional and contemporary. **Axe pillows** have been used in Thai homes for centuries, where it's normal to sit on the floor and lean against a densely stuffed *mawn khwaan*; in wealthier homes one reclines on a polished teak chaise longue and props one's head against a *mawn khwaan*.

Pillows are made up of seven or more triangular pods, each of which is packed with kapok, although the cheaper (but longer-lasting) versions are bulked out with cardboard. The **design** has been slightly adapted over the years, so it's now also possible to get *mawn khwaan* with up to four flat cushions attached, making lying out more comfortable. The trademark *khit* fabric used in traditional-style pillows is characterized by stripes of (usually yellow) supplementary weft and is mostly woven in north and northeast Thailand. Pillows made from the multi-coloured red, blue and green nylon *khit* are the most durable, but those covered in muted shades of cotton *khit* are softer and more fashionable. The price of a *mawn khwaan* depends on the number of triangular pods in the pillow: a stand-alone ten-triangle pillow costs around B300, or B1200 with three attached cushions, and a fifteen-triangle pillow costs about B600.

---

levels, with the main exception of household objects – particularly wickerware and tin bowls and basins – which get palmed off relatively expensively in Bangkok. Handicraft sellers in Banglamphu tend to tout a limited range compared to the shops downtown, but several places on Thanon Khao San sell reasonably priced triangular "axe" pillows (*mawn khwaan*) in traditional fabrics (see box above), which make fantastic souvenirs but are heavy to post home; some places, including one dedicated outlet between *Bella House* and *Baan Sabai* on Banglamphu's Soi Chana Songkhram, sell unstuffed versions which are simple to mail home, but a pain to fill when you return. The cheapest outlet for traditional northern and northeastern textiles – including sarongs, axe pillows and farmers' shirts – is **Chatuchak Weekend Market** (see p.129), where you'll also be able to nose out some interesting handicrafts. Bangkok is also rapidly establishing a reputation for its **contemporary interior design**, fusing minimalist Western ideals with traditional Thai and other Asian craft elements. The best places to sample this, as detailed in the reviews below, are on Floor 4 of the Siam Discovery Centre and Floor 4 of the Siam Paragon shopping centre, both on Thanon Rama I, and Floor 3 of the Gaysorn Plaza on Thanon Ploenchit.

Banglamphu

For a map of this area see p.80; for transport information see p.78.

Taekee Taekon 118 Thanon Phra Athit. Tasteful assortment of traditional textiles and scarves, plus a good selection of Thai art cards, black-and-white photocards and Nancy Chandler greetings cards.

Downtown: around Siam Square and Thanon Ploenchit

For a map of this area see p.113; for transport information see p.112.

Ayodhya Floor 4, Siam Paragon, Thanon Rama I, Floor 3, Gaysorn Plaza, Thanon Ploenchit and Floor 4, Emporium, Thanon Sukhumvit. With the same owners and designers as Panta (see p.214), but specializing in smaller items, such as gorgeous cushion covers, pouffes covered in dried water-hyacinth stalks, bowls, trays and stationery.

Come Thai Floor 3, Amarin Plaza, Thanon Ploenchit. Wide range of unusual handwoven silk and cotton fabrics from all over southeast Asia.

Earthasia 1045 Thanon Ploenchit (opposite Soi Ruam Rudee). Contemporary basketware, furniture, rugs and beautiful lotus-bud lamps in vivid colours.

Doi Tung by Mae Fah Luang Floor 4, Siam Discovery Centre, Thanon Rama I, and Suan Lum Night Bazaar, Thanon Rama IV ⓦwww .doitung.org. Part of the late Princess Mother's development project based at Doi Tung in northern Thailand, selling very attractive fabrics (silk, cotton and linen) in warm colours, either in bolts or made up into clothes, cushion covers, rugs and so on.

Exotique Thai Floor 4, Siam Paragon, Thanon Rama I. A collection of small outlets from around the city and the country – including silk-makers and clothes designers down from Chiang Mai – that makes a good, upmarket one-stop shop, much more interesting than Narai Phand (see below). There's everything from jewellery, through mother-of-pearl furniture, to beauty products, with a focus on home decor and contemporary adaptations of traditional crafts.

Lamont Contemporary Floor 3, Gaysorn Plaza, Thanon Ploenchit. Beautiful lacquerware bowls, vases and boxes in imaginative contemporary styles, as well as bronze and ceramic objects.

Narai (or Narayana) Phand 127 Thanon Rajdamri ⓦwww.naraiphand.com. This souvenir centre was set up to ensure the preservation of traditional crafts and to maintain standards of quality, as a joint venture with the Ministry of Industry in the 1930s, and it looks it: its layout is wholly unappealing, though it makes a reasonable one-stop shop for last-minute presents. It offers a huge assortment of very reasonably priced goods from all over the country, including silk and cotton, *khon* masks and musical instruments, *bencharong*, nielloware and celadon, woodcarving, silver, basketware and beauty products.

Niwat (Aranyik) Floor 3, Gaysorn Plaza, Thanon Ploenchit. A good place to buy that chunky, elegant Thai-style cutlery you may have been eating your dinner with in Bangkok's posher restaurants, with both traditional and contemporary handmade designs.

Panta Floor 4, Siam Discovery Centre, and Floor 4, Siam Paragon, both on Thanon Rama I. Modern design store which stands out for its experimental furniture, including way-out-there items made of woven rattan and wood and cushions covered in dried water-hyacinth stalks.

Thann Native Floor 3, Gaysorn Plaza, Thanon Ploenchit. Contemporary rugs, cushion covers and furniture, and some very striking glass candle-holders.

Triphum Floor 3, Gaysorn Plaza, Thanon Ploenchit, and Floor 4, Siam Paragon, Thanon Rama I. Affordable, hand-painted reproductions of temple mural paintings, Buddhist manuscripts from Burma, repro Buddha statues, lacquerware, framed amulets and even Buddha's footprints.

Downtown: south of Thanon Rama IV

For a map of this area see p.120; for transport information see p.119.

Jim Thompson's Thai Silk Company Main shop at 9 Thanon Suriwong (including a branch of their very good café – see p.189), plus branches in Isetan in the Central World Plaza, Central Chidlom department store on Thanon Ploenchit, at Emporium on Thanon Sukhumvit, at the Jim Thompson House Museum, and at many hotels around the city; ⓦwww.jimthompson.com. A good place to start looking for traditional Thai fabric, or at least to get an idea of what's out there. Stocks silk and cotton by the yard and ready-made items from dresses to cushion covers, which are well designed and of good quality, but pricey. They also have a home furnishings section and a good tailoring service. A couple of hundred metres along Thanon Suriwong from the main branch, at no. 149/4–6, a Jim Thompson Factory Sales Outlet sells remnant home-furnishing fabrics and home accessories at knock-down prices (if you're really keen on a bargain, they have a much larger factory outlet way out east of the centre on Soi 93, Thanon Sukhumvit).

The Legend Floor 3, Thaniya Plaza, Thanon Silom. Stocks a small selection of well-made Thai handicrafts, from wood and wickerware to pretty fabrics and celadon and other ceramics, at reasonable prices.

Silom Village 286/1 Thanon Silom. A complex of low-rise buildings that attempts to create a relaxing, upcountry atmosphere as a backdrop for its pricey fabrics and jewellery, and occasionally unusual souvenirs, such as woven rattan goods and grainy *sa* paper made from mulberry bark.

Tamnan Mingmuang Floor 3, Thaniya Plaza, Soi Thaniya, east end of Thanon Silom. Subsidiary of The Legend opposite (see above) which concentrates on basketry from all over the country. Among the unusual items on offer are trays and boxes for tobacco and betel nut made from *yan lipao* (intricately woven fern vines), and bambooware sticky-rice containers, baskets and lampshades. The Legend's other subsidiary, the adjacent Eros, sells rather tacky erotic craft items such as naked chess sets.

Thai Home Industries Oriental Avenue, in front of the Oriental Hotel. Huge, characterful museum-piece of an old shop, which seems to have surprisingly little for sale on its dusty shelves. However, you'll find attractive, traditional cutlery and some nice, plain cotton shirts and dressing gowns in amongst the basketware and bamboo trays.

Thanon Sukhumvit

For a map of this area see p.126; for transport information see p.127.

Rasi Sayam 82 Soi 33. Very classy handicraft shop, specializing in eclectic and fairly pricey decorative and folk arts such as tiny betelnut sets woven from *lipao* fern, sticky-rice lunch baskets, coconut wood bowls and *mut mee* textiles. Mon–Sat 9am–5.30pm.

Thai Celadon Soi 16 (Thanon Ratchadapisek). Classic celadon stoneware made without commercial dyes or clays and glazed with the archetypal blues and greens that were invented by the Chinese to emulate the colour of precious jade. Mainly dinner sets, vases and lamps, plus some figurines.

Tailored clothes

Inexpensive **tailoring shops** crowd Silom, Sukhumvit and Khao San roads, but the best single area to head for is the short stretch of Thanon Charoen Krung between the GPO and Thanon Silom, close by the Chao Phraya Express Boat stops at Tha Oriental and Tha Wat Muang Kae, or ten minutes' walk from either Saphan Taksin Skytrain station. It's generally best to avoid tailors in tourist areas such as Thanon Khao San, shopping malls and Thanon Sukhumvit's Soi Nana and Soi 11, although if you're lucky it's still possible to come up trumps here: one that stands apart is Banglamphu's well-regarded Chang Torn, located at 95 Thanon Tanao (☎02 282 9390). The tailors listed below are all recommended; see the box on p.216 for advice on having clothes made to measure.

For cheap and reasonable shirt and dress material other than silk go for a browse around **Pahurat** market (see p.95) and Chinatown's Sampeng Lane (see p.92) – though the suit materials are mostly poor, and best avoided.

△ Mah Boon Krong (MBK) Shopping Centre

Bangkok can be an excellent place to get **tailor-made** suits, dresses, shirts and trousers at a fraction of the price you'd pay in the West. Tailors here can copy a sample brought from home and will also work from any photographs you can provide; most also carry a good selection of catalogues. The bad news is that many tourist-oriented tailors aren't terribly good, often attempting to get away with poor work and shoddy materials, so lots of visitors end up wasting their time and money. However, with a little effort and thought, both men and women can get some fantastic clothes made to measure.

Choosing a tailor can be tricky, and unless you're particularly knowledgeable about material, shopping around won't necessarily tell you much. Don't make a decision based wholly on prices quoted – picking a tailor simply because they're the least expensive usually leads to poor work, and your cheap suit won't last. Special deals offering two suits, two shirts, two ties and a kimono for $99 should be left well alone. Above all, ignore recommendations by anyone with a vested interest in bringing your custom to a particular shop, such as tuk-tuk drivers.

Prices vary widely depending on material and the tailor's skill. As a very rough guide, for **labour alone** expect to pay B5000–6000 for a two-piece suit, though some tailors will charge rather more. For average **material** expect to pay about the same again, or anything up to four times as much for top-class cloth. With the exception of silk, local materials are frequently of poor quality and for suits in particular you're far better off using English or Italian cloth. Most tailors stock both imported and local fabrics, but bringing your own from home can work out significantly cheaper.

Give yourself as much **time** as possible. For suits, insist on two fittings. Most good tailors require around three days for a suit (some require ten days or more), although a few have enough staff to produce good work in a day or two. The more **detail** you can give the tailor the better. As well as deciding on the obvious features such as single- or double-breasted and number of buttons, think about the width of lapels, style of trousers, whether you want the jacket with vents or not, and so forth. Specifying factors like this will make all the difference to whether you're happy with your suit, so it's worth discussing them with the tailor; the tailors recommended below can give good advice. Finally, don't be afraid to be an awkward customer until you're completely happy with the finished product – after all, the whole point of getting clothes tailor-made is to get exactly what you want.

A Song Tailor 8 Trok Chartered Bank, off Thanon Charoen Krung, near the Oriental Hotel ☎02 630 9708. Friendly, helpful and a good first port of call if you're on a budget.

Ah Song Tailor 1203 Thanon Charoen Krung (opposite Soi 36) ☎02 233 7574. Meticulous tailor who takes pride in his work. Men's and women's suits.

Golden Wool 1340–1342 Thanon Charoen Krung ☎02 233 0149; also **World Group** 1302–1304 Thanon Charoen Krung ☎02 234 1527. Part of the same company, they can turn around decent work in a couple of days, though prefer to have a week. One of the tailors here has made suits for the king.

Marco Tailor Soi 7, Siam Square ☎02 252 0689 or 02 251 7633. Long-established tailor with a good reputation, though not cheap by Bangkok standards; they require two or three weeks for a suit. Men's only.

Marzotto Tailor 3 Soi Shangri-La Hotel, Thanon Charoen Krung ☎02 233 2880. Friendly business which makes everything from trousers to wedding outfits, and can make a suit in two days, with just one fitting, if necessary.

Fashions

Thanon Khao San is lined with stalls selling low-priced **fashions**: the tie-dyed vests, baggy cotton fisherman's trousers and embroidered blouses are all aimed at backpackers, but they're supplemented by cheap contemporary fashions that appeal to urban Thai trendies as well. The stalls of Banglamphu Market, near the post office on Soi Sibsam Hang and along nearby Trok Kraisi, have the best range of inexpensive Thai fashions in this area. For the best and latest trends from Thai designers, however, check out the shops in Siam Square and across the road in the more upmarket Siam Centre. Prices vary considerably: street gear in Siam Square is undoubtedly inexpensive, while genuine Western brand names, available in, for example, Siam Paragon, Siam Discovery, Gaysorn and Emporium shopping centres, are generally competitive but not breath-takingly cheaper than at home; larger sizes can be hard to find. **Shoes** and **leather goods** are good buys in Bangkok, being generally handmade from high-quality leather and quite a bargain: check out branches of the stylish, Italian-influenced Ragazze in the Silom Complex (Floor 2), Thanon Silom, in the menswear department at Isetan in the Central World Plaza or on Floor 3 of the MBK Shopping Centre (both Thanon Rama I).

Emporium Thanon Sukhumvit, between sois 22 and 24. Enormous and rather glamorous shopping plaza, with a good range of fashion outlets, from exclusive designer wear to trendy high-street gear. Brand-name outlets include Versace, Prada, Gucci, Chanel Louis Vuitton and Mango.

Gaysorn Plaza Thanon Ploenchit. The most chic of the city's shopping plazas: in amongst Burberry, Emporio Armani and Louis Vuitton, a few Thai names have made it, notably Fly Now, which mounts dramatic displays of women's party and formal gear, alongside more casual wear, and Fashion Society, a gathering of cutting-edge local designers in one store.

Mah Boon Krong (MBK) At the Rama I/Phrayat-hai intersection. Labyrinthine shopping centre which houses hundreds of small, mostly fairly inexpensive outlets, including plenty of high-street fashion shops.

Siam Centre Thanon Rama I, across the road from Siam Square. Particularly good for hip local labels, such as Greyhound, Jaspal and Fly Now, as well as international names like Ecko and Mambo.

Siam Square Worth poking around the alleys here, especially near what's styled as the area's "Centerpoint" between sois 3 and 4. All manner of inexpensive boutiques, some little more than booths, sell colourful street gear to the capital's fashionable students and teenagers.

Books

English-language **bookstores** in Bangkok are always well stocked with everything to do with Thailand and the rest of Southeast Asia, and most carry fiction classics and popular paperbacks as well. Imported books are quite pricey, however. The capital's **secondhand** bookstores are not cheap, but you can usually part-exchange your unwanted titles.

Aporia 131 Thanon Tanao, Banglamphu. This is one of Banglamphu's main outlets for new books and keeps a good stock of titles on Thai and Southeast Asian culture, a decent selection of travelogues, plus some English-language fiction. Also sells secondhand books.

Asia Books Branches on Thanon Sukhumvit between sois 15 and 19, in Landmark Plaza between sois 4 and 6, in Times Square between sois 12 and 14, and in Emporium between sois 22 and 24; in Peninsula Plaza and in the Central World Plaza, both on Thanon Rajdamri; in Siam Discovery Centre and in Siam Paragon, both on Thanon Rama I; and in Thaniya Plaza near Patpong off Thanon Silom. English-language bookstore that's especially recommended for its books on Asia

– everything from guidebooks to cookery books, novels to art (the Sukhumvit 15–19 branch has the very best Asian selection). Also stocks bestselling novels and coffee-table books.

B2S Floor 7, Central Chidlom, Thanon Ploenchit. Department-store bookshop with a decent selection of English-language books, but most notable for its huge selection of magazines and newspapers.

Bookazine Branches on Thanon Silom in the CP Tower (Patpong) and in the Silom Complex; on Thanon Rama I opposite the Siam Centre; in the Amarin Plaza on Thanon Ploenchit; in All Seasons Place on Thanon Witthayu; in Gaysorn Plaza on Thanon Ploenchit; and at the mouth of Sukhumvit Soi 5. Alongside a decent selection of English-language books about Asia and novels, these shops stock a huge range of foreign newspapers and magazines.

Books Kinokuniya Third Floor, Emporium Shopping Centre, between sois 22 and 24 on Thanon Sukhumvit, with branches at Floor 6, Isetan, in the Central World Plaza, Thanon Rajdamri, and Floor 3, Siam Paragon, Thanon Rama I. Huge English-language bookstore with a broad range of books ranging from bestsellers to travel literature and from classics to sci-fi; not so hot on books about Asia though.

Dasa Book Cafe Between sois 26 and 28, Thanon Sukhumvit Ⓦ www.dasabookcafe.com. Appealingly calm secondhand bookshop that's intelligently, and alphabetically, categorised, with sections on everything from Asia to chick lit, health to gay and lesbian interest. Browse its stock online, or enjoy coffee and cakes in situ. Daily 10am–9pm.

Rim Khob Fa Bookshop Democracy Monument roundabout, Rajdamnoen Klang, Banglamphu. Useful outlet for the more obscure and esoteric English-language books on Thailand and Southeast Asia, as well as mainstream titles on Thai culture.

Robinson's Department Store At the mouth of Sukhumvit Soi 19. The third-floor book department stocks a decent range of English-language fiction and nonfiction, plus lots of books about Asia as well as local and international magazines.

Shaman Books Thanon Khao San, Banglamphu. Well-stocked secondhand bookshop where all books are logged on the computer. Lots of books on Asia (travel, fiction, politics and history) as well as a decent range of novels and general interest books.

Siam Society Bookshop: Libreria 131 Sukhumvit Soi 21, inside the Ban Kamthieng compound. Extensive collection of esoteric and academic books about Thailand, including many ethnology studies published by White Lotus and by the Siam Society itself. Tues–Sat 9am–6pm, Sun noon–5pm.

Silpakorn Book Centre Corner of Na Phra Lan and Na Phra That roads. Very handily placed opposite the entrance to the Grand Palace, this smart little bookshop keeps a good selection of English-language titles, especially on Thailand and Southeast Asia.

Ton's Bookseller 327/5 Thanon Ram Bhuttri, Banglamphu. Exceptionally well stocked with titles about Thailand and Southeast Asia, particularly political commentary and language studies; also sells some English-language fiction.

Jewellery, gems and other rare stones

Bangkok boasts the country's best **gem and jewellery** shops, and some of the finest lapidaries in the world, making this *the* place to buy cut and uncut stones such as rubies, blue sapphires and diamonds. However, countless gem-buying tourists get badly **ripped off**, so be extremely wary. Never buy anything through a tout or from any shop recommended by a "government official", "student", "businessperson" or tuk-tuk driver who happens to engage you in conversation on the street, and note that there are no government jewellery shops – despite any information you may be given to the contrary. Always check that the shop is a member of the **Thai Gem and Jewelry Traders Association** by calling the association or visiting their website (Ⓣ02 630 1390–7, Ⓦ www.thaigemjewelry.or.th). To be doubly sure, you may want to seek out shops that also belong to the TGJTA's **Jewel Fest Club**

(W www.jewelfest.com), which guarantees quality and will offer refunds; see their website for a directory of members. For independent professional advice or precious stones certification, contact the Asian Institute of Gemological Sciences, located on the sixth floor of the Jewelry Trade Center Building, 919/1 Thanon Silom (T 02 267 4325–7, W www.aigsthailand.com), which also runs reputable **courses**, such as a five-day (15hr) introduction to gemstones (B7500) and one day on rubies and sapphires (B1500).

A common **scam** is to charge a lot more than what the gem is worth based on its carat weight. Get it tested on the spot, ask for a written guarantee and receipt. Don't even consider **buying gems in bulk** to sell at a supposedly vast profit elsewhere: many a gullible traveller has invested thousands of dollars on a handful of worthless multi-coloured stones, believing the vendor's reassurance that the goods will fetch a hundred times more when resold at home. Gem scams are so common in Bangkok that TAT has published a brochure about it and there are several websites on the subject, including the very informative W www.2bangkok.com/2bangkok/Scams/Sapphire.shtml, which describes the typical scam in detail and advises on what to do if you get caught out; it's also continuously updated with details of the latest scammers. Most victims receive no recompense at all, but you have more chance of doing so if you contact the website's recommended authorities while still in Thailand. See p.47 for more on common scams in Thailand.

The most exclusive of the reputable **gem outlets** are scattered along Thanon Silom, but many tourists prefer to buy from hotel shops, like the very upscale Kim's in Oriental Place in front of the *Oriental*, where reliability is assured. Other recommended outlets include Johnny's Gems at 199 Thanon Fuang Nakhon, near Wat Rajabophit in Ratanakosin, and Merlin et Delauney at 1 Soi Pradit, off Thanon Suriwong. Thongtavee, Floor 2, River City, an outlet of a famous Burmese **jade** factory in Mae Sai in northern Thailand, sells beautiful jade jewellery, as well as carved Buddha statues, chopsticks and the like. For cheap silver earrings, bracelets and necklaces you can't beat the traveller oriented jewellery shops along Trok Mayom in Banglamphu.

Among the more esoteric of Bangkok's outlets is the **Rare Stone Museum** at 1048–1054 Thanon Charoen Krung (T 02 236 5655, W www .rarestonemuseum.com), near Soi 26 and the GPO. Here, for B50–100, you can buy tektites, pieces of glassy rock found in Thai fields and thought to be the 750,000-year-old products of volcanic activity on the moon, as well as fossilized plants and shells, 60- to 200-million-year-old petrified dinosaur droppings (properly known as coprolite) unearthed in Thailand's Isaan region, and some fantastic rock formations. Of these last-mentioned, the best, resembling anything from owls and polar bears to grander scenes such as a dog contemplating the moon, are kept for display in the adjoining museum (daily 10am–5.30pm; B100).

Antiques and paintings

Bangkok is the entrepôt for the finest Thai, Burmese and Cambodian **antiques**, but the market has long been sewn up, so don't expect to happen upon any undiscovered treasure. Even experts admit that they sometimes find it hard to tell real antiques from fakes, so the best policy is just to buy on the grounds of attractiveness. The River City shopping complex, off Thanon Charoen Krung (New Road), devotes its third and fourth floors to a bewildering array of pricey treasures, as well as holding an auction on the first Saturday of every month (viewing during the preceding week). Worth singling out here are Old Maps and Prints on the fourth floor (Ⓦ www.classicmaps.com), which has some lovely old prints of Thailand and Asia (averaging around B3500), as well as rare books and maps; and Ingon on the third floor, which specializes in small Chinese pieces made of jade and other precious stones, such as snuff boxes, jewellery, statuettes and amulets. (The owners of Old Maps and Prints have a second outlet, the Old Siam Trading Company in the Nailert Building at the mouth of Thanon Sukhumvit Soi 5 (Ⓦ www.oldsiamtrading.com).) The other main area for antiques is the section of Charoen Krung that runs between the GPO and the bottom of Thanon Silom, and the stretch of Silom running east from here up to and including the multi-storey Silom Galleria. Here you'll find a good selection of largely reputable individual businesses specializing in woodcarvings, ceramics, bronze statues and stone sculptures culled from all parts of Thailand and neighbouring countries as well. To export antiques or religious artefacts – especially Buddha images – from Thailand, you need to have a licence granted by the Fine Arts Department; see p.53 for details.

Street-corner stalls all over the city sell poor-quality, mass-produced traditional Thai **paintings**, but for a huge selection of better-quality Thai art, especially oil paintings, visit Sombat Permpoon Gallery on Sukhumvit Soi 1, which carries thousands of canvases, framed and unframed, spanning the range from classical Ayutthayan-era-style village scenes to twenty-first-century abstracts. The gallery does have works by famous Thai artists like Thawan Duchanee, but prices for the more affordable works by less well-known painters start at B1500.

16

Kids' Bangkok

Thais are very tolerant of children, so you can take them almost anywhere without restriction. The only drawback might be the constant attention lavished on your kids by complete strangers, which can get tiring for adults and children alike.

Practicalities

Kids get **discounts** at most of the theme parks and amusement centres listed below, though not at the majority of the city's museums, and there are no reductions on Bangkok buses and boats. Bizarrely, when travelling on the State Railway (for example to Ayutthaya or Kanchanaburi) a child aged three to twelve qualifies for half fare only if under 150cm tall; in some stations you'll see a measuring scale painted onto the ticket-hall wall. Many of Bangkok's expensive hotels offer special deals for families (see p.168 for details), and an increasing number of guest houses offer three-person rooms. Decent **cots** are provided free in the bigger hotels, and in some smaller ones (though cots in these places can be a bit grotty).

Although most Thai babies don't wear them, **disposable nappies** (diapers) are sold at pharmacies, supermarkets, department stores and convenience stores across the city, as is international-brand formula and baby food (though some parents find restaurant-cooked rice and bananas go down just as well). Thai women do not **breastfeed** in public. A **changing mat** may be worth bringing with you as, although there are public toilets in every shopping plaza and department store, few have baby facilities (toilets at posh hotels being a useful exception). Opinions are divided on whether or not it's worth bringing a **buggy** or three-wheeled **stroller**. Bangkok's pavements are bumpy at best, and there's an almost total absence of ramps. Buggies and strollers do, however, come in handy for feeding and even bedding small children, as highchairs and cots are only provided in the most upmarket hotels. Taxis and car-rental companies never provide **children's car seats**, and even if you bring your own you'll often find there are no seatbelts to strap them in with.

Should you need to buy a crucial piece of **children's gear** while you're in Bangkok, you should find it in one of the department stores (see p.211), which all have children's sections, and there's a branch of Mothercare in Emporium between Sukhumvit sois 22 and 24 (see map on p.126). Children's clothes are very cheap in Thailand, and have the advantage of being designed for the climate.

Even more than their parents, children need protecting from the sun, unsafe drinking water, heat and unfamiliar **food**. All that chilli in particular may be a problem, even with older kids; consider packing a jar of Marmite or equivalent child's favourite, so that you can always rely on toast if the local food doesn't go down so well. As with adults, you should be careful about unwashed fruit and salads and about dishes that have been left uncovered for a long time (see p.181). As diarrhoea can be dangerous for a child, rehydration solutions (see under "Health", p.29) are vital if your child goes down with it. Other significant **hazards** include thundering traffic and the sun – sun hats and sunblock are essential, and can be bought anywhere in the city. You should also make sure, if possible, that your child is aware of the dangers of rabies; keep children away from animals, especially dogs, and ask your medical advisor about rabies jabs.

Information, advice and other resources

Bambi Ⓦ www.bambi-bangkok.org. The website of the Bangkok-based expat parents' group has tips on parents' common concerns, in particular health issues, as well as ideas for child-friendly activities in Thailand.

Kids To Go Ⓦ www.thorntree.lonelyplanet.com. The Kids To Go branch of this travel forum gets quite a lot of postings from parents who've already taken their kids to Thailand.

Nancy Chandler's Thailand Activity Book Ⓦ www .nancychandler.net. An activity book full of Thailand-related games, puzzles, colouring features and more. Also available is *Nancy Chandler's* Thailand Coloring Book. Both books can be bought online and at some English-language bookshops in the city.

Thailand 4 Kids Ⓦ www.thailand4kids.com. Sells an e-book guide covering the practicalities of family holidays in Thailand.

What Can We Do Today? Kids in Bangkok This guide to keeping kids entertained in Bangkok is designed as a pack of 52 cards, with each card describing a different activity, complete with practical information. Aims to appeal to all ages, from toddlers to teenagers, and is available online through Ⓦ www .nancychandler.net.

Activities for kids

The main drawback with Bangkok's kid-centred **activities** is that most of the theme parks and amusement centres listed below are located a long way from the city centre. However, a number of more accessible adult-oriented attractions also go down well with kids, including riding the pedalo boats in Lumphini Park (see p.121), taking longtail boat trips on the Thonburi canals (see p.100), the Snake Farm (see p.121), the Traditional Thai Puppet Theatre at Suan Lum Night Bazaar (see p.205), feeding the turtles at Wat Prayoon (see p.105), and cycling around the open-air museum and park at Muang Boran Ancient City (see p.138). In addition, there are Saturday afternoon classes in kids' traditional Thai dance at the Patravadi Theatre (see p.204), and if you're here in the right season, the annual spring kite festival is also fun (see p.171).

Children's Discovery Museum Opposite Chatuchak Weekend Market on Thanon Kamphaeng Phet 4 ☏ 02 615 7333, Ⓦ www .bkkchildrenmuseum.com/english. Tues–Fri 9am–5pm, Sat & Sun 10am–6pm; B150, kids B120. Interactive and hands-on displays covering science, the environment, human and animal life. Mo Chit Skytrain or Chatuchak Park subway or, from Banglamphu, any bus bound for Chatuchak or the Northern Bus Terminal (see p.78).

Dream World 10min drive north of Don Muang Airport at kilometre-stone 7 on Thanon Rangsit-Ongharak ☏ 02 533 1152, Ⓦ www .dreamworld-th.com. Mon–Fri 10am–5pm, Sat & Sun 10am–7pm; B120, children B95. Theme park with different areas such as Fantasy Land, Dream Garden and Adventure Land. Water rides, a hanging coaster and other amusements. Non-air-con buses #39 and #59 from Rajdamnoen Klang in Banglamphu to Rangsit, then songthaew or tuk-tuk to Dream World; or bus, Skytrain or subway to Mo Chit/Chatuchak Park, then air-con bus #523.

Dusit Zoo (Khao Din) Dusit. The main entrance is on Thanon Rajwithi, and there are others on Thanon U-Thong and Thanon Rama V; see map on p.106. Daily 8am–6pm; B30, children B5. The sizeable public park here is home to a fair number of creatures, including big cats, elephants, orang-utans, chimpanzees and reptiles, though conditions are fairly basic. The park also boasts a lake with pedalos, plenty of shade, and lots of foodstalls. From Banglamphu take bus #70, or use the express boat to Tha Thewes and then walk. From downtown Bangkok, easiest access is by bus from the Skytrain and subway stops at Victory Monument; there are many services from here, including air-con #510 and #16, both of which run all the way along Thanon Rajwithi (see box on p.36).

Safari World On the northeastern outskirts at 99 Thanon Ramindra, Minburi ℡02 518 1000, Ⓦ www.safariworld.com. Daily 9am–4.30pm; B700, children B450. Said to be Southeast Asia's largest wildlife park, Safari World centres on a drive-through safari park, which is home to an assortment of lions, rhinos, giraffes, zebras and monkeys. If you don't have your own car, you can drive through the park in a Safari World coach. There's also a sea-life area with dolphins and sea lions, and a bird park with a walk-in aviary. Take air-con bus #60

from Rajdamnoen Klang in Banglamphu or air-con #26 from Victory Monument, then a songthaew to Safari World.

Siam Ocean World In the basement of the Siam Paragon shopping centre on Thanon Rama I, ℡02 687 2000, Ⓦ www.siamoceanworld .com. Daily 9am–10pm, last admission 9pm; B450, children between 80 and 120cm tall B280. Huge, recently built aquarium housing over 400 species in various tanks, including one that's over eight metres deep. Also features a walk-through tunnel, touch-tanks for tickling the starfish, a 20min ride in a glass-bottomed boat (B150; be prepared to queue), penguin feeds (currently at 12.30pm and 4.30pm) and shark feeds (currently at 1.30pm and 5.30pm). If you pre-book, you can also dive with the sharks here (see p.116). Skytrain to Siam.

Siam Park On the far eastern edge of town at 101 Thanon Sukhapiban 2 ℡02 919 7200, Ⓦ www.siamparkcity.com. Daily 10am–6pm; B400, children B300. Popular water park that boasts some of the longest waterslides in the country, along with all manner of whirlpools, swimming pools, and pools that get churned up by artificial surf. There's also a mini-zoo, a botanical garden and roller-coasters. Air-con bus #60 from Rajdamnoen Klang in Banglamphu or air-con #501 from Hualamphong Station.

Contexts

Contexts

History

B
angkok is a comparatively new capital, founded in 1782 after Ayutthaya, a short way upriver, had been razed by the Burmese, but it has established an overwhelming dominance in Thailand. Its history over the last two centuries directly mirrors that of the country as a whole, and the city has gathered to itself, in the National Museum and elsewhere, the major relics of Thailand's previous civilizations, principally from the eras of Ayutthaya and its precursor, Sukhothai.

Early history

The region's first distinctive civilization, **Dvaravati**, was established around two thousand years ago by an Austroasiatic-speaking people known as the Mon. One of its mainstays was Theravada Buddhism, which had been introduced to Thailand during the second or third century BC by Indian missionaries. From the discovery of monastery boundary stones (sema), clay votive tablets and Indian-influenced Buddhist sculpture, it's clear that the Dvaravati city-states (including **Nakhon Pathom**) had their greatest flourishing between the sixth and ninth centuries AD. Meanwhile, in the eighth century, peninsular Thailand to the south of Dvaravati came under the control of the **Srivijaya** empire, a Mahayana Buddhist state centred on Sumatra which had strong ties with India.

From the ninth century onwards, however, both Dvaravati and Srivijaya Thailand succumbed to invading **Khmers** from Cambodia, who consolidated their position during the watershed reign of **Jayavarman II** (802–50). To establish his authority, Jayavarman II had himself initiated as a chakravartin or universal ruler, the living embodiment of the **devaraja**, the divine essence of kingship – a concept which was adopted by later Thai rulers. From their capital at **Angkor**, Jayavarman's successors took control over northeastern, central and peninsular Thailand, thus mastering the most important trade routes between India and China. By the thirteenth century, however, the Khmers had overreached themselves and were in no position to resist the onslaught of a vibrant new force in Southeast Asia, the Thais.

The earliest Thais

The earliest traceable history of the **Thai people** picks them up in southern China around the fifth century AD, when they were squeezed by Chinese and Vietnamese expansionism into sparsely inhabited northeastern Laos. Their first significant entry into what is now Thailand seems to have happened in the north, where some time after the seventh century the Thais formed a state known as Yonok. Theravada Buddhism spread to **Yonok** via Dvaravati around the end of the tenth century, which served not only to unify the Thais themselves but also to link them to the wider community of Buddhists.

By the end of the twelfth century they formed the majority of the population in Thailand, then under the control of the Khmer empire. The Khmers' main outpost, at Lopburi, was by this time regarded as the administrative capital of a land called **Syam** (possibly from the Sanskrit *syam*, meaning swarthy) – a mid-twelfth-century bas-relief at Angkor portraying the troops of Lopburi, preceded by a large group of self-confident Syam Kuk mercenaries, shows that the Thais were becoming a force to be reckoned with.

Sukhothai

At some time around 1238, Thais in the upper Chao Phraya valley captured the main Khmer outpost in the region at **Sukhothai** and established a kingdom there. For the first forty years it was merely a local power, but an attack by the ruler of the neighbouring principality of Mae Sot brought a dynamic new leader to the fore: the king's nineteen-year-old son, Rama, defeated the opposing commander, earning himself the name **Ramkhamhaeng**, "Rama the Bold". When Ramkhamhaeng himself came to the throne around 1278, he seized control of much of the Chao Phraya valley, and over the next twenty years, more by diplomacy than military action, gained the submission of most of Thailand under a complex tribute system.

Although the empire of Sukhothai extended Thai control over a vast area, its greatest contribution to the Thais' development was at home, in cultural and political matters. A famous **inscription** by Ramkhamhaeng, now housed in the Bangkok National Museum, describes a prosperous era of benevolent rule: "In the time of King Ramkhamhaeng this land of Sukhothai is thriving. There is fish in the water and rice in the fields… [The King] has hung a bell in the opening of the gate over there: if any commoner has a grievance which sickens his belly and gripes his heart… he goes and strikes the bell… [and King Ramkhamhaeng] questions the man, examines the case, and decides it justly for him."

Although this plainly smacks of self-promotion, it seems to contain at least a kernel of truth: in deliberate contrast to the Khmer god-kings (*devaraja*), Ramkhamhaeng styled himself as a **dhammaraja**, a king who ruled justly according to Theravada Buddhist doctrine and made himself accessible to his people. A further sign of the Thais' growing self-confidence was the invention of a new script to make their tonal language understood by the non-Thai inhabitants of the land.

The growth of Ayutthaya

After the death of Ramkhamhaeng around 1299, however, his empire quickly fell apart. By 1320 Sukhothai had regressed to being a kingdom of only local significance, though its mantle as the capital of a Thai empire was taken up shortly after at **Ayutthaya** to the south. Soon after founding the city in 1351, the ambitious king Ramathibodi united the principalities of the lower Chao Phraya valley, which had formed the western provinces of the Khmer empire. When he recruited his bureaucracy from the urban elite of Lopburi, **Ramathibodi** set the style of government at Ayutthaya, elements of which persisted into the Bangkok empire and up to the present day. The elaborate etiquette, language and rituals of Angkor were adopted, and, most importantly, the conception of the ruler as *devaraja*: when the king processed through the town, ordinary people were forbidden to look at him and had to be silent while he passed.

The site chosen by Ramathibodi was the best in the region for an international port, and so began Ayutthaya's rise to prosperity, based on exploiting the upswing in **trade** in the middle of the fourteenth century along the routes between India and China. By 1540, the Kingdom of Ayutthaya had grown to cover most of the area of modern-day Thailand. Despite a 1568 invasion by the Burmese, which led to twenty years of foreign rule, Ayutthaya made a spectacular comeback, and in the seventeenth century its **foreign trade** boomed. In 1511 the Portuguese had become the first Western power to trade with Ayutthaya, and a treaty with Spain was concluded in 1598; relations with Holland and England were initiated in 1608 and 1612 respectively. European merchants flocked to Thailand, not only to buy Thai products, but also to gain access to Chinese and Japanese goods on sale there.

The Burmese invasion

In the mid-eighteenth century, however, the rumbling in the Burmese jungle to the north began to make itself heard again. After an unsuccessful siege in 1760, in February 1766 the Burmese descended upon the city for the last time. The Thais held out for over a year, during which they were afflicted by famine, epidemics and a terrible fire which destroyed ten thousand houses. Finally, in April 1767, the walls were breached and the city taken. The Burmese savagely razed everything to the ground and led off tens of thousands of prisoners to Burma, including most of the royal family. The city was abandoned to the jungle, and Thailand descended into banditry.

Taksin and Thonburi

Out of this lawless mess, however, emerged **Phraya Taksin**, a charismatic and brave general, who had been unfairly blamed for a failed counterattack against the Burmese at Ayutthaya and had quietly slipped away from the besieged city. Taksin was crowned king in December 1768 at his new capital of **Thonburi**, on the opposite bank of the river from modern-day Bangkok. Within two years he had restored all of Ayutthaya's territories; more remarkably, by the end of the next decade Taksin had outdone his Ayutthayan predecessors by bringing Cambodia and much of Laos into a huge new empire.

However, by 1779 all was not well with the king. Taksin was becoming increasingly paranoid about plots against him, a delusion that drove him to imprison and torture even his wife and sons. At the same time he sank into religious excesses, demanding that the monkhood worship him as a god. By March 1782, public outrage at his sadism and dangerously irrational behaviour had reached such fervour that he was ousted in a coup.

Chao Phraya Chakri, Taksin's military commander, was invited to take power and had Taksin executed. In accordance with ancient etiquette, this had to be done without royal blood touching the earth: the mad king was duly wrapped in a black velvet sack and struck on the back of the neck with a sandalwood club. (Popular tradition has it that even this form of execution was too much: an unfortunate substitute got the velvet sack treatment, while Taksin was whisked away to a palace in the hills near Nakhon Si Thammarat, where he is said to have lived until 1825.)

The early Bangkok empire: Rama I

With the support of the Ayutthayan aristocracy, Chakri – reigning as **Rama I** (1782–1809) – set about consolidating the Thai kingdom. His first act was to move the capital across the river to what we know as **Bangkok**, on the more defensible east bank where the French had built a grand but short-lived fort in the 1660s. Borrowing from the layout of Ayutthaya, he built a new royal palace and impressive monasteries in the area of **Ratanakosin** – which remains the city's spiritual heart – within a defensive ring of two (later expanded to three) canals. In the palace temple, Wat Phra Kaeo, he enshrined the talismanic Emerald Buddha, which he had snatched during his campaigns in Laos. Initially, as at

Ayutthaya, the city was largely amphibious: only the temples and royal palaces were built on dry land, while ordinary residences floated on thick bamboo rafts on the river and canals, and even shops and warehouses were moored to the river bank.

During Rama I's reign, trade with China revived, and the style of government was put on a more modern footing: while retaining many of the features of a *devaraja*, he shared more responsibility with his courtiers, as a first among equals.

Rama II and Rama III

The peaceful accession of his son as **Rama II** (1809–24) signalled the establishment of the **Chakri dynasty**, which is still in place today. This Second Reign was a quiet interlude, best remembered as a fertile period for Thai literature. The king, himself one of the great Thai poets, gathered round him a group of writers including the famous Sunthorn Phu, who produced scores of masterly love poems, travel accounts and narrative songs.

In contrast, **Rama III** (1824–51) actively discouraged literary development and was a vigorous defender of conservative values. To this end, he embarked on an extraordinary redevelopment of **Wat Pho**, the oldest temple in Bangkok. Hundreds of educational inscriptions and mural paintings, on all manner of secular and religious subjects, were put on show, apparently to preserve traditional culture against the rapid change which the king saw corroding the country.

The danger posed by Western influence became more apparent in the Third Reign. As early as 1825, the Thais were sufficiently alarmed by **British colonialism** to strengthen Bangkok's defences by stretching a great iron chain across the mouth of the Chao Phraya River, to which every blacksmith in the area had to donate a certain number of links. In 1826 Rama III was obliged to sign the **Burney Treaty**, a limited trade agreement with the British by which the Thais won some political security in return for reducing their taxes on goods passing through Bangkok.

Mongkut

Rama IV, more commonly known as **Mongkut** (1851–68), had been a Buddhist monk for 27 years when he succeeded his brother. But far from leading a cloistered life, Mongkut had travelled widely throughout Thailand, had maintained scholarly contacts with French and American missionaries, and had taken an interest in Western learning, studying English, Latin and the sciences.

When his kingship faced its first major test, in the form of a threatening **British mission** in 1855 led by **Sir John Bowring**, Mongkut dealt with it confidently. Realizing that Thailand would be unable to resist the military might of the British, the king reduced import and export taxes, allowed British subjects to live and own land in Thailand and granted them freedom of trade. Furthermore, Mongkut quickly made it known that he would welcome diplomatic contacts from other Western countries: within a decade, agreements similar to the Bowring Treaty had been signed with France, the United States and a score of other nations.

Thus by skilful diplomacy the king avoided a close relationship with just one power, which could easily have led to Thailand's annexation. And as a result of the open-door policy, foreign trade boomed, financing the redevelopment of Bangkok's waterfront and, for the first time, the building of paved roads. However, Mongkut ran out of time for instituting the far-reaching domestic reforms which he saw were needed to drag Thailand into the modern world.

Chulalongkorn

Mongkut's son, **Chulalongkorn**, took the throne as Rama V (1868–1910) at the age of only 15, but he was well prepared by an excellent education which mixed traditional Thai and modern Western elements – provided by Mrs Anna Leonowens, subject of *The King and I*. When Chulalongkorn reached his majority after a five-year regency, he set to work on the reforms envisioned by his father.

One of his first acts was to scrap the custom by which subjects were required to prostrate themselves in the presence of the king. He constructed a new residential palace for the royal family in **Dusit**, north of Ratanakosin, and laid out that area's grand European-style boulevards. In the 1880s Chulalongkorn began to **restructure the government** to meet the country's needs, setting up a host of departments, for education, public health, the army and the like, and bringing in scores of foreign advisers to help with everything from foreign affairs to rail lines.

Throughout this period, however, the Western powers maintained their pressure on the region. The most serious threat to Thai sovereignty was the **Franco-Siamese Crisis** of 1893, which culminated in the French sending gunboats up the Chao Phraya River to Bangkok. Flouting numerous international laws, France claimed control over Laos and made other outrageous demands, which Chulalongkorn had no option but to concede. During the course of his reign the country was obliged to cede almost half of its territory, and forewent huge sums of tax revenue, in order to preserve its independence; but by Chulalongkorn's death in 1910, the frontiers were fixed as they are today.

The end of absolute monarchy

Chulalongkorn was succeeded by a flamboyant, British-educated prince, **Vajiravudh** (Rama VI, 1910–25). However, in 1912 a group of young army lieutenants, disillusioned by the absolute monarchy, plotted a **coup**. The conspirators were easily broken up, but this was something new in Thai history: the country was used to infighting among the royal family, but not to military intrigue by men from comparatively ordinary backgrounds. By the time the young and inexperienced **Prajadhipok** – seventy-sixth child of Chulalongkorn – was catapulted to the throne as Rama VII (1925–35), Vajiravudh's extravagance had created severe financial problems. The vigorous community of Western-educated intellectuals who had emerged in the lower echelons of the bureaucracy were becoming increasingly dissatisfied with monarchical government. The Great Depression, which ravaged the economy in the 1930s, came as the final shock to an already moribund system.

On June 24, 1932, a small group of middle-ranking officials, led by a lawyer, **Pridi Phanomyong**, and an army major, Luang Phibunsongkhram (**Phibun**), staged a **coup** with only a handful of troops. Prajadhipok weakly submitted to the conspirators, and 150 years of absolute monarchy in Bangkok came to a sudden end. The king was sidelined to a position of symbolic significance, and in 1935 he abdicated in favour of his ten-year-old nephew, **Ananda**, then a schoolboy living in Switzerland.

Up to World War II

The success of the 1932 coup was in large measure attributable to the army officers who gave the conspirators credibility, and it was they who were to dominate the constitutional governments that followed. Phibun emerged as prime minister after the decisive elections of 1938, and encouraged a wave of nationalistic feeling with such measures as the official institution of the name Thailand in 1939 – Siam, it was argued, was a name bestowed by external forces, and the new title made it clear that the country belonged to the Thais rather than the economically dominant Chinese.

The Thais were dragged into **World War II** on December 8, 1941, when, almost at the same time as the assault on Pearl Harbor, the Japanese invaded the east coast of peninsular Thailand, with their sights set on Singapore to the south. The Thais at first resisted fiercely, but realizing that the position was hopeless, Phibun quickly ordered a ceasefire.

The Thai government concluded a military alliance with Japan and declared war against the United States and Great Britain in January 1942, probably in the belief that the Japanese would win. However, the Thai minister in Washington, Seni Pramoj, refused to deliver the declaration of war against the US and, in cooperation with the Americans, began organizing a resistance movement called **Seri Thai**. Pridi Phanomyong, now acting as regent to the young king, furtively coordinated the movement under the noses of the occupying Japanese, smuggling in American agents and housing them in a European prison camp in Bangkok.

By 1944 Japan's defeat looked likely, and in July Phibun, who had been most closely associated with them, was forced to resign by the National Assembly. Once the war was over, American support prevented the British from imposing heavy punishments on the country for its alliance with Japan.

Postwar upheavals

With the fading of the military, the election of January 1946 was for the first time contested by organized political parties, resulting in Pridi becoming prime minister. A **new constitution** was drafted, and the outlook for democratic, civilian government seemed bright. Hopes were shattered, however, on June 9, 1946, when King Ananda was found dead in his bed, with a bullet wound in his forehead. Three palace servants were hurriedly tried and executed, but the murder has never been satisfactorily explained. Pridi resigned as prime minister, and in April 1948 Phibun, playing on the threat of communism, took over the premiership.

As **communism** developed its hold in the region with the takeover of China in 1949 and the French defeat in Indochina in 1954, the US increasingly viewed Thailand as a bulwark against the red menace. Between 1951 and 1957, when its annual state budget was only about $200 million a year, Thailand received a total $149 million in American economic aid and $222 million in military aid. This strengthened Phibun's dictatorship, while enabling leading military figures to divert American money and other funds into their own pockets.

Phibun narrowly won a general election in 1957, but only by blatant vote rigging and coercion. Although there's a strong tradition of foul play in Thai elections, this is remembered as the dirtiest ever: after vehement public outcry, **General Sarit**, the commander-in-chief of the army, overthrew the new government in September 1957. Believing that Thailand would prosper best under a unifying authority, Sarit set about re-establishing the monarchy as

△ King Bhumibol (Rama IX)

the head of the social hierarchy and the source of legitimacy for the government. Ananda's successor, **Bhumibol (Rama IX)**, was pushed into an active role, while Sarit ruthlessly silenced critics and pressed ahead with a plan for economic development, achieving a large measure of stability and prosperity.

The Vietnam War

Sarit died in 1963, whereupon the military succession passed to **General Thanom**, closely aided by his deputy prime minister, General Praphas. Their most pressing problem was the **Vietnam War**. The Thais, with the backing of the US, quietly began to conduct military operations in Laos, to which North Vietnam and China responded by supporting anti-government insurgency in Thailand. The more the Thais felt threatened by the spread of communism, the more they looked to the Americans for help – by 1968 around 45,000 US military personnel were on Thai soil, which became the base for US bombing raids against North Vietnam and Laos.

The effects of the **American presence** were profound. The economy swelled with dollars, and hundreds of thousands of Thais became reliant on the Americans for a living, with a consequent proliferation of prostitution – centred on Bangkok's infamous Patpong district – and corruption. The sudden exposure to Western culture also led many to question traditional Thai values and the political status quo.

The democracy movement and civil unrest

Poor farmers in particular were becoming increasingly disillusioned with their lot, and many turned against the Bangkok government. At the end of 1964, the **Communist Party of Thailand** and other groups formed a **broad left coalition** which soon had the support of several thousand insurgents in remote areas of the northeast and the north. By 1967, a separate threat had arisen in southern Thailand, involving **Muslim dissidents** and the Chinese-dominated **Communist Party of Malaya**, as well as local Thais.

Thanom was now facing a major security crisis, especially as the war in Vietnam was going badly. In November 1971 he reimposed repressive military rule, under a triumvirate of himself, his son Colonel Narong and Praphas, who became known as the "Three Tyrants". However, the 1969 experiment with democracy had heightened expectations of power-sharing among the middle classes, especially in the universities. **Student demonstrations** began in June 1973, and in October as many as 500,000 people turned out at Thammasat University in Bangkok to demand a new constitution. King Bhumibol intervened with apparent success, and indeed the demonstrators were starting to disperse on the morning of October 14, when the police tried to control the flow of people away. Tensions quickly mounted and soon a full-scale riot was under way, during which over 350 people were reported killed. The army, however, refused to provide enough troops to suppress this massive uprising, and later the same day, Thanom, Narong and Praphas were forced to resign and leave the country.

In a new climate of openness, **Kukrit Pramoj** formed a coalition of seventeen elected parties and secured a promise of US withdrawal from Thailand, but his government was riven with feuding. In October 1976, the students demonstrated again, protesting against the return of Thanom to Bangkok to become a monk at Wat Bowonniwet. This time there was no restraint: supported by elements of the military and the government, the police and reactionary students launched a massive assault on **Thammasat University**. On October 6, hundreds of students were brutally beaten, scores were lynched and some even burned alive; the military took control and suspended the constitution.

"Premocracy"

Soon after, the military-appointed prime minister, **Thanin Kraivichien**, forced dissidents to undergo anti-communist indoctrination, but his measures seem to have been too repressive even for the military, who forced him to resign in October 1977. **General Kriangsak Chomanand** took over, and began to break up the insurgency with shrewd offers of amnesty. He in turn was displaced in February 1980 by **General Prem Tinsulanonda**, backed by a broad parliamentary coalition.

Untainted by corruption, Prem achieved widespread support, including that of the monarchy. Overseeing a period of rapid economic growth, Prem maintained the premiership until 1988, with a unique mixture of dictatorship and democracy sometimes called **Premocracy**: although never standing for parliament himself, Prem was asked by the legislature after every election to become prime minister. He eventually stepped down because, he said, it was time for the country's leader to be chosen from among its elected representatives.

The 1992 demonstrations

The new prime minister was indeed an elected MP, **Chatichai Choonhavan**, a retired general with a long civilian career in public office. He pursued a vigorous policy of economic development, but this fostered widespread corruption in which members of the government were often implicated. Following an economic downturn and Chatichai's attempts to downgrade the political role of the military, the armed forces staged a bloodless **coup** on February 23, 1991, led by Supreme Commander **Sunthorn** and General **Suchinda**, the army commander-in-chief, who became premier.

When Suchinda reneged on promises to make democratic amendments to the constitution, hundreds of thousands of ordinary Thais poured onto the streets around Bangkok's Democracy Monument in **mass demonstrations** between May 17 and 20, 1992. Hopelessly misjudging the mood of the country, Suchinda brutally crushed the protests, leaving hundreds dead or injured. Having justified the massacre on the grounds that he was protecting the king from communist agitators, Suchinda was forced to resign when King Bhumibol expressed his disapproval in a ticking-off that was broadcast on world television.

The 1997 constitution

The elections on September 13, 1992 were won by the Democrat Party, led by **Chuan Leekpai**, a noted upholder of democracy and the rule of law. Despite many successes through a period of continued economic growth, he lost the 1995 poll to Chart Thai and its leader, Banharn Silpa-archa, who was nicknamed "the walking ATM" by the press for his vote-buying reputation. In the following year he in turn was replaced by **General Chavalit Yongchaiyudh**, leader of the New Aspiration Party (NAP), who just won what was dubbed as the most corrupt election in Thai history, with an estimated 25 million baht spent on vote-buying in rural areas.

The most significant positive event of his tenure was the approval of a **new constitution**. Drawn up by an independent drafting assembly, its main points included: direct elections to the senate, rather than appointment of senators by the prime minister, acceptance of the right of assembly as the basis of a democratic society and guarantees of individual rights and freedoms; greater public accountability; and increased popular participation in local administration. The eventual aim of the new charter was to end the traditional system of patronage, vested interests and vote buying.

The economic crisis

At the start of Chavalit's premiership, the Thai **economy** was already on shaky ground. In February 1997, foreign-exchange dealers began to mount speculative attacks on the baht, alarmed at the size of Thailand's private foreign debt – 250 billion baht in the unproductive property sector alone, much of it accrued through the proliferation of prestigious skyscrapers in Bangkok. The government valiantly defended the pegged exchange rate, spending $23 billion of the country's formerly healthy foreign-exchange reserves, but at the beginning of July was forced to give up the ghost – the baht was floated and soon went into freefall.

Blaming its traditional allies, the Americans, for neglecting their obligations, Thailand sought help from Japan; Tokyo suggested the **IMF**, who in August 1997 put together a **rescue package** for Thailand of $17 billion. Among the conditions of the package, the Thai government was to slash the national budget, control inflation and open up financial institutions to foreign ownership.

Chavalit's performance in the face of the crisis was viewed as inept, and in November, he was succeeded by **Chuan Leekpai**, who took up what was widely seen as a poisoned chalice for his second term. Chuan immediately took a hard line to try to restore confidence: he followed the IMF's advice, which involved maintaining cripplingly high interest rates to protect the baht, and pledged to reform the financial system. Although this played well abroad, at home the government encountered increasing hostility. Unemployment had doubled to 2 million by mid-1998 and there were frequent public protests against the IMF.

By the end of 1998, however, Chuan's tough stance was paying off, with the baht stabilizing at just under 40 to the US dollar, and interest rates and inflation starting to fall. Foreign investors slowly began returning to Thailand, and by October 1999 Chuan was confident enough to announce that he was forgoing almost $4 billion of the IMF's planned rescue package.

Thaksin

The 2001 general election was won by a new party, **Thai Rak Thai** (Thai Loves Thai), led by one of Thailand's wealthiest men, **Thaksin Shinawatra**, an ex-policeman who had made a personal fortune from government telecommunications concessions. Instead of a move towards greater democracy, as envisioned by the new constitution, Thaksin's government seemed to represent a full-blown merger between politics and big business, concentrating economic power in even fewer hands. Furthermore, the prime minister began to apply commercial and legal pressure, including several lawsuits, to try to silence critics in the media and parliament, and to manipulate the Senate and supposedly independent institutions such as the Election Commission to consolidate his own power. As his standing became more firmly entrenched, he rejected constitutional reforms designed to rein in his power – famously declaring that "democracy is only a tool" for achieving other goals. Thaksin did, however, live up to his billing as a populist reformer. In his first year of government, he issued a three-year loan moratorium for perennially indebted farmers and set up a one-million-baht development fund for each of the country's seventy thousand villages. To improve public health access, a standard charge of B30 per hospital visit was introduced nationwide.

In early 2004, politically and criminally motivated violence in the **Islamic southern provinces** escalated sharply, and since then, there have been over 1200 deaths on both sides in the troubles. The insurgents have targeted any representative of central authority, including monks and teachers, as well as setting off bombs in marketplaces and near tourist hotels. The authorities have inflamed opinion in the south by reacting violently, notably in crushing protests at Tak Bai and the much-revered Krue Se Mosque in Pattani in 2004, in which a total of over two hundred alleged insurgents died. In 2005, the government imposed **martial law** in Pattani, Yala and Narathiwat provinces and in parts of Songkhla province – this, however, has exacerbated economic and unemployment problems in what is Thailand's poorest region. Facing a variety of shadowy groups, whose precise aims are unclear, the authorities' natural instinct has been to get tough – which so far has brought the problem no nearer to a solution. Recent, constructive proposals by the **National Reconciliation Commission**, however, headed by former prime minister, Anand Panyarachun, may, if adopted, hold out some cause for hope.

Despite these problems, but bolstered by his high-profile response to the tsunami on December 26, 2004, in which over eight thousand people died on Thailand's Andaman Coast, Thaksin breezed through the **February 2005 election**, becoming the first prime minister in Thai history to win an outright majority at the polls. He promised an end to poverty, ambitious infrastructure projects and privatization of state companies, but the prospect of a one-party state alarmed a wide spectrum of opposition. When Thaksin's relatives sold their shares in the family's Shin Corporation in January 2006 for £1.1 billion, without paying tax, the tipping point was reached: tens of thousands of mostly middle-class Thais flocked to Bangkok to take part in peaceful demonstrations, which went on for weeks on end, under the umbrella of the **People's Alliance for Democracy**. The prime minister was eventually obliged to call a snap general election for April 2, but the three main opposition parties decided to boycott the poll, claiming that Thaksin was unfairly seeking a mandate without having to answer the corruption claims against him. Unsurprisingly, Thai Rak Thai won the election, but three days later, after an audience with King Bhumibol, Thaksin resigned. In May, the Constitutional Court ruled that the election had been unconstitutional and ordered a new poll. Thaksin was reinstalled as caretaker prime minister, but on September 19, while away at the United Nations General Assembly in New York, he was ousted by a military **coup d'état**, led by the army commander, General Sondhi Boonyaratkalin. At the time of going to press, it seems to have been a remarkably benign putsch, with the apparent support of the king and a large number of Thais. An interim caretaker prime minister, the senior royal advisor and former army general Surayud Chulanont, was inducted within a fortnight of the takeover, with General Sondhi promising that reform of the constitution and a general election would follow within the coming year.

Religion: Thai Buddhism

Over ninety percent of Thais consider themselves Theravada Buddhists, followers of the teachings of a holy man usually referred to as the Buddha (Enlightened One), though more precisely known as Gautama Buddha to distinguish him from three lesser-known Buddhas who preceded him, and from the fifth and final Buddha who is predicted to arrive in the year 4457 AD. Theravada Buddhism is one of the two main schools of Buddhism practised in Asia, and in Thailand it has absorbed an eclectic assortment of animist and Hindu elements into its beliefs as well. The other ten percent of Thailand's population comprises Mahayana Buddhists, Muslims, Hindus, Sikhs and Christians.

The Buddha: his life and beliefs

Buddhists believe that Gautama Buddha was the 500th incarnation of a single being: the stories of these five hundred lives, collectively known as the **Jataka**, provide the inspiration for much Thai art. (Hindus also accept Gautama Buddha into their pantheon, perceiving him as the ninth manifestation of their god Vishnu.)

In his last incarnation he was born in Nepal as **Prince Gautama Siddhartha** in either the sixth or seventh century BC, the son of a king and his hitherto barren wife, who finally became pregnant only after having a dream that a white elephant had entered her womb. At the time of his birth astrologers predicted that Gautama was to become universally respected, either as a worldly king or as a spiritual saviour, depending on which way of life he pursued. Much preferring the former idea, the prince's father forbade the boy to leave the palace grounds, and took it upon himself to educate Gautama in all aspects of the high life. Most statues of the Buddha depict him with elongated earlobes, a reference to his pampered early life, when he would have worn heavy precious stones in his ears.

The prince married and became a father, but at the age of 29 he flouted his father's authority and sneaked out into the world beyond the palace. On this fateful trip he encountered successively an old man, a sick man, a corpse and a hermit, and was thus made aware for the first time that pain and suffering were intrinsic to human life. Contemplation seemed the only means of discovering why this should be so – and therefore Gautama decided to leave the palace and become a **Hindu ascetic**.

For six or seven years he wandered the countryside leading a life of self-denial and self-mortification, but failed to come any closer to the answer. Eventually concluding that the best course of action must be to follow a "Middle Way" – neither indulgent nor overly ascetic – Gautama sat down beneath the famous riverside bodhi tree at Bodh Gaya in India, facing the rising sun, to meditate until he achieved enlightenment. For 49 days he sat crosslegged in the "lotus position", contemplating the causes of suffering and wrestling with temptations that materialized to distract him. Most of these were sent by **Mara**, the Evil One, who was finally subdued when Gautama summoned the earth goddess **Mae Toranee** by pointing the fingers of his right hand at the ground – the gesture known as *Bhumisparsa Mudra*, which has been immortalized by hundreds of Thai sculptors. Mae Toranee wrung torrents of water from her hair and engulfed Mara's demonic emissaries in a flood, an episode that also features in several sculptures and paintings, most famously in the statue in Bangkok's Sanam Luang.

Temptations dealt with, Gautama soon came to attain **enlightenment** and so became a Buddha. The Buddha preached his **first sermon** in a deer park in India, where he characterized his Dharma (doctrine) as a wheel. From this episode comes the early Buddhist symbol the **Dharmachakra**, known as the Wheel of Law, Wheel of Doctrine or Wheel of Life, which is often accompanied by a statue of a deer. Thais celebrate this first sermon with a public holiday in July known as Asanha Puja. On another occasion 1250 people spontaneously gathered to hear the Buddha speak, an event remembered in Thailand as Maha Puja and marked by a public holiday in February. For the next forty-odd years the Buddha travelled the region, converting non-believers and performing miracles. One rainy season he even ascended into the Tavatimsa heaven (Heaven of the thirty-three gods) to visit his mother and to preach the doctrine to her. His descent from this heaven is quite a common theme of paintings and sculptures, and the **Standing Buddha** pose of numerous Buddha statues comes from this story.

The Buddha "died" at the age of eighty on the banks of a river at Kusinari in India – an event often dated to 543 BC, which is why the Thai calendar is 543 years out of synch with the Western one, so that the year 2005 AD becomes 2548 BE (Buddhist Era). Lying on his side, propping up his head on his hand, the Buddha passed into **Nirvana** (giving rise to the classic pose, the Reclining Buddha), the unimaginable state of nothingness which knows no suffering and from which there is no reincarnation. Buddhists believe that the day the Buddha entered Nirvana was the same date on which he was born and he achieved enlightenment, a triply significant day that Thais honour with the Visakha Puja festival in May or June.

Buddhist doctrine

After the Buddha entered Nirvana, his **doctrine** spread relatively quickly across India, and probably was first promulgated in Thailand around the third century BC. His teachings, the *Tripitaka*, were written down in the Pali language – a derivative of Sanskrit – in a form that became known as Theravada or "The Doctrine of the Elders".

As taught by the Buddha, **Theravada Buddhism** built on the Hindu theory of perpetual reincarnation in the pursuit of perfection, introducing the notion of life as a cycle of suffering which could only be transcended by enlightened beings able to free themselves from earthly ties and enter into the blissful state of Nirvana. For the well-behaved but unenlightened Buddhist, each reincarnation marks a move up a vague kind of ladder, with animals at the bottom, women figuring lower down than men, and monks coming at the top – a hierarchy complicated by the very pragmatic notion that the more comfortable your lifestyle, the higher your spiritual status.

The Buddhist has no hope of enlightenment without acceptance of the **four noble truths**. In encapsulated form, these hold that desire is the root cause of all suffering and can be extinguished only by following the eightfold path or **Middle Way**. This Middle Way is essentially a highly moral mode of life that includes all the usual virtues like compassion, respect and moderation, and eschews vices such as self-indulgence and anti-social behaviour. But the key to it all is an acknowledgement that the physical world is impermanent and ever-changing, and that all things – including the self – are therefore not worth craving. Only by pursuing a condition of complete **detachment** can human beings transcend earthly suffering.

By the beginning of the first millennium, a new movement called **Mahayana** (Great Vehicle) had emerged within the Theravada school, attempting to make

Buddhism more accessible by introducing a Hindu-style pantheon of *bodhisattva*, or Buddhist saints, who, although they had achieved enlightenment, nevertheless postponed entering Nirvana in order to inspire the populace. Mahayana Buddhism subsequently spread north into China, Korea, Vietnam and Japan, also entering southern Thailand via the Srivijayan empire around the eighth century and parts of Khmer Cambodia in about the eleventh century. Meanwhile Theravada Buddhism (which the Mahayanists disparagingly renamed "**Hinayana**" or "Lesser Vehicle") established itself most significantly in Sri Lanka, northern and central Thailand and Burma.

The monkhood

In Thailand it's the duty of the 270,000-strong **Sangha** (monkhood) to set an example to the Theravada Buddhist community by living a life as close to the Middle Way as possible and by preaching the Dharma to the people. A monk's life is governed by 227 strict rules that include celibacy and the rejection of all personal possessions except gifts.

Each day begins with an alms round in the neighbourhood so that the laity can donate food and thereby gain themselves merit (see p.242), and then is chiefly spent in meditation, chanting, teaching and study. Always the most respected members of any community, monks act as teachers, counsellors and arbiters in local disputes. They also perform rituals at cremations, weddings and other events such as the launching of a new business or even the purchase of a new car. Although some Thai women do become nuns, they belong to no official order and aren't respected as much as the monks. Many young boys from poor families find themselves almost obliged to become **novice monks** because that's the only way they can get accommodation, food and, crucially, an education. This is provided free in exchange for duties around the wat, and novices are required to adhere to ten rather than 227 Buddhist precepts.

Monkhood doesn't have to be for life: a man may leave the Sangha three times without stigma and in fact every Thai male (including royalty) is expected

△ Receiving alms, Wat Benjamabophit

to **enter the monkhood** for a short period at some point in his life, ideally between leaving school and marrying, as a rite of passage into adulthood. So ingrained into the social system is this practice that Thai government departments and some private companies grant their employees paid leave for their time as a monk, but the custom is in decline as young men increasingly have to consider the effect their absence may have on their career prospects. Instead, many men now enter the monkhood for a brief period after the death of a parent, to make merit both for the deceased and for the rest of the family. The most popular time for temporary ordination is the three-month Buddhist retreat period – **Pansa**, sometimes referred to as "Buddhist Lent" – which begins in July and lasts for the duration of the rainy season. (The monks' confinement is said to originate from the earliest years of Buddhist history, when farmers complained that perambulating monks were squashing their sprouting rice crops.) **Ordination ceremonies** take place in almost every wat at this time and make spectacular scenes, with the shaven-headed novice usually clad entirely in white and carried about on friends' or relatives' shoulders. The boys' parents donate money, food and necessities such as washing powder and mosquito repellent, processing around the temple compound with their gifts, often joined by dancers or travelling players hired for the occasion.

Monks in contemporary society

In recent years, some monks have become influential activists in social and environmental issues, and some upcountry temples have established themselves as successful drug rehabilitation centres. Other monks have acquired such a reputation for giving wise counsel and bringing good fortune and prosperity to their followers that they have become national gurus and their temples now generate great wealth through the production of specially blessed amulets (see p.85) and photographs.

Though the increasing involvement of many monks in the secular world has not met with unanimous approval, far more disappointing to the laity are those monks who **flout the precepts** of the Sangha by succumbing to the temptations of a consumer society, flaunting Raybans, Rolexes and Mercedes cars (in some cases actually bought with temple funds), chain-smoking and flirting, even making pocket money from predicting lottery results and practising faith-healing. With so much national pride and integrity riding on the sanctity of the Sangha, any whiff of a deeper scandal is bound to strike deep into the national psyche. In recent years many have been shocked by the unprecedented litany of serious crimes involving monks, including several rapes and murders, and there's been an embarrassment of exposés of corrupt, high-ranking abbots caught carousing in disreputable bars, drug-dealing and even gun-running. This has prompted a stream of editorials on the state of the Sangha and the collapse of spiritual values at the heart of Thai society. The inclusivity of the monkhood – which is open to just about any male who wants to join – has been highlighted as a particularly vulnerable aspect, not least because donning saffron robes has always been an accepted way for criminals, reformed or otherwise, to repent of their past deeds.

Interestingly, back in the late 1980s, the influential monk Phra Bodhirak was unceremoniously defrocked after criticizing what he saw as a tide of decadence infecting Thai Buddhism and advocating an all-round purification of the Sangha. He now preaches from his breakaway **Santi Asoke** sect headquarters on the outskirts of Bangkok, but though his ascetic code of anti-materialist behaviour is followed by thousands of devotees across Thailand, it is not sanctioned by the more worldly figures of the Sangha Supreme Council. Nonetheless, Santi Asoke is often vocal on political issues: sect members were active in the democracy movement of 1992 and participated in the 2006 anti-Thaksin demonstrations as the self-fashioned Dharma Army. The sect is also famous across the country for its cheap vegetarian restaurants and for the back-to-basics uniform of the traditional blue farmer's shirt worn by many of its members.

Buddhist practice

A devout Buddhist layperson is expected to adhere to the **five basic precepts**, namely not to kill or steal, to refrain from sexual misconduct and incorrect speech (lies, gossip and abuse) and to eschew intoxicating liquor and drugs. There are three extra precepts for special *wan phra* holy days and for those laypeople including foreign students who study meditation at Thai temples: no eating after noon, no entertainment (including TV and music) and no sleeping on a soft bed; in addition, the no sexual misconduct precept turns into no sex at all.

In practice most Thai Buddhists aim only to be **reborn** higher up the incarnation scale rather than set their sights on the ultimate goal of Nirvana. The rank of the reincarnation is directly related to the good and bad actions performed in the previous life, which accumulate to determine one's **karma** or destiny – hence the Thai obsession with "making merit".

Merit-making (*tham bun*) can be done in all sorts of ways, from giving a monk his breakfast to attending a Buddhist service or donating money to the neighbourhood temple, and most festivals are essentially communal merit-making opportunities. Between the big festivals, the most common days for making merit and visiting the temple are *wan phra* (holy days), which are determined by the phase of the moon and occur four times a month. For a Thai man, temporary ordination is a very important way of accruing merit not only for himself but also for his mother and sisters – wealthier citizens might take things a step further by commissioning the casting of a Buddha statue or even paying for the building of a wat. One of the more bizarre but common merit-making activities involves **releasing caged birds**: worshippers buy one or more tiny finches from vendors at wat compounds and, by liberating them from their cage, prove their Buddhist compassion towards all living things. The fact that the birds were free until netted earlier that morning doesn't seem to detract from the ritual at all. In riverside and seaside wats, birds are sometimes replaced by fish or even baby turtles.

For a detailed introduction to Thai Buddhism, see Ⓦwww.thaibuddhism.net. Details of Thai temples that welcome foreign students of Buddhism and meditation are on p.209.

Spirits and non-Buddhist deities

While regular Buddhist merit-making insures a Thai for the next life, there are certain **Hindu gods** and **animist spirits** that most Thais also cultivate for help with more immediate problems. Sophisticated Bangkokians and illiterate farmers alike find no inconsistency in these apparently incompatible practices, and as often as not it's a Buddhist monk who is called in to exorcize a malevolent spirit. Even the Buddhist King Bhumibol employs Brahmin priests and astrologers to determine auspicious days and officiate at certain royal ceremonies and, like his royal predecessors of the Chakri dynasty, he also associates himself with the Hindu god Vishnu by assuming the title Rama, after the seventh avatar of Vishnu and hero of the Hindu epic the *Ramayana*.

If a Thai wants help in achieving a short-term goal, like passing an exam, becoming pregnant or winning the lottery, then he or she will quite likely turn to the **Hindu pantheon**, visiting an enshrined statue of either Brahma, Vishnu, Shiva, Indra or Ganesh, and making offerings of flowers, incense and maybe food. If the outcome is favourable, devotees will probably come back to show thanks, bringing more offerings and maybe even hiring a dance troupe to perform a celebratory *lakhon chatri* as well. Built in honour of Brahma, Bangkok's Erawan Shrine is the most famous place of Hindu-inspired worship in the country.

Whereas Hindu deities tend to be benevolent, **spirits** (*phi*) are not nearly as reliable and need to be mollified more frequently. They come in hundreds of varieties, some more malign than others, and inhabit everything from trees, rivers and caves to public buildings and private homes – even taking over people if they feel like it. So that these *phi* don't pester human inhabitants, each building has a special **spirit house** (*saan phra phum*) in its vicinity, as a dwelling for spirits ousted by the building's construction. Usually raised on a short column to set it at or above eye-level, the spirit house must occupy an auspicious location – not, for example, in the shadow of the main building – so help from the local temple is usually required when deciding on the best position. Spirit houses are generally about the size of a dolls' house and designed to look like a wat or a traditional Thai house, but their ornamentation is supposed to reflect the status of the humans' building, so if that building is enlarged or refurbished, the spirit house should be improved accordingly. And as architects become increasingly bold in their designs, so modernist spirit houses are also beginning to appear in Bangkok, where an eyecatching new skyscraper might be graced by a *saan phra phum* of glass or polished concrete. Figurines representing the relevant guardian spirit and his aides are sometimes put inside the little house, and daily offerings of incense, lighted candles and garlands of jasmine are placed alongside them to keep the *phi* happy – a disgruntled spirit is a dangerous spirit, liable to cause sickness, accidents and even death. As with any religious building or icon in Thailand, an unwanted or crumbling spirit house should never be dismantled or destroyed, which is why you'll often see damaged spirit houses placed around the base of a sacred banyan tree, where they are able to rest in peace.

Art and architecture

Aside from pockets of Hindu-inspired statuary and architecture, the vast majority of Thailand's cultural monuments take their inspiration from Theravada Buddhism, and so it is **temples** and **religious images** that constitute Bangkok's main sights. Few of these can be attributed to any individual artist, but with a little background information it becomes fairly easy to recognize the major artistic styles. Though Bangkok's temples nearly all date from the eighteenth century or later, many of them display features that originate from a much earlier time. The National Museum (see p.72) is a good place to see some of Thailand's more ancient Hindu and Buddhist statues, and a visit to the fourteenth-century ruins at Ayutthaya (see p.140), less than two hours from Bangkok, is also recommended.

The wat

The **wat** or Buddhist temple complex has a great range of uses, as home to a monastic community, a place of public worship, a shrine for holy images and a shaded meeting place for townspeople and villagers. Wat architecture has evolved in ways as various as its functions, but there remain several essential components which have stayed constant for some fifteen centuries.

The most important wat building is the **bot** (sometimes known as the *ubosot*), a term most accurately translated as the "ordination hall". It usually stands at the heart of the compound and is the preserve of the monks: lay persons are rarely allowed inside, and it's generally kept locked when not in use. There's only one bot in any wat complex, and often the only way to distinguish it from other temple buildings is by the eight **sema** or boundary stones which always surround it.

Often almost identical to the bot, the **viharn** or assembly hall is for the lay congregation, and as a tourist this is the building you're most likely to enter, since it usually contains the wat's principal **Buddha image**, and sometimes two or three minor images as well. Large wats may have several viharns, while strict meditation wats, which don't deal with the laity, may not have one at all.

Thirdly, there's the **chedi** or stupa, a tower which was originally conceived as a monument to enshrine relics of the Buddha, but has since become a place to contain the ashes of royalty – and anyone else who can afford it.

Buddhist iconography

In the early days of Buddhism, image-making was considered inadequate to convey the faith's abstract philosophies, so the only approved iconography comprised doctrinal **symbols** such as the Dharmachakra (Wheel of Law, also known as Wheel of Doctrine or Wheel of Life). Gradually these symbols were displaced by **images of the Buddha**, construed chiefly as physical embodiments of the Buddha's teachings rather than as portraits of the man.

Of the four postures in which the Buddha is always depicted – sitting, standing, walking and reclining – the seated Buddha, which represents him in meditation, is the most common in Thailand. A popular variation shows the Buddha **seated** on a coiled serpent, protected by the serpent's hood – a reference to the story about the Buddha meditating during the rainy season, when a serpent offered to raise him off the wet ground and shelter him from the storms. The **reclining** pose symbolizes the Buddha entering Nirvana at his death, while the **standing** and **walking** images both represent his descent from Tavatimsa heaven.

Hindu iconography

Hindu images tend to be a lot livelier than Buddhist ones, partly because there is a panoply of gods to choose from, and partly because these gods have mischievous personalities and reappear in all sorts of bizarre incarnations.

Vishnu has always been especially popular: his role of "Preserver" has him embodying the status quo, representing both stability and the notion of altruistic love. He is most often depicted as the deity, but frequently crops up in other human and animal incarnations. There are ten of these manifestations (or avatars) in all, of which **Rama** (number seven) is by far the most popular in Thailand. The epitome of ideal manhood, Rama is the superhero of the epic story the *Ramayana* (see p.65) and appears in storytelling reliefs and murals in every Hindu temple in Thailand; in painted portraits you can usually recognize him by his green face. Manifestation number eight is **Krishna**, more widely known than Rama in the West, but slightly less common in Thailand. Krishna is usually characterized as a flirtatious, flute-playing, blue-skinned cowherd and is a crucial moral figure in the *Mahabarata*. Confusingly, Vishnu's ninth avatar is the **Buddha** – a manifestation adopted many centuries ago to minimize defection to the Buddhist faith.

When represented as the **deity**, Vishnu is generally shown sporting a crown and four arms, his hands holding a conch shell (whose music wards off demons), a discus (used as a weapon), a club (symbolizing the power of nature and time), and a lotus (symbol of joyful flowering and renewal). The god is often depicted astride a **garuda**, a half-man, half-bird creature.

Statues and representations of **Brahma** (the Creator) are very rare. Confusingly, he too has four arms, but you should recognize him by the fact that he holds no objects, has four faces (sometimes painted red), and is generally borne by a goose-like creature called a *hamsa*.

Shiva (the Destroyer) is the most volatile member of the pantheon. He stands for extreme behaviour, for beginnings and endings, and for fertility, and is a symbol of great energy and power. His godlike form typically has four, eight or ten arms, sometimes holding a trident (representing creation, protection and destruction) and a drum (to beat the rhythm of creation). In abstract form, he is represented by a **lingam** or phallic pillar.

Close associates of Shiva include **Parvati**, his wife, and **Ganesh**, his elephant-headed son. Depictions of Ganesh abound, both as statues and, because he is the god of knowledge and overcomer of obstacles (in the path of learning), as the symbol of the Fine Arts Department – which crops up on all entrance tickets to museums and historical parks.

Lesser mythological figures include the **yaksha** giants who ward off evil spirits (like the enormous freestanding ones guarding Bangkok's Wat Phra Kaeo); the graceful half-woman, half-bird **kinnari**; and the ubiquitous **naga**, or serpent king of the underworld, often depicted with seven heads.

The schools

For Thailand's architects and sculptors, the act of creation was an act of merit and a representation of unchanging truths, rather than an act of expression, and thus Thai art history is characterized by broad schools rather than individual names. In the 1920s art historians and academics began to classify these schools along the lines of the country's historical periods.

Dvaravati (sixth to eleventh centuries)

Centred on the towns of Nakhon Pathom, U Thong, Lopburi and Haripunjaya (modern-day Lamphun), the Dvaravati state was populated by Theravada Buddhists who were strongly influenced by Indian culture.

In an effort to combat the defects inherent in the poor-quality limestone at their disposal, Dvaravati-era **sculptors** made their Buddhas quite stocky, cleverly dressing the figures in a sheet-like drape that dropped down to ankle level from each raised wrist, forming a U-shaped hemline – a style which they used when casting in bronze as well. Nonetheless many **statues** have cracked, leaving them headless or limbless. Where the faces have survived, Dvaravati statues display some of the most naturalistic features ever produced in Thailand, distinguished by their thick lips, flattened noses and wide cheekbones.

Srivijaya (eighth to thirteenth centuries)

While Dvaravati's Theravada Buddhists were influencing the central plains, southern Thailand was paying allegiance to the Mahayana Buddhists of the **Srivijayan** empire. Mahayanists believe that those who have achieved enlightenment should postpone their entry into Nirvana in order to help others along the way. These stay-behinds, revered like saints both during and after life, are called **bodhisattva**, and statues of them were the mainstay of Srivijayan art.

The finest Srivijayan *bodhisattva* statues were cast in bronze and show such grace and sinuosity that they rank among the finest sculpture ever produced in the country. Many are lavishly adorned, and some were even bedecked in real jewels when first made. By far the most popular *bodhisattva* subject was *Avalokitesvara*, worshipped as compassion incarnate and generally shown with four or more arms and clad in an animal skin. Bangkok's National Museum holds a beautiful example.

Khmer and Lopburi (tenth to fourteenth centuries)

By the end of the ninth century the **Khmers** of Cambodia were starting to expand from their capital at Angkor into the Dvaravati states, bringing with them the Hindu faith and the cult of the god-king (*devaraja*). As lasting testaments to the sacred power of their kings, the Khmers built hundreds of imposing stone sanctuaries across their newly acquired territory.

Each magnificent castle-temple – known in Khmer as a **prasat** – was constructed primarily as a shrine for a shiva lingam, the phallic representation of the god Shiva. Almost every surface of the sanctuary was adorned with intricate **carvings**, usually gouged from sandstone, depicting Hindu deities (notably Vishnu reclining on the milky sea of eternity in the National Museum – see p.73) and stories, especially episodes from the *Ramayana* (see p.65).

During the Khmer period the former Theravada Buddhist principality of Lopburi produced a distinctive style of Buddha statue. Broad-faced and muscular, the classic **Lopburi** Buddha wears a diadem or ornamental headband – a nod to the Khmers' ideological fusion of earthly and heavenly power – and the *ushnisha* (the sign of enlightenment) becomes distinctly conical rather than a mere bump on the head.

Sukhothai (thirteenth to fifteenth centuries)

Two Thai generals established the first real Thai kingdom in **Sukhothai** (some 400km north of modern-day Bangkok, in the northern plains) in 1238, and over the next two hundred years the artists of this realm produced some of Thailand's most refined art. Sukhothai's artistic reputation rests above all on its **sculpture**. More sinuous even than the Srivijayan images, Sukhothai Buddhas tend towards elegant androgyny, with slim oval faces and slender curvaceous bodies usually clad in a plain, skintight robe that fastens with a tassle close to the navel. Fine examples include the Phra Buddha Chinnarat image at Bangkok's Wat Benjamabophit, and the enormous Phra Sri Sakyamuni, in Bangkok's Wat Suthat. Sukhothai sculptors were the first to represent the walking Buddha, a supremely graceful figure with his right leg poised to move forwards.

Sukhothai-era architects also devised a new type of chedi, as elegant in its way as the images their sculptor colleagues were producing. This was the **lotus-bud chedi**, a slender tower topped with a tapered finial that was to become a hallmark of the Sukhothai era.

Ancient Sukhothai is also renowned for the skill of its potters, who produced a **ceramic ware** known as Sawankhalok, after the name of one of the nearby kiln towns. It is distinguished by its grey-green celadon glazes and by the fish and chrysanthemum motifs used to decorate bowls and plates.

Ayutthaya (fourteenth to eighteenth centuries)

From 1351 Thailand's central plains came under the thrall of a new power centred on **Ayutthaya**, and over the next four centuries, the Ayutthayan rulers commissioned some four hundred grand wats as symbols of their wealth and power. Though essentially Theravada Buddhists, the kings also adopted some Hindu and Brahmin beliefs from the Khmers – most significantly the concept of *devaraja* or god-kingship, whereby the monarch became a mediator between the people and the Hindu gods.

Retaining the concentric layout of the typical Khmer **temple complex**, Ayutthayan builders refined and elongated the prang into a **corncob-shaped tower**, rounding it off at the top and introducing vertical incisions around its circumference. The most famous example is Bangkok's Wat Arun, which though built during the subsequent Ratanakosin period is a classic Ayutthayan structure.

Ayutthaya's architects also adapted the Sri Lankan **chedi** so favoured by their Sukhothai predecessors, stretching the bell-shaped base and tapering it into a very graceful conical spire, as at Wat Phra Sri Sanphet in Ayutthaya. The **viharns** of this era are characterized by walls pierced by slit-like windows, designed to foster a mysterious atmosphere by limiting the amount of light inside the building; Wat Yai Suwannaram in Phetchaburi (see p.157) has a particularly fine example.

From Sukhothai's Buddha **sculptures** the Ayutthayans copied the soft oval face, adding an earthlier demeanour to the features and imbuing them with a hauteur in tune with the *devaraja* ideology. Like the Lopburi images, early Ayutthayan statues wear crowns to associate kingship with Buddhahood; as the court became ever more lavish, so these figures became increasingly adorned, until – as in the monumental bronze at Wat Na Phra Mane – they appeared in earrings, armlets, anklets, bandoliers and coronets. The artists justified these luscious portraits of the Buddha – who was, after all, supposed to have given up worldly possessions – by pointing to an episode when the Buddha transformed himself into a well-dressed nobleman to gain the ear of a proud emperor, whereupon he scolded the man into entering the monkhood.

Ratanakosin (eighteenth century to the 1930s)

When **Bangkok** emerged as Ayutthaya's successor in 1782, the new capital's founder was determined to revive the old city's grandeur, and the **Ratanakosin**

△ Detail from the Ramayana murals in Wat Phra Kaeo

(or Bangkok) period began by aping what the Ayutthayans had done. Since then neither wat architecture nor religious sculpture has evolved much further.

The first **Ratanakosin building** was the bot of Bangkok's Wat Phra Kaeo, built to enshrine the Emerald Buddha. Designed to a typical Ayutthayan plan, it's coated in glittering mirrors and gold leaf, with roofs ranged in multiple tiers and tiled in green and orange. To this day, most newly built bots and viharns follow a more economical version of this paradigm, whitewashing the outside walls but decorating the pediment in gilded ornaments and mosaics of coloured glass. The result is that modern wats are often almost indistinguishable from each other, though Bangkok does have a few exceptions, including Wat Benjamabophit, which uses marble cladding for its walls and incorporates Victorian-style stained-glass windows, and Wat Rajapobhit, which is covered all over in Chinese ceramics. The most dramatic chedi of the Ratanakosin era – the tallest in the world – was constructed in the mid-nineteenth century in Nakhon Pathom (see p.150), to the original Sri Lankan style.

Early Ratanakosin sculptors produced adorned **Buddha images** very much in the Ayutthayan vein, sometimes adding real jewels to the figures; more modern images are notable for their ugliness rather than for any radical departure from type. The obsession with size, first apparent in the Sukhothai period, has plumbed new depths, with graceless concrete statues up to 60m high becoming the norm (as in Bangkok's Wat Indraviharn), a monumentalism made worse by the routine application of browns and dull yellows. Most small images are cast from or patterned on older models, mostly Sukhothai or Ayutthayan in origin.

Painting has fared much better, with the *Ramayana* murals in Bangkok's Wat Pha Kaeo (see p.64) a shining example of how Ayutthayan techniques and traditional subject matters could be adapted into something fantastic, imaginative and beautiful.

Contemporary

Following the democratization of Thailand in the 1930s, artists increasingly became recognized as individuals, and took to signing their work for the first time. In 1933 the first school of fine art (now Bangkok's Silpakorn University) was established under the Italian sculptor Corrado Feroci (also known by his Thai name, Silpa Bhirasri), designer of the capital's Democracy and Victory monuments, and, as the new generation experimented with secular themes and styles adapted from their Western contemporaries, Thai art began to look a lot more **"modern"**. Nonetheless, with a few notable exceptions, the leading artistic preoccupation of the past 75 years has been Thailand's spiritual heritage, with nearly every major figure on the contemporary art scene tackling religious issues at some point. For some artists this has meant a straightforward modernization of Buddhist legends or a reworking of particular symbols, while others have sought to dramatize the moral relevance of their religion in the light of political, social and philosophical trends. A number of Thailand's more established contemporary artists have earned the title **National Artist**, an honour that has been bestowed on one or two artists, of any discipline, nearly every year since 1985.

Bangkok has a near-monopoly on Thailand's **art galleries**. While the permanent collections at the National Gallery (see p.75) are disappointing, regular exhibitions of more challenging contemporary work appear at the Silpakorn University Art Gallery (see p.75), The Queen's Gallery (see p.84), and the Queen Sirikit Convention Centre, as well as at smaller gallery spaces around the city. The listings magazine *Bangkok Metro* prints details of current exhibitions, and runs features on prominent artists, or there's the bi-monthly free Art Connection calendar of exhibitions, available from galleries. The headquarters of Bangkok's major banks and securities' companies also display works by modern Thai artists both established and lesser known, and in recent years have made a big show of backing substantial art prizes. For a preview of works by Thailand's best modern artists, visit the Rama IX Art Museum Foundation's website at ⓦwww.rama9art.org. Apinan Poshyananda's book *Modern Art In Thailand* provides an excellent introduction to twentieth-century Thai artists up to the early 1990s and is complemented by Steven Pettifor's *Flavours: Thai Contemporary Art*, which looks at the newly invigorated art scene in Thailand from 1992 to 2004.

Significant names to look out for at the city's art galleries include National Artist **Pichai Nirand** (b.1936), who is particularly well known for his fine-detail canvases of Buddha footprints; **Pratuang Emjaroen** (b.1935), who addresses issues of social injustice through a mix of Buddhist iconography and abstract imagery; and prolific traditionalist and National Artist **Chakrabhand Posayakrit** (b.1943), who is best known for his series of thirty-three *Life of the Buddha* paintings, and for his portraits, including many of members of the Thai royal family.

More controversial, and more of a household name, **Thawan Duchanee's** (b.1939) surreal juxtaposition of religious icons with fantastical Bosch-like characters and explicitly sexual images prompted a group of fundamentalist students to slash ten of his early paintings in 1971 – an unprecedented reaction to a work of Thai art. Since then, Thawan has continued to examine the spiritual tensions of modern life, but since the 1980s his street cred has waned as his saleability has mushroomed. Critics have questioned his integrity at accepting commissions from corporate clients, and his increasingly neo-conservative image was compounded when he was honoured as a National Artist in 2001.

Complacency is not a criticism that could be levelled at **Vasan Sitthiket** (b.1957), Thailand's most outspoken and iconoclastic living artist. A persistent crusader against the hypocrisies of establishment figures such as monks, politicians and military leaders, Vasan's is one of the loudest and most aggressive political voices on the contemporary art scene, expressed on canvas, in multi-media works and in performance art. Some of Vasan's most famous recent work has taken the form of enormous wooden puppets: typical were his grotesque representations of 49 Thai luminaries in his 2000 show *What's In Our Head*, an exhibit that had to be assembled in just a few days following the banning of his original show for being too provocative. He was one of the seven artists to represent Thailand at the 2003 Venice Biennale, where Thailand had its own pavilion for the first time.

Equally forthright is fellow Biennale exhibitor, the photographer, performance artist and social activist **Manit Sriwanichpoom** (b.1961). Manit is best known for his "Pink Man" series of photographs in which he places a Thai man (his collaborator Sompong Thawee), dressed in a flashy pink suit and pushing a pink shopping trolley, into different scenes and situations in Thailand and elsewhere. The Pink Man represents thoughtless, dangerous consumerism and his backdrop might be an impoverished hill-tribe village (*Pink Man on Tour*; 1998), or black-and-white shots from the political violence of 1976 (*Horror in Pink*; 2001).

Thaweesak Srithongdee (b.1970) is another increasingly important name on the Thai art scene. His style is very accessible, a distinctive blend of surreal, pop, erotic and figurative, and often cartoonlike. His subject is generally popular culture, often with a strong dose of sci-fi fantasy: in his 2006 exhibition, Flesh, he explores the way in which popular culture manifests itself through the human body.

Contemporary women artists tend to be less high-profile in Thailand, but **Pinaree Santipak** (b.1961) is becoming an important name: her mostly multi-media work focuses on gender issues and makes recurrent use of a female iconography in the form of vessels and mounds.

Books

We have included publishers' details for books that may be hard to find outside Thailand, though some of them can be ordered online through ⓦwww.dcothai .com. Other titles should be available worldwide.

Travel

Steve Van Beek *Slithering South* (Wind and Water, Hong Kong). An expat writer tells how he single-handedly paddled his wooden boat down the entire 1100-kilometre course of the Chao Phraya river, and reveals a side of Thailand that's rarely written about in English.

James O'Reilly and Larry Habegger (eds) *Travelers' Tales:* *Thailand*. An absorbing anthology of contemporary writings about Thailand, by Thailand experts, social commentators, travel writers and first-time visitors.

William Warren *Bangkok*. An engaging portrait of the unwieldy capital, weaving together anecdotes and character sketches from Bangkok's past and present.

Culture and society

Michael Carrithers *The Buddha: A Very Short Introduction*. An accessible account of the life of the Buddha, and the development and significance of his thought.

Philip Cornwel-Smith *Very Thai Why do Thais do out their* soft drinks into plastic bags, what lies behind their penchant for Neo-classical architecture, and how does one sniff-kiss? Answers and insights aplenty in this intriguingly observant and highly readable fully illustrated guide to contemporary Thai culture.

△ Secondhand bookstall, Banglamphu

James Eckardt *Bangkok People* (Asia Books, Bangkok). The collected articles of a renowned expat journalist, whose interviews and encounters with a gallery of different Bangkokians – from construction-site workers and street vendors to boxers and political candidates – add texture and context to the city.

Sandra Gregory with Michael Tierney *Forget You Had A Daughter: Doing Time in the "Bangkok Hilton" – Sandra Gregory's Story.* The frank and shocking account of a young British woman who was imprisoned in Bangkok's notorious Lard Yao prison after being caught trying to smuggle 89 grammes of heroin out of Thailand.

Roger Jones *Culture Smart! Thailand.* Handy little primer on Thailand's social and cultural mores, with plenty of refreshingly up-to-date insights.

Father Joe Maier *Welcome to the Bangkok Slaughterhouse: The Battle for Human Dignity in Bangkok's Bleakest Slums.* Catholic priest Father Joe shares the stories of some of the Bangkok street kids and slum-dwellers that his charitable foundation has been supporting since 1972 (see Basics, p.51).

Trilok Chandra Majupuria *Erawan Shrine and Brahma Worship in Thailand* (Tecpress, Bangkok). The most concise introduction to the complexities of Thai religion, with a much wider scope than the title implies.

Cleo Odzer *Patpong Sisters.* An American anthropologist's funny and touching account of her life with the prostitutes and bar girls of Bangkok's notorious red-light district.

Phra Peter Pannapadipo *Little Angels: The Real-Life Stories of Twelve Thai Novice Monks.* A dozen young boys, many of them from desperate backgrounds, tell the often poignant stories of why they became novice monks. For some, funding from the Students' Education Trust (described on p.52) has changed their lives.

Phra Peter Pannapadipo *Phra Farang: An English Monk in Thailand.* Behind the scenes in a Thai monastery: the frank, funny and illuminating account of a UK-born former businessman's life as a Thai monk.

Pasuk Phongpaichit and Sungsidh Piriyarangsan *Corruption and Democracy in Thailand.* Fascinating academic study, revealing the nuts and bolts of corruption in Thailand and its links with all levels of political life, and suggesting a route to a stronger society. Their sequel, a study of Thailand's illegal economy, *Guns, Girls, Gambling, Ganja*, co-written with Nualnoi Treerat, makes equally eye-opening and depressing reading.

Denis Segaller *Thai Ways* (Silkworm Books, Chiang Mai). Fascinating collection of short pieces on Thai customs and traditions written by a long-term English resident of Bangkok.

Richard Totman *The Third Sex: Kathoey – Thailand's Ladyboys* (Silkworm Books, Chiang Mai). As several *katoey* share their life-stories with him, social scientist Totman examines their place in modern Thai society and explores the theory, supported by Buddhist philosophy, that *katoey* are members of a third sex whose transgendered make-up is predetermined from birth.

William Warren *Living in Thailand.* Luscious gallery of traditional houses and furnishings, with an emphasis on the homes of Thailand's rich and famous; seductively photographed by Luca Invernizzi Tettoni.

Daniel Ziv and Guy Sharett *Bangkok Inside Out*. This A–Z of Bangkok quirks and cultural substrates is full of slick photography and sparky observations but was deemed offensive by Thailand's Ministry of Culture and so some Thai bookshops won't stock it.

History

Anna Leonowens *The English Governess at the Siamese Court*. The mendacious memoirs of the nineteenth-century English governess that inspired the Yul Brynner film *The King and I*; low on accuracy, high on inside-palace gossip.

Michael Smithies *Old Bangkok*. Brief, anecdotal history of the capital's early development, emphasizing what remains to be seen of bygone Bangkok.

William Stevenson *The Revolutionary King*. Fascinating biography of the normally secretive King Bhumibol, by a British journalist who was given unprecedented access to the monarch and his family. The overall approach is fairly uncritical, but lots of revealing insights emerge along the way.

John Stewart *To the River Kwai: Two Journeys – 1943, 1979* (Bloomsbury). A survivor of the horrific World War II POW camps along the River Kwai returns to the region, interlacing his wartime reminiscences with observations on how he feels 36 years later.

William Warren *Jim Thompson: the Legendary American of Thailand*. The engrossing biography of the ex-intelligence agent, art collector and Thai silk magnate whose disappearance in Malaysia in 1967 has never been satisfactorily resolved.

David K. Wyatt *Thailand: A Short History*. An excellent, recently updated treatment, scholarly but highly readable, with a good eye for witty, telling details. Good chapters on the story of the Thais before they reached what's now Thailand, and on recent developments. His *Siam in Mind* (Silkworm Books, Chiang Mai) is a wide-ranging and intriguing collection of sketches and short reflections that point towards an intellectual history of Thailand.

Art, architecture and film

Steve Van Beek *The Arts of Thailand*. Lavishly produced and perfectly pitched introduction to the history of Thai architecture, sculpture and painting, with superb photographs by Luca Invernizzi Tettoni.

Jean Boisselier *The Heritage of Thai Sculpture*. Expensive but accessible seminal tome by influential French art historian.

Susan Conway *Thai Textiles*. A fascinating, richly illustrated work which draws on sculptures and temple murals to trace the evolution of Thai weaving techniques and costume styles, and to examine the functional and ceremonial uses of textiles.

Sumet Jumsai *Naga: Cultural Origins in Siam and the West Pacific*. Wide-ranging discussion of water symbols in Thailand and other parts of Asia, offering a stimulating mix of art, architecture, mythology and cosmology.

Steven Pettifor *Flavours: Thai Contemporary Art*. Takes up the baton from Apinan Poshyananda (see p.254) to look at the newly invigorated art scene in Thailand from 1992 to 2004, with profiles of 23 leading lights including painters, multimedia and performance artists.

Apinan Poshyananda *Modern Art In Thailand*. Excellent introduction which extends up to the early 1990s, with very readable discussions on dozens of individual artists, and lots of colour plates.

Dome Sukwong and Sawasdi Suwannapak *A Century of Thai*

Cinema. Full-colour tome tracing the history of the Thai film industry and all the promotional artwork (billboards, posters, magazines and cigarette cards) associated with it.

William Warren and Luca Invernizzi Tettoni *Arts and Crafts of Thailand*. Good-value large-format paperback, setting the wealth of Thai arts and crafts in cultural context, with plenty of attractive illustrations and colour photos.

Literature

Alastair Dingwall (ed) *Traveller's Literary Companion: Southeast Asia*. A useful though rather dry reference, with a large section on Thailand, including a book list, well-chosen extracts, biographical details of authors and other literary notes.

M.L. Manich Jumsai *Thai Ramayana* (Chalermnit, Bangkok). Slightly stilted abridged prose translation of King Rama I's version of the epic Hindu narrative, full of gleeful descriptions of bizarre mythological characters and supernatural battles. Essential reading for a full appreciation of Thai painting, carving and classical dance.

Khammaan Khonkhai *The Teachers of Mad Dog Swamp* (Silkworm Books, Chiang Mai). The engaging story of a young teacher who encounters opposition to his progressive ideas when he is posted to a remote village school in the northeast. A typical example of the "novels for life" genre, which are known for their strong moral stance.

Chart Korpjitti *The Judgement* (Thai Modern Classics). Sobering modern-day tragedy about a good-hearted Thai villager who is ostracized by his hypocritical neighbours. Contains lots of interesting details on village life and traditions and thought-provoking passages on

the stifling conservatism of rural communities. Winner of the Southeast Asian Writers Award award in 1982.

Rattawut Lapcharoensap *Sightseeing*. This outstanding debut collection of short stories by a young Thai-born author now living overseas highlights big, pertinent themes – cruelty, corruption, racism, pride – in its neighbourhood tales of randy teenagers, bullyboys, a child's friendship with a Cambodian refugee, a young man who uses family influence to dodge the draft.

Nitaya Masavisut (ed) *The S.E.A. Write Anthology of Thai Short Stories and Poems* (Silkworm Books, Chiang Mai). Interesting medley of short stories and poems by Thai writers who have won Southeast Asian Writers Awards, providing a good introduction to the contemporary literary scene.

Kukrit Pramoj *Si Phaendin: Four Reigns* (Silkworm Books, Chiang Mai). A kind of historical romance spanning the four reigns of Ramas V to VIII (1892–1946). Written by former prime minister Kukrit Pramoj, the story has become a modern classic in Thailand, made into films, plays and TV dramas, with heroine Ploi as the archetypal feminine role model.

J.C. Shaw *The Ramayana through Western Eyes* (DK Books, Bangkok). The bare bones of the epic tale are retold between tenuously comparable excerpts from Western poets, including Shakespeare, Shelley and Walt Whitman. Much more helpfully, the text is interspersed with key scenes from the murals at Bangkok's Wat Phra Kaeo.

S.P. Somtow *Jasmine Nights*. An engaging and humorous rite-of-passage tale, of an upper-class boy

learning what it is to be Thai. *Dragon's Fin Soup and Other Modern Siamese Fables* is an imaginative and entertaining collection of often supernatural short stories, focusing on the collision of East and West.

Klaus Wenk *Thai Literature – An Introduction* (White Lotus, Bangkok). Dry, but useful, short overview of the last seven hundred years by a noted German scholar, with plenty of extracts.

Thailand in foreign literature

Dean Barrett *Kingdom of Make-Believe*. Despite the clichéd ingredients – the Patpong go-go bar scene, opium smuggling in the Golden Triangle, Vietnam veterans – this novel about a return to Thailand following a twenty-year absence turns out to be a rewardingly multidimensional take on the farang experience.

Botan *Letters from Thailand* (Silkworm Books, Chiang Mai). Probably the best introduction to the Chinese community in Bangkok, presented in the form of letters written over a twenty-year period by a Chinese emigrant to his mother. Branded as both anti-Chinese and anti-Thai, this 1969 prizewinning book is now mandatory reading in school social studies' classes.

Pierre Boulle *The Bridge Over the River Kwai*. The World War II novel which inspired the David Lean movie and kicked off the Kanchanaburi tourist industry.

John Burdett *Bangkok 8*. Absorbing Bangkok thriller that takes in Buddhism, plastic surgery, police corruption, the *yaa baa* drugs trade, hookers, jade-smuggling and the spirit world.

Alex Garland *The Beach*. Gripping cult thriller (later made into a film) that uses a Thai setting to explore the

way in which travellers' ceaseless quest for "undiscovered" utopias inevitably leads to them despoiling the idyll.

Spalding Gray *Swimming to Cambodia*. Entertaining and politically acute account of the late actor and monologist's time in Thailand on location for the filming of *The Killing Fields*.

Michel Houellebecq *Platform*. Sex tourism in Thailand provides the nucleus of this brilliantly provocative (some would say offensive) novel, in which Houellebecq presents a ferocious critique of Western decadence and cultural colonialism, and of radical Islam too.

Christopher G. Moore *God Of Darkness* (Asia Books, Bangkok). Thailand's bestselling expat novelist sets his most intriguing thriller during the economic crisis of 1997 and includes plenty of insights on endemic corruption and the desperate struggle for power within family and society.

Darin Strauss *Chang & Eng*. An intriguing imagined autobiography of the famous nineteenth-century Siamese twins (see p.102), from their impoverished Thai childhood via the freak shows of New York and London to married life in smalltown North Carolina. Unfortunately marred by lazy research and a confused grasp of Thai geography and culture.

Food and cookery

Vatcharin Bhumichitr *The Taste of Thailand*. Another glossy introduction to this eminently photogenic country, this time through its food. The author runs a Thai restaurant in London and provides background colour as well as about 150 recipes adapted for Western kitchens.

Jacqueline M. Piper *Fruits of South-East Asia*. An exploration of the bounteous fruits of the region, tracing their role in cooking, medicine, handicrafts and rituals. Well illustrated with photos, watercolours and early botanical drawings.

David Thompson *Thai Food*. Comprehensive, impeccably researched celebration of Thai food, with over 300 recipes, by the owner of the first Thai restaurant ever to earn a Michelin star.

Language

Language

Language

T hai belongs to one of the oldest families of languages in the world, Austro-Thai, and is radically different from most of the other tongues of Southeast Asia. Being tonal, Thai is extremely difficult for Westerners to master, but by building up from a small core of set phrases, you should soon have enough to get by. Most Thais who deal with tourists speak some English, but once you stray off the beaten track you'll probably need at least a little Thai. Anywhere you go, you'll impress and get better treatment if you at least make an effort to speak a few words.

Thai script is even more of a problem to Westerners, with 44 consonants to represent 21 consonant sounds and 32 vowels to deal with 48 different vowel sounds. However, street signs in touristed areas are nearly always written in Roman script as well as Thai, and in other circumstances you're better off asking than trying to unscramble the swirling mess of symbols, signs and accents. For more information on transliteration into Roman script, see the box in the Introduction.

Among **language books**, *Thai: The Rough Guide Phrasebook* covers the essential phrases and expressions in both Thai script and phonetic equivalents, as well as dipping into grammar and providing a menu reader and fuller vocabulary in dictionary format (English–Thai and Thai English). Probably the best pocket dictionary is Paiboon Publishing's (⊛www.ThaiLao.com) *Thai-English, English-Thai Dictionary*, which lists words in phonetic Thai as well as Thai script, and features a very handy table of the Thai alphabet in a dozen different fonts; it's also available as a searchable dictionary for Palm PDAs. Among the rest, G.H. Allison's *Mini English Thai and Thai-English Dictionary* (Chalermnit) has the edge over *Robertson's Practical English-Thai Dictionary* (Asia Books), although it's more difficult to find.

The best **teach-yourself course** is the expensive *Linguaphone Thai*, which includes six CDs or six cassettes. *Thai for Beginners* by Benjawan Poomsan Becker (Paiboon Publishing; ⊛www.ThaiLao.com) is a cheaper, more manageable textbook and is especially good for getting to grips with the Thai writing system; you can also buy accompanying CDs or tapes to help with listening skills. For a more traditional textbook, try Stuart Campbell and Chuan Shaweevongse's *The Fundamentals of the Thai Language*, which is comprehensive, though hard going. G.H. Allison's *Easy Thai* is best for those who feel the urge to learn the alphabet. The **website** ⊛www.thai-language.com is an amazing free resource, featuring a searchable dictionary of over 27,000 Thai words, complete with Thai script and audio clips, plus a guide to the language and forums.

Pronunciation

Mastering **tones** is probably the most difficult part of learning Thai. Five different tones are used – low, middle, high, falling, and rising – by which the meaning of a single syllable can be altered in five different ways. Thus, using four of the five tones, you can make a sentence just from just one syllable: "mái mài mâi măi" meaning "New wood burns, doesn't it?" As well as the natural difficulty in becoming attuned to speaking and listening to these different tones, Western efforts are complicated by our habit of denoting the overall meaning of a sentence by modulating our tones – for example, turning a statement into a question through a shift of stress and tone. Listen to native Thai speakers and you'll soon begin to pick up the different approach to tone.

The pitch of each tone is gauged in relation to your vocal range when speaking, but they should all lie within a narrow band, separated by gaps just big enough to differentiate them. The **low tones** (syllables marked `` ` ``), **middle tones** (unmarked syllables), and **high tones** (syllables marked ´) should each be pronounced evenly and with no inflection. The **falling tone** (syllables marked ^) is spoken with an obvious drop in pitch, as if you were sharply emphasizing a word in English. The **rising tone** (marked ˇ) is pronounced as if you were asking an exaggerated question in English.

As well as the unfamiliar tones, you'll find that, despite the best efforts of the transliterators, there is no precise English equivalent to many **vowel and consonant sounds** in the Thai language. The lists below give a rough idea of pronunciation.

Vowels

a	as in dad.		eu	as in sir, but heavily nasalized.
aa	has no precise equivalent, but is pronounced as it looks, with the vowel elongated.		i	as in tip.
			ii	as in feet.
			o	as in knock.
ae	as in there.		oe	as in hurt, but more closed.
ai	as in buy.		oh	as in toe.
ao	as in now.		u	as in loot.
aw	as in awe.		uay	"*u*" plus "*ay*" as in pay.
e	as in pen.		uu	as in pool.

Consonants

r	as in rip, but with the tongue flapped quickly against the palate – in everyday speech, it's often pronounced like "l".		k	is unaspirated and unvoiced, and closer to "g".
			p	is also unaspirated and unvoiced, and closer to "b".
kh	as in keep.		t	is also unaspirated and unvoiced, and closer to "d".
ph	as in put.			
th	as in time.			

General words and phrases

Greetings and basic phrases

When you speak to a stranger in Thailand, you should generally end your sentence in *khráp* if you're a man, *khâ* if you're a woman – these untranslatable politening syllables will gain good will, and are nearly always used after *sawàt dii* (hello/goodbye) and *khàwp khun* (thank you). *Khráp* and *khâ* are also often used to answer "yes" to a question, though the most common way is to repeat the verb of the question (precede it with *mâi* for "no"). *Châi* (yes) and *mâi châi* (no) are less frequently used than their English equivalents.

Hello	sawàt dii	My name is…	phŏm (men)/ diichăn (women) chêu…
Where are you going?	pai năi? (not always meant literally, but used as a general greeting)	I come from…	phŏm/diichăn maa jàak…
		I don't understand	mâi khâo jai
I'm out having fun/ I'm travelling	pai thîaw (answer to pai năi, almost indefinable pleasantry)	Do you speak English?	khun phûut phasăa angkrìt dâi măi?
		Do you have…?	mii…măi?
Goodbye	sawàt dii/la kàwn	Is there…?	…mii măi?
Good luck/cheers	chôk dii	Is…possible?	…dâi măi?
Excuse me	khăw thâwt	Can you help me?	chûay phŏm/ diichăn dâi măi?
Thank you	khàwp khun		
It's nothing/it doesn't matter	mâi pen rai	(I) want…	ao…
How are you?	sabai dii reŭ?	(I) would like to…	yàak jà…
I'm fine	sabai dii	(I) like…	châwp…
What's your name?	khun chêu arai?	What is this called in Thai?	nîi phasăa thai rîak wâa arai?

Getting around

Where is the…?	…yùu thîi năi?	east	tawan àwk
How far?	klai thâo rai?	west	tawan tòk
I would like to go to…	yàak jà pai…	near/far	klai/klai
		street	thanŏn
Where have you been?	pai năi maa?	train station	sathàanii rót fai
		bus station	sathàanii rót meh
Where is this bus going?	rót nîi pai năi?	airport	sanăam bin
		ticket	tŭa
When will the bus leave?	rót jà àwk mêua rai?	hotel	rohng raem
		post office	praisanii
What time does the bus arrive in…?	rót theŭng…kìi mohng?	restaurant	raan ahăan
		shop	raan
Stop here	jàwt thîi nîi	market	talàt
here	thîi nîi	hospital	rohng pha-yaabaan
there/over there	thîi nâan/thîi nôhn	motorbike	rót mohtoesai
right	khwăa	taxi	rót táksîi
left	sái	boat	reua
straight	trong	bicycle	jàkràyaan
north	neŭa		
south	tâi		

Accommodation and shopping

How much is…?	…thâo rai/kìi bàat?	Do you have a cheaper room?	mii hâwng thùuk kwàa măi?
How much is a room here per night?	hâwng thîi nîi kheun lá thâo rai?	Can I/we look at the room?	duu hâwng dâi măi?

I/We'll stay two nights	jà yùu săwng kheun	air-con room	hăwng ae
Can you reduce the price?	lót raakhaa dâi măi?	ordinary room	hăwng thammadaa
Can I store my bag here?	fàak krapăo wái thîi nîi dâi măi?	telephone	thohrásàp
cheap/expensive	thùuk/phaeng	laundry	sák phâa
		blanket	phâa hòm
		fan	phát lom

General adjectives

alone	khon diaw	easy	ngâi
another	ìik…nèung	fun	sanùk
bad	mâi dii	hot (temperature)	ráwn
big	yài	hot (spicy)	phèt
clean	sa-àat	hungry	hiŭ khâo
closed	pìt	ill	mâi sabai
cold (object)	yen	open	pòet
cold (person or weather)	năo	pretty	sŭay
		small	lek
delicious	aròi	thirsty	hiŭ nám
difficult	yâak	tired	nèu-ai
dirty	sokaprok	very	mâak

General nouns

Nouns have no plurals or genders, and don't require an article.

bathroom/toilet	hăwng nám	foreigner	fàràng
boyfriend or girlfriend	faen	friend	phêuan
		money	ngoen
food	ahăan	water/liquid	nám

General verbs

Thai verbs do not conjugate at all, and also often double up as nouns and adjectives, which means that foreigners' most unidiomatic attempts to construct sentences are often readily understood.

come	maa	sit	nâng
do	tham	sleep	nawn làp
eat	kin/thaan khâo	take	ao
give	hâi	walk	doen pai
go	pai		

Numbers

zero	sŭun	six	hòk
one	nèung	seven	jèt
two	săwng	eight	pàet
three	săam	nine	kâo
four	sìi	ten	sìp
five	hâa	eleven	sìp èt

twelve, thirteen, etc	sìp săwng, sìp săam...	thirty, forty, etc	săam sìp, sìi sìp...
twenty	yîi sìp/yiip	one hundred, two	nèung rói, săwng
twenty-one	yîi sìp èt	hundred, etc	rói...
twenty-two,	yîi sìp săwng,	one thousand	nèung phan
twenty-three, etc	yîi sìp săam...	ten thousand	nèung mèun

Time

The commonest system for telling the time, as outlined below, is actually a
confusing mix of several different systems. The State Railway and government
officials use the 24-hour clock (9am is *kâo naalikaa*, 10am *sìp naalikaa*, and so
on), which is always worth trying if you get stuck.

1–5am	tii nèung–tii hâa	hour	chûa mohng
6–11am	hòk mohng cháo–	day	waan
	sìp èt mohng cháo	week	aathít
noon	thîang	month	deuan
1pm	bài mohng	year	pii
2–4pm	bài săwng mohng–	today	wan níi
	bài sìi mohng	tomorrow	phrûng níi
5–6pm	hâa mohng yen–	yesterday	mêua wan
	hòk mohng yen	now	diăw níi
7–11pm	nèung thûm–	next week	aathít nâa
	hâa thûm	last week	aathít kàwn
midnight	thîang kheun	morning	cháo
What time is it?	kìi mohng láew?	afternoon	bài
How many hours?	kìi chûa mohng?	evening	yen
How long?	naan thâo rai?	night	kheun
minute	naathii		

Days

Sunday	wan aathít	Thursday	wan pháréuhàt
Monday	wan jan	Friday	wan sùk
Tuesday	wan angkhaan	Saturday	wan săo
Wednesday	wan phút		

Food and drink

Basic ingredients

Ahăan thaleh	Seafood	Mŭu	Pork
Hŏy	Shellfish	Néua	Beef, meat
Hŏy nang rom	Oyster	Pèt	Duck
Kài	Chicken	Plaa	Fish
Khài	Egg	Plaa dùk	Catfish
Kleua	Salt	Plaa mèuk	Squid
Kûng	Prawn, shrimp	Puu	Crab

Vegetables (phàk)

Hèt	Mushroom	Phrík	Chilli
Krathiam	Garlic	Phrík yùak	Green pepper
Makěua	Aubergine	Taeng kwaa	Cucumber
Makěua thêt	Tomato	Tôn hŏrm	Spring onions
Man faràng	Potato	Tùa	Peas, beans or lentils
Man faràng thâwt	Chips	Tùa ngâwk	Bean sprouts
Nàw mái	Bamboo shoots		

Noodles

Ba mìi	Egg noodles	Kwáy tiăw/ ba mìi rât nâ (mŭu)	Rice noodles/egg noodles fried in gravy-like sauce with vegetables (and pork slices)
Ba mìi kràwp	Crisp fried egg noodles		
Kwáy tiăw (sên yaì/sên lék)	White rice noodles (wide/thin)		
Kwáy tiăw/ ba mìi haêng	Rice noodles/egg noodles fried with egg, small pieces of meat and a few vegetables	Phàt siyú	Wide or thin noodles fried with soy sauce, egg and meat
		Phàt thai	Thin noodles fried with egg, bean sprouts and tofu, topped with ground peanuts
Kwáy tiăw/ba mìi nám (mŭu)	Rice noodle/egg noodle soup, made with chicken broth (and pork balls)		

Rice

Khâo	Rice	Khâo nâ kài/pèt	Chicken/duck served with sauce over rice
Khâo kaeng	Curry over rice		
Khâo man kài	Slices of chicken served over marinated rice	Khâo niăw	Sticky rice
		Khâo phàt	Fried rice
Khâo mŭu daeng	Red pork with rice	Khâo tôm	Rice soup (usually for breakfast)

Curries and soups

Kaeng jèut	Mild soup with vegetables and usually pork	Kaeng phánaeng	Thick, savoury curry
		Kaeng phèt	Hot, red curry
		Kaeng sôm	Fish and vegetable curry
Kaeng karìi	Mild, Indian-style curry		
Kaeng khiăw wan	Green curry	Tôm khà kài	Chicken coconut soup
Kaeng liang	Aromatic vegetable soup		
Kaeng mátsàman	Rich Muslim-style curry, usually with beef and potatoes	Tôm yam kûng	Hot and sour prawn soup

LANGUAGE — Food and drink

Names and descriptions of Thai **fruits** are given on p.184.

Salads

Lâap	Spicy ground meat salad	Yam plaa dùk foo	Crispy fried catfish salad
Nám tòk	Grilled beef or pork salad	Yam plaa mèuk	Squid salad
Sôm tam	Spicy papaya salad	Yam sôm oh	Pomelo salad
Yam hua plee	Banana flower salad	Yam thuù phuu	Wing-bean salad
Yam néua	Grilled beef salad	Yam wun sen	Noodle and pork salad

Other dishes

Hâwy thâwt	Omelette stuffed with mussels	Néua phàt krathiam phrík thai	Beef fried with garlic and pepper
Kài phàt bai kraprao	Chicken fried with basil leaves	Néua phàt nám man hâwy	Beef in oyster sauce
Kài phàt khǐng	Chicken with ginger	Pàw pía	Spring rolls
Kài phàt mét mámûang	Chicken with cashew nuts	Phàt phàk bûng fai daeng	Morning glory fried in garlic and bean sauce
Kài phàt nàw mái	Chicken with bamboo shoots	Phàt phàk lǎi yàng	Stir-fried vegetables
Kài yâang	Grilled chicken	Plaa nêung páe sá	Whole fish steamed with vegetables and ginger
Khài yát sài	Omelette with pork and vegetables		
Khǎnǒm jìin nám yaa	Noodles topped with fish curry	Plaa rôt phrík	Whole fish cooked with chillies
Kûng chúp paêng thâwt	Prawns fried in batter	Plaa thâwt	Fried whole fish
		Sàté	Satay
Mǔu prîaw wǎan	Sweet and sour pork	Thâwt man plaa	Fish cake

Thai desserts (khanǒm)

Khanǒm beuang	Small crispy pancake folded over with coconut cream and strands of sweet egg inside	Khâo niǎw thúrian/ mámûang	Sticky rice mixed with coconut cream and durian/ mango
		Klûay khàek	Fried banana
Khâo lǎam	Sticky rice, coconut cream and black beans cooked and served in bamboo tubes	Lûk taan chêum	Sweet palm kernels served in syrup
		Sǎngkhayaa	Coconut custard
		Tàkôh	Squares of transparent jelly (jello) topped with coconut cream
Khâo niǎw daeng	Sticky red rice mixed with coconut cream		

Drinks (khreûang deùm)

Bia	Beer	Kaafae ráwn	Hot coffee
Chaa ráwn	Hot tea	Kâew	Glass
Chaa yen	Iced tea	Khúat	Bottle

Mâekhŏng (or anglicized "Mekong")	Thai brand-name rice whisky	Nám sŏdaa	Soda water
		Nám tan	Sugar
		Nám yen	Cold water
Nám klûay	Banana shake	Nom jeùd	Milk
Nám mánao/sôm	Fresh, bottled or fizzy lemon/orange juice	Ohlíang	Iced coffee
		Thûay	Cup
Nám plào	Drinking water (boiled or filtered)		

Ordering

Can I see the menu?	Khăw duù menu?	I would like...	Khăw...
I am vegetarian/ vegan	Phŏm (male)/ diichăn (female) kin ahăan mangsàwirát/ jeh	With/without...	Sài/mâi sài...
		Can I have the bill please?	Khăw check bin?

Glossary

Amphoe District.

Amphoe muang Provincial capital.

Ao Bay.

Apsara Female deity.

Avalokitesvara Bodhisattva representing compassion.

Avatar Earthly manifestation of a deity.

Ban Village or house.

Bang Village by a river or the sea.

Bencharong Polychromatic ceramics made in China for the Thai market.

Bhumisparsa mudra Most common gesture of Buddha images; symbolizes the Buddha's victory over temptation.

Bodhisattva In Mahayana Buddhism, an enlightened being who postpones his or her entry into Nirvana.

Bot Main sanctuary of a Buddhist temple.

Brahma One of the Hindu trinity – "The Creator". Usually depicted with four faces and four arms.

Celadon Porcelain with distinctive grey-green glaze.

Changwat Province.

Chao ley/chao nam "Sea gypsies" – nomadic fisherfolk of south Thailand.

Chedi Reliquary tower in Buddhist temple.

Chofa Finial on temple roof.

Deva Mythical deity.

Devaraja God-king.

Dharma The teachings or doctrine of the Buddha.

Dharmachakra Buddhist Wheel of Law (also known as Wheel of Doctrine or Wheel of Life).

Doi Mountain.

Erawan Mythical three-headed elephant; Indra's vehicle.

Farang Foreigner/foreign.

Ganesh Hindu elephant-headed deity, remover of obstacles and god of knowledge.

Garuda Mythical Hindu creature – half-man half-bird; Vishnu's vehicle.

Gopura Entrance pavilion to temple precinct (especially Khmer).

Hamsa Sacred mythical goose; Brahma's vehicle.

Hanuman Monkey god and chief of the monkey army in the *Ramayana*; ally of Rama.

Hat Beach.

Hin Stone.

Hinayana Pejorative term for Theravada school of Buddhism, literally "Lesser Vehicle".

Ho trai A scripture library.

Indra Hindu king of the gods and, in Buddhism, devotee of the Buddha; usually carries a thunderbolt.

Isaan Northeast Thailand.

Jataka Stories of the five hundred lives of the Buddha.

Khaen Reed and wood pipe; the characteristic musical instrument of Isaan.

Khao Hill, mountain.

Khlong Canal.

Khon Classical dance-drama.

Kinnari Mythical creature – half-woman, half-bird.

Kirtimukha Very powerful deity depicted as a lion-head.

Ko Island.

Ku The Lao word for *prang*; a tower in a temple complex.

Laem Headland or cape.

Lakhon Classical dance-drama.

Lak muang City pillar; revered home for the city's guardian spirit.

Lakshaman/Phra Lak Rama's younger brother.

Lakshana Auspicious signs or "marks of greatness" displayed by the Buddha.

Lanna Northern Thai kingdom that lasted from the thirteenth to the sixteenth century.

Likay Popular folk theatre.

Longyi Burmese sarong.

Luang pho Abbot or especially revered monk.

Maenam River.

Mahathat Chedi containing relics of the Buddha.

Mahayana School of Buddhism now practised mainly in China, Japan and Korea; literally "the Great Vehicle".

Mara The Evil One; tempter of the Buddha.

Mawn khwaan Traditional triangular or "axe-head" pillow.

Meru/Sineru Mythical mountain at the centre of Hindu and Buddhist cosmologies.

Mondop Small, square temple building to house minor images or religious texts.

Moo/muu Neighbourhood.

Muang City or town.

Muay thai Thai boxing.

Mudra Symbolic gesture of the Buddha.

Mut mee Tie-dyed cotton or silk.

Naga Mythical dragon-headed serpent in Buddhism and Hinduism.

Nakhon Honorific title for a city.

Nam Water.

Nam tok Waterfall.

Nang thalung Shadow-puppet entertainment, found in southern Thailand.

Nielloware Engraved metalwork.

Nirvana Final liberation from the cycle of rebirths; state of non-being to which Buddhists aspire.

Pak Tai Southern Thailand.

Pali Language of ancient India; the script of the original Buddhist scriptures.

Pha sin Woman's sarong.

Phi Animist spirit.

Phra Honorific term – literally "excellent".

Phu Mountain.

Prang Central tower in a Khmer temple.

Prasat Khmer temple complex or central shrine.

Rama/Phra Ram Human manifestation of Hindu deity Vishnu; hero of the *Ramayana*.

Ramakien Thai version of the *Ramayana*.

Ramayana Hindu epic of good versus evil: chief characters include Rama, Sita, Ravana, Hanuman.

Ravana/Totsagan Rama's adversary in the *Ramayana;* represents evil.

Reua hang yao Longtail boat.

Rishi Ascetic hermit.

Rot ae/rot tua Air-conditioned bus.

Rot thammadaa Ordinary bus.

Sala Meeting hall, pavilion, bus stop – or any open-sided structure.

Samlor Passenger tricycle; literally "three-wheeled".

Sanskrit Sacred language of Hinduism; also used in Buddhism.

Sanuk Fun.

Sema Boundary stone to mark consecrated ground within temple complex.

Shiva One of the Hindu trinity – "The Destroyer".

Shiva lingam Phallic representation of Shiva.

Soi Lane or side road.

Songkhran Thai New Year.

Songthaew Pick-up used as public transport; literally "two rows", after the vehicle's two facing benches.

Takraw Game played with a rattan ball.

Talat Market.

Talat nam Floating market.

Talat yen Night market.

Tambon Subdistrict.

Tavatimsa Buddhist heaven.

Tha Pier.

Thale Sea or lake.

Tham Cave.

Thanon Road.

That Chedi.

Thep A divinity.

Theravada Main school of Buddhist thought in Thailand; also known as Hinayana.

Totsagan Rama's evil rival in the *Ramayana*; also known as Ravana.

Tripitaka Buddhist scriptures.

Trok Alley.

Tuk-tuk Motorized three-wheeled taxi.

Uma Shiva's consort.

Ushnisha Cranial protuberance on Buddha images, signifying an enlightened being.

Viharn Temple assembly hall for the laity; usually contains the principal Buddha image.

Vipassana Buddhist meditation technique; literally "insight".

Vishnu One of the Hindu trinity – "The Preserver". Usually shown with four arms, holding a disc, a conch, a lotus and a club.

Wai Thai greeting expressed by a prayer-like gesture with the hands.

Wang Palace.

Wat Temple.

Wiang Fortified town.

Yaksha Mythical giant.

Yantra Magical combination of numbers and letters, used to ward off danger.

LANGUAGE | Glossary

Travel
store

D: Rough Guide
DIRECTIONS for
short breaks

Available from all good bookstores

ROUGH **GUIDES** Complete Listing

For more information go to www.roughguides.com

Avoid Guilt Trips

Buy fair trade coffee + bananas ✓

Save energy - use low energy bulbs ✓

– don't leave tv on standby ✓

Offset carbon emissions from flight to Madrid ✓

Send goat to Africa ✓

Join Tourism Concern today ✓

Slowly, the world is changing.
Together we can, and will, make a difference.

Tourism Concern is the only UK registered charity fighting exploitation in one of the largest industries on earth: people forced from their homes in order that holiday resorts can be built, sweatshop labour conditions in hotels and destruction of the environment are just some of the issues that we tackle.

Sending people on a guilt trip is not something we do. We know as well as anyone that holidays are precious. But you can help us to ensure that tourism always benefits the local communities involved.

Call 020 7133 3330
or visit **tourismconcern.org.uk** to find out how.

*A year's membership of Tourism Concern costs just £20 (£12 unwaged)
– that's 38 pence a week, less than the cost of a pint of milk, organic of course.*

Fighting Exploitation in Tourism

TourismConcern

Small print and

A Rough Guide to Rough Guides

Published in 1982, the first Rough Guide – to Greece – was a student scheme that became a publishing phenomenon. Mark Ellingham, a recent graduate in English from Bristol University, had been travelling in Greece the previous summer and couldn't find the right guidebook. With a small group of friends he wrote his own guide, combining a highly contemporary, journalistic style with a thoroughly practical approach to travellers' needs.

The immediate success of the book spawned a series that rapidly covered dozens of destinations. And, in addition to impecunious backpackers, Rough Guides soon acquired a much broader and older readership that relished the guides' wit and inquisitiveness as much as their enthusiastic, critical approach and value-for-money ethos.

These days, Rough Guides include recommendations from shoestring to luxury and cover more than 200 destinations around the globe, including almost every country in the Americas and Europe, more than half of Africa and most of Asia and Australasia. Our ever-growing team of authors and photographers is spread all over the world, particularly in Europe, the USA and Australia.

In the early 1990s, Rough Guides branched out of travel, with the publication of Rough Guides to World Music, Classical Music and the Internet. All three have become benchmark titles in their fields, spearheading the publication of a wide range of books under the Rough Guide name.

Including the travel series, Rough Guides now number more than 350 titles, covering: phrasebooks, waterproof maps, music guides from Opera to Heavy Metal, reference works as diverse as Conspiracy Theories and Shakespeare, and popular culture books from iPods to Poker. Rough Guides also produce a series of more than 120 World Music CDs in partnership with World Music Network.

Visit www.roughguides.com to see our latest publications.

Rough Guide travel images are available for commercial licensing at www.roughguidespictures.com

ROUGH
GUIDES

SMALL PRINT

Rough Guide credits

Text editor: Matthew Teller
Layout: Pradeep Thapliyal
Cartography: Ashutosh Bharti
Picture editor: Siobhan Donoghue
Production: Aimee Hampson
Proofreader: Martin Moore
Cover design: Chloë Roberts
Photographer: Karen Trist
Editorial: London Kate Berens, Claire Saunders, Ruth Blackmore, Polly Thomas, Richard Lim, Alison Murchie, Karoline Densley, Andy Turner, Keith Drew, Edward Aves, Nikki Birrell, Helen Marsden, Alice Park, Sarah Eno, Joe Staines, Duncan Clark, Peter Buckley, Matthew Milton, Tracy Hopkins, David Paul, Lucy White, Ruth Tidball; **New York** Andrew Rosenberg, Steven Horak, April Isaacs, AnneLise Sorensen, Amy Hegarty, Sean Mahoney, Ella Steim, Anna Owens, Joseph Petta
Design & Pictures: London Scott Stickland, Dan May, Diana Jarvis, Mark Thomas, Jj Luck, Harriet Mills; **Delhi** Madhavi Singh, Umesh Aggarwal, Ajay Verma, Jessica Subramanian, Ankur Guha, Pradeep Thapliyal, Sachin Tanwar, Anita Singh

Production: Sophie Hewat, Katherine Owers
Cartography: London Maxine Repath, Ed Wright, Katie Lloyd-Jones; **Delhi** Rajesh Chhibber, Jai Prakash Mishra, Rajesh Mishra, Animesh Pathak, Jasbir Sandhu, Karobi Gogoi, Amod Singh, Alakananda Bhattacharya, Athokpam Jotinkumar
Online: New York Jennifer Gold, Suzanne Welles, Kristin Mingrone; **Delhi** Manik Chauhan, Narender Kumar, Shekhar Jha, Rakesh Kumar, Amit Verma, Amit Kumar, Rahul Kumar, Ganesh Sharma, Debojit Borah
Marketing & Publicity: London Niki Hanmer, Louise Maher, Anna Paynton, Jess Carter; **New York** Geoff Colquitt, Megan Kennedy, Katy Ball; **Delhi** Reem Khokhar
Special projects editor: Philippa Hopkins
Manager India: Punita Singh
Series editor: Mark Ellingham
Reference Director: Andrew Lockett
Publishing coordinator: Megan McIntyre
Publishing Director: Martin Dunford

Publishing information

This fourth edition published January 2007 by
Rough Guides Ltd,
80 Strand, London WC2R 0RL
345 Hudson St, 4th Floor,
New York, NY 10014, USA
14 Local Shopping Centre, Panchsheel Park,
New Delhi 110017, India
Distributed by the Penguin Group
Penguin Books Ltd,
80 Strand, London WC2R 0RL
Penguin Putnam, Inc.
375 Hudson Street, NY 10014, USA
Penguin Group (Australia)
250 Camberwell Road, Camberwell,
Victoria 3124, Australia
Penguin Books Canada Ltd,
10 Alcorn Avenue, Toronto, Ontario,
Canada M4V 1E4
Penguin Group (NZ)
67 Apollo Drive, Mairangi Bay, Auckland 1310,
New Zealand
Cover concept by Peter Dyer.

Typeset in Bembo and Helvetica to an original
design by Henry Iles.
Printed in Italy by LegoPrint S.p.A.
© Paul Gray and Lucy Ridout 2007

300pp includes index
A catalogue record for this book is available from
the British Library
ISBN 1-84353-780-X
ISBN 13: 9-78184-353-780-9

The publishers and authors have done their best
to ensure the accuracy and currency of all the
information in **The Rough Guide to Bangkok**,
however, they can accept no responsibility for
any loss, injury, or inconvenience sustained by
any traveller as a result of information or advice
contained in the guide.

1   3   5   7   9   8   6   4   2

Help us update

We've gone to a lot of effort to ensure that the
fourth edition of **The Rough Guide to Bangkok**
is accurate and up-to-date. However, things
change – places get "discovered", opening hours
are notoriously fickle, restaurants and rooms raise
prices or lower standards. If you feel we've got it
wrong or left something out, we'd like to know,
and if you can remember the address, the price,
the time, the phone number, so much the better.
We'll credit all contributions, and send a copy of
the next edition (or any other Rough Guide if you

prefer) for the best letters. Everyone who writes
to us and isn't already a subscriber will receive
a copy of our full-colour thrice-yearly newsletter.
Please mark letters: **"Rough Guide Bangkok
Update"** and send to: Rough Guides, 80 Strand,
London WC2R 0RL, or Rough Guides, 4th Floor,
345 Hudson St, New York, NY 10014. Or send an
email to **mail@roughguides.com**
Have your questions answered and tell others
about your trip at
www.roughguides.atinfopop.com

Acknowledgements

The **authors** jointly would like to thank: Abigail Batalla and Richard Hume at London TAT; Fran Sandham for the feature on Bangkok tailors; Victor Borg for information on drugs penalties; Phil Cornwel-Smith; and our editor, Matthew Teller.

Readers' letters

Thanks to all the readers who have taken the time to write in with comments and suggestions (and apologies if we've inadvertently omitted anyone's name):

Philip Ampofo, Roger Baker, Arden Bashforth, Sue Bayliss, Paul Bonner, Andy & Claire Brice, Meredith Byers, Brian Candler, Paula Carter, John Clements, Varry Cocker, Andy Conner, Joanna Cox, B.M. Dobson, Colin Doyle, Don Dunlop, Heather Engley, Mike Fletcher, Johanna Ford and Chris Porter, George, Adrian Greenwood, Joan Gregoire, Lesley & Bob Hamson, Alan Hickey, Paul Jeffries, Monica Kearns, Harm Jan Kinkhorst, Liz Kirby, Alexander MacArthur, Lyn McCoy, Orlaith Mannion, Bill & Sandra Martin, Shelley Mason, Ken Mays, Bernard Nalson, Terry J. Nixon, Hubert de Paor, Miranda Pattinson, Bryan Pittman, Geoff Pocket, Sarah Riches, Emily De Ruyter, Rob Samborn, Maya Smith, Jeremy Tilden-Smith, Jim Snaith, Ian Spinney, Allan Tyrer, Sarah Valencik, A. Watson, Philip Wong, Helen Williams, Roger S. Windsor, Linda Wylie & Stephen Rodgers.

Photo credits

All pictures © Rough Guides except the following:

Things not to miss
06 Detail of a Thai Manuscript Depicting a Royal Parade, National Museum,Thailand © Luca Tettoni/Corbis
07 Joe Luis Puppet Theatre, Bangkok © Tourism Board of Thailand
11 Ancient City, Muan Boran, Bangkok © Cris Haigh/Alamy
14 Thai Boxing, Bangkok © Tourism Board of Thailand
19 Songkran, Water Festival © Tourism Board of Thailand

ROUGH GUIDES

SMALL PRINT

Index

Map entries are in colour.

INDEX

Map symbols

maps are listed in the full index using coloured text

‒ ‒ ‒ ‒	Chapter division boundary	☉	Statue
═══	Road	✈	Airport
------	Path	★	Transport stop
▬▬▬	Railway	♥	Museum
‒ ‒ ‒	Ferry route	@	Internet
———	Waterway	ⓘ	Information office
———	Wall	ℂ	Telephone
〰	Mountain range	⊞	Hospital
) (	Bridge	⊠	Post office
♦	Point of interest	🎵	Market
▣	Accommodation	◯	Stadium
◉	Restaurants & bars	▬	Building
⚲	Temple	⊞	Church
⊙	Cave	⊤	Christian cemetery
⊠	Gate	▦	Park
∩	Arch		

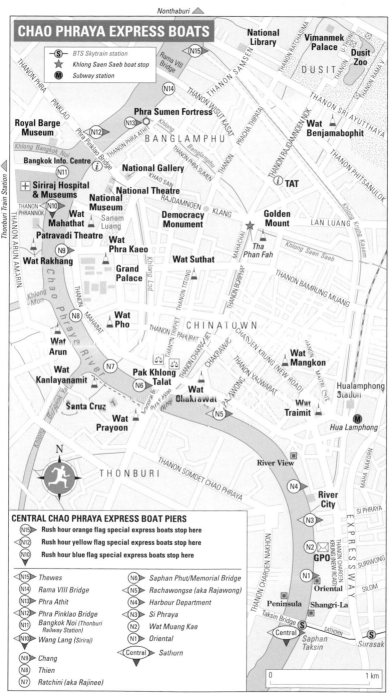

CHAO PHRAYA EXPRESS BOATS

Nonthaburi

(S) BTS Skytrain station
★ Khlong Saen Saeb boat stop
(M) Subway station

National Library
Vimanmek Palace
Dusit Zoo
DUSIT

THANON PHRA PINKLAO
Rama VIII Bridge
N15
N14
THANON WISUT KASAT
THANON SAMSEN
THANON RATCHASIMA
THANON U-THONG
THANON RAMA V
THANON SRI AYUTTHAYA

Royal Barge Museum
N13
N12
Phra Sumen Fortress
Khlong Banglamphu
BANGLAMPHU
THANON PHRA ATHIT
Phra Pinklao Bridge
THANON PRACHA THIPATAI
THANON RAJDAMNOEN NOK
Wat Benjamabophit
THANON PHITSANULOK

Bangkok Info. Centre
(i)
N11
National Gallery
THANON PHRA SUMEN
KHAO SAN
Siriraj Hospital & Museums
National Theatre
N10
National Museum
THANON PHRANNOK
Wat Mahathat
Sanam Luang
RAJDAMNOEN KLANG
Democracy Monument
(i) TAT
Golden Mount
LAN LUANG
Khlong Krung Kasem

Patravadi Theatre
Wat Phra Kaeo
N9
Wat Rakhang
Grand Palace
Wat Suthat
Tha Phan Fah
MAHACHAI
Khlong Saen Saeb
THANON BAMRUNG MUANG

Chao Phraya River
THANON MAHARAT
N8
Wat Pho
THANON TITONG
THANON BORPHIT
Khlong Lod
Khlong Mon

Wat Arun
N7
THANON TRIPHET
THANON PAHURAT
CHINATOWN
Wat Mangkon
THANON MAITRI CHIT
Hualamphong Stadium

Wat Kanlayanamit
Pak Khlong Talat
N6
THANON CHAKRAPHET
CHAKRAWAT
CHAROEN KRUNG (NEW ROAD)
THANON YAOWARAT

Santa Cruz
Wat Chakrawat
PA-AYWONG
Wat Traimit
Hua Lamphong (M)

Wat Prayoon
N5
MAHA NAKORN

N
THONBURI
THANON SOMDET CHAO PHRAYA
River View

N4
River City
SI PHRAYA

CENTRAL CHAO PHRAYA EXPRESS BOAT PIERS

N15 ▷ Rush hour orange flag special express boats stop here
N12 ◁ Rush hour yellow flag special express boats stop here
N10 ▽ Rush hour blue flag special express boats stop here

N3
Si Phraya
N2
GPO
THANON CHAROEN KRUNG (NEW ROAD)
SURIWONG
SILOM
EXPRESSWAY

N15 ▷ Thewes	N6 ▷ Saphan Phut/Memorial Bridge
N14 ▷ Rama VIII Bridge	N5 ◁ Rachawongse (aka Rajawong)
N13 ▷ Phra Athit	N4 ▷ Harbour Department
N12 ◁ Phra Pinklao Bridge	N3 ▷ Si Phraya
N11 ▷ Bangkok Noi (Thonburi Railway Station)	N2 ▷ Wat Muang Kae
N10 ▷ Wang Lang (Siriraj)	N1 ▷ Oriental
N9 ▷ Chang	Central ◁ Sathorn
N8 ▷ Thien	
N7 ▷ Ratchini (aka Rajinee)	

N1
Oriental
Peninsula
Shangri-La
Taksin Bridge
Central (S)
Saphan Taksin
SATHORN
Surasak (S)

THANON CHAROEN NAKHON

0   1 km

Thonburi Train Station
THANON ARUN AMARIN
Khlong Bangkok Noi
Khlong Bangkok Yai

▽ Krungthep Bridge

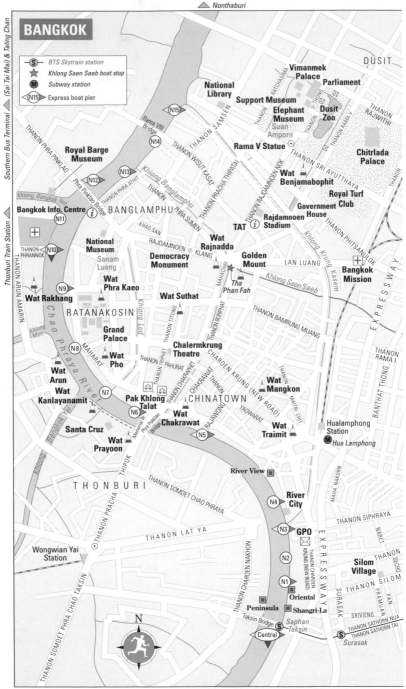

△ Nonthaburi

BANGKOK

- Ⓢ BTS Skytrain station
- ★ Klhong Saen Saeb boat stop
- Ⓜ Subway station
- N15 Express boat pier

DUSIT

National Library

Vimanmek Palace   Parliament

Support Museum

Elephant Museum   Dusit Zoo

Suan Amporn

Chitrlada Palace

Rama V Statue

Wat Benjamabophit

Royal Turf Club

Government House

Rajdamnoen Stadium

THANON PHITSANULOK

Bangkok Mission

Royal Barge Museum

BANGLAMPHU

Bangkok Info. Centre ⓘ

KHAO SAN

RAJDAMNOEN

Wat Rajnadda

KLANG

Golden Mount

LAN LUANG

Khlong Saen Saeb

National Museum

Sanam Luang

Democracy Monument

Tha Phan Fah

Wat Phra Kaeo

Wat Suthat

Wat Rakhang

RATANAKOSIN

THANON BAMRUNG MUANG

Grand Palace

Chalermkrung Theatre

Wat Pho

Wat Arun

CHAROEN KRUNG (NEW ROAD)

Wat Mangkon

Wat Kanlayanamit

Pak Khlong Talat

CHINATOWN

Wat Chakrawat

YAOWARAT

Wat Traimit

Santa Cruz

Wat Prayoon

Hualamphong Station

Ⓜ Hua Lamphong

THONBURI

River View

THANON SOMDET CHAO PHRAYA

River City

Wongwian Yai Station

THANON LAT YA

GPO

THANON SIPHRAYA

Silom Village

THANON SILOM

Peninsula
Shangri-La

Oriental

Ⓢ Saphan Taksin

Taksin Bridge

Ⓢ Central

THANON SATHORN NUA
THANON SATHORN TAI

Surasak

N

▽ Bangkok Marriott Resort & Krungthep Bridge

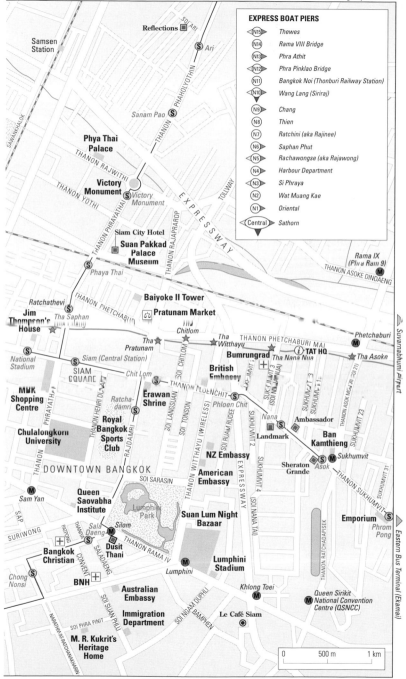

EXPRESS BOAT PIERS

N15	Thewes
N14	Rama VIII Bridge
N13	Phra Athit
N12	Phra Pinklao Bridge
N11	Bangkok Noi (Thonburi Railway Station)
N10	Wang Lang (Siriraj)
N9	Chang
N8	Thien
N7	Ratchini (aka Rajinee)
N6	Saphan Phut
N5	Rachawongse (aka Rajawong)
N4	Harbour Department
N3	Si Phraya
N2	Wat Muang Kae
N1	Oriental
Central	Sathorn

Samsen Station

Reflections

Soi Ari

Ari

Phaholyothin

Sanam Pao

Phya Thai Palace

Thanon Rajwithi

Thanon Yothi

Victory Monument

Thanon Phrayathai

Victory Monument

Expressway

Tollway

Thanon Rajaprarop

Siam City Hotel

Suan Pakkad Palace Museum

Phaya Thai

Rama IX (Phra Ram 9)

Thanon Asoke Dindaeng

Ratchathevi

Jim Thompson's House

Tha Saphan

Baiyoke II Tower

Pratunam Market

Thanon Phetchaburi

Chitlom

Tha Pratunam

Tha Witthayu

Thanon Phetchaburi Mai

TAT HQ

Phetchaburi

Bumrungrad

Tha Nana Nua

Tha Asoke

National Stadium

Siam (Central Station)

Siam Square

Chit Lom

Thanon Ploenchit

British Embassy

Phloen Chit

Ambassador

Ban Kamthieng

Sukhumvit

Asok

MBK Shopping Centre

Ratchadamri

Erawan Shrine

Royal Bangkok Sports Club

Chulalongkorn University

Soi Langsuan

Soi Tonson

Thanon Witthayu (Wireless)

Nana

Landmark

Soi Ruam Rudee

DOWNTOWN BANGKOK

Soi Sarasin

Queen Saovabha Institute

NZ Embassy

American Embassy

Expressway (Soi Nana Tai)

Sheraton Grande

Thanon Sukhumvit

Sam Yan

Lumphini Park

Sala Daeng

Silom

Suan Lum Night Bazaar

Emporium

Phrom Pong

Suriwong

Dusit Thani

Thanon Rama IV

Lumphini

Bangkok Christian

Convent

Salakdaeng

Lumphini Stadium

Chong Nonsi

BNH

Australian Embassy

Khlong Toei

Queen Sirikit National Convention Centre (QSNCC)

Immigration Department

Soi Suan Phlu

Soi Ngam Duphli

Soi Phra Pinit

M. R. Kukrit's Heritage Home

Narathiwat Ratchanakharin

Le Café Siam

Suvarnabhumi Airport

Eastern Bus Terminal (Ekamai)

0   500 m   1 km

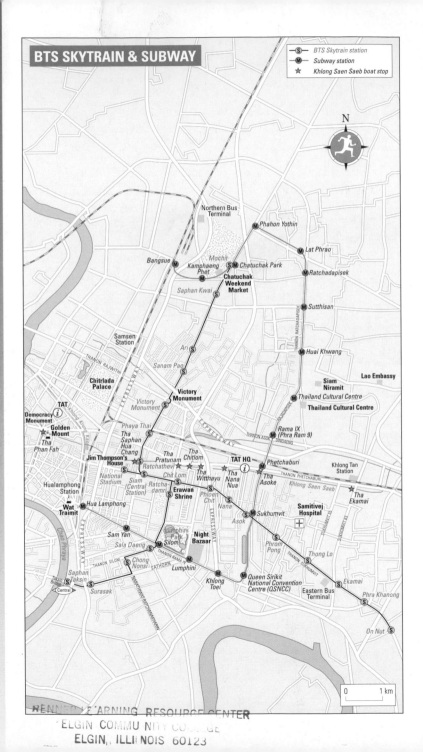

BTS SKYTRAIN & SUBWAY

Ⓢ BTS Skytrain station
Ⓜ Subway station
★ Khlong Saen Saeb boat stop

N

Northern Bus Terminal

Phahon Yothin

Ⓜ Lat Phrao

Bangsue

Mochit
Kamphaeng Phet
Ⓢ Chatuchak Park

Ⓜ Ratchadapisek

Chatuchak Weekend Market

Saphan Kwai

Ⓢ Sutthisan

Samsen Station

Ari

Ⓜ Huai Khwang

THANON RAJWITHI

Sanam Pao

Chitrlada Palace

Siam Niramit

Lao Embassy

EXPRESSWAY

Victory Monument

Ⓜ Thailand Cultural Centre

TAT
Democracy Monument

Victory Monument

THANON RATCHADAPISEK

Thailand Cultural Centre

Golden Mount

Phaya Thai

EXPRESSWAY

THANON ASOK

Rama IX (Phra Ram 9)

Tha Phan Fah

Tha Saphan Hua Chang

Tha Chitlom

TAT HQ

Ⓜ Phetchaburi

Khlong Tan Station

Jim Thompson's House

Tha Pratunam
Ⓢ Ratchathevi

THANON PHETCHABURI

Khlong Saen Saeb

National Stadium

Chit Lom
Siam (Central Station)
Ratcha-damri

Tha Witthayu

Tha Nana Nua

Tha Asoke

Tha Ekamai

Hualamphong Station

Erawan Shrine

Phloen Chit

Nana

Samitivej Hospital

Hua Lamphong

Wat Traimit

Sam Yan

Lumphini Park

Night Bazaar

Asok

Ⓢ Sukhumvit

Phrom Pong

THANON SUKHUMVIT

Thong Lo

Sala Daeng
Ⓢ Silom

Ⓜ Silom

Chao Phraya

Saphan Taksin

Chong Nonsi

THANON SILOM

SATHORN

THANON RAMA IV

Lumphini

Khlong Toei

Queen Sirikit National Convention Centre (QSNCC)

Ekamai

Eastern Bus Terminal

Phra Khanong

Surasak

On Nut

0   1 km